Global Youth Development Index and Report

2020

The Commonwealth

Commonwealth Secretariat
Marlborough House
Pall Mall
London SW1Y 5HX
United Kingdom

Published by the Commonwealth Secretariat.

Typeset by Nova Techset Private Ltd
Printed by APS Group

Views and opinions expressed in this publication are the responsibility of the author(s) and should in no way be attributed to the institutions to which they are affiliated or to the Commonwealth Secretariat. Wherever possible, the Commonwealth Secretariat uses paper sourced from sustainable forests or from sources that minimise a destructive impact on the environment.

Copies of this publication may be obtained from:

Publications Section
Commonwealth Secretariat
Marlborough House
Pall Mall
London SW1Y 5HX
United Kingdom
Tel: +44 (0)20 7747 6534
Email: publications@commonwealth.int
Web: https://books.thecommonwealth.org/

A catalogue record for this publication is available from the British Library.

ISBN (paperback): 978-1-84929-200-9
ISBN (e-book): 978-1-84859-992-5

The Commonwealth is an association of 54 independent countries, comprising large and small, developed and developing, landlocked and island economies. As the main intergovernmental body of the association, the Commonwealth Secretariat works with member governments to deliver on priorities agreed by Commonwealth Heads of Government and promotes international consensus building. It provides technical assistance and advisory services to members, helping governments achieve sustainable, inclusive and equitable development. The Secretariat's work programme encompasses areas such as democracy, rule of law, human rights, governance and social and economic development.

The Youth Development Index 2020 was intended to be published at CHOGM 2020. The impact of the COVID-19 pandemic has delayed its publication until 2021 but it remains as the 2020 report to reflect its conception. The report is also based upon data up to 2018 as this is the most up to date comparable global data available. This does mean that the report cannot take proper account of the significant impact of the global pandemic.

Rather our hope is that it serves as a baseline for use by policy makers, governments and the public in their discussion of and decisions on policies effecting young people and how we invest in them to help us build back better, both nationally and internationally, from the devastation of COVID-19.

Foreword

Taking Charge of our Future: youth development issues and policy directions

Foreword

The Rt Hon Patricia Scotland QC

Secretary General of the Commonwealth

As we work together to recover and rebuild from the heart-breaking losses and far-reaching consequences of the COVID-19 pandemic, we need to draw as fully as possible on the energy and imagination of young people. Following a period of immense social and economic dislocation and turmoil, our focus for the future must be on reconnecting with one another, and on innovating and transforming to build greater resilience into our systems.

In the Commonwealth, we are fortunate to be able to draw on the resourcefulness and creativity of the more than 1.2 billion young people between the ages of 15 and 29 years who live in our 54 member countries, and who are indispensable to delivering a common future that is fairer and more inclusive, more sustainable and more resilient.

Continuing progress towards achieving the Sustainable Development Goals is vital to building the world we want to see, and to do so we need to be able reliably and progressively to measure and monitor the ways in which young people live, learn and work in our communities. We need to be able to assess the extent to which youth are encouraged and empowered to add their contributions to our societies, and supported with enabling policies and tools.

The Commonwealth's global Youth Development Index (YDI) is one of the tools that has significantly enhanced our capacity to interrogate and assess

that progress and which we hope will be of use not just to the Commonwealth, but to the whole world. Now in its third iteration, this index has been strengthened to measure new dimensions of progress – on equality and inclusion, and on peace and security – while continuing to analyse changes in the foundational elements of the index: education, health and well-being, employment and opportunity, and political and civic participation.

The data used to compile the index was gathered before the COVID-19 pandemic and uses the latest available data to enable global comparability. As a result, this data and iteration of the index does not take into account the pandemics impact. However, it sets a baseline for us as we begin the work of rebuilding nationally and internationally, in our communities and collectively in the Commonwealth, from the many impacts of COVID-19, it will be important to focus on the fundamentals of human capital development. This means paying attention to the depredations and disproportionate disruption to education and employment experienced by young people. We need transformative programmes for investing in the health and well-being of youth, and for mobilising their advocacy and practical action to build a more equal, just and peaceful world.

Let us be inspired by the profiles featured in this report of Commonwealth youth who, through their imagination and innovation, with commitment to collective action and inclusiveness, are driving forward in fairer and more sustainable ways the delivery of our common future.

Foreword

Hon Florence Nakiwala Kiyingi
*Minister of State for Youth and Children Affairs, Government of Uganda and Chair
of the Commonwealth Youth Ministerial Task Force*

At the 9th Meeting of Commonwealth Youth Ministers in 2017, we committed to *inter alia* strengthening our mainstreamed approach to supporting youth participation in governance, to building youth work capacity, to developing new ideas for financing youth development and improving data for monitoring our progress on pursuing positive outcomes for youth in relation to the Sustainable Development Goals (SDGs).

We mandated the Secretariat to strengthen the global youth development index, including to consider the differential experiences of vulnerable young people including those living in poverty and those with disabilities. We also mandated improved measurement of youth participation – a critical part of the youth development experience which has been the most challenging to measure at a global level.

Those mandates have been fulfilled with this 2020 global Youth Development Index and report which outlines an index significantly updated in scope and depth. The inclusion of new domains and indicators on Equality and Inclusion and Peace and Security are positive developments in understanding the experiences of young people across the world, including differences between young men and young women and those facing economic marginalization. The report also includes analysis of the differential experiences of young people with disabilities in the education and employment sectors. Significantly, the revised domain on Political and Civic Participation includes new measures of the extent to which young people have accessed opportunities for participation as well as measures of the state of the enabling policy and institutional environment for participation.

This global report stands alongside the other investments in youth data we have made within the Commonwealth including working with national statistical offices and international partners to produce regional state of youth reports in Africa and the Pacific, a regional youth development index in ASEAN and embarking on national YDI projects in several countries including Australia, Namibia and Pakistan.

The message of this report is clear. We have made some progress on key development outcomes for young people between 2010 and 2018. We have also improved our capacity to monitor that progress at a global level. However, with the significant effects and disruptions of the COVID-19 pandemic which have occurred since the completion of this index, we must prepare to respond to an anticipated negative impact on the gains that have been achieved over the last decade. This report calls on us to redouble efforts on youth data collection so that we can account for some of these effects in the next iteration of the index; and we can use that evidence to inform new and effective strategies to build resilience into our youth development policies and programmes and support young people to continue to take charge of leading us sustainably and inclusively into a common future of peace and prosperity.

Foreword

Tijani Christian, JP
Chairperson of the Commonwealth Youth Council

Today, the world has the largest population of youth people in existence, with the Commonwealth alone having 60 per cent of its population below the age of 30. These extremely important assets must be protected and upskilled for countries to truly advance their economic growth and development agendas.

The Youth Development Index (YDI) 2020 underscores this point. It suggests that the participation of young people remains critical to the achievement of Agenda 2030, while the low scores in the Political and Civic Participation domain of the YDI call for increased support and investment in youth participation. Therefore, in many cases, countries are being left behind because they are leaving young people behind.

The YDI 2020 and report offer some compelling lessons for youth development. It brings together critical data for analysis to guide the development of policies and initiatives for global and country-specific youth development. It allows us to see the youth development journey as it unfolds and the realities of young people in a comprehensive snapshot.

The Commonwealth Youth Council appreciates that the YDI 2020 and report provide insights into how the role of young people is being facilitated in the global development agenda and the investment, or lack thereof, being made to create the space for their safe and inclusive development. The report highlights that, on average, youth development has been improving, although progress is slow. Between 2010 and 2018, the global average youth development score has improved by 3.1 per cent.

While progress is growth, no matter how small, and should be celebrated, the YDI allows us to see beyond averages and aggregates to a clearer picture of the situation of youth within countries. The YDI provides evidence to give greater support to youth-led advocacy, ensuring that we are more evidence-based and well researched.

This year and last, we have and are still facing a different and unique global threat – the COVID-19 pandemic. We have all been affected, no one spared. The most vulnerable, those within the lowest socio-economic grouping, such as young people, are experiencing the worse effect of the pandemic. As policy-makers, the private sector and civil society collectively chart recovery responses to the growing needs, let us utilise the YDI to ensure that the policies and strategies that are being developed and implemented do not create more challenges than opportunities, and that policies with attractive short-run gains do not overshadow long-term effects or impact.

The active inclusion of young people to safeguard a sustainable future cannot take time off during a crisis, nor should we as young people, who must stand as the gatekeepers of accountability, equality and equity. Therefore, now more than ever, we must ensure that young people are given more opportunities for economic empowerment and safeguard their freedoms against any further growing inequality in our societies. It's your country, it's our world, and we must guarantee that we build back better for all, inclusively and sustainably.

Acknowledgements

The 2020 Global Youth Development Index and Report is a knowledge product which has been realised through partnership and collaboration. Our team from the Social Policy Development section of the Commonwealth Secretariat including Sushil Ram, Tamara Babao-Sadgrove, Azimin Ibrahim, Amina Hussein, Puja Bajad, Mike Armstrong, Saurabh Mishra, Sita Patel and Terri-Ann Gilbert-Roberts, who coordinated the final report. We received critical support from colleagues across the Secretariat including the Climate Change, Communications, ICT and Trade sections. We also thank Kirk Haywood, Jevanic Henry, Sherry Dixon, Alison Arnold and Vicky Bates for their contributions. We owe a debt of gratitude to Osmal Wood and Lydia Ebert-Robert who led the design of the interactive data dashboard which accompanies this report.

The methodology, data and analysis for the 2020 YDI was updated by the Institute of Economics and Peace (IEP), led by David Hammond and Nadia Sorenson. Our partners in the United Nations Population Division, UNESCO Institute for Statistics, International Labour Organization (ILO), World Health Organisation (WHO) and the World Bank, among others, provided access to suitable data for global comparison. We are also grateful for the advice of the YDI Technical Group of Experts – comprising representatives from governments, development organisations, youth networks and research and academic institutions – who were instrumental in refining and validating the methodology and data choices for the 2020 index. The members of the expert group are listed in Annex 3.

Our guest contributors, including many young people, have been invaluable in helping us to demonstrate how young people have been and are 'Taking Charge of Our Common Future'; and have provided insight and policy advice on how various stakeholders can support them. We thank each of our contributors for sharing their analysis, experiences, ideas and recommendations in the pages of this report.

Without a doubt, this report prompts us to reflect on how we can invest more in what has worked and avoid a reversal of the gains achieved for young people. Across the Commonwealth and globally, up to 2018, youth development outcomes for young people were trending in a positive direction. Education scores had improved by 3 per cent between 2010 and 2018, with higher literacy rates and secondary school completion rates. More young people were financially empowered through access to their own bank accounts and mobile money. Fewer young women were becoming pregnant before the age of 20, increasing their chances to pursue a career and achieve financial independence. Fewer young people were dying from direct violence such as armed conflict and terrorism over the period, leading to a 3.41 per cent improvement in the global average score on Peace and Security.

Significantly, all countries, regardless of their overall levels of youth development, were scoring very highly on the Health and Well-being domain, with 12.1 per cent improvement in the world's average mortality rate score. The scores for HIV, self-harm, alcohol abuse and tobacco consumption rates improved by less than 2 per cent each.

The COVID-19 pandemic has significantly affected that progress, particularly in education and employment. With less than 40 per cent of young people estimated to be digital natives – that is, having five or more years' experience using the Internet – we must now heed the recommendations contained in this report about advancing human capital development, including leveraging partnerships towards skilling for the digital economy. And in taking our next steps, we must ensure the full participation of young people in the decision-making process – ensuring none of them is left behind.

Layne Robinson

Head of Social Policy Development
Economic Youth and Sustainable Development
Directorate, Commonwealth Secretariat

Contents

Guest Contributions

List of Figures

List of Tables

List of Boxes

Abbreviations and Acronyms

ADB	Asian Development Bank
AIDS	Acquired Immune Deficiency Syndrome
ASIRT	Association for Safe International Road Travel
AU	African Union
BIAC	Business at OECD
CCFAH	Commonwealth Climate Finance Access Hub
CCYDN	Commonwealth Children and Youth Disability Network
CEDAW	Convention on the Elimination of All Forms of Discrimination Against Women
CEDEL	Centre for Entrepreneurship and Labour Development
CEMM	Commonwealth Education Ministers Meeting
CHOGM	Commonwealth Heads of Government Meeting
COP21	21st session of the Conference of the Parties
CRPD	Convention on the Rights of Persons with Disabilities
CRS	Creditor Reporting System
CRSI	Commonwealth Road Safety Initiative
CSA	Commonwealth Student Association
CYC	Commonwealth Youth Council
CYCN	Commonwealth Youth Climate Change Network

CYHN	Commonwealth Youth Health Network
CYMM	Commonwealth Youth Ministers Meeting
CYSDP	Commonwealth Youth Sport for Development and Peace Network
DAC	Development Assistance Committee
DAP	Digital Ambassador Programme
DHS	Demographic and Health Survey
EU	European Union
GAN	Global Apprenticeship Network
GBD	Global Burden of Disease
GCF	Green Climate Fund
GDP	Gross Domestic Product
GPI	Gender Parity Index
GPI	Global Peace Index
GWP	Gallup World Poll
HDI	Human Development Index
HDRO	Human Development Report Office
HIV	Human Immunodeficiency Virus
IEP	Institute for Economics & Peace
IHME	Institute for Health Metrics and Evaluation
IOE	International Organisation of Employers
IIEP	International Institute for Educational Planning
IISD	International Institute for Sustainable Development

ILO	International Labour Organization
INFORM	Index for Risk Management
IOC	International Olympic Committee
IoT	Internet of Things
IPC	International Paralympic Committee
IPU	Inter-Parliamentary Union
ISCO	International Standard Classification of Occupations
ITU	International Telecommunication Union
IUCN	International Union for Conservation of Nature
LGBTQIA	Lesbian, Gay, Bisexual, Transgender, Queer and/or Questioning, Intersex and Asexual and/or Ally
MENA	Middle East and North Africa
MP	Member of Parliament
NbS	Nature-Based Solution
NDC	Nationally Determined Contribution
NDP	National Development Plan
NEET	Not in Education, Employment or Training
NGO	Non-Governmental Organisation
OCHA	UN Office for the Coordination of Humanitarian Affairs
ODA	Official Development Assistance
OECD	Organisation for Economic Co-operation and Development
OEWG	Open-Ended Working Group
PAYM	Pan-African Youth Movement
PCA	Principal Components Analysis
PIL	Labour Integration Programme
PYU	Pan-African Youth Union
R&D	Research and Development
QPE	Quality Physical Education
S4YE	Solutions for Youth Employment
SDG	Sustainable Development Goal
SeyCCAT	Seychelles' Conservation and Climate Adaptation Trust

SGBV	Sexual and Gender-Based Violence
SIDS	Small Island Developing State
SRHIN	Slum and Rural Health Initiative
SROI	Social Return on Investment
SST	Seychelles Support Team
STEAM	Science, Technology, Engineering, Art and Maths
STEM	Science, Technology, Engineering and Maths
STI	Sexually Transmitted Infection
TOL	Transfer of Learning
UK	United Kingdom
UNAIDS	Joint United Nations Programme on HIV/AIDS
UNCDP	United Nations Committee for Development Policy
UNDESA	United Nations Department of Economic and Social Affairs
UNDP	United Nations Development Programme
UNEP	United Nations Environment Programme
UNESCO	United Nations Educational, Scientific and Cultural Organization
UNFCCC	United Nations Framework Convention on Climate Change
UN-Habitat	United Nations Human Settlements Programme
UNICEF	United Nations Children's Fund
UNSC	UN Security Council
UNSCR	United Nations Security Council Resolution
UNOY	United Network of Young Peacebuilders
USA	United States of America
USAID	US Agency for International Development
USDOL	US Department of Labor
WBL	Work-Based Learning
WEF	World Economic Forum
WHO	World Health Organization

Y20	Youth 20	YOURS	Youth for Road Safety
YCL	Youth Climate Lab	YP	Young Professional
YDI	Youth Development Index	YPP	Young Professionals Programme
YLL	Years of Life Lost	YPS	Youth, Peace and Security

Executive Summary

What is the Youth Development Index?

The YDI is a resource for researchers, policy-makers and civil society, including young people, to track progress on the Sustainable Development Goals (SDGs) associated with youth development. This is a process that enhances the status of young people, empowering them to build on their competences and capabilities for life and enabling them to contribute and benefit from a politically stable, economically viable and legally supportive environment, ensuring their full participation as active citizens in their countries.

The 2020 YDI measures progress in 181 countries, including 48 of the 54 Commonwealth countries, across 6 domains of youth development: Health and Wellbeing, Education, Employment and Opportunity, Political and Civic Participation, Equality and Inclusion and Peace and Security. Changes in 27 indicators across the 6 domains are tracked over the period 2010–2018. Where indicators are used that refer specifically to the situation of the youth population, the definition of youth is of persons 15–29 years old, though data is sometimes available only for those 15–24 years old.

The methodology and indicators used to compile the YDI have been updated since the 2016 report and, for the first time, levels of Peace and Security and Equality and Inclusion are being measured. Full details of the indicators comprising the index and the methodology are found in Chapter 1 and Annex 1.

How should we interpret the YDI?

The YDI score is a number between 0 and 1, with 1 representing the highest possible level of youth development attainable across all indicators. A score of 0, therefore, reflects little to no youth development.

In Chapter 2, which outlines the overall and domain scores achieved by countries, reference is made to four levels of youth development – "very high", "high", "medium" and "low." A country's level of youth development is dependent on the country's position relative to other countries on a spectrum of "relatively good" to "relatively poor." This relative approach acknowledges that a score of 1 is idealistic and practically impossible and a score of 0 is also practically impossible.

As a global comparison tool, the YDI uses national-level data, which can sometime mask variations in youth development at sub-national levels. It compares scores between countries and regions but does not provide insight on variations or inequalities in youth development within a country. It also does not measure every aspect of youth development – focusing instead on a core set of indicators that expert literature has shown heavily influences development outcomes for young people. There is a strong relationship between the YDI and most of the SDGs – meaning that countries that perform well on youth development also tend to have made greater progress towards the SDGs.

In summary, the YDI allows us to take a temperature check on progress towards youth development in the world. Increasing or declining scores signal the need for further investigation and dialogue on the situation of young people and prompt action to scale up good practice or undertake reforms. It is not a definitive diagnosis or situation analysis of each country's policies or programmes. However, it is an indication of collective progress or decline towards ensuring that young people are not left behind in the pursuit of the SDGs.

The index was compiled, before the COVID-19 pandemic, using the latest available data for global comparability. Notwithstanding the commentary included in this report on the preliminary effects of the pandemic on young people, the 2020 index does not take into account these more recent changes. Indeed, it would not be wise to seek to measure those effects too early in a continually evolving context. However, the next iteration of the index is likely to take into account the impact of the pandemic on young people's lives.

What have we learnt from the 2020 YDI?

On average, youth development has been improving, although progress is slow. Between 2010 and 2018, the global average youth development score improved by 3.1 per cent. Similarly, 156 of the

181 countries included in the index (86 per cent) improved their scores. Singapore had the highest level of youth development and Chad the lowest.

Tracking progress in the Commonwealth is important, given that more than 60 per cent of its population of over 2 billion is under 30 years old. Of the 48 Commonwealth countries included in the 2020 YDI, 40 (83 per cent) improved their scores. The Commonwealth average score improved by 2.8 per cent compared with the 3.1 per cent improvement in the global average. Although two Commonwealth countries (Singapore and Malta) are in the top 10 of global countries, one (Mozambique) is in the lowest-ranked countries. More than half of the Commonwealth countries included in the index are still in the low or medium youth development categories.

Progress by thematic domain of the index has been varied.

Health and Wellbeing

Up to 2018, more than half of countries were performing well in this domain – consistent with high and very high levels of youth development, given the traditionally strong policy focus on heavy investment in health. The world's mortality score improved by 12.1 per cent up to 2018. The rates of HIV, self-harm, alcohol abuse and tobacco consumption also improved over the period, though by only 2 per cent each.

The Health and Wellbeing domain recorded the largest improvement at 4.39 per cent. With the advent of the COVID-19 pandemic, these marginal gains are under threat, from weakened health systems and restrictions on movement, which have hampered access to health services, as well as isolation, unemployment and educational disruptions, which negatively affect mental health. The implications of the COVID-19 context are discussed in Chapter 2.

Chapter 4 highlights ways in which young people are contributing to promoting good health and wellbeing, with special recognition of the work of the 2021 Commonwealth Young Person of the Year and the Commonwealth COVID-19 Heroes. In addition, it highlights two important areas requiring special attention going forward – revision of legislation governing youth access to mental health services; and the worrisome levels of road traffic fatalities among young people. Chapter 5 explores the potential for measuring progress on health, alongside education, employment and peace, by monitoring contribution of sports and physical activity.

Less than half of Commonwealth countries register scores on Health and Well-being consistent with high and very high levels of youth development. Careful attention will have to be paid to recent changes in light of the effects of COVID-19 on health systems.

Education

Globally, scores in the Education domain improved by on average 3 per cent over the period, driven by a 5.3 per cent improvement in lower secondary school completion rates and a 2.4 per cent improvement in literacy rates. Half of the Commonwealth countries received scores consistent with HIGH AND VERY HIGH levels of youth development.

At the same time, it is estimated that only 38 per cent of young people can be considered "digital natives" based on five or more years of internet use. This estimate derives from 2014 data from the International Telecommunication Union because evidence is still insufficient in this area. In addition to the lack of time-series data on digital natives, there is a lack of other data to measure more comprehensively young people's skills and engagement online. The kinds of skills required to take advantage of the digital economy are explored in Chapters 6 and 7, which also explore a variety of opportunities for human capital development in this area.

South Asia recorded the largest improvement in the Education domain, with 16.13 per cent improvement on the regional average. Sub-Saharan Africa also made substantial progress, posting nearly 10 per cent improvement.

Employment and Opportunity

The global average score in this area improved by over 3 per cent up to 2018. Seven of the top ten countries in this domain were small states, including five small island developing states (SIDS).

Over the period, global levels of underemployment and shares of young people not in education, employment or training (NEET) largely remained constant. However, disruptions caused by the COVID-19 pandemic have had disproportionate effects on the educational and employment opportunities of young people, especially young women. While more young people have access to a bank account or mobile money and there are fewer adolescent pregnancies before age 20 – both trends indicating increased opportunity for young people – these gains may be reversed in a post-COVID era. At the same time, the pandemic has created new opportunities for online work. However, as we see in Chapter 7, greater investment in skilling for the digital economy will be required if young people are to reap the benefits.

Political and Civic Participation

The strong correlation between the YDI and the indicators for the SDGs suggests that participation of young people remains critical to the achievement of Agenda 2030. However, performance in the Political and Civic Participation domain of the YDI has been universally poor. This is the only domain in which the average global score has deteriorated. No country scored more than 0.50.

On average in 2018, 20 per cent of youth in each country reported that they had volunteered their time, while 16.2 per cent reported that they had voiced an opinion to an official in the previous 30 days. In contrast, recognition of young people's investments in improving their communities has increased on average by over 10 per cent.

The low scores call for a more rounded evaluation of and greater investment in participation processes and structures. The YDI measures formal institutional aspects of participation,

based on globally comparable indicators. However, the stories and experiences shared in this report demonstrate that young people in some contexts are on their own initiative making innovative contributions and #TakingCharge of our common future. Profiles of youth participation and contribution are featured in each chapter of the report. The work ahead of stakeholders is to strengthen the formal institutional environment, removing barriers to participation and making connections to and investments in less formal youth initiatives at local, regional, national and international levels.

Equality and Inclusion

This new domain of the YDI allows us to track the differential progress of young men and women in education, employment, peace and security; and differential progress between young people living above or below the poverty line.

A 2 per cent improvement in the domain score suggests greater equality among young people. The 5.71 per cent improvement in the score for economic marginalisation suggests that more young people are being pulled out of extreme poverty and have improved opportunities for economic security and inclusion. Improvements have been made towards gender equality, with improved scores for gender parity in literacy (improved by 2.13 per cent), proportion of youth NEET (improved by 1.85 per cent) and incidents of early marriage among young women (improved by 1.1 per cent). Combined with the fact that fewer young women are becoming pregnant before age 20, chances to pursue a career and achieve financial independence are increasing for young women.

These gains for young women will have to be reconsidered in the post-COVID analysis. Preliminary research from the International Labour Organization has highlighted the disproportionately negative impact of socio-economic disruptions of the pandemic on young women.

There has been no significant change in gender parity in safety and security. Significantly more young men than young women around the world report feeling safe in their communities. The gender gap in feelings of safety is widest in the world's most peaceful countries, suggesting that gains in peacefulness have, thus far, disproportionately accrued to men.

Chapter 8 provides an opportunity to highlight Commonwealth Youth Awardees working towards greater equality and inclusion in their communities, including initiatives focusing on gender equality and disability inclusion. This index has not been able to directly capture the differential experiences of young people with disabilities. In this regard, Chapter 9 provides insight into the educational and employment experiences of young people with disabilities, making recommendations for greater policy equality and better data collection to support monitoring progress.

Peace and Security

The second largest global improvement in scores was recorded in the Peace and Security domain, improving by 3.41 per cent between 2010 and 2018.

The improvement in the domain is driven by a 5.32 per cent improvement in the Index for Risk Management (INFORM) score, which measures country-level risk of armed conflict and climate change-induced disasters. Young people continue to develop in a context of increasing environmental hazard. However, country coping capacity seems to be rising. The index does not capture any specific measure of youth participation in climate change decision-making but perspectives on the needs in this area are covered in Chapter 10.

Fewer young people are dying from direct violence – from armed conflict, terrorism and homicide around the world – with improved scores on the conflict and terrorism scores. This is reflective of the overall trends of fewer lives lost owing to armed conflict in the past decade. However, the internal peace indicator deteriorated by 1.28 per cent, suggesting young people are experiencing more violent environments.

Data availability

Notwithstanding the updates to the 2020 YDI, the report highlights the fact that youth-disaggregated data is still limited in many areas. Data on youth-specific digital engagement, road traffic fatalities,

climate change and peace and security-related goals is still inadequate. At the same time, there exist opportunities to measure progress on the contribution of sports to positive outcomes for youth in education, health, employment and peace.

A renewed focus on data collection and disaggregation for youth, as well as continued updating of the YDI as a tool for consistent monitoring, is imperative.

What are the implications for the YDI and youth development policy?

Following the presentation of the 2020 YDI results and analysis in Chapters 1 and 2, the report offers a variety of perspectives from specialist researchers, policy-makers, youth workers and youth leaders that identify key opportunities and entry points for connecting, innovating and transforming the situation for youth development. These varied perspectives and analyses outline opportunities for change in four key areas.

Supporting young people #TakingCharge of the future

Continued recognition of the contributions of young people, who are taking charge of our future through their own small initiatives with big impact, is an important policy priority, against a background of declining satisfaction and participation in formal institutions of governance.

Deeper research and evaluation of participation at local, national, regional and international levels is required to obtain a more comprehensive picture of youth engagement in political and civic life and guidance on principles, processes and structures that prove effective.

Strengthening the measurement of participation will perhaps lead to more progress in this area and will encourage exchange of good practice across the Commonwealth and beyond on youth

mainstreaming and strengthening informal and formal structures.

Opportunities for human capital development

The progress on health, education and employment for young people observed over the past decade has been the result of consistent investment in these sectors. Now, in the context of a pandemic that has had a direct and negative impact on young people, there is a need to ensure that we are able to prioritise policy action in areas that specifically affect young people.

This will include policy reform on access to mental health, reducing road traffic fatalities, promoting sport and physical activity and investing in capacity-building for young people to take advantage of decent work and entrepreneurship opportunities in an increasingly digital economy.

Opportunities for equality and inclusion

The measurement of differential impact is critical for effective youth policy-making. The continued updating of the global YDI to take into account of gender and economic marginalisation is critical.

The disproportionately limited opportunities for young people with disabilities mean that greater attention is required to adopting anti-discrimination legislation to ensure equal access to education, employment and full participation in society for youth with disabilities. In addition, it will be necessary to adapt data collection methodologies to ensure that high-quality data is available on youth with disabilities to both inform policy and raise public awareness of the rights of persons with disabilities.

Capacity for equitable and evidence-based policy-making will be significantly increased through the creation and tracking of national youth development indices that can more sensitively capture indicators required for equality and inclusion across racial, ethnic, religious and other groups, relevant to each country context.

Opportunities for security

The new domain on Peace and Security helps us understand the environment in which young people are living with respect to climate hazard and violence. However, the indicators are not yet available at a global level to measure youth participation in climate action and peace-building, even though young people continue to lead global movements and action on these issues.

Mainstreaming of youth in climate and security policies and plans is critical to enabling investment in youth-led initiatives that promote change. Inclusion of the concerns of young people in Nationally Determined Contributions and in national action plans for youth, peace and security should be encouraged.

Increased participatory monitoring and evaluation of the social and economic value created by youth-led initiatives to build social cohesion, peace and security will provide better evidence for policy-making and investment in effective programming.

The Youth Development Index at a Glance

01

Chapter 1

The Youth Development Index at a Glance

The primary objective of the Youth Development Index (YDI) is to deliver an evidence-based overview of the conditions of youth across the world, focusing on opportunities for their development. Chapter 1 provides a brief overview of the 2020 YDI, including:

- Purpose;

- Definitions and theoretical underpinnings;

- Discussion of the availability of youth-disaggregated data.

1.1 Why measure youth development?

Today's youth are coming of age at a unique moment in time. On top of facing colliding climate, economic and health crises, Generation Z could be the last youth boom for the foreseeable future. Economic development and advances in health and medicine mean that families are smaller and people are living longer, leading to an ageing global population. Figure 1.1 shows the world's expected population distributions in 2018 and 2100.

Over the next century, the world will face overlapping trends: an increase in the number of young people and a decline in their share of the population. In 2018, the world population was approximately 7.6 billion people, with 15–29 year olds amounting to 1.8 billion, or nearly

24 per cent (UNDESA, 2019). The proportion of young people is projected to decrease to 19 per cent by 2075, despite an increase in the total number of young people to over 2 billion. In contrast, the share of people aged 60 and older, who currently account for about 13 per cent of the global population, is expected to rise to more than 25 per cent by 2075.

Conventional wisdom suggests this demographic trend will create risks for both the near and the far future. In the near term, despite evidence to the contrary, youth bulges are thought to lead to social unrest and higher rates of crime and violence. Larger youth populations are also more difficult to serve, which partially explains the trend shown in Figure 1.2, whereby countries with a youth bulge generally have lower levels of youth development. In the longer term, an ageing population means there are fewer people of working age to support the economy and the elderly. Meanwhile, an elder bulge creates the same strain on service delivery as a youth bulge, when too many people of the same age need the same care at the same time. However, the findings of the 2020 YDI reveal two countervailing trends suggesting that, rather than a social or economic risk factor, today's global youth boom represents a much-needed opportunity.

Overall, development for young people has improved steadily, albeit slowly, for the past decade. For the most part, more young people are completing their

Figure 1.1 World population pyramids, 2018 and 2100

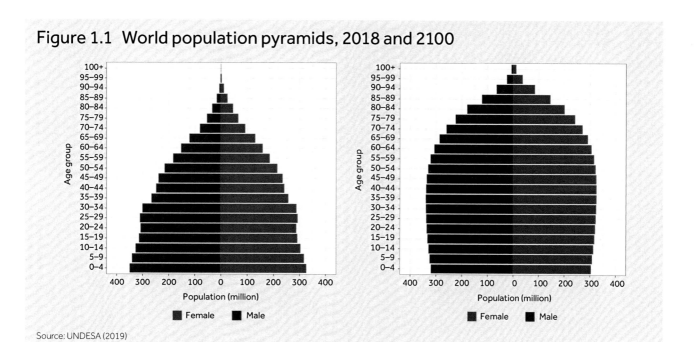

Source: UNDESA (2019)

education, achieving economic independence and engaging productively in their community and country. Today's youth will be well prepared to become the leaders their societies need.

In addition, while global peacefulness has mostly deteriorated over the same period, the YDI shows that the peace and security context for young people has improved significantly over the period. Despite the terrorism, civil wars, displacement and natural disasters of the past decade, young people today face fewer years of life lost from violence and are coming of age in societies better prepared to prevent and address crises. This is a promising finding in light of the recent United Nations Security Council Resolution 2250, which requires the world to engage young people as active peace-builders

rather than threats to security, and the mandate of the Sustainable Development Goals (SDGs) to leave no one behind in creating a safer, more sustainable world.

These demographic projections highlight the need to seize the opportunity of today's youth boom, while the YDI offers one of the tools needed to do so. Figure 1.3 shows that high levels of youth development are correlated with high levels of development for everyone. The findings presented in this report highlight the progress of the past decade, and the areas that need urgent attention in order to lay the groundwork for addressing future challenges. Now is the moment to lay the foundations for a century of sustainable human development – while today's global population is young.

Figure 1.2 Correlation between youth proportion and YDI score by region, 2018

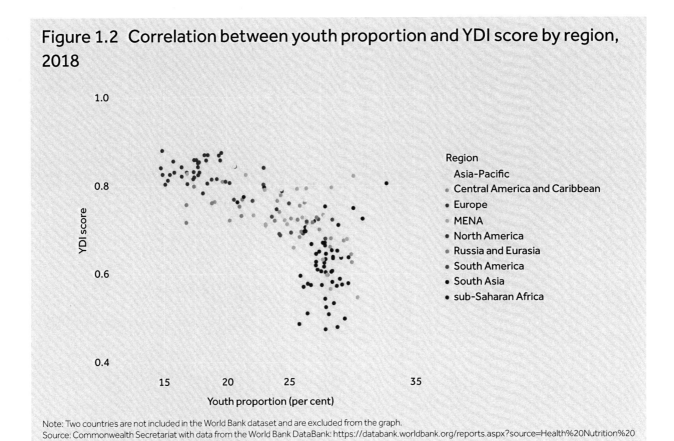

Note: Two countries are not included in the World Bank dataset and are excluded from the graph.
Source: Commonwealth Secretariat with data from the World Bank DataBank: https://databank.worldbank.org/reports.aspx?source=Health%20Nutrition%20
and%20Population%20Statistics:%20Population%20estimates%20and%20projections#

Figure 1.3 Correlation between YDI score and HDI score, 2018

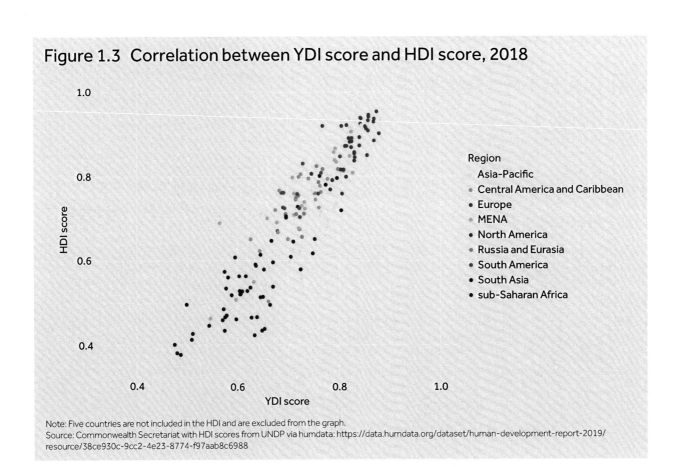

Note: Five countries are not included in the HDI and are excluded from the graph.
Source: Commonwealth Secretariat with HDI scores from UNDP via humdata: https://data.humdata.org/dataset/human-development-report-2019/
resource/38ce930c-9cc2-4e23-8774-f97aab8c6988

1.2 What is the YDI?

The global Youth Development Index (YDI) is a composite index of 27 indicators that measures youth development in 181 countries, including 48 of the 54 Commonwealth countries. The YDI comprises six domains, measuring levels of *Health and Wellbeing, Education, Employment and Opportunity, Equality and Inclusion, Political and Civic Participation* and *Peace and Security.* It provides researchers, policy-makers and civil society, including youth, with a resource to compare countries on their relative levels of youth development. The 2020 YDI measures youth development over an eight-year time span, from 2010 to 2018, tracking trends in youth development across regions and within countries. The YDI scores range between 0 and 1, with 1 indicating the highest possible level of youth development.

The YDI and the accompanying report of findings are but two tools in the Commonwealth Secretariat's Youth Programme. The global YDI measures youth development at the national level and sets out the framework for measuring progress in youth development. The Commonwealth Secretariat also works with member countries and regional bodies to develop regional and sub-national YDIs that can further illuminate local youth development successes and challenges.

These local indices follow the framework developed collaboratively by experts at the global level and also lead the way in terms of metrics that cannot be included in the global YDI. Some of these metrics include context-specific indicators measuring local challenges; others fill indicator gaps where local data coverage outperforms global datasets. The periodically published global YDI report represents the flagship publication in the series, paving the way for additional research and data on youth development around the world, while regions, countries and communities are encouraged to develop additional metrics and tools to advance youth development and its measurement.

1.3 What is youth development?

"Human development is about giving people more freedom to live lives they value" (HDRO Outreach, 2015). The process of human development is therefore about developing people's abilities and ensuring they have the opportunity to use them. The YDI defines youth development as "enhancing the status of young people, empowering them to build on their competencies and capabilities for life. It will enable them to contribute and benefit from a politically stable, economically viable, and legally supportive environment, ensuring their full participation as active citizens in their countries." The theoretical framework that underpins the development of the YDI is derived from the work of Sen (1985) and Nussbaum (2000, 2003) on capabilities, which has similarly been used as the theoretical framework for the United Nations Development Programme's (UNDP's) Human Development Report.

Nussbaum (2003) distinguishes between first-generation rights, such as civil liberties and opportunities for political participation, and second-generation rights, such as opportunities for education and employment. In addition, Sen (1985) advocates for a broad capability approach to development, not one that focuses simply on economic measures. Sen illustrates this by pointing out that, while the gross domestic products of Brazil and Mexico are significantly higher than that of Sri Lanka, life expectancy and child mortality are far better in the latter country. The YDI adopts this broad approach to capabilities and includes domains that cover both first- and second-generation rights in youth development.

1.4 Who are youth?

The YDI uses the Commonwealth Secretariat's definition of youth: young people aged 15–29. However, there is no universal definition of the ages that start and end the period called "youth." *Young people* or *youth* are often defined more by "who they are not" than by who they are (Furlong and Cartmel, 1997). Often, *youth* are taken to be a group between childhood and adulthood but the actual age range is debatable. And yet data and policy necessitate defining youth within an age bracket. As Table 1.1 shows, regional and international organisations use varying age ranges to categorise young people, and the same is true of national governments.

In constructing the YDI, in some instances data was unavailable for the 15–29 age bracket. For example, International Labour Organization (ILO) data covers only 15–24 year olds. As a consequence, indicators in the YDI unavoidably cover slightly different age cohorts, but the best available datasets, with a range as close to 15–29 years as possible, have been selected.

Table 1.1 Age group defined as youth by various regional and international organisations

Organisation	Age group defined as youth
The Commonwealth	15–29
United Nations Educational, Scientific and Cultural Organization (UNESCO)	15–24
International Labour Organization (ILO)	15–24
United Nations Human Settlements Programme (UN-Habitat) (Youth Fund)	15–32
World Health Organization (WHO)	10–24
World Bank	15–24
Organisation for Economic Co-operation and Development (OECD)	15–29
African Union Commission	18–35
European Commission	15–29
United Nations Security Council Resolution 2250 on Youth, Peace and Security	18–29

1.5 What does the YDI add to existing measures?

Similar to human development, it is not possible to measure youth development via one single indicator. Youth development is a multidimensional concept that can be better understood via an aggregation of multiple indicators. Many governments, non-governmental organisations (NGOs) and youth service providers publish data on specific aspects of youth development but do not provide a holistic picture of youth development. The YDI provides this by compiling the available data into one comprehensive and harmonised measure. This enables youth development advocates and policy-makers to gain a better understanding of youth development across time and space, as the index covers 181 countries over an 8-year time span.

In addition, in constructing the 2020 YDI, the data scoping process has drawn attention to key gaps in data and has highlighted particular areas where data collection efforts can be improved. While some countries face greater challenges in collating data, youth-specific datasets appear to be a global challenge. As an ambiguously defined group, young people are often not specifically addressed in the statistics. Evidently, there is a need for more youth-specific data. In addition, some countries face greater challenges in collecting data owing to limited capacities and are, therefore, falling behind on youth development already.

1.6 What does the YDI measure?

The YDI measures six distinct domains that are considered key aspects of youth development: *Health and Wellbeing, Education, Employment and Opportunity, Equality and Inclusion, Political and Civic Participation* and *Peace and Security.* In total, the YDI compiles 27 indicators, as presented in Table 1.2, grouping between 3 and 7 indicators in each domain.

1.7 How should one interpret the YDI?

The YDI score is a number between 0 and 1, with 1 representing the highest possible level of youth development attainable across all indicators. A score of 0, therefore, reflects little to no youth development. The scoring system resembles that of UNDP's Human Development Index (HDI).

In addition, the results section refers to four categories of youth development: "very high," "high," "medium" and "low." These categories are calculated as the three quartiles – that is, the 25th, 50th and 75th percentiles – of all country scores. Categorising countries' level of youth development is, therefore, dependent on the individual country's position relative to other countries on a spectrum from "relatively good" to "relatively poor." By using the quartiles, the categorisation takes the actual scoring range into account, adopting a relative approach and acknowledging that a score of 1 is idealistic and practically impossible.

Finally, the YDI is constrained in its application of national-level data, which can sometimes mask variations in youth development on the sub-national levels. As a global index, the YDI facilitates a comparison of scores between countries and regions but does not provide any insight on variations or inequalities in youth development within a country.

Table 1.2 2020 YDI indicators

Domain	Indicator	Definition	Source
Health & Wellbeing	Mortality rate	Deaths from all causes, ages 15–29	Institute for Health Metrics and Evaluation (IHME), Global Burden of Disease (GBD)
	HIV rate	HIV rate, ages 15–24	Joint United Nations Programme on HIV/AIDS (UNAIDS) estimates
	Self-harm	Years of life lost (YLL) from self-harm, ages 15–29	IHME GBD
	Mental health	YLL from mental disorders, ages 15–29	IHME GBD
	Drug abuse	YLL from drug use disorders, ages 15–29	IHME GBD
	Alcohol abuse	YLL from alcohol use disorders, ages 15–29	IHME GBD
	Tobacco consumption	Tobacco smokers, % of ages 15–29	IHME GBD
Education	Literacy rate	Literacy rate, youth total, % of ages 15–24	UNESCO Institute for Statistics
	School completion	Lower secondary completion rate, total, % of country-specific age group	UNESCO Institute for Statistics
	Digital natives	Five or more years' experience using the internet, % of ages 15–29	International Telecommunication Union (ITU)
Employment & Opportunity	Not in education, employment or training (NEET)	NEET youth, % of ages 15–24	ILO
	Underemployment	Time-related underemployment, ages 15–24	ILO modelled estimates
	Adolescent fertility rate	Adolescent fertility rate, births per 1,000 women ages 15–19	United Nations Population Division, World Population Prospects
	Account	Respondents who report having an account (by themselves or together with someone else) at a bank or other financial institution or report using mobile money in the past 12 months, % ages 15–24	World Bank Global Findex Database

(*Continued*)

Table 1.2 2020 YDI indicators (*Continued*)

Domain	Indicator	Definition	Source
Equality & Inclusion	Gender parity in NEET	Distance from parity between percentages of NEET young women and NEET young men, ages 15–24	United Nations Department of Economic and Social Affairs (UNDESA) Global Sustainable Development Goal (SDG) Indicators Database, Institute for Economics & Peace (IEP) calculations
	Gender parity in safety and security	Distance from parity between percentages of young women and young men who report feeling safe walking alone in their neighbourhood at night	Gallup World Poll (GWP), IEP calculations
	Gender parity in literacy	Literacy rate, youth, ages 15–24, Gender Parity Index (GPI)	UNESCO Institute for Statistics
	Early marriage	Women first married by age 18, % of women ages 20–24	Country surveys collected by the World Bank and OECD
	Economic marginalisation	Population percentage classified as extremely poor (< US$ 1.90 PPP) or moderately poor (>= US$ 1.90 and <US$ 3.20 PPP), ages 15–24	ILO modelled estimates
Political & Civic Participation	Youth policy score	Scores on youth policy and legislation, public institutions, youth representation, and public budget and spending	Youth Policy Labs, IEP calculation
	Voiced opinion to an official	Responding that they have voiced their opinion to an official in the past 30 days, % ages 15–29	GWP
	Volunteered time	Responding that they have volunteered time in the past 30 days, % ages 15–29	GWP
	Recognition for community improvement	Responding "agree" or "strongly agree' with the statement "In the last 12 months, you have received recognition for helping to improve the city or area where you live," % ages 15–29	GWP
Peace & Security	Internal peace score	Composite score for domestic peace and safety and security	IEP Global Peace Index (GPI)
	Interpersonal violence	YLL from interpersonal violence, ages 15–29	IHME GBD
	Conflict and terrorism	YLL from armed conflict and terrorism, ages 15–29	IHME GBD
	Index for Risk Management (INFORM) score	Risk of humanitarian crisis and disaster, including climate change related risks	EU INFORM

Box 1.1 What is new in the 2020 YDI?

The 2020 YDI includes two new domains, as well as some changes to the previous domains and indicators, in order to improve the overall metric. Section 1.8 outlines the rationale for each of the 2020 YDI domains while the methodology annex (Annex 1) details specific updates to the domains and indicators compared with the 2016 YDI. In addition to the use of ever-better data on youth development, the chief improvements introduced in the 2020 YDI involve the addition of the *Peace and Security* and *Equality and Inclusion* domains – both of which represent global firsts.

Each domain of the YDI is a sub-index in itself, in that it brings together distinct indicators to create a composite measure of the topic. The YDI's *Peace and Security* domain is the first global youth-specific peace and security index, and the 2020 findings highlight the value of youth-specific metrics. In spite of the fact that world peace has deteriorated for most of the past decade, the experiences and context for young people have improved on *Peace*

and Security more than for any other domain of the YDI. Youth are globally recognised as being heavily affected by breakdowns in peacefulness, making the YDI results particularly promising.

The YDI's *Equality and Inclusion* domain is the first global index on youth inclusion, with an important emphasis on gender equality. The domain is designed to measure multiple aspects of inclusion, recognising that the factors that create social exclusion for young people are diverse and intersectional and have wide-ranging impacts. However, global datasets on the prevalence and exclusionary impacts of factors like disability and mental ill-health remain unavailable. It is chiefly the progress that the world has made in acknowledging and tracking gender gaps that has made the development of this domain possible in 2020. In its inaugural iteration, this domain measures economic inclusion and gender equality, while creating the framework to add additional indicators as they become available.

1.8 How is the YDI weighted?

Composite indices often apply weights to the indicators or domains within the index, for a variety of reasons. Index weights can indicate conceptual importance, correct for poor data quality (by underweighting less reliable datasets) or statistically adjust the overall index score so that it better reflects the multidimensional concept being measured. The YDI employs indicator and domain weights for all three of these purposes.

The most heavily weighted domains in the YDI are those that align with the three domains of the HDI: *Health and Wellbeing*, *Education* and *Employment and Opportunity*. Similarly, each of these three domains includes a primary indicator, weighted to comprise 10 per cent of the domain score. The remaining indicators in these domains complete the picture.

The other three YDI domains are included in order to capture additional key aspects of the youth development and are weighted using all three approaches. The *Equality and Inclusion* domain includes high-quality data and directly measures the experiences of young people. As such, this domain is weighted most heavily of the three secondary domains. The *Peace and Security* domain includes a mix of indicators measuring youth experiences and the

enabling environment, and as such is weighted slightly less, as it is important but less directly relevant. As discussed elsewhere in this report, the *Political and Civic Participation* domain suffers from data limitations. In addition, a principal component analysis (PCA) revealed that indicators in this domain contribute the least, statistically, to variations in the YDI overall score.

The weighting scheme used in the 2020 YDI helps in constructing an accurate composite measure of the broad concept of youth development, by leading with the critical, foundational aspects of human development but also incorporating youth-specific needs and experiences. Detailed domain and indicator weights are provided in the methodology annex (Annex 1) of this report.

1.9 Rationale for the 2020 YDI domains

The domains that constitute the YDI reflect some of the essential areas of youth development. As a multidimensional concept, youth development is dependent on a wide range of factors, influencing the individual in the transition from childhood to full adulthood. Backed by research evidence and directed by data availability, three of the six domains

Figure 1.4 Youth Development Index domains

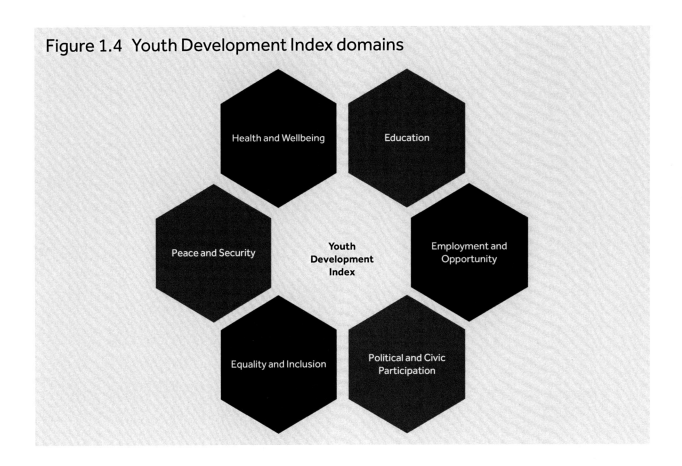

are weighted more heavily in the 2020 YDI: *Health and Wellbeing, Education* and *Employment and Opportunity.* These domains are weighted at 22 per cent of the overall index score each, while *Equality and Inclusion* is weighted at 14 per cent and the two remaining domains, *Political and Civic Participation* and *Peace and Security,* are both weighted at 10 per cent each.

The domains of the 2020 YDI have been developed with the sustainability and scalability of the index in mind. While several domains still lack key indicators – such as those capturing the experiences of youth with disabilities – the conceptual framework and the domain themes have been developed so as to allow for the inclusion of better data as it becomes available.

1.9.1 Health and Wellbeing

While young people are often thought to be in the prime of their lives, suicide, communicable diseases (including HIV) and non-communicable diseases remain a challenge to their development globally. Moreover, some suffer from chronic illnesses that hinder their ability to grow and develop their full potential. Health is closely related to socio-economic status and habits established in youth, such as smoking or drinking alcohol, which subsequently affect patterns of mortality (West, 2009). To grow and progress in

life, young people require access to good health care and, crucially, should engage in healthier practices to guard against premature death and to ensure a healthy adult life. The seismic impact of COVID-19 upon global health systems and the necessary initial focus on those most vulnerable to the virus, generally older populations, will inevitably have had an impact upon health care outcomes for younger people.

This health emergency will have been compounded by the spill over socio-economic impacts of the pandemic which seem likely to have adversely impacted younger people more and which unless addressed could have significant longer term ramifications for their health.

"Education opens opportunities and improves life chances."

1.9.2 Education

Education opens opportunities and improves life chances. It plays a vital role in occupation entry, financial security and life satisfaction. However, there are still vast numbers of young people who lack basic literacy skills, and educational opportunities are restricted for some groups, such as girls and young women, rural youth and young people with disabilities (Furlong et al., 2016).

Education continues to be one of the development areas where we see large and persistent inequalities in performance and progression (Shavit and Blossfeld, 1993). Improving access to quality education, especially with growing concern about the impact of COVID-19, by eliminating barriers, is key to youth development.

1.9.3 Employment and Opportunity

Opportunities to gain employment in secure and meaningful jobs or to pursue financial independence are key features of a well-functioning society. Without access to employment or dignity of labour, young people are unable to develop skills, become established as independent citizens or maintain an adequate standard of living. Therefore, measures of employment, employment opportunities and financial independence are important indicators of youth development. Employment is an area of immediate importance for youth development as the economic shock caused by the COVID-19 pandemic is expected to disproportionately affect young workers and those hoping to enter the job market (ILO, 2020).

1.9.4 Equality and Inclusion

The *Equality and Inclusion* domain was newly developed for the 2020 YDI. Its goal is to capture the degree to which various groups of young people are enjoying equal opportunities in society. In the 2020 YDI, owing to limited availability of cross-country data, this domain is included with scalability in mind. In the 2020 YDI, the domain indicators measure gender parity and economic marginalisation, while the overall domain holds space in the index for the incorporation of improved data. More detail about additional possible metrics is included in Annex 1 detailing the YDI methodology.

Young women and young men have demonstrably distinct experiences in the transition from adolescence to adulthood. Disparities can be harmful to both the individual and society as a whole. Systematic discrimination, such as discrimination against women, limits not only the individual's prospect of self-realisation but also the national economy, which, for example, misses out on valuable contributions. By excluding certain segments of the population from education, employment opportunities and political participation, the whole country suffers. In light of this, the YDI includes a basket of indicators that measure gender parity on key development outcomes.

Economic inequalities have a similar effect on youth development, limiting both the individual and broader society. For example, an interest in politics and political participation is more common among young people from affluent families and those who are better educated (Henn et al., 2005), at least in part because inequality reduces social, civic and political participation as more work hours are required to achieve economic security.

1.9.5 Political and Civic Participation

Participation combats exclusion and promotes social integration as well as youth development by giving young people a stake in their society. Young people's participation in their communities' political life shows the extent to which they are empowered and engaged in the political process. In addition, stronger intergenerational bonds are formed when young people are given a say in the development of their community. Similarly, civic engagement is a vital component in community development. Civic participation is a complementary element to political participation and can take many forms, such as volunteering in the local sports club. It is a key marker of human development as it provides youth the opportunity to fully integrate into society.

1.9.6 Peace and Security

The *Peace and Security* domain captures both the direct effects of interpersonal violence and the enabling environment for youth development. Violence, threats of violence or exposure to natural disasters have psychological, economic and developmental impacts on youth, and violent or hazardous environments can be detrimental to development initiatives. We are also now seeing growing evidence that the COVID-19 pandemic has also significantly increased the prevalence of domestic and gender based violence across all societies. Failure to keep young people safe, as well as the potential for young people to be drawn into criminal organisations, militias or violent movements, ultimately undermines development efforts. A peaceful and secure environment is, therefore, essential to ensure young people can face the challenges of their generation.

1.10 Availability of youth-disaggregated data

Data availability has been one of the primary challenges in constructing the 2020 YDI. The research process has found that many relevant indicators are not disaggregated by age. In general, data on "youth" as a distinct category is limited, with datasets focusing on childhood, adulthood or the total population. The need for comprehensive data to ensure effective youth development is especially important in developing contexts. And yet data availability is a more pressing problem in these countries, where the capacity to invest in data collection is limited.

Annex 1 of this report explains in detail how data limitations were addressed in the construction of the index. However, it is useful to note some key areas for improvement in youth development data:

- Improved country coverage: One of the chief limitations relates to the absence of several Commonwealth countries and other small states from global datasets. In order to include as many Commonwealth countries as possible, the index imputes up to half of country data in some cases. While several developing countries have levels of data coverage that outpace those of the developed world, small states will need particular support to improve. Accurate and complete data is critical to tracking everything from YDI metrics to progress on the SDGs. The percent of data coverage for each country is detailed in Annex 1. Countries for which a large portion of data is imputed should interpret their results with care.

- Engagement and participation data: Youth engagement in their community is a critical aspect of development, which is acknowledged through the inclusion of the *Political and Civic Participation* domain in the YDI. However, datasets that capture this are scarce. Globally comparable data measuring concepts such as mentorship, healthy relationships, participation in sport, and government policy to facilitate constructive youth engagement range from nascent to non-existent. The datasets used in the YDI provide the best possible picture of youth participation in civic and political spaces; however, with the *Political and Civic Participation* domain showing the only deteriorating trend since 2010, the area remains critical for improved metrics, to make it possible to understand the drivers of the trend and possible solutions.

- Digital data: Access to the internet – and the skills to use it effectively – is of ever-increasing importance in the 21st century. However, there remains no globally comparable dataset that tracks trends in digital skills or engagement over time. The YDI uses country-level estimates of the proportion of youth that can be considered "digital natives," but the data is available for only one year. The extent of digital exposure extended to broader youth populations remains

unmeasured, as do the digital skills that are prioritised in the SDGs, and levels of constructive online engagement, such as the ability to apply for a job or to differentiate between true and false information. Arguably, these represent the most critical data gaps for youth development going forward.

References

Furlong, A. and F. Cartmel (1997) *Young People and Social Change: Individualization and Risk in Late Modernity* (Repr). Milton Keynes: Open University Press.

Furlong, A., J. Goodwin, H. O'Connor, S. Hadfield, S. Hall, K. Lowden and R. Plugor (2016) *Young People in the Labour Market: Past, Present, Future*. London: Routledge.

HDRO (Human Development Report Office) Outreach (2015). *What is Human Development*. New York: United Nations Development Programme. http://hdr.undp.org/en/content/what-human-development

Henn, M., M. Weinstein and D. Wring (2005) "A Generation Apart? Youth and Political Participation in Britain". *The British Journal of Politics and International Relations* **4**(2): 167–192.

ILO (International Labour Organization) (2020) "A Policy Framework for Responding to the COVID-19 Crisis". Policy Brief, 18 May. http://www.ilo.org/global/topics/coronavirus/impacts and-responses/WCMS_739047/lang--en/index.htm

Nussbaum, M. C. (2000) *Women and Human Development: The Capabilities Approach*. Cambridge: Cambridge University Press.

Nussbaum, M. C. (2003) "Capabilities as Fundamental Entitlements: Sen and Social Justice". *Feminist Economics* **9**(2–3): 33–59.

Sen, A. (1985) *Commodities and Capabilities*. Oxford: Oxford University Press.

Shavit, Y. and H.-P. Blossfeld (eds) (1993) *Persistent Inequality: Changing Educational Attainment in Thirteen Countries*. Boulder, CO: Westview Press.

UNDESA (United Nations Department of Economic and Social Affairs) (2019) *World Population Prospects 2019*. New York: Population Division, UNDESA.

West, P. (2009) "Health in Youth: Changing Times and Changing Influences". In Furlong, A. (ed.) *Handbook of Youth and Young Adulthood: New Perspectives and Agendas*. London: Routledge.

2020 Youth Development Index: Analysis and Results

02

Chapter 2

2020 Youth Development Index: Analysis and Results

Key findings

- The global average youth development score improved by 3.1 per cent between 2010 and 2018.

- Singapore had the highest level of youth development on the 2020 YDI, followed by Slovenia, Norway, Malta and Denmark.

- Chad had the lowest level, followed by Central African Republic, Afghanistan, South Sudan and Niger.

- Of the 181 countries included on the 2020 YDI, 156 or 86 per cent, recorded improvements in the eight-year period.

- The top five risers from 2010 to 2018 were Afghanistan, India, Russia, Ethiopia and Burkina Faso.

- Syria, Ukraine, Libya, Yemen and Jordan were the largest fallers.

- On average, the top five risers improved their score by 15.74 per cent while the five largest fallers saw an average deterioration of 10.28 per cent.

- The global average improved in five out of the six domains on the YDI.

- The largest global improvement was recorded in Health and Wellbeing, which improved by 4.39 per cent between 2010 and 2018.

- Political and Civic Participation was the only domain to record an average global deterioration, albeit minimal, at 0.18 per cent.

- Eight out of the nine world regions recorded improvements on their average YDI scores between 2010 and 2018.

- South Asia recorded the largest improvement in its average youth development levels, at 9.5 per cent, followed by Sub-Saharan Africa, Russia and Eurasia and South America.

- Over the eight-year period from 2010 to 2018, the Commonwealth countries recorded an average improvement in youth development of 2.8 per cent, compared with the 3.1 per cent improvement in the global average.

- Of the 48 Commonwealth countries included on the 2020 YDI, 40, or 83 per cent, improved their YDI scores. One country maintained its score.

- On average, the Commonwealth has made progress in all six YDI domains, with the largest improvement seen in the Health and Wellbeing, Peace and Security and Education domains.

2.1 Youth development in a time of a pandemic

Key findings

Youth development improved globally from 2010 to 2018 but the COVID-19 pandemic poses great challenges to the continuous efforts of youth-centred initiatives.

- Sixty-five per cent of youth say they have learnt less since the beginning of the pandemic because of the transition to new ways of learning.

- A study in the UK shows that young people's wellbeing has been declining at a faster rate during the lockdown compared with that of older respondents.

- Prior to the pandemic, young people were almost three times more likely to be unemployed than adults, and youth unemployment tends to increase at a higher rate than overall unemployment during crises.

- Young women, young people with disabilities and other marginalised groups are expected to experience the worst consequences of the pandemic.

- Of the projected 2.3 percentage point increase in people living in poverty as a consequence of COVID-19, more than 82 per cent of this population will be in South Asia and Sub-Saharan Africa, which is home to 42 per cent of the world's youth population.

The results of the 2020 YDI show the promising progress in youth development that youth around the globe have enjoyed in the past decade. Global improvements have been made across all areas, except in the Political and Civic Participation domain, and, with the exception of the Middle East and North Africa (MENA) region, youth in all regions of the world have experienced promising advancements. But the COVID-19 pandemic has proven difficult, particularly for young people, with government-enforced lockdowns leading to sharp increases in youth unemployment, and increased reports of mental anguish among young people, compared with other age groups, even in the most developed countries (Eurofound, 2020a).

The pandemic also poses unforeseen long-term threats to the continuous efforts of youth development. As highlighted by the International Labour Organization (ILO 2020c), "COVID-19 does not discriminate against its victims but the economic impact of the pandemic does" and young people are particularly vulnerable to fluctuations in the economy, during the pandemic as well as through the long-term impact it will have on the economy, health and education systems and opportunities, such as travelling.

Young people are already at higher risk of suffering the economic consequences of lockdowns, as young people more often work in the gig economy, under temporary contracts or informal work-arrangements (ILO, 2020a). In addition to age-based inequalities, young women are at even higher risk of losing out on education and employment opportunities. Particularly in developing countries with poor health systems, care-taking responsibilities often fall on young women, forcing them to leave education behind and limiting their future employment prospects (IIEP, 2020a). Therefore, the long-term impacts of the pandemic will be unequal not only between countries but also within countries, with young people disproportionately affected, and this will require policy-makers and advocates to rethink youth development initiatives in a post-COVID world. This addition to Chapter 2 provides insights into the current impact of the COVID-19 pandemic on youth (as of November 2020), and explains how the 2020 YDI can be used as a timely tool to assist in the planning and prioritisation of youth development initiatives in the future.

2.1.1 Being young during a pandemic

Young people around the globe have already seen challenges as a result of COVID-19 in the diverse areas covered by the YDI. Some of the core challenges for youth caused by the pandemic so far have included disparities in educational performance as a consequence of school closures, rising youth unemployment and the disproportionate mental and physical health challenges facing young people, in particular young women, during government-enforced lockdowns.

COVID-19 has disrupted and halted critical mental health services in 93 per cent of countries worldwide, leaving many young people without the essential services needed to get through the pandemic (WHO, 2020a). Additionally, the increased consumption of alcohol and tobacco and use of illicit substances in Australia have been found to be strongly associated with physiological distress for both sexes, but for males in particular (Biddle et al., 2020). Many youth helpline support services have also recorded a rise in traffic during the pandemic, and widespread lockdowns have made it increasingly difficult for victims of domestic violence to escape their perpetrator.

A study in the UK shows that young people's wellbeing has been declining at a faster rate during the lockdown than that of older respondents (Etheridge and Spantig, 2020). The study also shows a disproportionate decline in women's mental health during lockdown compared with men's, indicating a gender-based inequality. Young women are further disadvantaged during lockdowns, with limited access to sexual and reproductive health care services (Azcona et al., 2020). Migrant women and women from marginalised ethnic groups are also overrepresented in personal care jobs, which require close contact with others and place them at higher risk of contracting COVID-19 (ibid.).

Youth unemployment has increased significantly around the globe since the outbreak early this year. Many young people work in the so-called gig economy, with informal work arrangements or casual contractual work, which is why youth unemployment tends to be higher than the overall unemployment rate. Despite a slight improvement in youth unemployment (15–24 year olds) since February 2020 in Organisation for Economic Co-operation and Development (OECD), the average youth unemployment rate was more than twice as large as that for over 25 year olds in July 2020 (OECD, 2020a). As of September 2020, the OECD estimates youth unemployment to be 15.15 per cent on average, with female youth unemployment

slightly higher, at 15.42 per cent on average (OECD, 2020b). Employment during lockdown not only ensures financial stability but also supports mental well-being, as young people in employment are almost twice as likely to be optimistic about the future, compared with their unemployed peers (Eurofound, 2020b). Yet 38 per cent of young people feel uncertain about their future career prospects (ILO, 2020b).

Part of the uncertainty about future career prospects for young people can be accredited to school closures, which has led to a forcible revolution in learning and teaching methods. School closures impact all young learners and, according to the International Labour Organization (ILO) (2020b), 65 per cent of youth say they have learnt less since the beginning of the pandemic because of the transition. Closing educational institutions does, meanwhile, disproportionately affect disadvantaged youth's career prospects. The need for young people to become digital natives has never been more important, but these opportunities are currently limited to families that can afford the technological equipment required to support such learning.

> *"The COVID-19 crisis has not only highlighted the critical role of information and communication technologies (ICTs) for continued functioning of societies but has also brought to the fore the startling digital inequalities between and within countries"* (IIEP, 2020b).

Again, young women face greater difficulties in attaining these skills, as domestic chores and care-taking responsibilities often fall on females (IIEP, 2020a).

However, the COVID-19 pandemic has also presented new opportunities for youth to participate in and contribute to civil society. Many young people have volunteered to assist with service delivery in their local community, and as such the global downward trend in volunteered time recorded in the 2020 YDI may be reversed in the near future. In the OECD countries, for which data is available, youth volunteered more than older people in 2019, and OECD Director of the Directorate for Public Governance Elsa Pilichowski expects this to increase even more in 2020 as a result of the pandemic (OECD, 2020c). Multiple governments, including those in Canada and France, have set up volunteer platforms to mobilise young volunteers and youth workers during the pandemic – posting great success so far (OECD, 2020d). Evidently, youth volunteers and workers have played a critical role in helping some of the most vulnerable in society throughout the pandemic, from elderly people shielding in their homes to children with limited out-of-school activities (OECD, 2020e). The pivotal role that youth play in protecting some of the most vulnerable in society will be essential in supporting governments to carry out the necessary measures to mitigate the impacts of the pandemic in both the short and the long term.

2.1.2 Youth development post-COVID

The 2020 YDI analysis was conducted in February 2020, only a month before the World Health Organization (WHO) declared the COVID-19 epidemic a global pandemic (WHO, 2020b). The results presented in this chapter reflect this and posit a more optimistic narrative on youth development for the years to come. While youth development has improved globally over the past decade, the pandemic presents cause for concern on whether long-term youth policies will be deprioritised to make room for the short-term necessary prioritisation of health services and the economy. Fortunately, the global improvement over the past decade leaves many countries in a stronger position to deal with the challenges COVID-19 poses, and the 2020 YDI represents a timely tool that can be used for planning and prioritisation of youth development in a time of a pandemic.

Health and Wellbeing, Education, Employment and Opportunity and Equality and Inclusion are the domains expected to be hit the hardest by the long-term consequences of the COVID-19 pandemic. In particular, lockdown measures and school closures will have, and already have had, a substantial impact on educational outcomes, young people's opportunities in the labour market and their prospects of participating in civil and political life. It is also expected that marginalised groups will carry most of the financial burden, potentially increasing global inequality as well as national inequality gaps.

The World Bank projects that an additional 176 million people live below the US$3.20 a day poverty line and an additional 177 million people below $5.50 a day compared with estimates for 2020 prior to the pandemic – almost half of this population will be in

South Asia and more than a third in Sub-Saharan Africa (World Bank, 2020). These two regions recorded some of the largest percentage progress in youth development in the 2020 YDI, at 6.91 and 3.02 per cent, respectively, but the COVID-19 pandemic poses a serious threat to the continuous youth development efforts here. While poverty projections from the World Bank DataBank are not youth-specific, they highlight how youth in some regions face a greater risk of falling into poverty relative to youth in other regions. Young people who are financially dependent on their parents face great challenges when their parents fall into poverty, but also young people who are currently financially independent may find themselves financially dependent on family and their social network. These challenges are expected to be particularly relevant in countries in South Asia and Sub-Saharan Africa, which are home to 42 per cent of the world's youth population and where young people (15–29 year olds) account for 25 per cent of the population.

School closures are expected to lead to a knowledge gap between generations, putting young people at even greater risk at falling behind older generations. Young people will find themselves competing with more experienced and possibly better-skilled candidates in an increasingly strained labour market (Nigro, 2020). In addition, Hanushek and Woessmann (2020) point to existing research that estimates that students in Grades 1–12 who lose one-third of a school year's learning could expect a 3 per cent lower income over their entire lifetime. In addition, these losses are expected to be reflected in countries' annual gross domestic product growth, which is expected to be 1.5 per cent lower per year for the remainder of the century (ibid.). It is, therefore, essential that governments continue to invest heavily in the education sector and support young people's opportunities to develop the skills demanded by the labour market. Government support is particularly important in countries where funding of the education sector relies heavily on international student mobility, as international students typically pay higher fees than domestic students (Schleicher, 2020).

The global financial crisis of 2007/08 highlighted that youth make up a particularly vulnerable group that is disproportionally challenged during times of crises. Underutilisation of youth labour supply, so-called underemployment, is often higher than the national average underemployment rate and, following the global financial crisis, global youth underemployment (15–24 year olds) was more than double that of adult underemployment (25+ years) (ILOSTAT 2020).

The trend was similar in the Commonwealth countries, where youth underemployment peaked at 31.09 per cent in 2013, compared with an adult underemployment rate of 14.99 per cent on average (ibid.).

"Youth make up 25 per cent of the global working-age population, yet they account for 40 per cent of total unemployment. Young people are almost three times more likely to be unemployed than adults" (ILO, 2019).

MENA had one of the highest youth unemployment rates in the world prior to the pandemic (ILO, 2017). In addition, it was the only region to record an average deterioration from 2010 to 2018 on the 2020 YDI. This deterioration was driven primarily by worsened Peace and Security conditions in the region, and this reflects the extent to which some regions face greater challenges in mitigating the impacts of COVID-19, given their predisposition.

The emphasis on Equality and Inclusion has been a key addition to this year's YDI, stressing the importance of including all young people when planning and implementing youth policies, and the COVID-19 pandemic has only reinforced the need for inclusive policies. Young women are at particularly high risk of being excluded from the labour market and are already overrepresented in NEET (not in education, employment or training) statistics (OECD, 2017). On average, women spend nearly three times more hours on unpaid household and care work than men – so-called invisible work – which is not recorded in economic measures, although it is essential work (ILO, 2018). One study has also linked female youth unemployment to higher HIV rates for young women in developing countries, particularly in Sub-Saharan Africa, proving that economic hardship can lead to hardship in other areas of life (Austin et al., 2017). Limited access to sexual and reproductive health care services during lockdowns also affects women disproportionately (Azcona et al., 2020) and declines in national screening programmes risk causing more health challenges in the future (Australian Institute of Health and Welfare, 2020).

Young people with disabilities are also particularly susceptible to the worst consequences of COVID-19, especially people with pre-existing health conditions who are more vulnerable to COVID-19, as well as those who have limited online access and whose support services are disrupted. National lockdowns have, however, challenged the conventional ideas of work-life balance and have potentially opened more flexible employment opportunities for marginalised young people, who would otherwise have been kept out of employment as a result of inflexible work arrangements. Nevertheless, it is important that any measures taken to support young people in the years following the COVID-19 outbreak, whether health policies, employment support initiatives or educational reforms, are co-designed with young people and particularly marginalised youths (OECD, 2020e).

"Investments in youth-responsive policies and services pay off … and everybody gains", as OECD Secretary-General Angel Gurría stated at the launch of the report Governance for Youth, Trust and Intergenerational Justice: Fit for All Generations? on 22 October 2020 (OECD, 2020c). Yet, with only 22 per cent of parliamentarians in the OECD being under the age of 40, in a context where 34 per cent of the population in these countries is between 20 and 40 years, it is even more important that youth advocacy groups are included in the political process. The 2020 YDI can work as a collective starting-point for these conversations and help direct future efforts to ensure that challenges for young people, which vary significantly between countries, are addressed as the COVID-19 pandemic unfolds and further intensifies some of these.

The advent of vaccines have brought hope for recovery; however the uncertainty about long-term effectiveness of such vaccines in light of emerging variants of the virus, requires policy-makers to continuously monitor the health situation and readjust policies when necessary. It is also not guaranteed that a vaccine can be distributed equally, which could lead to further marginalisation of some groups in society, such as youth. These challenges make it even more important for policy-makers, youth advocates and young people to reconsider how to support young people's meaningful participation in civil as well as political life.

Governments must also continue to invest in research on youth issues. Age-disaggregated data is already scarce, and the COVID-19 pandemic poses further challenges to data collection. It is therefore essential that governments continue to invest in data collection and research concerning the pressing challenges to youth and youth development. The Commonwealth Secretariat's 2020 YDI is as an example of a research tool that seeks to deliver information on and support fruitful youth development initiatives around the globe in the current COVID-19 era, and beyond.

2.2 2020 Global YDI results

Figure 2.1 shows the worldwide results of the 2020 YDI. The countries in dark blue – mostly in Europe – have very high levels of youth development relative to the rest of the world. Countries in the lightest blue – mostly in Africa – have the most room for improvement. Box 2.1 explains the criteria for grouping countries by low, medium, high and very high levels of youth development.

On average, youth development has been improving, although the rate of progress is slow. The Global YDI improved by 3.1 per cent between 2010 and

2018, as Figure 2.2 shows. Development indicators typically advance slowly, so the improvement in the global average over the past decade can be taken as encouragement for policy-makers that progress is possible, even though it materialises only gradually.

On a global level, youth development is on the up and up, but not all young people around the world have benefited in equal measure. Of the 181 countries included on the 2020 YDI, 156, or 86 per cent, recorded improvements on their YDI score over the eight-year period, as Figure 2.3 shows, with the largest gains seen in Afghanistan, India and Russia. Twenty-five countries saw a fall in their YDI score between 2010 and 2018, with the greatest deteriorations recorded in Syria, Ukraine and Libya.

Progress was made in five out of the six domains in the YDI, with the largest global improvement recorded in Health and Wellbeing, which improved by 4.39 per cent

Figure 2.1 YDI world map, 2018 scores

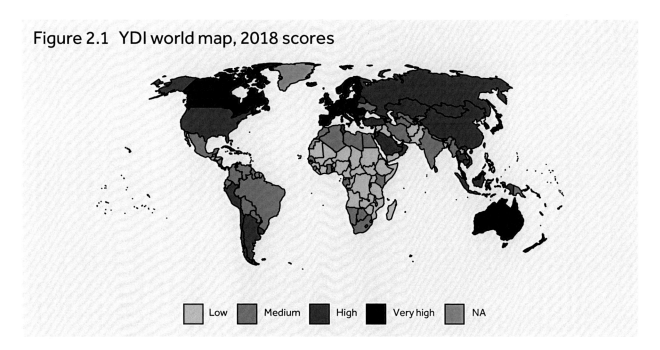

| Low | Medium | High | Very high | NA |

Box 2.1 Definition of YDI categories

The YDI score is a number between 0 and 1, with a score of 1 representing the highest level of youth development.

By calculating the quartiles, countries have been grouped into "very high", "high", "medium" and "low" levels of youth development categories on the 2020 YDI. This categorisation reflects the position of a country on a spectrum ranging from "relatively good" to "relatively poor". The scoring system is the same

as the one that underpins the HDI. The 2020 YDI categories by score are:

Youth development level category	Score range
Low	0.000–0.595
Medium	0.595–0.691
High	0.691–0.78
Very high	0.78–1.000

Figure 2.2 Trend in youth development, global average, 2010–2018

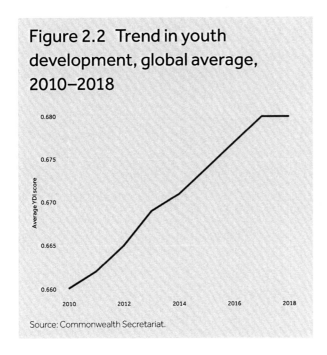

Source: Commonwealth Secretariat.

Figure 2.3 Country improvements and deteriorations in YDI score, 2010–2018

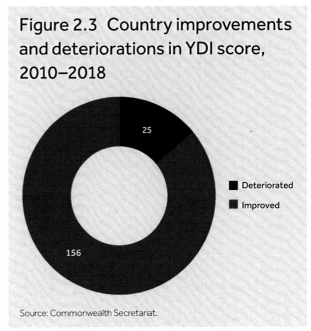

Source: Commonwealth Secretariat.

between 2010 and 2018. Peace and Security saw the second-largest average improvement, at 3.41 per cent, followed by Employment and Opportunity, Education, and Equality and inclusion. Political and Civic Participation was the only domain to record an average global deterioration, albeit minimal, at 0.18 per cent. Figure 2.4

Figure 2.4 Global change in the average YDI score and domain scores, 2010–2018

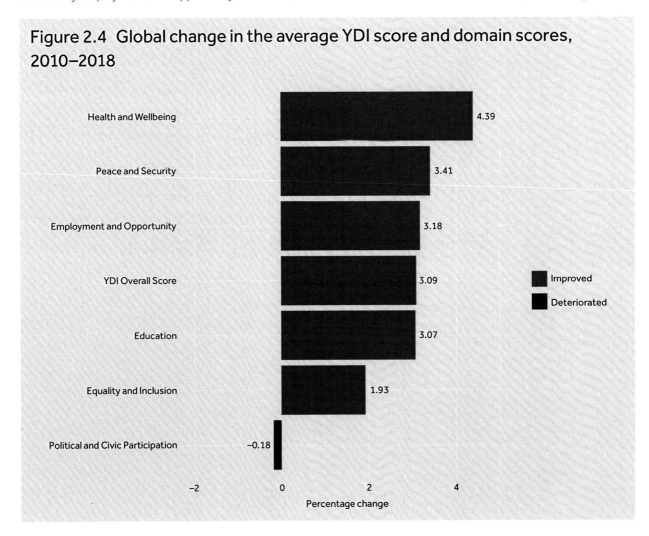

Figure 2.5 Change in average regional YDI score, 2010–2018

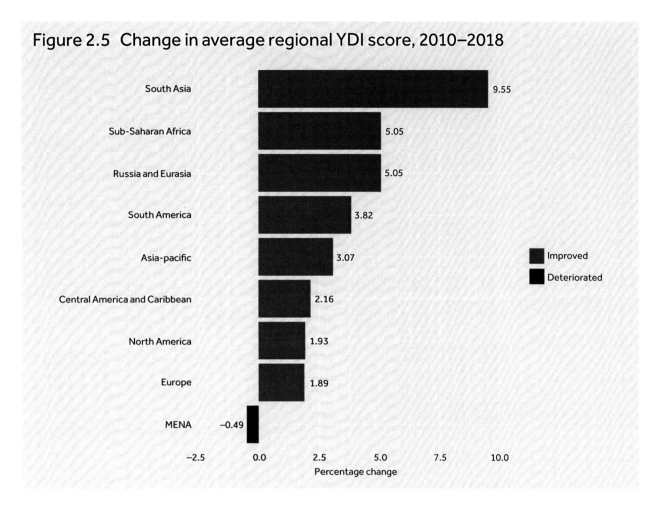

Eight out of the nine world regions recorded
improvements on their average YDI scores from 2010

shows the percentage change in the Global YDI score
and each of the six YDI domains between 2010 and 2018.

Eight out of the nine world regions recorded
improvements on their average YDI scores from 2010
to 2018. MENA was the only region to record an average
deterioration in youth development, though this was
relatively low, at 0.49 per cent. Of the eight improving
regions, South Asia recorded the largest increase in
its average youth development levels, at 9.5 per cent,
followed by Sub-Saharan Africa, Russia and Eurasia,
and South America. Figure 2.5 shows the percentage
change in regional YDI scores between 2010 and 2018.

Despite having made significant progress since
2010, Sub-Saharan Africa remained the region with
the lowest average level of youth development in
the world in 2018, at 0.549, as Figure 2.6 shows.
Furthermore, eight of the ten lowest-ranked countries
in the 2020 YDI are in Sub-Saharan Africa. Europe had
the highest average level of youth development at
0.818, followed by North America and Asia-Pacific.
With the exception of Singapore, which is the highest
scoring country on the 2020 YDI, all other countries
in the top 10 on the 2020 YDI are in Europe (see
Table 2.1).

Countries with the largest improvement in YDI
score between 2010 and 2018 are referred to as the
largest risers. On the 2020 YDI, the top five risers are
Afghanistan, India, Russia, Ethiopia and Burkina Faso.
Afghanistan improved its YDI score 19.9 per cent,
India improved by 18.7 per cent; while the remaining
risers recorded improvements of over 12 per cent
each – Russia (13.9%), Ethiopia (13.2%) and Burkina
Faso (12.6%).

Syria, Ukraine, Libya, Yemen and Jordan are the
largest fallers on the 2020 YDI, with Syria recording a
deterioration in youth development of 19.9 per cent.
On average, the top five risers improved their score by
15.74 per cent between 2010 and 2018 while the five
largest fallers saw an average deterioration of 10.28 per
cent (see Figure 2.7).

2.3 Inequality in youth development

While the global average level of youth development
improved between 2010 and 2018, progress has
been uneven. There are significant disparities in youth
development between and within different regions. The
extent of inequality between countries can be assessed

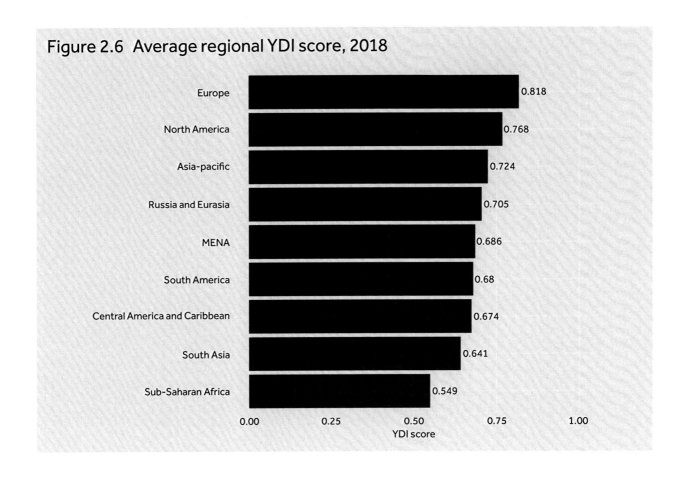

Figure 2.6 Average regional YDI score, 2018

Region	YDI score
Europe	0.818
North America	0.768
Asia-pacific	0.724
Russia and Eurasia	0.705
MENA	0.686
South America	0.68
Central America and Caribbean	0.674
South Asia	0.641
Sub-Saharan Africa	0.549

by analysing the gap between countries with different levels of youth development.

Figure 2.8 compares average domain scores for the four YDI level categories. The largest discrepancies between countries at low YDI levels and countries at very high YDI levels are recorded in the Education and

Table 2.1 Ten highest-ranking countries, 2020 YDI

YDI rank	Country	Region	YDI score
1	Singapore	Asia-Pacific	0.875
2	Slovenia	Europe	0.866
3	Norway	Europe	0.862
4	Malta	Europe	0.859
5	Denmark	Europe	0.858
6	Sweden	Europe	0.857
7	Switzerland	Europe	0.849
8	Netherlands	Europe	0.848
9	Ireland	Europe	0.846
10	Luxembourg	Europe	0.845
10	Portugal	Europe	0.845

Table 2.2 Ten lowest-ranking countries, 2020 YDI

YDI rank	Country	Region	YDI score
172	Yemen	MENA	0.474
173	Mozambique	Sub-Saharan Africa	0.46
174	Cote d'Ivoire	Sub-Saharan Africa	0.457
175	Mali	Sub-Saharan Africa	0.447
176	Somalia	Sub-Saharan Africa	0.436
177	Niger	Sub-Saharan Africa	0.424
178	Afghanistan	South Asia	0.421
179	South Sudan	Sub-Saharan Africa	0.421
180	Central African Republic	Sub-Saharan Africa	0.399
181	Chad	Sub-Saharan Africa	0.398

Figure 2.7 Largest improvements and deteriorations in YDI score, 2010–2018

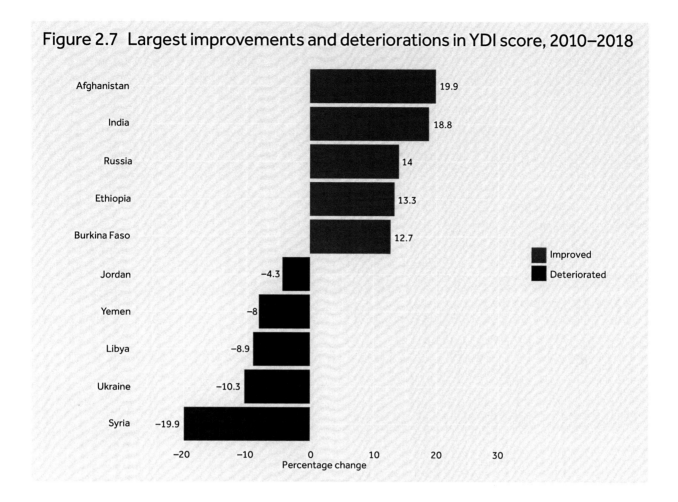

Figure 2.8 Average domain scores by YDI category, 2018

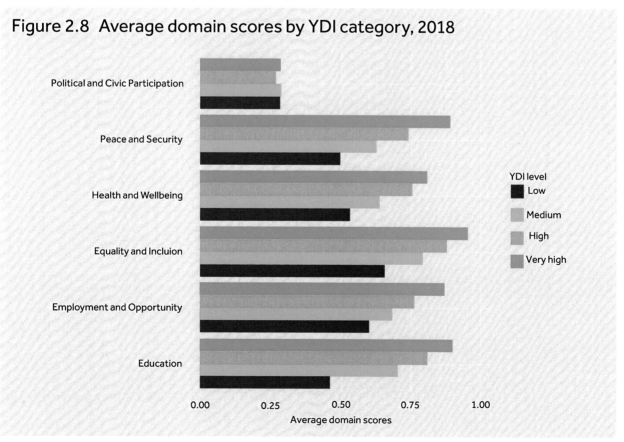

Peace and Security domains. In the Education domain, the difference between the lowest and highest YDI-level countries' average scores is 0.441 on the YDI scale of 0 to 1. In the Peace and Security domain, the difference in average scores amounts to 0.396.

All countries, regardless of their level of youth development, scored relatively low in the Political and Civic Participation domain. This can be explained in part by the relatively low level of political and civic participation recorded on the volunteered time and voiced opinion to official indicators across the globe. On average, roughly 20 per cent of youth in each country reported volunteering their time on the 2018 survey, while 16.2 per cent stated that they had voiced their opinion to an official in the past 30 days.

Figure 2.9 compares the average indicator scores for the 10 best and ten worst performing countries in the 2020 YDI. The difference between the 10 highest-

and the 10 lowest-ranked countries worldwide was substantial for digital natives, economic marginalisation and conflict and terrorism, all with a difference over 0.828. Conflict and terrorism recorded the largest difference in average scores, amounting to 0.930 on the scale from 0 to 1. Evidently, the difference between the countries with the highest youth development and those with the lowest youth development is recorded across indicators from different domains.

Figure 2.9 also highlights indicators on which the 10 highest-ranked countries worldwide score worse than the 10 lowest-ranked countries. These indicators are particularly behavioural health indicators (alcohol consumption, tobacco abuse and drug abuse) as well as the mental health and self-harm indicators. Thus, the 2020 YDI highlights how countries with high levels of youth development, overall, are still challenged in the area of Health and Wellbeing, particularly in ensuring young people's long-term physical and mental health. In

Figure 2.9 Average YDI indicator scores for the 10 countries with the highest and lowest YDI scores, 2018

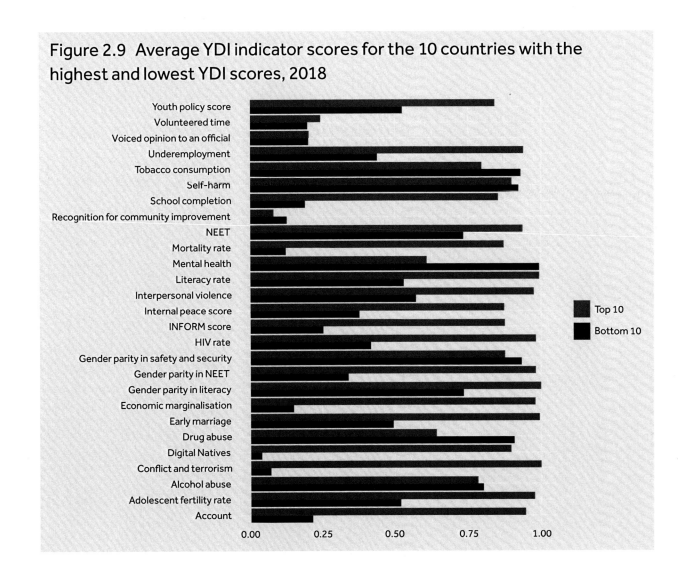

addition, data on mental health may suffer from reliability issues as mental illnesses are still stigmatised, especially in lower- and middle-income countries, and, therefore, may go underreported (Mascayano et al., 2015).

The disparate distribution of youth development was also present across the 48 Commonwealth countries on the 2020 YDI, with more than half of the Commonwealth countries falling within the low and medium category – 15 and 13 countries, respectively. Twelve countries recorded a high level of youth development and eight countries recorded very high levels of youth development in 2018.

2.4 Youth development and the Sustainable Development Goals

The Sustainable Development Goals (SDGs) represent the global agenda for development by the year 2030. There are 17 SDGs, which have 169 targets and 230 indicators in total, representing the global commitment to "leave no one behind." The goals are integrated and indivisible, and can be understood through 5Ps (Commonwealth Secretariat, 2016):

1. People: The SDGs are goals for everyone, everywhere. Regardless of gender, ethnicity, sexuality or ability - we have promised to leave no one behind in this agenda.

2. Planet: We have one planet with finite resources, that sustains life for all of us. It is critical that we are good stewards of the earth and take serious action to tackle and reverse climate change.

3. Peace: There can be no development without peaceful, just communities and countries. The institutions that govern us should be transparent, responsive and accountable.

4. Prosperity: We need sustainable economic growth and decent livelihoods throughout our lifetimes.

5. Partnerships: Everyone must work together and bring their best selves to this global agenda in order for it to succeed.

In order to achieve the aim of "leaving no one behind", the SDGs must not only consider but also include the 1.8 billion youth across the globe.

2.4.1 Youth development and the Sustainable Development Goals

The SDGs that explicitly refer to young people fall into two categories: those that require that the goal must be met and measured for disaggregated age groups and those that specifically apply to young people. Eight SDGs refer to age disaggregation or age groups in the Goal, targets or indicators. These are SDGs 1 (poverty), 3 (health), 5 (gender equality), 8 (decent work), 10 (inequality), 11 (sustainable cities), 16 (peaceful, just

Figure 2.10 Number of Commonwealth countries at different YDI levels, 2018

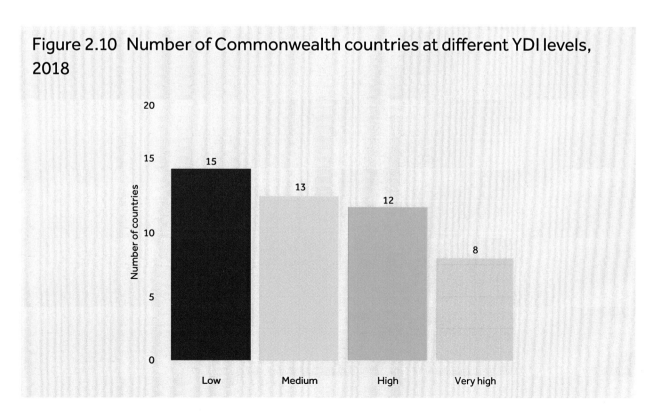

and inclusive societies) and 17 (partnership). Similarly, there are explicit references to youth, young men and women, adolescents, girls and boys in the targets or indicators of nine SDGs: 1 (poverty), 2 (hunger), 3 (health), 4 (education), 5 (gender equality), 6 (clean water and sanitation), 8 (decent work), 13 (climate action) and 16 (peaceful, just and inclusive societies) (Commonwealth Secretariat and Youth Division, 2016). Table 2.3 lists these goals in more detail.

Table 2.3 also demonstrates that there is a strong conceptual overlap between the YDI and the SDGs that

Table 2.3 Youth in the Sustainable Development Goals and the 2020 YDI

SDG	SDG target		YDI domain
SDG 1	**End poverty in all its forms everywhere**		Employment and Opportunity, Equality and Inclusion
	1.1	By 2030, eradicate extreme poverty for all people everywhere, currently measured as people living on less than $1.25 a day	
	1.2	By 2030, reduce at least by half the proportion of men, women and children of all ages living in poverty in all its dimensions according to national definitions	
	1.3	Implement nationally appropriate social protection systems and measures for all, including floors, and by 2030 achieve substantial coverage of the poor and the vulnerable	
SDG 2	**End hunger, achieve food security and improved nutrition and promote sustainable agriculture**		Employment and Opportunity, Equality and Inclusion, Health and Wellbeing
	2.2	By 2030, end all forms of malnutrition, including achieving, by 2025, the internationally agreed targets on stunting and wasting in children under 5 years of age, and address the nutritional needs of adolescent girls, pregnant and lactating women and older persons	
SDG 3	**Ensure healthy lives and promote well-being for all at all ages**		Health and Wellbeing
	3.1	By 2030, reduce the global maternal mortality ratio to less than 70 per 100,000 live births	
	3.3	By 2030, end the epidemics of AIDS, tuberculosis, malaria and neglected tropical diseases and combat hepatitis, water-borne diseases and other communicable diseases	
	3.4	By 2030, reduce by one third premature mortality from non-communicable diseases through prevention and treatment and promote mental health and well-being	
	3.5	Strengthen the prevention and treatment of substance abuse, including narcotic drug abuse and harmful use of alcohol	
	3.6	By 2020, halve the number of global deaths and injuries from road traffic accidents	
	3.7	By 2030, ensure universal access to sexual and reproductive health-care services, including for family planning, information and education, and the integration of reproductive health into national strategies and programmes	
	3.8	Achieve universal health coverage, including financial risk protection, access to quality essential health-care services and access to safe, effective, quality and affordable essential medicines and vaccines for all	
	3.a	Strengthen the implementation of the World Health Organization Framework Convention on Tobacco Control in all countries, as appropriate	

(Continued)

Table 2.3   Youth in the Sustainable Development Goals and the 2020 YDI (*Continued*)

SDG	SDG target		YDI domain
SDG 4	**Ensure inclusive and equitable quality education and promote lifelong learning opportunities for all**		Education, Employment and Opportunity, Equality and Inclusion, Political and Civic Participation
	4.1	By 2030, ensure that all girls and boys complete free, equitable and quality primary and secondary education leading to relevant and effective learning outcomes	
	4.3	By 2030, ensure equal access for all women and men to affordable and quality technical, vocational and tertiary education, including university	
	4.4	By 2030, ensure that all youth and adults have relevant skills, including technical and vocational skills, for employment, decent work and entrepreneurship	
	4.6	By 2030, ensure that all youth and adults, both men and women, reach a proficiency level in literacy and numeracy sufficient to fully participate in society	
	4.7	By 2030, ensure that all learners acquire knowledge and skills needed to promote sustainable development, including, among others, through education for sustainable development and sustainable lifestyles, human rights, gender equality, promotion of a culture of peace and nonviolence, global citizenship and appreciation of cultural diversity and of culture's contribution to sustainable development	
	4.a	Build and upgrade education facilities that are child, disability and gender sensitive and provide safe, non-violent, inclusive and effective learning environments for all	
SDG 5	**Achieve gender equality and empower all women and girls**		Education, Employment and Opportunity, Equality and Inclusion
	5.1	End all forms of discrimination against all women and girls everywhere	
	5.2	Eliminate all forms of violence against all women and girls in the public and private spheres, including trafficking and sexual and other types of exploitation	
	5.3	Eliminate all harmful practices, such as child, early and forced marriage and female genital mutilation	
	5.4	Recognize and value unpaid care and domestic work through the provision of public services, infrastructure and social protection policies and the promotion of shared responsibility within the household and the family as nationally appropriate	
	5.6	Ensure universal access to sexual and reproductive health and reproductive rights as agreed in accordance with the Programme of Action of the International Conference on Population and Development and the Beijing Platform for Action and the outcome documents of their review conferences	
	5.c	Adopt and strengthen sound policies and enforceable legislation for the promotion of gender equality and the empowerment of all women and girls at all levels	

(Continued)

Table 2.3 Youth in the Sustainable Development Goals and the 2020 YDI (*Continued*)

SDG	SDG target		YDI domain
SDG 6	**Ensure availability and sustainable management of water and sanitation for all**		Health and Wellbeing
	6.2	By 2030, achieve access to adequate and equitable sanitation and hygiene for all and end open defecation, paying special attention to the needs of women and girls and those in vulnerable situations	
SDG 8	**Promote sustained, inclusive and sustainable economic growth, full and productive employment and decent work for all**		Education, Employment and Opportunity, Equality and Inclusion, Political and Civic Participation
	8.5	By 2030, achieve full and productive employment and decent work for all women and men, including for young people and persons with disabilities, and equal pay for work of equal value	
	8.6	By 2020, substantially reduce the proportion of youth not in employment, education or training	
	8.7	Take immediate and effective measures to eradicate forced labour, end modern slavery and human trafficking and secure the prohibition and elimination of the worst forms of child labour, including recruitment and use of child soldiers, and by 2025 end child labour in all its forms	
	8.10	Strengthen the capacity of domestic financial institutions to encourage and expand access to banking, insurance and financial services for all	
	8.b	By 2020, develop and operationalize a global strategy for youth employment and implement the Global Jobs Pact of the International Labour Organization	
SDG 10	**Reduce inequality within and among countries**		Equality and Inclusion
	10.2	By 2030, empower and promote the social, economic and political inclusion of all, irrespective of age, sex, disability, race, ethnicity, origin, religion or economic or other status	
	10.7	Facilitate orderly, safe, regular and responsible migration and mobility of people, including through the implementation of planned and well-managed migration policies	
SDG 11	**Make cities and human settlements inclusive, safe, resilient and sustainable**		Political and Civic Participation, Equality and Inclusion
	11.2	By 2030, provide access to safe, affordable, accessible and sustainable transport systems for all, improving road safety, notably by expanding public transport, with special attention to the needs of those in vulnerable situations, women, children, persons with disabilities and older persons	
	11.7	By 2030, provide universal access to safe, inclusive and accessible, green and public spaces, in particular for women and children, older persons and persons with disabilities	
SDG 13	**Take urgent action to combat climate change and its impacts**		Health and Wellbeing, Political and Civic Participation
	13.b	Promote mechanisms for raising capacity for effective climate change-related planning and management in least developed countries, including focusing on women, youth and local and marginalized communities	

(*Continued*)

Table 2.3 Youth in the Sustainable Development Goals and the 2020 YDI (*Continued*)

SDG	SDG target		YDI domain
SDG 16	**Promote peaceful and inclusive societies for sustainable development, provide access to justice for all and build effective, accountable and inclusive institutions at all levels**		Health and Wellbeing, Equality and Inclusion, Peace and Security
	16.1	Significantly reduce all forms of violence and related death rates everywhere	
	16.2	End abuse, exploitation, trafficking and all forms of violence against and torture of children	
	16.3	Promote the rule of law at the national and international levels and ensure equal access to justice for all	
	16.7	Ensure responsive, inclusive, participatory and representative decision-making at all levels	
	16.a	Strengthen relevant national institutions, including through international cooperation, for building capacity at all levels, in particular in developing countries, to prevent violence and combat terrorism and crime	
	16.b	Promote and enforce non-discriminatory laws and policies for sustainable development	
SDG 17	**Strengthen the means of implementation and revitalize the global partnership for sustainable development**		Political and Civic Participation
	17.2	By 2020, enhance capacity-building support to developing countries, including for least developed countries and small island developing States, to increase significantly the availability of high-quality, timely and reliable data disaggregated by income, gender, age, race, ethnicity, migratory status, disability, geographic location and other characteristics relevant in national contexts.	

pertain to youth, especially with the inclusion of the new domains in the 2020 YDI. The rows shaded in green are the SDG targets that directly mention youth, young men and women, and/or adolescents. The remaining table rows are SDG targets that have indicators pertaining to different age groups, which include young people. Targets that do not apply to young people have been omitted here for space.

The United Nations provides over 500 different variables that can be used for tracking progress on the SDGs.[1] While not all of these have global coverage, correlating the YDI with available SDG indicators provides an indication of how strongly youth development aligns with each goal. Figure 2.11 visualises the results of this analysis and shows there is a strong relationship between the YDI and the SDGs, in particular between SDG 3, SDG 4, SDG 7 and SDG 16.

The yellow circles represent specific indicators while the blue circles represent the percentage of indicators within each goal that correlate with the YDI. The larger the yellow circle, the more strongly the YDI correlates with that indicator. The larger the blue circle, the greater the percentage of indicators that correlate with the YDI.

2.4.2 Youth participation in the Sustainable Development Goals

The strong statistical link between the SDGs and the 2020 YDI highlights that countries that perform well on youth development also tend to have made greater progress towards the SDGs. This highlights the relationship between youth development and society and vice versa. In countries that have strong development pathways for youth, this is not just a reflection of youth being recognised as a priority but also evidence that society has sufficient capacity in its institutions to provide health, education and employment outcomes for its citizens.

With the strong correlation between the YDI and the SDGs, many young people will be benefactors of a

Figure 2.11 Significant correlations between the YDI and available SDG indicators

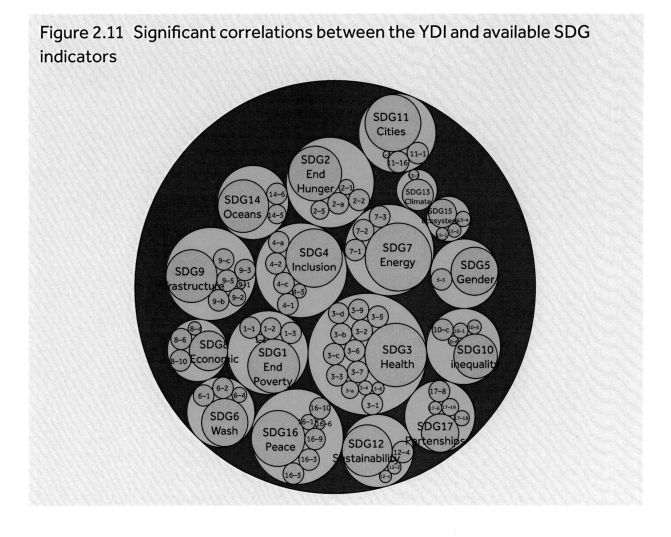

country's broader progress on the SDGs. In addition, better outcomes can be achieved when youth participate actively in this development. By nature of their position, youth bring fresh perspectives and unique experiences. The United Nations, in collaboration with Search for Common Ground, explicitly states that "young people are valuable innovators of change, and their contributions should be actively supported, solicited and regarded as essential to building peaceful communities and supporting democratic governance and transition" (United Nations and Search for Common Ground, 2014). With regard to the SDGs, youth can participate and contribute in the following ways (Plan International and ADB, 2018):

- Help deliver programmes responsive to the real needs of youth;

- Seek out networks and partnerships within and between generations;

- Act as "mobilisers" in person and online;

- Influence parents, communities and national governments;

- Envision what will happen in the future to frame policy and implementation;

- Act as provocateurs across all SDGs, especially in education, gender and employment.

Despite this, there are many barriers to actively engaging youth in development policy. While more than half of the world is currently under the age of 30, decision-making processes remain largely in the hands of older generations (Commonwealth Secretariat, 2016). Young people, especially young women, are underrepresented in formal political processes or institutions – including parliaments, political parties and public administrations (ibid.). In addition, youth, especially young males, are seen as a "threat" because of their tendency towards "civil disobedience" (Plan International and ADB, 2018). Credibility remains a challenge, with the result that suggestions from young people are either not being taken seriously or,

Figure 2.12 Political and Civic Participation score by region

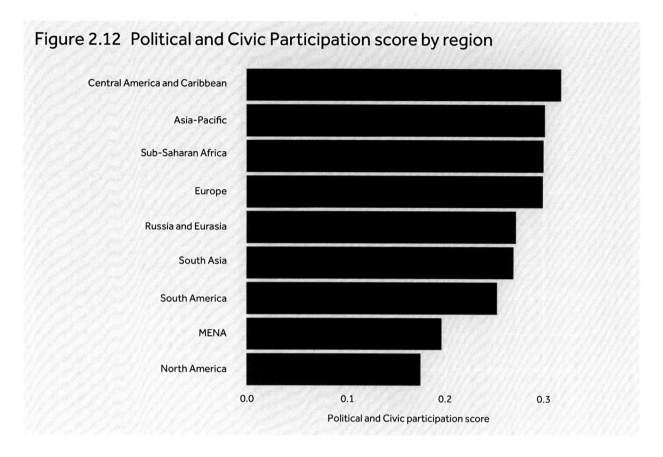

worse, are completely disregarded (Commonwealth Secretariat, 2016).

The above challenges act as barriers for youth to provide meaningful contributions to the SDGs, their implementation and society as a whole. In the YDI, this is reflected by low performance in the Political and Civic Participation domain. The Political and Civic Participation domain in the YDI has the lowest levels of achievement globally.

Figure 2.12 shows the regional averages for the Political and Civic Participation domain score. The Central America and the Caribbean region scores the highest while North America records the lowest average performance. This should be a priority for the SDGs: empowering young people to hold governments and duty-bearers accountable is one of the most important means of implementation for an agenda that "leaves no one behind" (Commonwealth Secretariat, 2016).

On a positive note, there are actionable opportunities for countries to build on and strengthen existing youth participation. Governments and development partners can (Plan International and ADB, 2018):

- Invest to optimise the "youth dividend" by pursuing innovation, creativity and risk for youth cohorts to participate;

- Build an evidence base to show the impact of youth engagement;

- Ensure young people are welcomed into the inner circles of policy- and decision-making processes.

The Commonwealth Secretariat provides practical actions that national governments can take to promote this across four areas (Commonwealth Secretariat, 2016):

- Youth participation in review and accountability mechanisms:

  o Assess and strengthen spaces for institutionalising youth participation;

  o Develop co-management structures for national and local accountability platforms;

  o Implement regular dialogues and action planning with young constituents;

  o Create official roles for youth at the national and regional levels.

- Data for monitoring and review:

  o Empower a generation of SDG infomediaries;

  o Develop "shadow" indicators grounded in lived experiences.

- Transparency and access to information:

  ○ Ensure open access to information for young people on the SDGs and state-led reviews.

- Emerging accountability approaches and practices:

  ○ Develop communities of practice on data-driven social accountability.

  ○ Put ground level panels and platforms at the forefront of accountability.

  ○ Embed review in everyday life and popular culture.

2.5 Youth development in the Commonwealth

Of the Commonwealth's population of over 2 billion, more than 60 per cent are under the age of 30,[2] underscoring the importance of high levels of youth development in Commonwealth countries. However, the Commonwealth showed less progress over the measurement period than the world at large. Over the eight-year period from 2010 to 2018, the

Commonwealth recorded an average improvement in youth development of 2.8 per cent, compared with a 3.1 per cent improvement in the global average. Of the 48 Commonwealth countries included in the 2020 YDI, 40 or 83 per cent, improved their YDI score. Seven countries deteriorated. Brunei maintained its score.

On average, the Commonwealth has made progress in all six YDI domains, with the largest improvement seen in the Health and Wellbeing and Peace and Security domains (see Figure 2.13). Health and Wellbeing improved by almost 5.78 per cent while Peace and Security improved by 3.54 per cent from 2010 to 2018. The Commonwealth countries saw an improvement in Education of 2.8 per cent. The three remaining domains improved by approximately 1–2 per cent.

As evidenced by Table 2.4, most of the 10 highest-ranked Commonwealth countries on the 2020 YDI are in Europe and Asia Pacific. With the exception of Pakistan, all of the 10 lowest-ranked countries in the Commonwealth are in Sub-Saharan Africa.

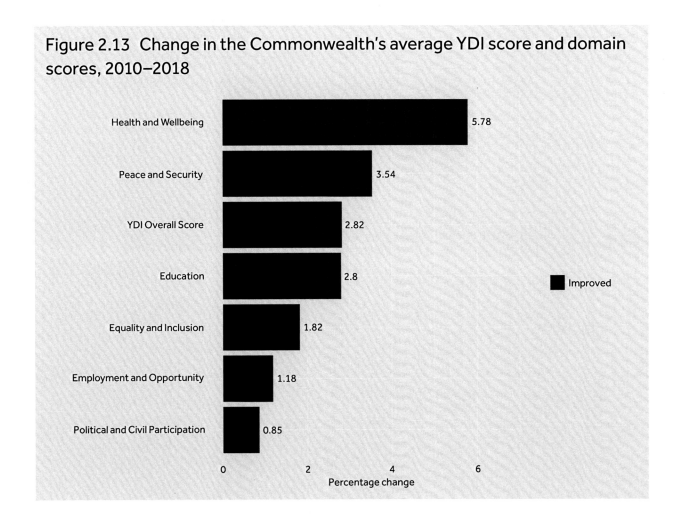

Figure 2.13 Change in the Commonwealth's average YDI score and domain scores, 2010–2018

Table 2.4 Commonwealth countries with the highest 2020 YDI ranks

YDI rank	Country	Region	YDI score
1	Singapore	Asia-Pacific	0.875
4	Malta	Europe	0.859
18	Cyprus	Europe	0.825
19	New Zealand	Asia-Pacific	0.824
29	Australia	Asia-Pacific	0.807
36	Canada	North America	0.798
39	Maldives	South Asia	0.794
40	United Kingdom	Europe	0.793
47	Barbados	Central America And Caribbean	0.779
49	Brunei	Asia-Pacific	0.777

2.6 Global results by domain

2.6.1 Health and Wellbeing

The Health and Wellbeing domain recorded the largest improvement, at 4.39 per cent, driven by improvements on five out of seven indicators. The largest was a 12.1 per cent improvement in the world's average mortality rate score. The HIV rate, self-harm, alcohol abuse and tobacco consumption scores also improved by less than 2 per cent. In contrast, the global average for drug abuse and mental health deteriorated, but by less than 1 per cent each. Figure 2.14 shows the trend in Health and Wellbeing, as well as each of its component indicators.

Worldwide, 148 countries improved in Health and Wellbeing, while 33 deteriorated. Russia had the largest improvement, with its domain score increasing by 38.8 per cent from 2010 to 2018. Gabon had the next largest improvement, at 33.6 per cent, followed by similar gains in Botswana, Tanzania and Sri Lanka. Syria had the largest deterioration globally, at 40.5 per cent over the period, with a sharp decline from 2010 but some recovery after 2016. Yemen followed, but with a deterioration of 17.7 per cent, as did Ukraine, Iraq and Libya.

Figure 2.15 compares the change by region in Health and Wellbeing from 2010 to 2018. Seven of the nine regions improved in this domain, offset by deteriorations in MENA and North America.

2.6.2 Education

Globally, the Education domain improved 3 per cent from 2010 to 2018, driven by a 5.3 per cent improvement in school completion, indicating that more young people around the world are completing a basic education.[3] The global average score for the literacy rate indicator also improved, by 2.4 per cent over the decade. Figure 2.16 shows the trend in Education, as well as each of its component indicators.

The digital natives indicator recorded a constant score of just under 0.4 because, unfortunately, time series data is not available to measure global progress in young people's skills and engagement online. In 2014, the International Telecommunication Union (ITU) estimated that roughly 38 per cent of youth worldwide could be considered "digital natives," based on five or more years of internet use.

Two-thirds of countries worldwide showed an improvement in this domain, led by Burkina Faso, Afghanistan, Burundi, Bangladesh and Laos. The 61 countries that have deteriorated in Education since 2010 are spread around the world, with Chad recording the largest deterioration globally, followed by Qatar, Jordan, Ukraine and Jamaica.

All nine world regions improved in the Education domain, on average, except for North America, which maintained its score of 0.936. Figure 2.17 gives the change in each region's average score from 2010 to 2018.

Table 2.5 Commonwealth countries with the lowest 2020 YDI ranks

YDI rank	Country	Region	YDI score
148	Tanzania	Sub-Saharan Africa	0.559
152	Eswatini	Sub-Saharan Africa	0.553
154	Zambia	Sub-Saharan Africa	0.548
157	Uganda	Sub-Saharan Africa	0.534
160	Cameroon	Sub-Saharan Africa	0.527
161	Nigeria	Sub-Saharan Africa	0.52
162	Pakistan	South Asia	0.517
163	Lesotho	Sub-Saharan Africa	0.511
171	Malawi	Sub-Saharan Africa	0.484
173	Mozambique	Sub-Saharan Africa	0.46

Figure 2.14 Global trend in Health and Wellbeing, 2010–2018

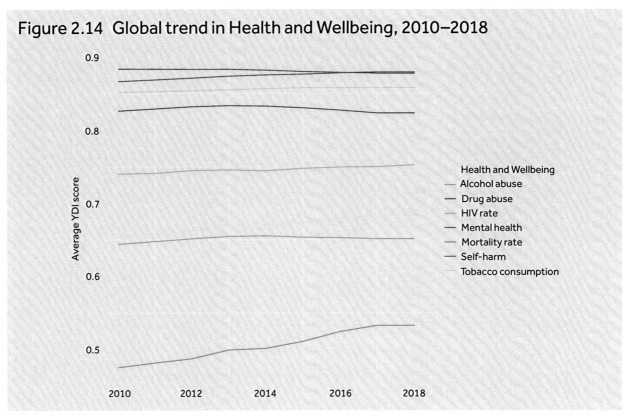

Figure 2.15 Change in Health and Wellbeing by region, 2010–2018

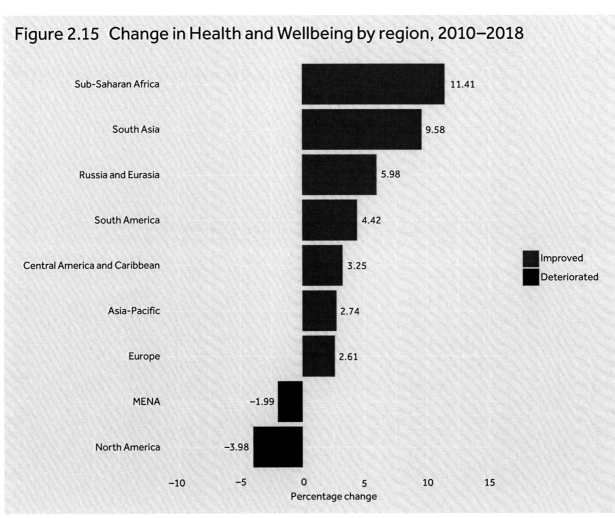

Figure 2.16 Global trend in Education, 2010–2018

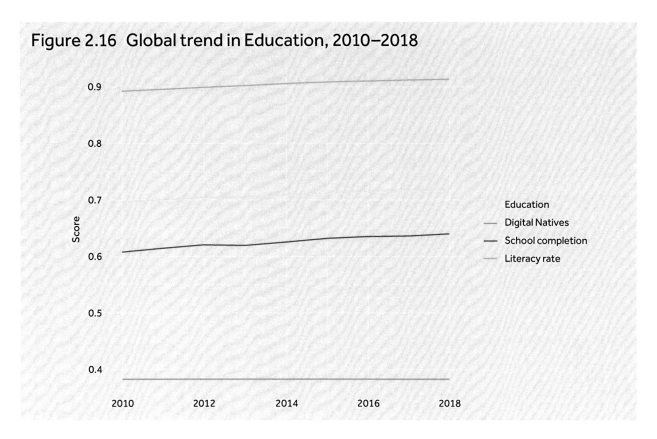

South Asia was the region to record the largest improvement, with a 16.13 per cent increase in the regional average and educational gains recorded in seven out of eight countries. Afghanistan had the largest improvement in the region – and the second-largest in the world –

followed in South Asia by Bangladesh, Nepal, Bhutan and India.

Sub-Saharan Africa also made substantial progress, posting nearly a 10 per cent improvement. Improvements were even seen in regions where educational attainment was already high, such as Europe.

Figure 2.17 Change in Education by region, 2010–2018

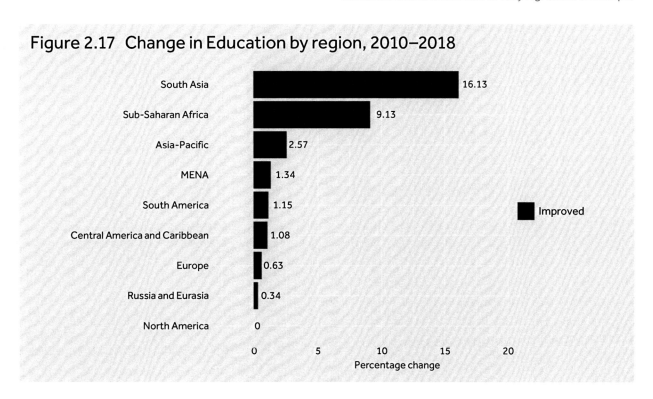

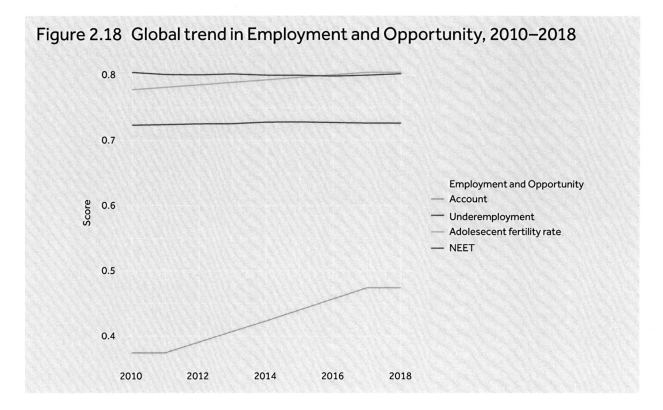

Figure 2.18 Global trend in Employment and Opportunity, 2010–2018

Legend:
Employment and Opportunity
— Account
— Underemployment
— Adolesecent fertility rate
— NEET

2.6.3 Employment and Opportunity

The Employment and Opportunity domain recorded an average improvement from 2010 to 2018, of just over 3 per cent. Worldwide, 145 countries improved, while 36 deteriorated. Peru had the largest improvement, followed by Vietnam, Malawi, Indonesia and Nicaragua. Laos had the largest deterioration, followed by Ghana, Zimbabwe, Côte d'Ivoire and Rwanda.

Progress in this domain was driven largely by a 27 per cent improvement in the account indicator score, which measures access to the financial system, including mobile money. Figure 2.18 shows the trend in Employment and Opportunity, as well as each of its component indicators.

The next most improved indicator in this domain was the score for adolescent fertility, which increased 3.4 per cent between 2010 and 2018, indicating that fewer young women are getting pregnant before age 20. Early pregnancies can limit young women's opportunities to achieve financial independence and pursue a career. Progress in this indicator is a positive sign for economic progress and greater gender quality.

Underemployment was fairly constant, with the global average improving by less than 1 per cent. The share of youth not in education, employment or training (NEET) showed a similar trend, with the score declining by less than 1 per cent. On the whole, the domain results suggest that more young people around the world are poised for economic independence, but rates of formal and full economic engagement are stubborn.

The widespread global improvement in *Employment and Opportunity* boosted the average for all nine world regions, as shown in Figure 2.19. Results in North America and South America drove the trend, with each recording about an 8 per cent improvement in the average domain score. The rest of the world saw more modest improvements, ranging from 6.4 per cent in Russia and Eurasia to just over 2 per cent in Europe.

2.6.4 Equality and Inclusion

The Equality and Inclusion domain improved nearly 2 per cent from 2010 to 2018, driven by a 5.71 per cent improvement in the score for economic marginalisation. Improvements in economic marginalisation mean that more youth are being pulled out of extreme poverty and thus have improved opportunities for economic security and inclusion.

Gains were also made in gender equality, with a 2.13 per cent improvement toward gender parity in literacy, as the global average score rose from 0.94 out of 1 in 2010 to 0.96 in 2018. Average scores for gender parity in NEET and early marriage were more stubborn, but improved by 1.85 and 1.1 per cent, respectively.

Gender parity in safety and security was more or less flat over the decade, with significantly more young men

Figure 2.19 Change in Employment and Opportunity by region, 2010–2018

Percentage change

- North America 8.08
- South America 8
- Russia and Eurasia 6.4
- South Asia 4.07
- MENA 3.85
- Central America and Caribbean 2.87
- Asia-Pacific 2.7
- Sub-Saharan Africa 2.19
- Europe 2.17

■ Improved

around the world reporting that they felt safe in their communities than young women did. The gender gap in feelings of safety is widest in the world's most peaceful countries, indicating that gains in peacefulness have, thus far, disproportionately accrued to men (IEP, 2018). Figure 2.20 shows the trend in Equality and Inclusion, as well as each of its component indicators.

Worldwide, 135 countries improved in Equality and Inclusion, while 46 deteriorated, resulting in an average improvement in every region. Egypt had the largest improvement globally, followed by Afghanistan, Qatar,

India and Guinea. Yemen had the largest deterioration, followed by Côte d'Ivoire, Syria, Botswana and Sri Lanka.

Figure 2.21 shows the change in each region's average Equality and Inclusion score from 2010 to 2018. South Asia had the largest improvement, nearing 7 per cent. Seven out of eight countries in South Asia improved, with Afghanistan recording the largest improvement in the region, followed by India, Maldives, Pakistan and Bangladesh. Afghanistan improved in gender parity in literacy, economic marginalisation, early marriage and gender parity in safety and security.

Figure 2.20 Global trend in Equality and Inclusion, 2010–2018

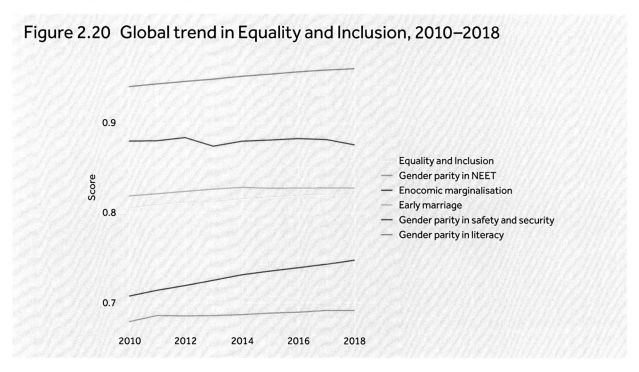

Score

- Equality and Inclusion
- Gender parity in NEET
- Enocomic marginalisation
- Early marriage
- Gender parity in safety and security
- Gender parity in literacy

2010   2012   2014   2016   2018

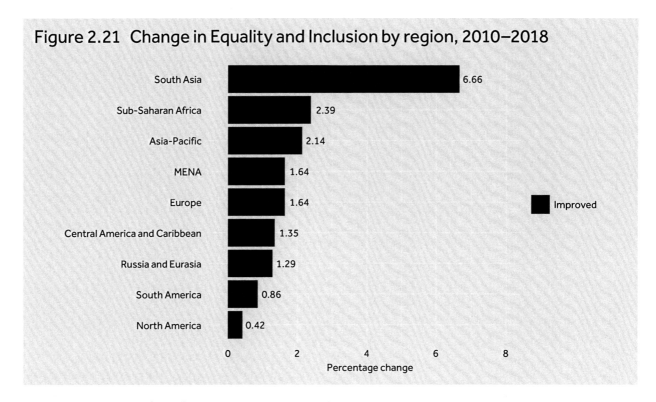

Figure 2.21 Change in Equality and Inclusion by region, 2010–2018

2.6.5 Political and Civic Participation

Political and Civic Participation was the only domain in the 2020 YDI to show an average deterioration over the past decade. Worldwide, 102 countries deteriorated while 79 improved.

Progress in Political and Civic Participation for young people deteriorated by 0.18 per cent from 2010 to 2018, driven by a 3.41 per cent deterioration in the average global score for the volunteered time indicator. The score for voiced opinion to an official also declined, by just under 3 per cent.

In contrast, recognition for community improvement improved by more than 10 per cent, indicating that an increasing share of young people around the world are receiving recognition for their investments in improving their communities. This indicator is included in the YDI on the premise that being recognised, or seeing one's peers recognised, for efforts to improve the community encourages community engagement. Young people around the world will respond to this survey question differently, as they understand community improvement, and recognition for it, differently in their own context. However, a 10 per cent improvement on this indicator suggests that some avenues for youth engagement are increasingly encouraging, even though others are in decline. Figure 2.22 shows the trend in Political and Civic Participation, as well as each of its component indicators.

North America posted the greatest regional average decline in Political and Civic Participation, at 17 per cent. Both countries in North America – Canada and the USA – deteriorated over the decade, at 26 and 12 per cent, respectively. The deterioration in Canada was the fifth-largest worldwide.

Figure 2.23 gives the change in each region's average Political and Civic Participation score from 2010 to 2018. Russia and Eurasia followed North America with a 12.2 per cent deterioration; South Asia, MENA, South America and Central America and the Caribbean had single-digit declines.

In contrast, Sub-Saharan Africa recorded nearly a 5 per cent improvement and marginal gains were made in Asia-Pacific and Europe. Of Sub-Saharan Africa's 31 risers, Madagascar had the largest improvement, followed by Kenya, Sierra Leone, Côte d'Ivoire and Comoros.

2.6.6 Peace and Security

The Peace and Security domain recorded the second largest improvement of any domain on the 2020 YDI, with the average domain score increasing by 3.41 per cent from 2010 to 2018, driven by a 5.32 per cent improvement in the INFORM score. INFORM measures country-level risk of armed conflict and climate change-induced natural disasters, giving an indication of the context today's young people are coming of age in. The world's average INFORM score has improved over the past decade based on gains in

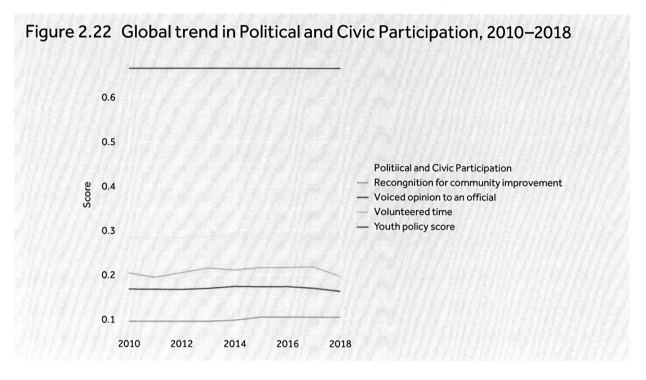

Figure 2.22 Global trend in Political and Civic Participation, 2010–2018

socio-economic development and coping capacity, which reduces the severity of disasters when they do occur. The prevalence of environmental hazards has continued to rise for the past 10 years, but the INFORM score trend suggests the world is increasingly rising to meet the challenge.

The average conflict and terrorism and interpersonal violence scores had nearly concomitant improvements, at 5 and 4.5 per cent, respectively. This indicates that fewer young people are dying from armed conflict, terrorism and homicide around the world. However, the internal peace indicator deteriorated 1.28 per cent

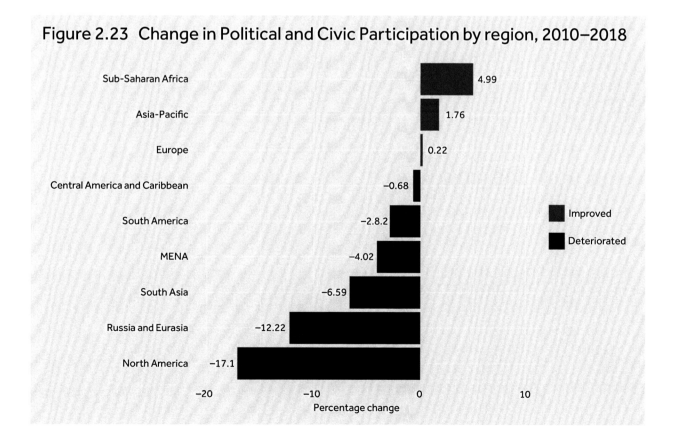

Figure 2.23 Change in Political and Civic Participation by region, 2010–2018

on average, suggesting that youth are experiencing more violent environments. This contrast is an important area for exploration for the Youth, Peace and Security Agenda adopted in United Nations Security Council Resolution 2250. Historically, youth have been considered those seeing the most impacts from direct violence. However, a decline in years of life lost amid ever more violent contexts is consistent with the overall trend of changes in the nature of armed conflict that has taken place in the past decade. Figure 2.24 shows the trend in Peace and Security, as well as each of its component indicators.

The progress in this domain was shared by more countries than not, with 131 countries improving while 50 deteriorated. Somalia had the largest improvement globally, followed by Colombia, Sri Lanka, Eritrea and Russia – all countries that emerged from armed conflicts over the decade. Unsurprisingly, Libya had the largest deterioration, followed by Ukraine, Syria, Burkina Faso and Cameroon.

Figure 2.25 gives the change in each region's average score from 2010 to 2018. Results in Russia and Eurasia drove the improving trend, with a 31 per cent increase in the region's average score and gains in 11 out of 12 countries. Russia recorded the region's largest improvement, followed by Kazakhstan, Kyrgyzstan, Turkmenistan and Uzbekistan.

In contrast, MENA deteriorated by 13.63 per cent. Following Libya and Syria, Egypt, Lebanon and Bahrain made up the top five deteriorations in Peace and Security

in the region. MENA has generally been the region most affected by armed conflict over the past decade.

2.7 Global results by region

While the YDI focuses on youth development at a national level, it is also important to understand similarities and differences between and within the world's regions. Highlighting distinct regional characteristics of youth development leads to a better understanding of common challenges faced by countries in the region, and this may encourage greater intra-regional co-operation.

The 2020 YDI results show that Europe had the highest average YDI score among the nine world regions in 2018. Sub-Saharan Africa saw the lowest ranking region, on average. Table 2.6 shows the 2020 regional ranks for the overall YDI score as well as the regional rankings for each YDI domain. Most regions vary substantially in domain ranks, highlighting youth development strengths and weaknesses. Asia-Pacific is the exception, which is the most consistent, ranking third and fourth across all domains.

2.7.1 Asia-Pacific

The third highest-ranking region in the 2020 YDI was Asia-Pacific, with an average country score of 0.724. In addition, the region ranks third out of the nine regions in Employment and Opportunity and Peace and Security and fourth in the four remaining domains. The region scored higher than the global average

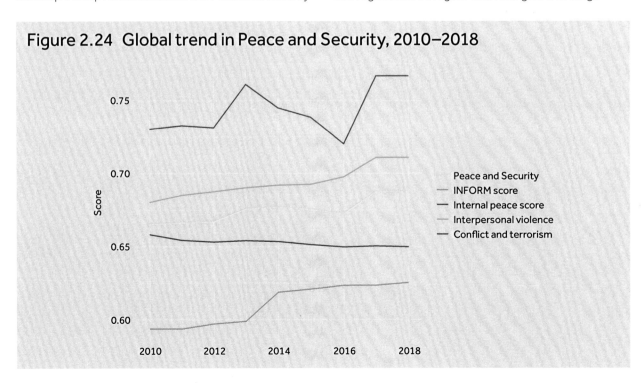

Figure 2.24 Global trend in Peace and Security, 2010–2018

Figure 2.25 Change in Peace and Security by region, 2010–2018

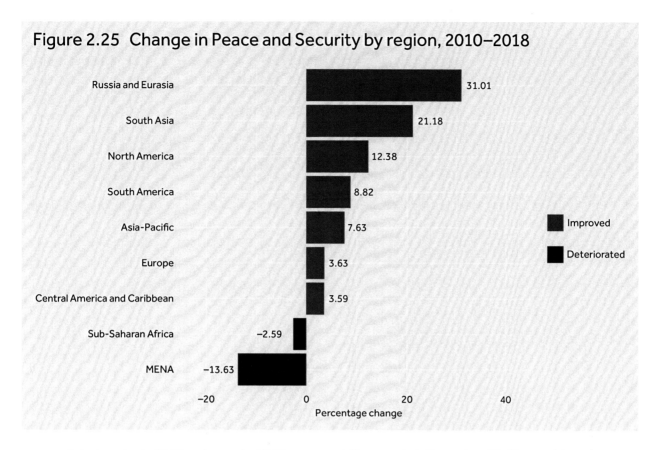

across all six domains in 2018 and recorded 3.07 per cent improvement in the average country score from 2010 to 2018.

Asia-Pacific is home to almost half a billion young people, making up 27.6 per cent of the world's youth population. With a total population of approximately 2.4 billion people in the region, 15–29 year olds make up 21.1 per cent of the region's population. This is slightly lower than the global youth proportion at 23.7 per cent.[4]

Only two countries in the region fall in the low YDI level category: Laos and Papua New Guinea. Seven

Table 2.6 Regional ranking for domain scores and YDI score, 2018

Region	YDI score rank	Education rank	Employment & Opportunity rank	Health & Wellbeing rank	Political & Civic Participation rank	Equality & Inclusion rank	Peace & Security rank
Europe	1	2	1	1	3	1	1
North America	2	1	2	8	9	2	2
Asia-Pacific	3	4	3	4	4	4	3
Russia and Eurasia	4	3	5	6	5	3	4
MENA	5	7	4	2	8	6	8
South America	6	5	7	5	7	5	5
Central America And Caribbean	7	6	6	7	1	7	7
South Asia	8	8	8	3	6	8	6
Sub-Saharan AfricaSub-Saharan	9	9	9	9	2	9	9

countries in the region experienced medium levels of youth development in 2018, while eleven and five countries, respectively, recorded high and very high levels of youth development.

Of the 25 Asia-Pacific countries included on the 2020 YDI, only two, Kiribati and Samoa, recorded deteriorations, both at less than 1 per cent, from 2010 to 2018. Brunei is the only country in the region to have recorded no change in youth development, while 22 countries improved (see Figure 2.26).

On average, Asia-Pacific improved across all six domains between 2010 and 2018 (see Figure 2.27). Peace and Security saw the largest progress, at 7.14 per cent, while the region improved around 2 per cent for the remaining domains.

All countries in the region improved in Peace and Security from 2010 to 2018, except Japan, having recorded a slight deterioration of 0.75 per cent, and Taiwan, whose score remained unchanged. Peace and Security is the domain to record the largest progress for any single country, with Thailand improving its score from 0.387 in 2010 to 0.653 in 2018, an increase of

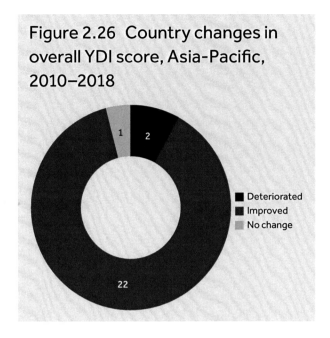

Figure 2.26 Country changes in overall YDI score, Asia-Pacific, 2010–2018

Legend:
- Deteriorated
- Improved
- No change

68.74 per cent. Similarly, Mongolia's score increased by 66.74 per cent, while Myanmar and South Korea recorded progress of 47.42 and 26.84 per cent, respectively. All other countries in the region improved

Figure 2.27 Trend in YDI domain scores, Asia-Pacific, 2010–2018

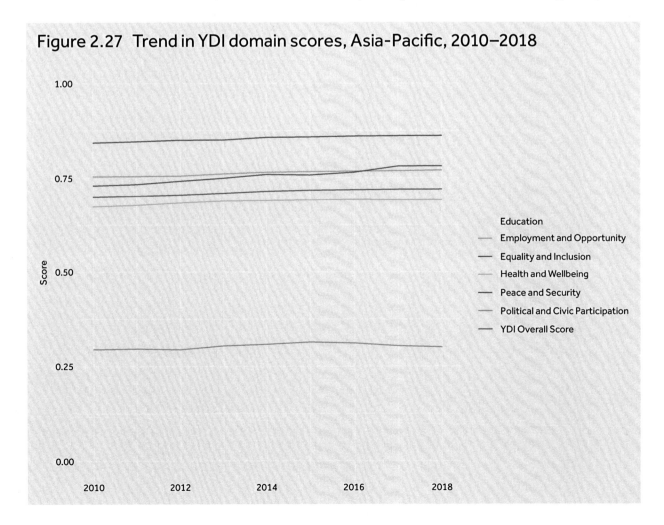

Legend:
- Education
- Employment and Opportunity
- Equality and Inclusion
- Health and Wellbeing
- Peace and Security
- Political and Civic Participation
- YDI Overall Score

between 0 and 6 per cent, and Asia-Pacific's youth continue to experience levels of Peace and Security that are substantially higher than the global average. In 2018, the region scored 0.781 on average, compared with the global average score at 0.688.

Myanmar recorded the largest progress in youth development in the region from 2010. With improvement seen across all six domains, the country's YDI score increased by 10.5 per cent. This was based on progress across most areas of youth development, with the exception of Political and Civic Participation. Myanmar's improvement was primarily driven by progress in Peace and Security, which increased by 47.42 per cent from a score of 0.445 in 2010 to 0.656 in 2018. In addition, Myanmar's Education score increased by 8.45 per cent and Employment and Opportunity improved by 5.14 per cent.

Indonesia recorded the second-largest improvement in the region, at 9.4 per cent. The country recorded a significant increase in Political and Civic Participation, at 62.21 per cent. In addition, Indonesia's youth experienced improvements in Employment and Opportunity of 17.12 per cent and progress in Equality and Inclusion of 11.35 per cent.,

Samoa's relatively small decrease in its YDI score from 2010 to 2018 was driven by deteriorations in Equality and Inclusion, particularly worsened parity in NEET. In addition to the decrease in Samoa's Equality and Inclusion score by 3.93 per cent, Samoa's youth have experienced worsened conditions in Education, falling by 1.34 per cent from 2010. Similarly, Kiribati's deterioration in youth development was driven by worsened Education outcomes, with the domain score decreasing by 3.10 per cent.

2.7.2 Central America and the Caribbean

Central America and the Caribbean ranked seventh out of the nine regions on the 2020 YDI, with an average score of 0.674. The region recorded progress on youth development of 2.16 per cent from 2010. While all regions scored relatively low in the Political and Civic Participation domain compared with other domains, Central America and the Caribbean ranked first of the nine regions in this domain, with an average score of 0.318. This is despite the region recording a slight deterioration of 0.68 per cent between 2010 and 2018.

With a total population of 217.3 million people, Central America and the Caribbean is home to a youth population of approximately 56.7 million. Thus, 15–29 year olds constitute 26.1 per cent of the region's total

population. This is slightly higher than global youth proportion at 23.66 per cent[5] Of the region's 17 countries included on the 2020 YDI, only 2, Honduras and Guatemala, fell within the low YDI group. Eight countries fell within the medium youth development category, while seven countries were classified as high.

Since 2010, only three countries in the region, Jamaica, and Saint Lucia have recorded average deteriorations in youth development. Fifteen countries have therefore recorded average improvements, with Haiti recording the most significant progress in youth development, of 5.4 per cent, between 2010 and 2018. On average, countries in Central America and the Caribbean improved in five out of the six domains. The largest increase was in the region's Health and Wellbeing and Peace and Security score, at 2.1 per cent. Following this, the region progressed in Employment and Opportunity, recording improvements of about 2 per cent. Equality and Inclusion as well as Education also recorded improvements, at around 1 per cent.

As mentioned, Haiti recorded the region's largest progress on youth development. Haiti has seen substantial progress in Health and Wellbeing in particular, with its score improving by 34.5 per cent. Haiti faced a devastating earthquake in 2010, which had a substantial impact on the country's mortality rate that year, which led to the country ranking last on the youth mortality indicator in 2010.

Similar to other regions, Central America and the Caribbean saw varying developments in Peace and Security between 2010 and 2018, despite an average improvement. Belize recorded the largest improvement, at 75.76 per cent, increasing its score from 0.330 in 2010 to 0.580 in 2018. Peace and Security in Nicaragua has improved by 6.33 per cent, while Barbados has recorded the third-largest improvement in its score, of 5.45 per cent. Four countries have recorded deteriorations since 2010, with Mexico seeing the largest deterioration, of 7.91 per cent. Conditions for young people in El Salvador have deteriorated by 3.13 per cent since 2010. Similarly, Cuba and The Bahamas recorded worsened conditions, though changes were of less than 1 per cent. Saint Lucia is the only country to have maintained its Peace and Security score between 2010 and 2018.

Central America and the Caribbean's average deterioration in Political and Civic Participation was minimal, at 0.68 per cent, with five countries improving, seven deteriorating and five maintaining their score. However, the relatively flat trend in the average regional score is the result of some large improvements and

Figure 2.28 Country changes in overall YDI score, Central America and the Caribbean, 2010–2018

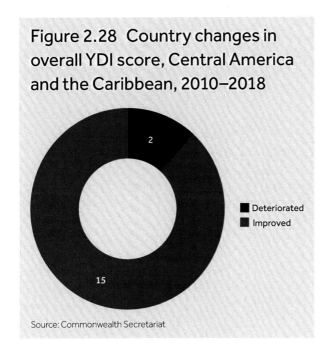

- Deteriorated
- Improved

Source: Commonwealth Secretariat

some large deteriorations. Nicaragua recorded the greatest progress, at 14.62 per cent, followed by Trinidad and Tobago and Haiti, both of which saw improvements above 11 per cent. Honduras' youth ranked highest on Political and Civic Participation in the region, and, having improved by 7.85 per cent since 2010, Honduras had the world's fourth-highest youth participation score. On the other hand, Panama and Mexico recorded deteriorations at 17.89 and 16.67 per cent, respectively, and young people's Political and Civic Participation has worsened by around 6 per cent in Jamaica and Guatemala.

2.7.3 Europe

The highest-ranking region in the world in the 2020 YDI was Europe, with an average overall score of 0.818. Europe also ranked first in Employment and Opportunity, Health and Wellbeing, Equality and Inclusion and Peace and Security among the nine

Figure 2.29 Trend in YDI domain scores, Central America and the Caribbean, 2010–2018

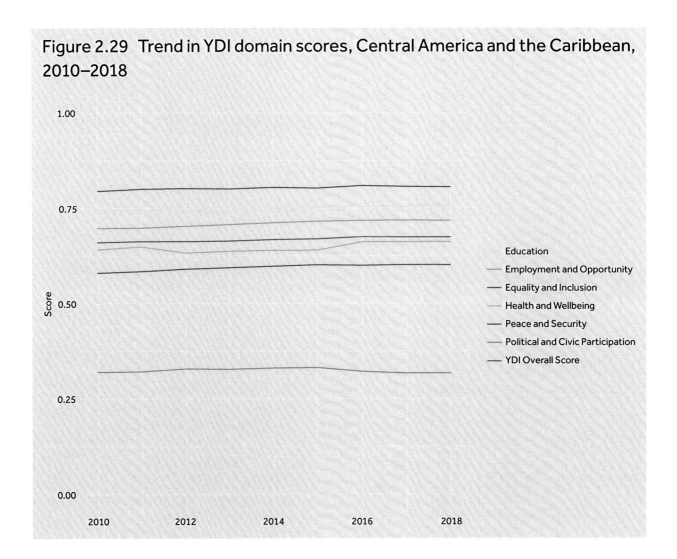

- Education
- Employment and Opportunity
- Equality and Inclusion
- Health and Wellbeing
- Peace and Security
- Political and Civic Participation
- YDI Overall Score

Figure 2.30 Country changes in overall YDI score, Europe, 2010–2018

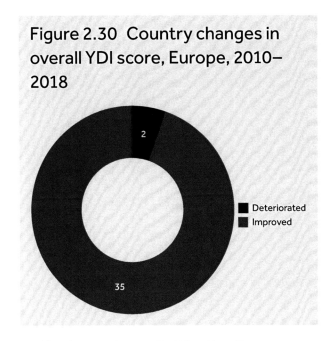

Deteriorated
Improved

2

35

world regions, and second in Education. On average, European countries scored higher than the global average across all six domains on the 2020 YDI,

based on improvements across all domains over the past decade.

Europe's youth proportion is relatively low, at 17.8 per cent, with a total population of almost 626 million people and a youth population close to 112 million people in 2018. Compared with other regions and the global youth proportion (23.66 per cent), young people make up a relatively low percentage of the region's total population, and young Europeans only make up 6.19 per cent of the global youth population.[6] These young Europeans enjoy particularly high levels of youth development, with 32 countries falling within the very high YDI level and the remaining five in the high category.

Starting at a relatively high average level of youth development in 2010, the region only saw minor changes from 2010 to 2018. Only two countries, out of thirty-seven, recorded deteriorations in their YDI score: North Macedonia and Slovenia. Europe's largest progress was recorded in the Peace and Security domain, which improved 3.63 per cent over the eight-

Figure 2.31 Trend in YDI domain scores, Europe, 2010–2018

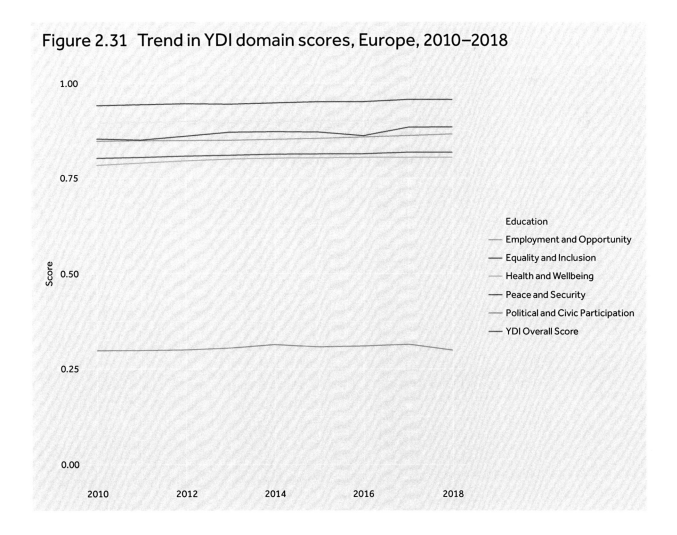

Education
Employment and Opportunity
Equality and Inclusion
Health and Wellbeing
Peace and Security
Political and Civic Participation
YDI Overall Score

Figure 2.32 Country changes in overall YDI score, North America, 2010–2018

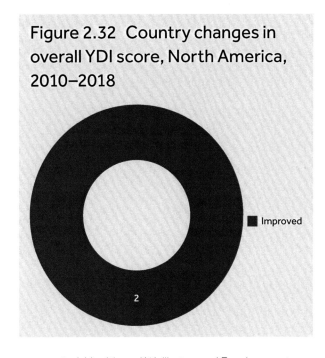

Improved

2

year period. Health and Wellbeing and Employment and Opportunity improved by 2.6 and 2.2 per cent, respectively. Yet, as mentioned, these small changes

must be evaluated relative to the region's actual scores, which were already at relatively high levels in 2010.

Despite a relatively small average change of 0.22 in Europe's Political and Civic Participation score, countries in the region recorded varying developments. Political and Civic Participation was the domain to see Europe's biggest divergence in progress and deterioration in youth development between 2010 and 2018. Fourteen countries deteriorated, with three counties, Slovenia, Netherlands and Czech Republic, seeing particularly deteriorations of above 20 per cent. On the other hand, 22 countries recorded improvements in young people's Political and Civic Participation. Five of these countries, Bosnia and Herzegovina, Norway, France, Turkey and Montenegro, recorded progress above 20 per cent. Bulgaria is the only country in the region to have recorded no changes in its domain score over the eight-year period.

All European countries except Turkey and Poland improved in Peace and Security between 2010 and 2018. Estonia recorded the largest improvement at 27.09 per cent, while the UK, Norway and Croatia

Figure 2.33 Trend in YDI domain scores, North America, 2010–2018

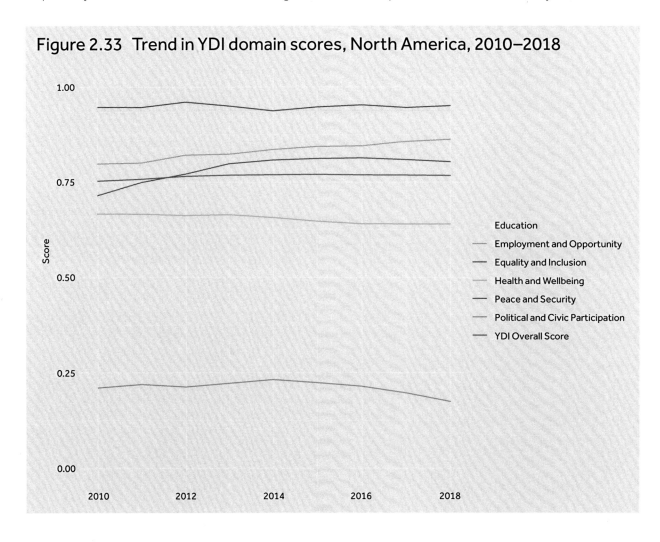

Legend:
- Education
- Employment and Opportunity
- Equality and Inclusion
- Health and Wellbeing
- Peace and Security
- Political and Civic Participation
- YDI Overall Score

improved more than 10 per cent. Poland recorded no change over the eight-year period, while Peace and Security in Turkey deteriorated by 11.86 per cent. Turkey remains the lowest-scoring country in the region with a score of 0.446, significantly lower than the region's average at 0.885 in 2018.

Employment and Opportunity for youth in Europe is on average the best in the world and the region's youth continue to see improvements in this area. Only seven countries recorded deteriorations in this domain, while youth in thirty countries experienced progress. In spite of the deterioration in Peace and Security, Turkey recorded the largest improvement in Employment and Opportunity in the region between 2010 and 2018. Lithuania and Italy both recorded progress around 7 per cent, while young Germans and Poles saw improvements of around 6 per cent. The remaining 25 countries to improve in Employment and Opportunity recorded progress of less than 5 per cent. While the percentage increase in European countries' Employment and Opportunity scores since 2010 are relatively small compared with those of other regions, Europe was already the highest-ranking region in 2010, with an average score of 0.848. Thus, Europe continues to be home to the best Employment and Opportunity conditions for young people.

2.7.4 North America

With an average YDI score of 0.768, North America was the second-highest ranking region on the 2020 YDI. In addition, the region ranked first in Education and second in Employment and Opportunity, Equality and Inclusion and Peace and Security. The region does, however, score lower than the global average in Political and Civic Participation.

The youth population in North America was 20.5 per cent in 2018, with approximately 74.6 million young people.[7]

With only two countries in the region, the overall improvement in youth development of 1.9 per cent was driven primarily by progress in the USA, at 3.1 per cent, leaving the country in the high YDI category in 2018. Youth development in Canada improved slightly between 2010 and 2018, at 0.9 per cent. Canada's young people enjoy very high levels of youth development, with an overall score of 0.798 in 2018.

North America recorded its largest percentage progress in Peace and Security, with Canada and the USA improving their scores by 6.58 and 20.54 per cent, respectively. Similarly, the region recorded an impressive improvement in Employment and

Opportunity, at 8.83 per cent. While Canada's percentage improvement was relatively low compared with that of the USA, at 3.92 per cent and 13.03 per cent, respectively, Canada's score was still nearly 10 per cent above that of the USA.

On the other hand, both Canada and the USA recorded significant deteriorations in Political and Civic Participation between 2010 and 2018. Canada's score decreased by 25.81 per cent while the USA recorded a 12.03 per cent deterioration. These percentage changes should, however, be evaluated relative to the already low scores. Despite the significant percentage decrease, Canada has recorded an absolute deterioration in Political and Civic Participation only from 0.155 in 2010 to 0.115 in 2018. Similarly, the USA has seen only a marginal deterioration in its score, going from 0.266 to 0.234.

The region's average decline in the Health and Wellbeing score of 2.6 per cent reflects how both countries have recorded worsened conditions for young people's physical and mental health. The USA's score fell from 0.574 in 2010 to 0.538 in 2018, a decrease of 6.3 per cent. Canada saw a similar decrease at 2.2 per cent, albeit from a relatively higher level in 2010. Thus, Canada's score remains relatively higher in 2018, at 0.742.

2.7.5 Middle East and North Africa

The MENA region records an average score of 0.686 in the 2020 YDI and ranked fifth out of the nine regions. The region saw a slight deterioration in youth development of 0.5 per cent in its overall score between 2010 and 2018.

In 2018, MENA was home to 489.1 million people, of whom 124.2 were between 15 and 29 years of age. Thus, more than a quarter of the population are considered youth (25.4 per cent), and the 20 counties in the region account for 6.88 per cent of the world's youth population.[8] Eleven of the twenty countries in the region fall within the low and medium youth development categories on the 2020 YDI. These countries are home to almost 103.5 million young people, thus 83.29 per cent of youth in the region live in countries with relatively low and medium levels of youth development. This highlights how youth development is disparate and not equally available within a region.

The disparate development within the region is evident in Figure 2.34, which shows that half of the countries improved while the other half deteriorated their YDI score between 2010 and 2018. MENA's average

Figure 2.34 Country changes in overall YDI score, MENA, 2010–2018

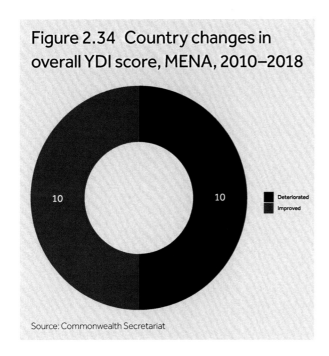

10   10

■ Deteriorated
■ Improved

Source: Commonwealth Secretariat

was the fall in the region's average Peace and Security score, which declined by 13.63 per cent. The remaining domains, Education, Employment and Opportunity and Equality and Inclusion have, however, recorded average improvements.

The largest percentage increases in overall scores in the region were recorded in Algeria and Morocco, at 8.2 and 6.5 per cent, respectively. Algeria progressed across all domains in the 2020 YDI. Education improved by 16.64 per cent, while Peace and Security and Political and Civic Participation both improved by more than 10 per cent between 2010 and 2018. Similarly, Morocco has recorded substantial improvements in four of the six YDI domains: Education, Equality and Inclusion, Employment and Opportunity, Health and Wellbeing and Peace and Security. The largest increase was recorded in Education, at 15.41 per cent.

deterioration was driven by worsening results in Peace and Security, Political and Civic Participation and Health and Wellbeing over the decade. Particularly substantial

Syria recorded the largest deterioration in youth development in the region, at 19.9 per cent, from 2010 to 2018. The instability in the country led to a 51.9 per cent decline in its Peace and Security score, from

Figure 2.35 Trend in YDI domain scores, MENA, 2010–2018

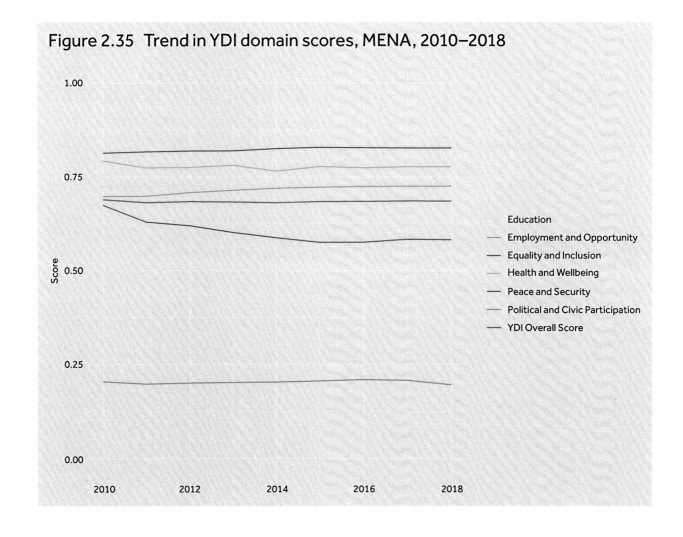

0.742 in 2010 to 0.357 in 2018. Syria recorded the second-largest deterioration in Peace and Security in the region, only topped by Libya, which saw its score worsen by 53.4 per cent.

It is evident that Peace and Security remains a core challenge to youth development in some countries in the region, with eight countries measuring deteriorations from 2010 to 2018 above 20 per cent. Simultaneously, however, eight MENA countries recorded progress in Peace and Security in this period, with improvements in Iran and Israel measured at 33.88 and 24.21 per cent, respectively. Evidently, disparity in Peace and Security in the region is substantial, with Qatar scoring an impressive 0.906 and Iraq ranking last in the region with a score of 0.311 in 2018.

2.7.6 Russia and Eurasia

Since 2010, Russia and Eurasia has improved youth development by 5.1 per cent overall and scores slightly higher than the global average in 2018, 0.705 compared with 0.671. In addition, the region has seen significant improvements in Peace and Security and Employment

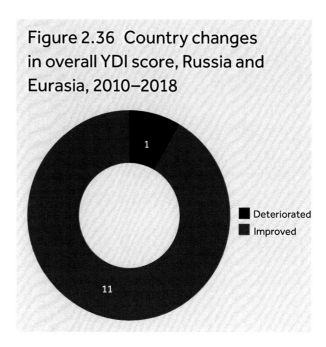

Figure 2.36 Country changes in overall YDI score, Russia and Eurasia, 2010–2018

and Opportunity, at 31 and 6.4 per cent, respectively. The region ranked fourth out of the nine regions in its average YDI score in 2018, based on improvements in 11 out of 12 countries over the prior decade.

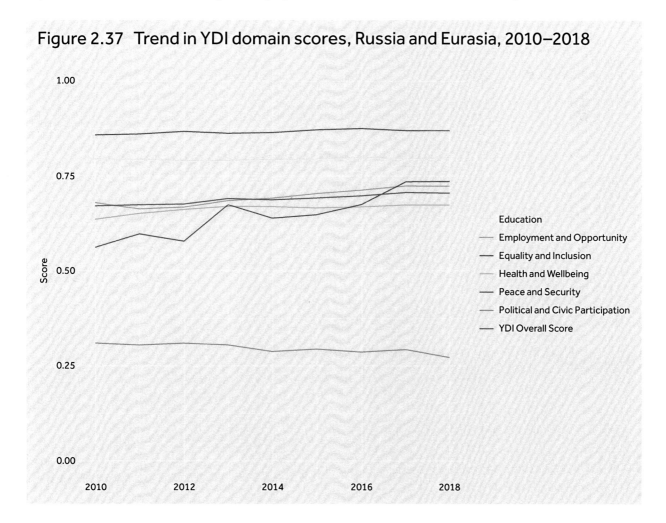

Figure 2.37 Trend in YDI domain scores, Russia and Eurasia, 2010–2018

Figure 2.38 Country changes in overall YDI score, South America, 2010–2018

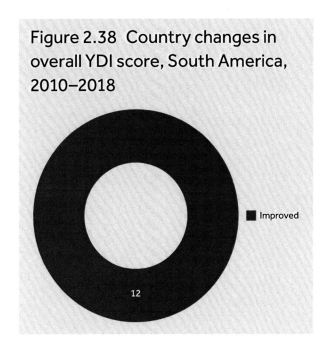

■ Improved

12

Youth in Russia and Eurasia account for only 3.12 per cent of the world's youth population. However, with a relatively small population of 292 million, the 56 million

15–29 year olds make up 19.3 per cent of the region's population.[9] In six of the twelve countries in the region, young people are experiencing relatively high levels of youth development, while the remaining six countries in the region fall within the medium YDI category.

The relatively high levels of youth development in the region are driven mainly by high average scores in Education, Equality and Inclusion and Peace and Security and Health and Wellbeing, with all domains scoring higher than the global average. The region falls behind the global average in the remaining domains: Employment and Opportunity, and Political and Civic Participation.

Ukraine was the only country in the region to deteriorate on the YDI from 2010 to 2018. The country's deterioration in youth development was driven by deteriorations across five out of the six domains. Only the Employment and Opportunity domain recorded progress, at 4.85 per cent, between 2010 and 2018. Particularly significant were regressions in the Political and Civic Participation, Health and Wellbeing and Peace and Security domains. The

Figure 2.39 Trend in YDI domain scores, South America, 2010–2018

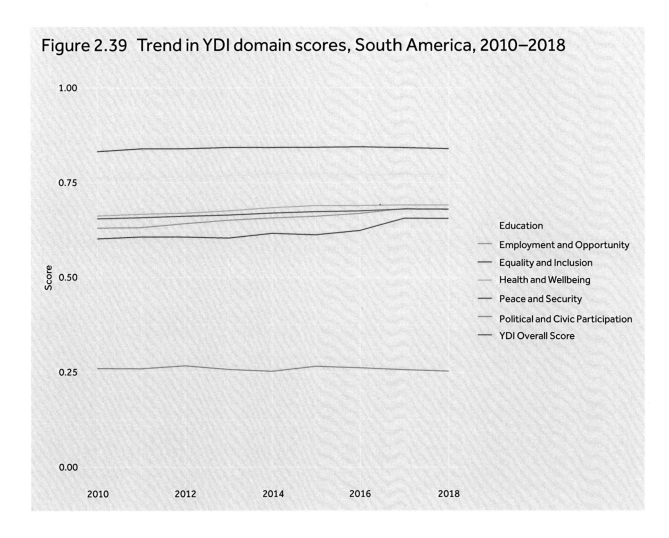

Figure 2.40 Country changes in overall YDI score, South Asia, 2010–2018

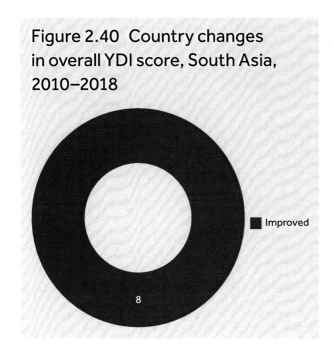

Improved

8

Political and Civic Participation domain fell from 0.382 in 2010 to 0.322 in 2018, a decrease of 15.71 per cent. Health and Wellbeing deteriorated by 16.9 per cent.

Most substantial, however, is Ukraine's deterioration in Peace and Security of 52.11 per cent between 2010 and 2018, highlighting the impact of the ongoing armed conflict on the young people of Ukraine.

As mentioned, all other countries in the region recorded improvements in youth development between 2010 and 2018, with the largest progress recorded in Russia at 14 per cent. Second, Khazakstan improved 8.3 per cent; Armenia, Tajikistan and Kyrgyzstan all saw improvements in youth development above 7 per cent.

With the exception of Ukraine, all countries in the region have recorded significant progress in Peace and Security. Most countries have made double-digit gains. Moldova recorded the smallest improvement, at 3.17 per cent, while the next smallest was in Belarus, at an impressive 18.8 per cent. Peace and Security in Uzbekistan and Turkmenistan improved more than 50 per cent between 2010 and 2018, and Kyrgyzstan and Kazakhstan recorded progress above 60 per cent.

Russia's position as the fifth top riser globally was driven particularly by the significant increase in its Peace and Security score, of 81.31 per cent. Yet, despite the

Figure 2.41 Trend in YDI domain scores, South Asia, 2010–2018

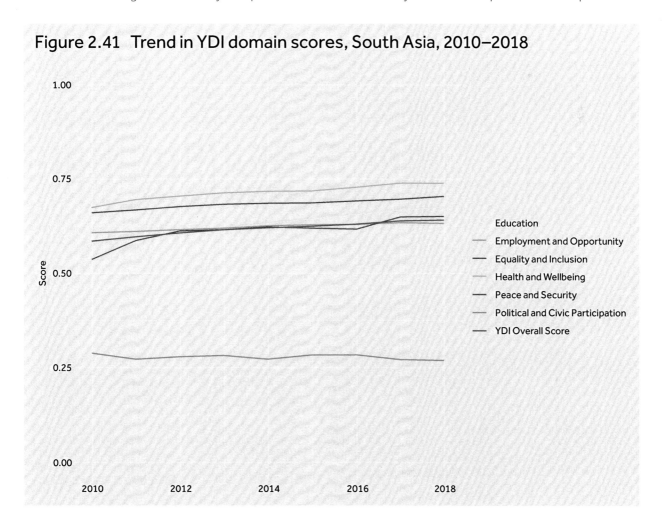

Figure 2.42 Country changes in overall YDI score, Sub-Saharan Africa, 2010–2018

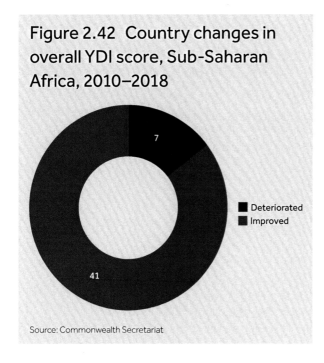

Source: Commonwealth Secretariat

significant percentage increase, Russia's level of Peace and Security, at a score of 0.582, remains lower than the global average (0.688). The country also continues to

rank low regionally, going from the lowest-ranking country in this domain in 2010 to the second-lowest in 2018.

While the region has recorded a marginal actual deterioration in Political and Civic Participation, several countries have recorded substantial percentage changes in this domain. Turkmenistan saw a 30.74 per cent deterioration in this domain, while Azerbaijan and Kazakhstan recorded deteriorations of 26 and 24.33 per cent, respectively. Four other countries in the region saw deteriorations in Political and Civic Participation above 12 per cent, and only three countries, Tajikistan, Armenia and Georgia, have recorded improvements.

2.7.7 South America

South America ranked sixth out of the nine regions on the 2020 YDI. The region outperformed the global average in the Education, Health and Wellbeing and Equality and Inclusion domains, but fell behind the global average in Political and Civic Participation as well as Peace and Security in 2018. The region's average YDI score, at 0.680.

Figure 2.43 Trend in YDI domain scores, Sub-Saharan Africa, 2010–2018

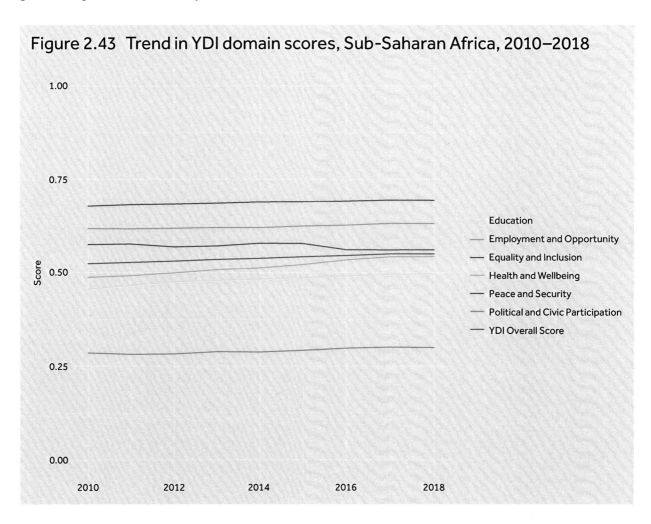

In 2018, South America was home to 104.4 million young people, with youth making up 24.7 per cent of the region's population. It is thus home to 5.78 per cent of the world's youth population.[10] Most South American countries have medium levels of youth development, although Chile, Uruguay, Peru and Argentina do all fall within the high category, contributing to the regional average YDI score of 0.723.

All 12 South American countries included in the 2020 YDI improved their overall score from 2010 to 2018, averaging a 2.5 per cent increase. The region recorded substantial progress in the Employment and Opportunity and Peace and Security domains, at 8 and 8.82 per cent, respectively. Education improved slightly in the region, at 1.15 per cent, while Equality and Inclusion and Health and Wellbeing recorded improvements of less than 1 per cent. Political and Civic Participation was the only domain to record a deterioration, with the average country score declining by 2.82 per cent from 2010 to 2018.

The region's three largest risers improved their YDI scores by more than 5 per cent between 2010 and 2018: Peru, Colombia and Ecuador. Peru recorded a substantial increase in its YDI score of 10 per cent, while Ecuador and Colombia improved their score by 6.8 per cent and 7.3 per cent, respectively. Yet the development in each domain varies across the three countries.

Peru progressed in five out of the six domains and maintained its score in Political and Civic Participation. The greatest improvement was recorded in Employment and Opportunity, improving by 25.92 per cent, and Peace and Security, up by 20.16 per cent. In addition, Peru's Education score improved by 5.57 per cent and Equality and Inclusion recorded a 2.36 per cent increase.

Similarly, Paraguay's improvement was driven primarily by substantial gains in the Employment and Opportunity and Peace and Security domains, recording improvements of 16.19 per cent and 12.39 per cent, respectively. In addition, Paraguay improved across all domains, except Political and Civic Participation (which deteriorated by 6.25 per cent), between 2010 and 2018.

Colombia recorded the most significant domain improvement in the region, more than doubling its Peace and Security score. This progress should, however, be interpreted relative to Colombia's low score on Peace and Security. Colombian youth continue to face great challenges in this area and

instability in the country poses barriers to youth development progress. Colombia also recorded substantial improvement in Employment and Opportunity, of 13.28 per cent. In contrast, its Political and Civic Participation and Education scores deteriorated by 1.56 and 6.73 per cent, respectively.

Brazil, Argentina, Uruguay, Bolivia and Guyana saw the region's smallest improvements in youth development, all improving their overall score by less than 2 per cent. In addition, Bolivia recorded the region's largest domain deterioration, with a 32.31 per cent deterioration in Political and Civic Participation between 2010 and 2018.

The region saw the most countries deteriorate in the Political and Civic Participation domain between 2010 and 2018. Seven countries in the region recorded deteriorations, while three maintained their scores and Ecuador and Venezuela improved theirs. Ecuador recorded an increase of 5.77, while Venezuela improved its score by a staggering 20.60 per cent. All countries do, however, continue to score relatively low on this domain, which reflects the global trend.

2.7.8 South Asia

South Asia ranked eighth out of the nine regions in the 2020 YDI, with an average 2018 score of 0.641. Thus, despite a 9.5 per cent increase from 2010 to 2018, the region's average YDI score remained lower than the global average.

With 492.4 million young people in 2018, South Asian youth made up 27.28 per cent of the world's youth population. The region's eight countries are home to more than 1.8 billion people and young people made up 27.1 per cent of South Asia's population in 2018.[11] Three countries in the region scored in the high YDI category, while two countries fell within the medium category and the final three in the low category.

From 2010 to 2018, all eight South Asian countries included on the 2020 YDI improved their overall score, with substantial progress particularly in the Education and Peace and Security domains. The region's average Education score improved by 16.13 per cent, while Peace and Security improved by 21.18 per cent from 2010 to 2018. Political and Civic Participation was the only domain to record deterioration across the eight-year period, with the average country score deteriorating by 6.91 per cent.

South Asia's substantial progress in Peace and Security was driven primarily by positive developments recorded in five countries: Afghanistan, India, Sri Lanka,

Bangladesh and Nepal. This progress, measured as substantial percentage improvements, put Afghanistan and India among the largest YDI risers in the 2020 YDI.

Sri Lanka recorded an impressive increase in Peace and Security of 98.98 per cent, almost doubling its score from 0.391 in 2010 to 0.778 in 2018. India also recorded improvements in Peace and Security of 44.47 per cent. The substantial increase in Afghanistan's Peace and Security score of 29.09 per cent has, however, led to only a marginal absolute improvement in the score, which remained at a relatively low level (moving from 0.110 to 0.142). Hence, youth development continues to face great challenges in Peace and Security in South Asia.

Similarly, South Asia's impressive progress in the Education domain, at 26.13 per cent, was driven by improvements of greater than 10 per cent in six of the eight countries. Afghanistan's score improved by 54.39 per cent, while Bangladesh and Nepal recorded improvements of 40.16 and 24.01 per cent, respectively. Sri Lanka was the only country in the region to deteriorate in the Education domain, albeit marginally, at 0.13 per cent. Sri Lanka remained the second-highest scoring country in the region, with an Education score of 0.769 in 2018. Maldives maintained its first place in Education in the region, scoring an impressive 0.857 in 2018, much higher than the regional average at 0.676. Maldives also scored higher than the global average, despite a relatively small improvement of 1.88 per cent since 2010.

Political and Civic Participation was the only domain to record an average deterioration in the region since 2010. Three countries have contributed significantly to this development: Pakistan, Afghanistan and Sri Lanka. Pakistan's score deteriorated by 64.29 per cent, though from a relatively low score of 0.168 in 2010. Afghanistan and Sri Lanka saw deteriorations above 11 per cent each, while Bangladesh and Bhutan recorded deteriorations in Political and Civic Participation at less than 5 per cent. Nepal and India were the only two countries in the region to improve their Political and Civic Participation scores, by 7.53 and 7.79 per cent, respectively. Maldives maintained its score at 0.243 from 2010 to 2018.

2.7.9 Sub-Saharan Africa

Despite an improvement in youth development of 5 per cent, Sub-Saharan Africa continued be the lowest-ranking region on the 2020 YDI, with an average score of 0.549. The region ranked last in five out of the six domains – Education, Health and Wellbeing,

Employment and Opportunity, Equality and Inclusion and Peace and Security. It did however rank second in Political and Civic Participation. Sub-Saharan

Sub-Saharan Africa was home to 14.45 per cent of the world's youth population in 2018, with almost 261 million young people. With a total population of 947.4 million people, 15–29 year olds made up 27.5 per cent of the region's population.[12] With only three countries in the high YDI level category and 10 countries in the medium category, young people in the remaining 35 Sub-Saharan African countries faced low levels of youth development in 2018.

As the largest world region in the 2020 YDI, Sub-Saharan Africa saw varying changes in youth development between 2010 and 2018. Forty-one countries in the region improved their overall score, while seven countries recorded deteriorations. The region recorded its largest improvement in youth development in the Health and Wellbeing domain, increasing by 11.4 per cent. Progress was also recorded in the Education domain, improving by 9.05 per cent. As the only domain recording average deteriorations, Peace and Security worsened by 2.46 per cent over the eight-year period and remains a core challenge to youth development in the region.

In addition, the worsened average Peace and Security score in the region masks disparate developments. A total of 23 countries saw deteriorations in their score from 2010 to 2018, with 11 of these recording deteriorations above 25 per cent. On the other hand, 25 countries recorded improvements in Peace and Security, with eight countries increasing their score by more than 25 per cent. Somalia recorded a substantial increase, more than doubling its score between 2010 and 2018, while Eritrea recorded an increase of 95.82 per cent. Despite doubling its score, Somalia remained the lowest scoring country in the region, at 0.213 in 2018.

The significant progress in the Education domain in Sub-Saharan Africa was driven by significant progress in several countries' average score. In fact, 21 countries improved their score more than 10 per cent and eight countries by above 25 per cent. Burkina Faso improved its score by a staggering 70 per cent. It should be noted, however, that all these countries, except São Tomé and Príncipe, despite their progress, continued to score significantly lower than the global average.

Endnotes

1   https://unstats.un.org/sdgs/indicators/database/

2   https://thecommonwealth.org/youth

3   UNESCO defines a basic education as comprising primary and lower secondary education, according to the International Standard Classification of Education (ISCED) (http://uis.unesco.org/en/glossary-term/basic-education). The YDI indicator measures the rate of lower secondary school completion.

4   https://databank.worldbank.org/source/population-estimates-and-projections

5   https://databank.worldbank.org/source/population-estimates-and-projections

6   https://databank.worldbank.org/source/population-estimates-and-projections

7   https://databank.worldbank.org/source/population-estimates-and-projections

8   https://databank.worldbank.org/source/population-estimates-and-projections

9   https://databank.worldbank.org/source/population-estimates-and-projections

10 https://databank.worldbank.org/source/population-estimates-and-projections

11 https://databank.worldbank.org/source/population-estimates-and-projections

12 https://databank.worldbank.org/source/population-estimates-and-projections

References

Austin, K.F., M.M. Choi and V. Berndt (2017) "Trading Sex for Security: Unemployment and the Unequal HIV Burden among Young Women in Developing Nations". *International Sociology* **32**: 343–368.

Australian Institute of Health and Welfare (2020) "New Report Shows Impact of COVID-19 on Cancer Screening". https://www.aihw.gov.au/news-media/media-releases/2020/october/new-report-shows-impact-of-covid-19-on-cancer-scre

Azcona, G., A. Bhatt, J. Encarnacion, J. Plazaola-Castaño, P. Seck, S. Staab and L. Turquet (2020) From Insights to Action: Gender Equality in the Wake of COVID-19. New York: UN Women.

Biddle, N., B. Edwards, M. Gray and K. Sollis (2020) "Alcohol Consumption during the COVID-19 Period: May 2020". Canberra: Australia National University.

Commonwealth Secretariat (2016) *Youth-Led Accountability for the SDGs: A Guide to National Action*. London: Commonwealth Secretariat.

Commonwealth Secretariat and Youth Division (2016) *Global Youth Development Index and Report 2016*. London: Commonwealth Secretariat.

Etheridge, B. and L. Spantig (2020) "The Gender Gap in Mental Well-Being During the Covid-19 Outbreak: Evidence from the UK". ISER Working Paper 2020-08. Colchester: University of Essex.

Eurofound (2020a) *Living, Working and COVID-19*. Luxembourg: EU Publication Office.

Eurofound (2020b) *Living, Working and COVID-19 – First Findings, April 2020*. Luxembourg: EU Publication Office.

Hanushek, E.A. and L. Woessmann (2020) "The Economic Impacts of Learning Losses". Education Working Paper 225. Paris: OECD.

IEP (Institute for Economics & Peace) (2018). *Global Peace Index: Measuring Peace in a Complex World*. Sydney: IEP.

IIEP (International Institute for Educational Planning) (2020a) "COVID-19 School Closures: Why Girls Are More At Risk". UNESCO, 29 April. http://www.iiep.unesco.org/en/covid-19-school-closures-why-girls-are-more-risk-13406

IIEP (International Institute for Educational Planning) (2020b) "What Price Will Education Pay for COVID-19?" UNESCO, 7 April. http://www.iiep.unesco.org/en/what-price-will-education-pay-covid-19-13366

ILO (International Labour Organization) (2017) "Where Is Youth Unemployment the Highest?" http://www.ilo.org/global/about-the-ilo/multimedia/maps-and-charts/enhanced/WCMS_600072/lang--en/index.htm

ILO (2018) "The Gender Gap in Employment: What's Holding Women Back? What Does Vulnerable Employment Look Like?" https://www.ilo.org/infostories/en-GB/Stories/Employment/barriers-women#unemployed-vulnerable/vulnerable-employment

ILO (2019) "Skills for Youth Employment". http://www.ilo.org/skills/areas/skills-for-youth-employment/WCMS_672181/lang--en/index.htm

ILO (2020a) *Global Challenges, Global Solutions: Tackling the COVID-19 Pandemic and the Youth Employment Crisis*. Geneva: ILO.

ILO (2020b) "COVID-19 Disrupts Education of More than 70 Per Cent of Youth". Press Release, 11 August. http://www.ilo.org/global/about-the-ilo/newsroom/news/WCMS_753060/lang--en/index.htm

ILO (2020c) "Youth hit hard by COVID-19's economic fallout". YouTube video, 17 April. https://www.youtube.com/watch?v=ZPo09WPVTwk&list=TLGGxZVgNPAChD4yNjA0MjAyMQ&t=7s

Mascayano, F., J.E. Armijo and L.H. Yang (2015) "Addressing Stigma Relating to Mental Illness in Low- and Middle-Income Countries". *Frontiers in Psychiatry*, 11 March. https://doi.org/10.3389/fpsyt.2015.00038

Nigro, S. (2020) "Not in Education, Employment or Training... and Locked Out of the Labour Market". *Youth Employ*, 28 July. https://youthemploymentmag.net/2020/07/28/not-in-education-employment-or-training-and-locked-out-of-the-labour-market/

OECD (Organisation for Economic Co-operation and Development) (2017) "NEET Rates Are Significantly Higher among Young Women: Percentage-Point Difference in NEET Rates between Women and Men, by Age Group, 2015 or Latest Available". https://www.oecd-ilibrary.org/social-issues-migration-health/the-pursuit-of-gender-equality/neet-rates-are-significantly-higher-among-young-women_9789264281318-graph72-en

OECD (2020a) "Unemployment Rates, OECD – Updated: September 2020". https://www.oecd.org/newsroom/unemployment-rates-oecd-update-september-2020.htm

OECD (2020b) "Unemployment – Youth Unemployment Rate – OECD Data". http://data.oecd.org/unemp/youth-unemployment-rate.htm

OECD (2020c) "Governance for Youth, Trust and Intergenerational Justice: Fit for all Generations?" Launch Webinar.

OECD (2020d) "Youth and COVID-19: Response, Recovery and Resilience". 11 June. https://www.oecd.org/coronavirus/policy-responses/youth-and-covid-19-response-recovery-and-resilience-c40e61c6/

OECD (2020e) *Governance for Youth, Trust and Intergenerational Justice: Fit for All Generations?* Public Governance Review. Paris: OECD.

Plan International and ADB (Asian Development Bank) (2018) *What's the Evidence? Youth Engagement and the Sustainable Development Goals*. Woking and Manila: Plan International and ADB.

Schleicher, A. (2020) "The Impact of COVID-19 on Education – Insights from Education at a Glance 2020". Brochure. https://www.oecd.org/education/the-impact-of-covid-19-on-education-insights-education-at-a-glance-2020.pdf

United Nations and Search for Common Ground (2014) *Guiding Principles on Young People's Participation in Peacebuilding*. https://www.undp.org/content/undp/en/home/librarypage/democratic-governance/guiding-principles-on-young-peoples-participation-in-peacebuildi.html

World Bank (2020) *Projected Poverty Impacts of COVID-19*. Washington, DC: World Bank.

WHO (World Health Organization) (2020a) "COVID-19 Disrupting Mental Health Services in Most Countries". WHO Survey, 5 October. https://www.who.int/news/item/05-10-2020-covid-19-disrupting-mental-health-services-in-most-countries-who-survey

WHO (2020b) "WHO Director-General's Opening Remarks at the Media Briefing on COVID-19". 11 March. https://www.who.int/director-general/speeches/detail/who-director-general-s-opening-remarks-at-the-media-briefing-on-covid-19---11-march-2020

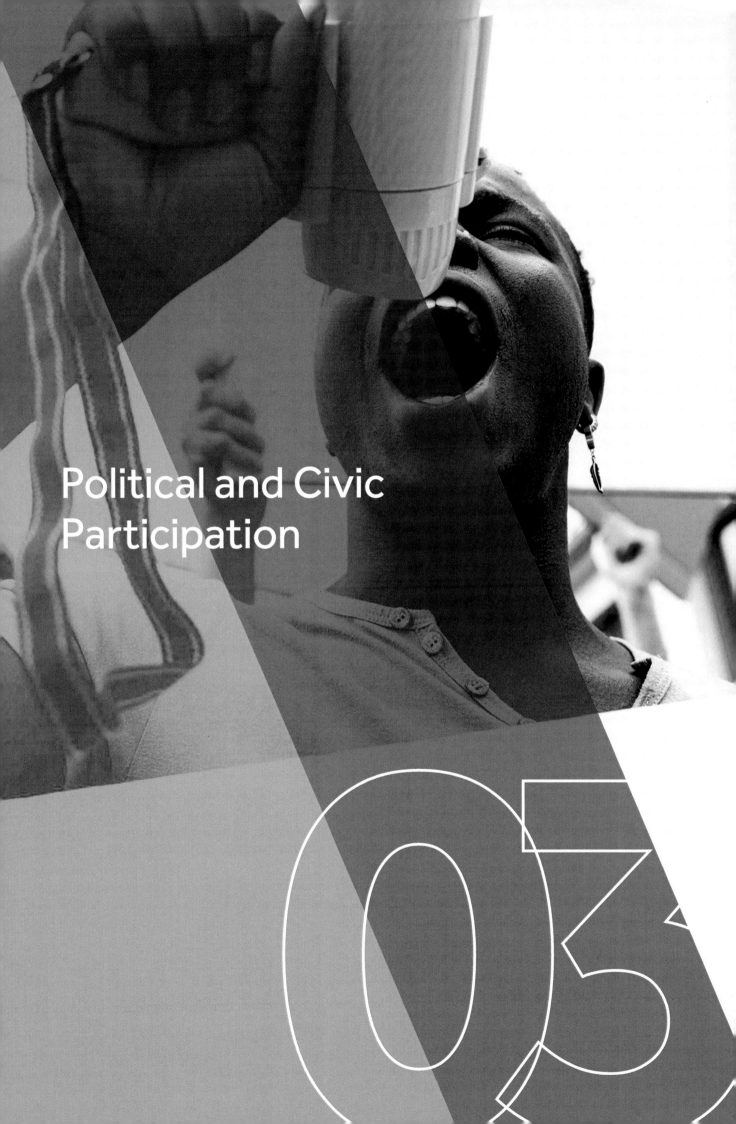

Political and Civic
Participation

03

Chapter 3

Political and Civic Participation

Global performance in this area of the Youth Development Index (YDI) has been disappointing. Notwithstanding improved scores in 79 countries across the board, all countries scored less than 0.50 on this domain, reflecting very low levels of participatory youth development. The scores reflect declining estimates of reported volunteerism and voicing opinions to officials over the 2010–2018 period. At the same time, we cannot deny observable trends of continued youth engagement – whether expressed in the form of political protest, declaration or civic contribution – particularly against the background of the COVID-19 pandemic and global resistance against racism, oppression and corruption. The juxtaposition of these two realities reveals the limitations of the YDI's capacity to measure participation – owing to the necessary reliance on globally available data on formal processes – and suggests the need for deeper analysis (qualitative and quantitative) of participation as a phenomenon that occurs at multiple levels and in multiple ways.

This chapter presents a perspective on participation that draws on principles, processes and structures advanced by the Commonwealth, as well as barriers to political participation, and recommends areas that could represent entry-points to reimagining participation. It also highlights youth-led initiatives that respect the right to participation and reflect the value of youth participation. The chapter concludes with messages from global leaders, outlining their views on the index and recommendations for change.

Guest Contributor

Inspiring a Collective Future

Puja Bajad, Consultant, youth and social policy

As young people around the world put themselves on the frontline to challenge historic and systematic forms of oppression and exclusion, their demands and voices resonate with a sense of resolve and urgency. Separated by space, time and geographical contexts, they nevertheless are joining in a common call for institutions to be more responsive to their rights and freedoms. Through diverse slogans, calls and action, young people have made known to the world their frustrations regarding the incremental nature of change. They have spoken powerfully and demanded a more just world by challenging various forms of inequalities and injustices arising as a result of climate change, slow or incomplete democratic reform, racism and other forms of systematic oppression, police brutality, corruption and ineffective governance.

Youth participation speaks directly to the sustainability of democratic representation – it concerns the modern dilemmas of young people, their expression of dissent, their affirmations, their hopes and despairs (Tisdall, 2014). Consequently, it is a phenomenon that encompasses online and offline spaces; traditional democratic dialogue and direct action; and formal youth networks and councils and informal groupings.

In addition, local contexts are linked to national and transnational mechanisms. There has been a renewed focus within development planning, policy circles and national politics over the past decade. With regard to the United Nations Sustainable Development Goals (SDGs), youth participation appears in over one-third of the 169 indicators of Agenda 2030. The Commonwealth Secretariat has asserted its commitment to youth participation through the establishment of the Commonwealth Youth Council (CYC), the Commonwealth Student Association (CSA) and various thematic youth networks, as well as the provision of technical assistance to member countries in setting up National Youth Councils and developing toolkits and guidance on strengthening youth representation and participation. This increased international focus has encouraged collaborative policy, action and research on participation.

However, global trends highlight growing youth disengagement with traditional participation structures and a general dip in political participation. On average, youth political and civic participation declined

globally between 2010 and 2018. "Political and Civic Participation" was the only one out of six YDI domains to record a decline in the global average score (by 0.18 per cent) and the only one in which all countries scored relatively lower than in other domains. In 2018, roughly 20 per cent of youth reported volunteering their time, and 16.2 per cent stated that they had voiced their opinion to an official in the previous 30 days. In contrast, there was a 10 per cent improvement in the scores for the indicator on "recognition for time spent improving communities", which suggests that young people are not completely disengaged.

The opportunities and challenges of youth participation cannot be seen within silos, nor can they be understood or articulated through individual numbers and rankings. The issue calls for critical broad inter-sectoral, inter-disciplinary research and practice so it can be a true marker in development programmes and a basis for policy formulation. While the much-needed quantitative assessment draws attention to areas of concerns, it also underlines the need for a more holistic framework for use in conceptualising, assessing and formulating strategies and solutions that enhance or at the very least explain the broad spectrum of participation phenomena, which go beyond traditional spaces of involvement.

In pursuit of such a holistic framework, this discussion outlines the principles, processes and structures that have guided the work of the Commonwealth Secretariat with its member countries. It describes core principles and processes that serve as enabling factors for effective participation; discusses barriers to political participation identified by young people; and highlights Commonwealth formal structures that play an important role in facilitating participation but that must be complementary to other structures to be effective.

Table 3.1 Principles, processes and structures of rights-based youth participation

Rights-based youth participation principles respect rights to...	Rights-based youth participation structures have...	Rights-based youth participation processes promote...
1. Self-determination	1. Inclusive membership	1. Subsidiarity in practice
2. Equitable treatment and inclusion, regardless of gender, age, ethnicity, religion, language, disability	2. Mechanisms that facilitate organised participation	2. Principles of equality and equity
3. Be heard	3. Varied types of democratic youth organisations	3. Youth inclusion in the design of democratic decision-making mechanisms
4. Freedom of expression, assembly and association	4. Representative/accountable leadership	4. Participatory strategic planning
5. Subsidiarity – having decisions taken at the most local level where appropriate	5. Autonomyv	
6. Direct and indirect political participation		
7. Participation in formulation of policy and programmes		

3.1 Commonwealth youth participation

3.1.1 Rights-based youth participation: A Commonwealth perspective

A recent study revealed key principles for rights-based youth participation, drawing on commitments member countries have made via international conventions and charters and drawing on observations of the experiences of youth organisations across the Commonwealth (Reddy et al., 2020). Applied at any level of governance, these principles, summarised in Table 3.1, encourage the implementation of processes and the establishment of structures that facilitate effective participation.

Member countries, as duty-bearers, have the responsibility to ensure that the necessary structures, mechanisms and processes are in place for the realisation of youth rights to participation, as well as to operationalise and sustain them. While encouraging the adoption of the aforementioned principles and characteristic processes and structures, the study by Reddy et al.(2020) does not prescribe a specific institutional model of participation at national level. Rather, it acknowledges the need for a participation ecosystem that respects youth rights and considers the varied socio-cultural,

economic and political conditions in each member country (see Figure 3.1). At the same time, the study also emphasises the need for young people to lead on the conceptualisation and implementation of participation initiatives.

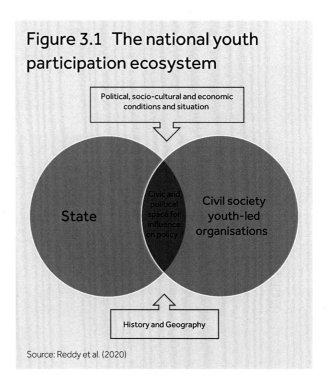

Figure 3.1 The national youth participation ecosystem

Political, socio-cultural and economic conditions and situation

State

Civic and political space for influence on policy

Civil society youth-led organisations

History and Geography

Source: Reddy et al. (2020)

3.1.2 Commonwealth processes: Youth mainstreaming

One of the ways in which the Commonwealth has applied the rights-based framework of participation is through the promotion of youth mainstreaming in development planning. A recent guidebook on mainstreaming situates youth participation firmly as fundamental to whole-of-government planning processes (Seneviratne, 2017). The guide describes mainstreaming as:

- Ensuring youth-centric institutions and processes in development planning within and across all sectors to realise equitable development for youth and society;

- Ensuring youth participation in all spheres and levels of development planning, without which positive and equitable outcomes for youth are not possible; and

- Acknowledging the implications of intergenerational relations among youth and adults, and young people's unique developmental rights and evolving capacities in conceiving and delivering policies and plans for them.

Consistent with the principles of rights-based participation, the youth mainstreaming process requires equitable, multi-level and comprehensive inclusion of young people. The guide also outlines that mainstreaming has been effective when:

- participation is free, voluntary and informed;

- participation influences policy and practice;

- all youth groups representing gender, ethic and geographic groups are included without discrimination;

- young people can "claim" their own space without having it "conferred" on them but receive support to participate in governance structures led by older persons;

- solidarity among youth social and cultural groups is encouraged and more privileged youth support marginalised groups by sharing access to decision-making domains;

- there is solidarity among younger and older youth and older youth make space for younger youth groups;

- participation extends beyond formal and official structures like National Youth Councils to engage youth social movements and unaffiliated youth;

- attention is paid to ideological tensions and differential experiences of politics and economics, but all participants are able to work constructively with dissent;

- there is cross-sectoral structures for youth participation in all areas of development planning (political, economic, social, cultural), and youth participation at all levels of governance.

3.1.3 Commonwealth structures

In pursuit of rights-based participation, the Commonwealth has encouraged the establishment of mechanisms at pan-Commonwealth, regional and national levels for young people to engage in governance and planning. Since the establishment of the Commonwealth Youth Programme, ministers and senior officials have asserted the importance of National Youth Councils and other participation structures.

Historically, critical contributions have included the creation of the United Nations Children's Fund-Commonwealth Secretariat toolkit on youth participation, technical assistance in setting up National Youth Councils and the creation of positions of Regional Youth Coordinators who represent national networks of young people engaged in the decision-making processes of youth ministries and departments.

More recently, in 2013, the Secretariat established the CYC and the CSA, which are global representative structures that link youth participation mechanisms in member countries to global platforms. The model connects representatives of National Youth Councils and students' unions or a parallel nationally recognised network to international decision-making fora. The CYC engages with governments through Youth Forums during the Commonwealth Heads of Government Meeting (CHOGM), the Commonwealth Youth Ministers Meeting (CYMM) and Youth Forums related to selected thematic Ministerial Meetings. The CSA's primary engagement with decision-makers is through the Commonwealth Education Ministers Meeting (CEMM).

Other thematic networks cover sport, climate change, entrepreneurship, journalism, peace, health, human rights and democracy, and disability. The networks connect young experts, activists and their organisations across borders and regions, so that informed, united and representative youth voices can advocate and collaborate with policy-makers.

They ensure that voices of youth from small and vulnerable states are heard in debates that can often be dominated by those from wealthier and more powerful countries. Importantly, the networks also provide a platform for young people to share innovation and good practice across borders and between regions and cultures, which enhances collaborative, youth-led action for change and peace.

Key advances made through these formal pan-Commonwealth structures have included affirming young people's rights to participation in decision-making in national and global planning structures, including in educational governance and higher education processes. The outcomes and impacts of the networks are emerging, and require critical monitoring and evaluation and impact assessment. At the same time, if we are to abide by the principles of the rights-based participation framework, it must be acknowledged that there are limitations to these structures. In particular:

- They cannot and should not replace national and sub-national, including community and school, structures.

- They are likely to privilege young people who have strong communication skills in English for international engagement and high-level policy dialogue with national decision-makers.

The biggest challenge for pan-Commonwealth structures going forward will be to develop ways of effectively incorporating views from local contexts, as well as marginalised voices, including young people below the voting age. Deeper and more deliberate engagement and consultation are needed to strengthen and/or transform these spaces. A solution recommended by the CYC has been to develop deeper engagement between youth wings of political parties with youth who have not attained the voting age in their country.

3.1.4 Commonwealth youth political participation

At the same time, attention is needed to issues related to youth participation in formal politics. As one young politician said, "[We must] ensure inclusion of young people in political processes and decisions - for they will defend the interests and dreams of the young generation, [and] most importantly build the capacity of young people to be part of the national legislative institutions through actively seeking for elective positions" (young politician, in Thibodeau et al., 2018).

A CYC-commissioned study on "Meaningful Youth Engagement in Political Parties" (Thibodeau et al., 2018) highlights the barriers to youth participation in political processes. Given an overall decrease in voter turnout across countries, including among young people, whether mandatory or voluntary voting is in place, a survey of young people across the Commonwealth, conducted as a part of the study, revealed several barriers to participation.

Young people were shown to have limited knowledge of the processes involved in formally signing up to a political party. Lack of interest in politics, lack of resonance with party ideologies and lack of trust in politics and politicians emerged as other key factors in youth disengagement. Furthermore, among surveyed youth who were already a part of a political party, only 47 per cent felt valued within the decision-making processes of the party (Thibodeau et al., 2018).

Membership fees, which are an important source of revenue for political parties, were also identified as a barrier to youth participation, since young people often lack the requisite income to take advantage of membership. In most cases, meanwhile, eligibility to join a political party is gained only after attaining the official voting age, which restricts the political participation of younger youth. Even young people over the voting age are restricted by age requirements in terms of standing for election to the highest levels of office, such as president or prime minister. Recently, though, there have been some changes to age restrictions in some member countries. For example, Nigeria has reduced the age to contest presidential elections from 40 to 35 through a campaign called "Not Too Young to Run." The Green Party in Canada allows party membership applications at 12 years of age without voting rights until the age of 14, when they can cast votes on policy resolutions (Thibodeau et al., 2018).

Notwithstanding these barriers, many political parties in the Commonwealth have established youth branches or youth wings to try to engage young people. Across the Commonwealth, the lower age limit for participation in a youth branch is 14 years and the upper age limit varies between 25 and 35 years. The youth branches or wings of political parties can be further strengthened by improving internal governance. This might involve limiting the length of the term an individual can serve as the chair to ensure full representation; ensuring complete autonomy within the branch; or providing access to a budget for activities. The existence of these youth wings is positive but the CYC is concerned to ensure that they have what is needed for meaningful engagement of members in party affairs; that they have the resources and tools to advocate for the policies they believe in; and that youth are viewed as serious and full members of the party (Thibodeau et al., 2018).

3.1.5 Dropping traditional norms

The above analysis suggests that there is a need for change in the way that we view, measure and facilitate participation. The following are key areas in which a reimagining of participation is recommended.

Broadening spaces online and offline

The Fourth Industrial Revolution has led to the emergence of new power structures within the digital sphere. While questions around access to the internet suggest unequal representation and engagement, the scale of connectivity has influenced how movements and mobilisation are conceptualised and executed. Youth are at the helm of this technological advancement, as the largest group of content consumers/producers, innovators, strategists, influencers and activists. Youth participation through new media is essential to modern political activism, and the confluence of youth voices in online forums, petition campaigns, online campaigning, mobilising, information production and dissemination, fact checking, etc. has shaken up the *status quo*. Traditional spaces reserved for youth participation no longer provide a litmus test for enhanced or reduced participation.

Applying inter-sectionality

Participation and representation are closely related but the former does not guarantee the latter. If inclusive participation structures are to emerge or exist, there is an urgent need to address the exclusionary socio-political norms that omit marginalised voices. Youth participation in national unions and politics has been on a constant decline while the existing members of these structures continue to age further, increasing the generational gap. The cause, and the consequence, of this disconnect might well be lack of interest or scepticism but underlying this are perceptions of the inefficacy of formal systems that no longer adequately represent or serve young people.

Youth are a heterogeneous group composed of individuals. Just like any other social group, their challenges and successes cannot be measured or reflected in binaries or reduced to conventional sub-divisions. There is thus a need for responsive and inclusive youth participation modalities, so as

to be representative of this diversity. To ensure that diverse ideologies can thrive, participation structures and processes will need to eliminate all exclusionary socio-political norms. Participation processes and frameworks can be responsive only if they consider the intersections of race, sexuality, gender, class, caste, ethnicity and economic status that could obstruct inclusive youth participation. The efficacy of a formal participation structure to meaningfully engage youth thus depends highly on its ability to challenge existing norms of exclusion. This resistance to change and challenge is often an underlying factor determining the youthfulness of these structures.

The World Programme of Action for Youth demands that governments take effective action against the violation of human rights and fundamental freedoms of youth and promotes non-discrimination, tolerance and respect for diversity. For the effective implementation of programmes and policies, it mandates institutions to value and integrate diverse religious and ethical ideologies, cultural backgrounds and philosophical convictions of youth and to ensure equality of opportunity, solidarity, security and participation for all young women and men.[1]

Engendering youth participation is an important part of this process. When considering the areas of education, health, economic participation, educational attainment and political empowerment, the greatest gender disparity is seen in women's political empowerment, with the gap measuring 75.3 per cent. At the current rate, the world is projected to close this gap in 94.5 years (WEF, 2020). Young men hold twice as many parliamentary seats (4.9 per cent) as their counterparts (2.3 per cent) (IPU, 2018). Young people, especially young women, are under-represented in formal political processes or institutions – including parliaments, political parties and public administrations (Commonwealth Secretariat, 2016).

Young women face disproportionate challenges in exercising their rights to participate in governance, political life and civic action and at the decision-making table. Young women and sexual minorities negotiate a complex web of gender-, generation- and class-based exclusion on the pathway to participation. Quotas and reservations in political parties, national youth associations and other traditional spaces are demonstrating an institutional focus and inclination towards encouraging women's participation in politics and governance. More than half the countries in the world now use some form of quota to ensure women constitute a minimum 30–40 per cent minority in political institutions.[2]

"We are not going to be beneficiaries. That's not happening anymore. It's 2019. Give us power." Natasha Mwansa from Zambia, aged 18, received a standing ovation from heads of states and the audience at the Women Deliver 2019 Conference for making a case for young girls' active role in decision-making.[3]

The obstacles to young women's pathways to participation cross their public and private lives (Salih et al., 2017). Care responsibilities and issues related to access to support networks, funding and gendered spaces define the personal experiences of young women. For young women and marginalised groups, the mere removal of formal institutional fences and the incentivising of participation will not necessarily guarantee meaningful participation. A complex network of hidden barriers influences women's participation in governance, and gendered power differentials intersecting with other forms of exclusion define women's participation in governance, direct action and civic space (Bowman, 2020).

Promoting localisation

Free and open spaces for young people at local governance levels are considered a key pathway towards building sustainable holistic solutions and enhancing overall youth participation at the national and sub-national levels. An example of this bottom-up approach comes from Uganda, where quotas have reinforced the participation of women and youth with disabilities. With a proportion of positions in the Youth Council reserved for young people in these categories, one young man on a local council, with cerebral palsy and accompanying speech difficulties, has presented the specific concerns of youth with disabilities and influenced local-level decisions. Another relevant example is Oldham Youth Council in the UK, which provides for co-opting young people from under-represented groups such as young carers, young people with disabilities, young people who are parents and young offenders, among others. A co-opted member is elected by the group he or she represents, has full voting rights and serves a term of office until the next election, when he or she is eligible to stand for re-election. In the UK, the national participatory structures do not have formal provisions for inclusion; interestingly, the proportion of women and ethnic and sexual minorities in the UK Youth Parliament is significantly higher than is the case in the regular Parliament.

Evaluating formality and giving space to non-formality

Evidence suggests that non-formal spaces of participation for young people opposing hegemonic power provide a relatively more inclusive sense of participation for minorities, marginalised communities and women (Anstead et al., 2016). These structures may have complexities similar to those of more formal spaces but, in defining their scope and space, many youth-led movements have shown a resistance to exclusionary socio-cultural norms (Craddock, 2019).

The overall youth participation ecosystem would benefit from a nuanced socio-political analysis of existing structures at local, national, regional and global level. Such an analysis would suggest ways to strengthen existing youth-led participatory structures through financial assistance, the scaling-up of best practices, ensuring inclusive spaces, consultation and further replication. Formal spaces like National Youth Councils, the CYC, student associations, etc., will benefit from a thorough evaluation, in consultation with young people and civil society groups, youth workers and other youth development agencies. An expression of the distinct challenges facing marginalised groups, women, younger youth, LGBTQIA groups, persons with disabilities and dissenting youth, among others, will not only provide a deeper understanding of the structural barriers in existence but also inform the development of a holistic youth participation strategy.

Investing in mainstreaming

Mainstreaming youth voices within institutional, policy and development planning forms the core of meaningful participation. Regularly consulting and engaging with youth in the decision-making process has a direct linkage with youth participation. The development of inclusive and responsive structures calls for greater investment in the capacity-building of youth workers, civil society, political parties, decision-makers, bureaucrats, youth leaders and youth themselves. This need is further heightened in times of ideological polarisation, state sanctions against dissenting youth and systemic oppression. Ensuring youth, especially historically excluded groups, find a seat at the decision-making table is a decisive policy and advocacy goal. To achieve this, policy-makers need to focus on overall institutional efficacy in engaging with youth and acting on their recommendations.

3.1.6 Conclusion

Reimagining youth participation in 2020 calls for a closer look at the systematic barriers that oppress and disenfranchise youth groups, minorities, women and other historically marginalised groups. A rights-based framework for discerning, evaluating and reformulating participation structures is required, along with focused and recurring consultation with youth. Youth demand non-exclusionary spaces. Re-envisioning formal and non-formal participation spaces as both necessary and complementary is vital to ensure inclusive structures. Youth have built and promoted non-formal inclusive spaces for participation. Concepts and tools such as youth mainstreaming and the rights-based participation principles for youth participation, as laid out in the sections above, provide strategies to strengthen a truly inclusive, responsive and powerful youth participation ecosystem. Youth participation is no longer a question of when and how; it is now about political will and the equitable distribution of power to inspire our collective future.

3.2 Youth participation in the design of YDIs

In this section, we outline the value of participation in the design of the YDI process. Young people's advice has been critical to the decisions taken by the YDI Technical Group of Experts who guided the design of the global index. Similarly, youth participation has been invaluable to the formulation of regional and national YDIs which are recommended tools to deepen the analysis that the global YDI provides.

Guest Contributor

Youth Consultation in National and Regional YDIs

Gemma Wood, Co-Founder/Principal Statistician, Numbers and People Synergy

Numbers and People Synergy (NAPS) has provided technical support on several national and regional YDIs since 2016. Below is a summary of the youth voice from consultations during these projects funded by the Commonwealth Secretariat, UNFPA and the Australian Government.

Youth participation is an indispensable part of the development of priorities for the YDI. At global, regional and national levels, youth consultation workshops and surveys have been conducted, alongside the consultations with other key government and non-government stakeholders, to inform the development of indices that include lessons from other countries whilst reflecting local priorities. The scope of consultation varies from, on the one hand, multiple youth consultations within a country covering all sub-national geographical territories to, on the other hand, singular national-level youth representative forums. Drawing on the experiences of preparing indices and reports for the Global YDI, the ASEAN secretariat, the African Union, Barbados, Indonesia, Cambodia, Bangladesh, Namibia, Pakistan and Australia, I share insights on how youth participation shaped the design of YDIs, in identifying unique priorities that did not emerge from broader stakeholder consultation.

Size and methods of consultations

The most extensive and most recent youth consultation for the design of a YDI, in which NAPS has been involved, was the second iteration of the Australian YDI. Several youth consultation workshops were conducted in each State and territory in partnership with youth organisations in those areas. In these workshops, as has been done on a smaller scale in Indonesia, Cambodia and Namibia, young people were given the opportunity to review existing YDIs and rank the domains and indicators which they felt related most to their lived experiences. They were also given the opportunity

to suggest new domains and indicators which were not seen in other YDIs. This kind of process consistently leads to a more detailed, nuanced insight into youth priorities, and expands the list of priorities beyond what is covered in past YDIs.

These ranking processes often revealed new concerns about culture, racism, housing and social and family networks. In developing the Australian YDI, young people ranked domains in order of priority as follows: 1) Health and Wellbeing; 2) Education; 3) Employment and Opportunity; 4) Civic and Political Participation; 5) Safety; 6) Community and Culture; 7) Racism; 8) Housing; 9) Social and Family Network and 10) Poverty. This directly led to the inclusion of "Safety and Security" and "Community and Culture" domains for the first time in the second Australian YDI. In other country contexts where this ranking process was undertaken, youth identified Gender Equality as a priority, this was particularly clear from the youth voice in Indonesia, Bangladesh, Cambodia and Pakistan where Gender and Inclusion domains were subsequently added to the national YDIs.

In Namibia and Pakistan, the youth voice was broadened past the design phase with the inclusion of national surveys to bolster the data available. These surveys aim to capture information on data gaps identified through the YDI design phases and provide up-to-date information on the lived experiences of young people and can be used for research, policy and programme design processes even after the YDI has been completed. The Pakistan survey used multiple methods of collection, including online and phone surveys, and was available in multiple local languages. It had over 16,000 responses allowing for a comprehensive district-level dashboard to be created and shared publicly. It has enabled collection of data on: Health and Wellbeing; Education and Skills; Employment and Opportunity; Participation and Engagement; Equity and Inclusion; Safety and Security; and more detailed data on mental health and COVID-19.

Education and Employment

While all stakeholders, both youth and others, consistently consider opportunity for employment and quality of education to be priorities; young people tend to link these two priorities as the quality of education holds a direct relationship with the ability to secure suitable and available employment. In addition, good government and economic management have been identified as priorities that youth associate with employment, as has been the case of Namibia.

With respect to education, the priorities for youth have included: support for student wellbeing; affordability for cost of living; alternative forms of education such as technical and vocational training; respecting diverse levels of educational attainment as well as practical experience in the field; and preparation for real life experiences. Youth, particularly those living in small islands or mountainous regions, have highlighted the view that opportunities there are fewer opportunities for youth in remote areas than in urban areas and quality of education often suffers in these areas, exacerbating the lack of employment opportunities.

In respect of employment, across all consultations, youth priorities have included: the availability of employment; the rate of underemployment; ensuring adequate rate of pay; opportunities for entrepreneurship; and affordability of living, coupled with financial literacy for budgeting and managing personal finances.

Health and Wellbeing

For health and wellbeing, the main priorities highlighted by young people are: greater access to mental health services, particularly in remote areas; support for drug and alcohol abuse; suicide ideation; and the affordability of healthcare.

Youth consultations have tended to raise issues around the impact of drug and alcohol abuse on wellbeing; vulnerability to mental health stressors and suicidal tendencies; and a need for the voice of youth to be welcomed and incorporated into policy development as key priorities for their wellbeing. The demands and expectations of family; poverty; and living with a disability have been identified throughout youth consultations as issues which lead to vulnerability in both physical and mental health. They also stand as reasons why adequate services are not received to deal with physical and mental health conditions.

Safety and Security

Youth describe feeling deeply affected by disruptions to family and community networks caused by lack of safety in the home; gender-based violence and other forms of gender inequality; suppressed political freedoms; and having to move

Guest Contributor

to urban areas or overseas to find employment. The desire for greater social connection is evident in both developed and developing countries.

In respect to safety, youth want to see greater justice in the policing, the judiciary and detention; reduced rates of sexual and other violence particularly in the family home; and greater equality between genders. For youth, equality also includes fair access to public spaces, particularly for young women, that is equal to the access of older people. Youth believe that greater participation and involvement in the community will increase feelings of safety.

Participation and Engagement

Youth want to see higher youth participation rates, in formal political processes and in elected positions within government, with stronger gender equity, to ensure greater direct youth influence on policy development.

Potential ways to increase youth civic participation, as suggested by young people included: increasing funding from government and non-government sources to youth organisations; increasing government focus on youth leadership; providing youth access to government, including for advocacy and funding; creating enabling environments for youth volunteer programmes; and ensuring young people have access to transparent, accurate and relevant information through the media and the internet.

A more inclusive multicultural society where governance institutions are trustworthy, transparent and accountable were key priorities in this domain. Strong youth representation both in elected positions and through consultation was important to ensure that laws protect youth. Changes affecting youth should be communicated to them before decisions are made. Young people reported this can be achieved by: raising civic and political education in schools; tracking the number of youth in positions with decision-making power; creating formal positions for youth and advocacy; establishing a minister dedicated to equality and the needs of vulnerable and marginalised youth; and awareness-raising programmes dedicated to priority youth concerns.

Equality, inclusion and gender discrimination

In developing countries, particularly in Pakistan, Bangladesh and Cambodia, improved access to the internet and accurate information has been important for young people as well as greater freedom of movement and opportunity for female youth, particularly in rural areas. Youth, from all consultations, wish to see an end to the practice of child marriage and associated family violence.

Of particular note, was the attention paid by youth to having greater access to quality health services and reduced "taboo" of sexual reproductive health services. There were discussions around "taboo" issues including Lesbian, Gay, Bisexual, Transgender, Queer or Questioning, Intersex and Asexual (LGBTQIA+), sexual relations and menstruation which need to be better understood but the pathway to do this is seen to be difficult given generational and cultural impediments.

Disability, both visible and hidden, was a topic raised in consultations which should be treated as a crosscutting indicator. There was a focus on equal access and appropriate support for people with different disabilities. National Disability Surveys were recommended as a place to get more detailed information on youth with disabilities who should be supported to thrive in all aspects of their lives.

There were discussions around who are included in national statistics as youth. For example, some countries only include citizens born in the country but not migrants or refugees. Many minority groups have distinct experiences which should be considered; even as all youth face multiple challenges to accessing achieving financial, spiritual and educational independence.

Equitable access to space, including government buildings and spaces to hold gatherings was also raised as a concern since building healthy and productive relationships requires space and support.

Community and Culture

Youth are seeking greater involvement in cultural practices such as rites of passage ceremonies and events; for cultural heritage to be taught as part of education; and the opportunity to volunteer and hold a position within youth-oriented forums. With regards to racism, youth wish to see educational curricula that acknowledge different cultures and the elimination of racism from institutions including prisons.

Housing is also identified by youth as a specific priority that relates to various domains, including safety; connectedness to community; relationship to family; and wellbeing. Youth describe poverty in terms of the need for social inclusion, housing, transport and equality of opportunity.

Conclusion

The results of youth consultations compared to broader stakeholder consultations differ in that there is a greater emphasis on mental health including suicide, drug and alcohol issues; cost of living pressures; the impacts of racism; the need for real life practical skills for living and managing personal finances; and a need for greater connection to culture and community. Youth articulate a unique perspective on the priorities required to foster development.

3.3 Youth Taking Charge

As we have seen, spaces and initiatives that allow young people to lead and to voice their views and ideas are critical to the achievement of a positive common future. The connection between participation, leadership, mainstreaming and empowerment cannot be underestimated. Participatory spaces allow young people to connect, innovate and transform the contexts that hamper development at the organisational, community, national and international levels. The preceding sections have highlighted various types of structures and processes at pan-Commonwealth, regional and national levels that create opportunities for formal and informal participation. Here, we complement this analysis by highlighting examples of new and emerging youth-led initiatives that also support youth political and civic participation.

3.3.1 The Commonwealth Young Professionals Foundry

The Commonwealth Secretariat has prioritised youth participation in decision-making in its own work, as part of a broader strategy for innovation and youth mainstreaming. The Young Professionals Programme (YPP), which has been operating since 2015, provides an exciting development opportunity for qualified young citizens to contribute their technical expertise, innovation, energy and perspectives to the work of the Secretariat. Highly skilled, technology-savvy professionals from across the Commonwealth have been embedded as Young Professionals (YPs) across the Secretariat, comprising around 10 per cent of staff. More recently, space has been created for an innovation lab lead by the YPs to harness their skills and fresh ideas.

The innovation lab – known as The Foundry – engages all the YPs across the various directorates of the Secretariat to design and collaborate on the implementation of innovative cross-sectoral projects that advance the strategic objectives of Commonwealth member countries and citizens. The Foundry is expected to strengthen the Secretariat's innovation and partnership efforts through increased collaboration, cross-fertilisation, the introduction of new ideas, including new ways of working, and the development of an enabling and empowering organisational culture. In turn, YPs will expand their knowledge, skills and networks within a new framework for full engagement in the work of the Secretariat.

The members of the Foundry will develop evidence-based, new technology-driven and results-oriented projects that are built on:

- Innovation, through the development and application of novel solutions to enhance the reach, efficiency, effectiveness, impact and sustainability of thematic projects;

- Digitalisation, through the incorporation and use of digital technologies and tools to improve the delivery, user experience and enhance value creation of the project;

- Synergy, by enhancing the representation and fairness in delivery and results achieved through the inclusion and/or mainstreaming of cross cutting-themes such as youth, gender and climate change; and

- Partnerships, which involve collaboration internally, across departments and with external with partner organisations.

3.3.2 Democracy in colour

Tim Lo Surdo of Australia is a 2021 Commonwealth Youth Award Finalist who was recognised for his work related to the attainment of SDG 10 on reducing inequalities. Tim founded Democracy in Colour, a racial and economic justice organisation created to tackle structural racism and address critical civic issues facing people of colour in Australia. The programme has grown a membership of over 57,000 people and engaged over 85,000 people in advocacy and capacity-building leadership training, including young people, women and persons with disabilities.

Message from the Pan-African Youth Union on behalf of African youth

Bora Kamwanya, Deputy Secretary General, Pan-African Youth Union

The PYU welcomes the Global Youth Development Index Report. The call of duty that inspired the founders of the Pan-African Youth Movement (PAYM) in 1962 is the same that is driving African youth today through the PYU. The COVID-19 pandemic has deepened inequalities and shown the gaps in the health sector on a continent where 60 per cent of people are under the age of 25. The scores for *Health and Wellbeing* in 2018 show good signs; however, the exodus of some leaders to seek medical attention abroad during the pandemic proves that proper health infrastructure on the continent is in most cases non-existent, and we remain largely dependent on foreign assistance. The continent has doctors and should make bold investments in the sector.

Africa's policy priorities for supporting young people to build a resilient and sustainable future should be in line with the SDGs. It is alarming to note that, in the 10 countries with the lowest level of youth development, we find 8 African countries. And yet, as alarming as it is, it is unsurprising.

In 2020, we witnessed an increased demand for justice, the respect of human rights and improved democratisation by young people in Africa. In 1962, the founders of the PAYM were aiming to "foster and consolidate the process of democracy and reinforce peace and African integration; develop the political conscience of young Africans; co-operate with other international organisations with respect to liberty, progress and peace on the African continent." Today's African youth are actively but unofficially participating in the political and civic life of their nations. We say "unofficially" because there are still barriers preventing them from effectively occupying public offices.

What, we, African youth, demand is fair and good management of national resources, investment in long-lasting infrastructure and the creation of strong and just institutions. Post-COVID, our economic and social recovery should be inclusive and focused on enabling young people to take charge of our future.

The inclusion of young people from all demographics in the design, implementation and monitoring of all policies is crucial to ensure a sustainable and competitive future for Africa, as youth represent the demographic that is both the most affected by our current unsustainable lifestyle and the one on the forefront in fighting for a sustainable future – the essential workers.

To our leaders we say, freedom, justice and democracy are not Western concepts, they are human concepts.

Message from the Commonwealth Students Association on behalf of young people in Asia

Dr Musarrat Maisha Reza, Chair, Commonwealth Students' Association, and Lecturer, University of Exeter, UK

I am really delighted at the launch of the Global Youth Development Index Report. This is an excellent tool that indicates areas of success and highlights areas that require greater attention and investment. It also provides a reference for data-driven policy-making, implementation, monitoring and evaluation of the SDGs. My vision for all of us is that we come together as one Commonwealth, learn from one another and adapt policies that have worked for other nations within our own countries.

It is encouraging to see the progress the Commonwealth has been making on youth development and to see that we are scoring in the high category for five out of six YDI domains. Of notable success, Asia has collectively recorded excellence on the overall YDI as well as in the *Education* domain, with South Asia seeing the most significant improvement in the past decade. Overall, Singapore tops the YDI ranking table, and two of the top five risers are Commonwealth Asian nations – India and Bangladesh. The CSA celebrates the rapid development of young persons in Asia, especially through education, an integral tool for youth empowerment and upward mobility.

While we acknowledge the wins and keep pressing forward, it is important that we seriously investigate the YDI domains on which countries are falling behind. Particularly disappointing for young people globally is the *Political and Civic Participation* score, which hovers at an alarmingly low level. Of note, the 2018 average score on this domain in the Commonwealth Asia region was below the global (0.282) and Commonwealth (0.309) average scores in this domain. Young people of the Commonwealth under the age of 30 make up over 60 per cent of the population and cannot be left behind in decision-making, at any level of society. We must be involved not as a tokenistic measure but in a holistic and inclusive manner, as all SDG goals impact us all directly. Governments must commit greater support to and investment in youth participation.

I implore government leaders, policy-makers and civil society not just to tap on the brilliance, passion, talents and exuberance of youth but also to embed them systematically and institutionally, which I wholeheartedly believe is a highly strategic policy direction. Including young people in all six domains of the YDI is critical for us to reach our Agenda 2030 and to deliver national and global goals. Young people are now more connected than ever and are standing united to work with you to accelerate progress on all aspects of the YDI and take charge of our future. Youth empowerment must become a priority for all countries. As we pledge our dedication and partnership, we look forward to your promise in creating an enabling ecosystem for us to shape and direct our common future.

Guest Contributor

Meaningful Youth Engagement for an Inclusive, Prosperous, Resilient and Sustainable Asia and the Pacific

Guest Contribution by Chris Morris, Head of NGO and Civil Society Center and Concurrent Manager of ADB's Youth for Asia initiative

It gives me great honor to congratulate the Commonwealth Secretariat on their most recent update and expansion of their flagship Youth Development Index (YDI) and Report. The expansion to six domains featured in this latest YDI to include equality and opportunity and peace and security are particularly relevant as these highlight significant areas of vulnerability of young people. I am also particularly hearted by the emphasis taken over the last few years, which I witnessed first-hand at the Commonwealth Youth Senior Officials Meeting (Asia Region) in Brunei Darussalam (August 2019), of using the YDI to inform and drive local and national government policy reforms. We at ADB share a common view with the Commonwealth recognizing young people are crucial to a country's social, economic, and political development. Investments are needed in youth development and empowerment resulting in growth of youth's human capital and leadership behaviors, realization of their full potential, and attaining sustainable development outcomes.[4]

Accelerating progress towards a prosperous, inclusive, resilient, and sustainable Asia and the Pacific will require mobilizing the potential of its one billion young people[5]. The COVID-19 pandemic has demonstrated the risk of creating a "lockdown generation" with youth bearing disproportionate long-term economic and social costs of such major disasters and crises in a region which is home to 54 per cent of the world's youth.[6] A strong and renewed intergenerational contract is urgently required to recover from the COVID-19 pandemic and achieve the Sustainable Development Goals. While the region is aging, the poorer low income and lower middle income developing member countries have very youthful populations. For these countries, making the most of their demographic dividend is an urgent priority and one that the Asian Development Bank is well placed to support through its Strategy 2030 and partnering with young people through ADB's unique Youth for Asia (YfA) initiative.[7]

YfA's youth-led approach is operationalized through the placement of young leaders in a core team at ADB's headquarters. This team identifies meaningful spaces for the engagement and empowerment of youth across the Asia and the Pacific region and has become the first initiative amongst IFIs with the explicit goal of mainstreaming meaningful youth engagement (MYE)[8] in operations.

On the basis of enhancing delivery of ADB's Strategy 2030, YfA's vision is: **"An inclusive, prosperous, resilient and sustainable Asia and the Pacific driven by young people engaging as active citizens".** YfA

is uniquely placed to facilitate collaboration between young people, governments and citizens of the region; the Commonwealth's YDI provides solid insights to drive national and local policy reform and direct project planning and investments. We look forward to continue to work with the Commonwealth supporting youth human capital, youth leadership and youth-led policy and project interventions across Asia and the Pacific.

Guest Contributor

Supporting the Development of Today's Young People

Mamta Murthi, Vice President of Human Development, World Bank

The COVID-19 pandemic has caused significant setbacks for the prospects of young people all over the world, but particularly in developing countries. Even before the COVID crisis there were significant challenges, with a third of all young people globally not in work, education, or training.

The pandemic has exacerbated inequalities, both within and across countries, hitting women and youth especially hard. More than a billion young people have been affected by school closures. For many young people and their societies, the disruption may have lifelong consequences. Recent estimates suggest that a global school shutdown of five months will reduce lifetime earnings by as much as $10 trillion. Overall, up to 255 million full-time jobs were lost globally in 2020 and the job losses are expected to expand further in 2021, resulting in a more severe impact than experienced in the aftermath of the 2008 financial crisis.

At the World Bank, we are taking fast, comprehensive action to fight the impacts of the pandemic. Between April 2020 and June 2021, WBG financing commitments reached over $150 billion, including an unprecedented $12 billion response to improve social protection and create employment opportunities in 56 developing countries, including 15 countries facing fragility and conflict. These projects will benefit over one billion individuals worldwide. In Nepal, for example, World Bank financing is being used to provide temporary income support and temporary employment opportunities to young people who have lost or been unable to find employment.

Protecting and investing in young people builds human capital, which is key to enabling them to realize their full potential, for sustaining long-term economic growth and preventing millions of people from falling into poverty. The pandemic threatens to reverse a decade of gains in human capital worldwide due to school closures, job losses, and interruptions to routine health care. This erosion could undermine economic recovery and prosperity for a generation. Protecting and investing in people must be the top

priority for countries to cope with the ongoing crisis, restore setbacks to human capital, and strengthen the education, health, and social protection systems that will lead to a more resilient recovery.

Action needs to be timely: the longer young people are unemployed, the harder it is to get back into productive employment. To address the growing levels of stress and anxiety experienced by young people, the World Bank is supporting projects which provide psychosocial support and the creation of safe spaces where young people can express their concerns. We also support services for young entrepreneurs and the self-employed, for example with emergency cash in the short term as well as medium-term support to increase digital capacity and online presence.

To empower youth for a productive future, countries must prepare members of the "COVID-19 generation" for a changing and uncertain world. Young people must be provided with skills that are in demand in the labor market, help them adapt and take advantage of new opportunities, and enable them to secure a livelihood by launching their own businesses where jobs are unavailable. The pandemic has intensified the pace of change in the labor market and the demand for new skills. Education and training systems must evolve in response, to make sure the supply of skills remains relevant and forward-looking. It may be that governments should prioritize the planning, financing, and oversight of training programs, and engage private sector providers in their design and delivery. Demand-led training can also combine the classroom with on-the-job experience and apprenticeships. The World Bank-supported Kenya Youth Empowerment Program showed that those young men and women who had been placed in internships were more likely to be in paid work a year later.

As we know, vocational and technical training by themselves are no longer sufficient: in the 21st century, employers require creative workers who can solve problems and engage in teamwork. Jobs are evolving from routine tasks with fixed and explicit rules to open-ended tasks that require flexibility, creativity, and judgment. These ostensibly "soft" skills – the skills one needs to learn – also enable people to adapt and deal with adversity. The acquisition of these non-technical skills begins in early childhood and continues throughout one's life. Happily, while socioemotional skills contribute to success in school and beyond, recent reviews have confirmed the effectiveness of both school-based and out-of-school programs to help young people build these skills.

Governments, the private sector, and the global community must target investments and services to young job seekers and entrepreneurs to ensure that the pandemic does not leave debilitating and lasting scars on this generation of young people or on the economy. The Youth Development Index clearly shows parallels between progress on youth development and advances toward the Sustainable Development Goals. Our commitment to support the healthy development of today's young people will determine our ability to engender sustainable and broad-based growth and the durable escape from poverty, as well as to prevent and endure future crises such as COVID-19.

Endnotes

1   https://www.un.org/esa/socdev/unyin/
documents/wpay2010.pdf

2   https://www.idea.int/data-tools/data/gender-
quotas

3   womendeliver.org/2019/19-ways-youth-
delivered-for-gender-equality-in-2019/

4   Schusler, T. M., et al (2009). Developing citizens and
communities through youth environmental action.
Environmental Education Research, *15*(1), 111–127.

5   ADB. 2018. *Strategy 2030: Achieving a Prosperous,
Inclusive, Resilient, and Sustainable Asia and the
Pacific.* Manila.

6   H. Osborne, P. Vandenberg, and C. Morris. 2020.
How to avoid creating a "lockdown generation".
Asian Development Blog. 7 September 2020.

7   **Youth for Asia** is ADB's initiative to empower the
youth of the Asia and the Pacific region to have
meaningful roles in ADB's operations. YfA is led
by young people based at ADB HQ in Manila who
work on ADB projects, research, partnerships
and events, each of which are guided by youth
leadership principles.

8   C. Morris and J. Corpus. 2021. Meaningful Youth
Engagement Strengthens Post-Pandemic
Response and Recovery Initiatives. Development
Asia an initiative of Asia Development Bank. 19
July 2021.

References

Anstead, N., S. Banaji, M. Bruter, B. Cammaerts and S.
Harrison (2016) *Youth Participation in Democratic
Life*. Basingstoke: Palgrave Macmillan.

Bowman, B. (2020) *Imagining Future Worlds Alongside
Young Climate Activists: A New Framework
for Research*. Manchester: Manchester
Metropolitan University,

Commonwealth Secretariat (2016) *Youth-Led
Accountability for the SDGs: A Guide to
National Action*. London:
Commonwealth Secretariat.

Craddock, E. (2019) "Doing 'Enough' of the 'Right'
Thing: The Gendered Dimension of the 'Ideal
Activist' Identity and Its Negative Emotional
Consequences". *Social Movement Studies* **18**(2):
137–153.

IPU (Inter-Parliamentary Union) (2018) *Youth
Participation In National Parliaments: 2018*. Geneva:
IPU.

Reddy, N., J. Kramer and K. Ratna (2020) "Rights
Based Youth Participation in Governance – A
Commonwealth Perspective". Bangalore:
Dhruva, Consultancy Unit of The Concerned for
Working Children.

Salih, R., L. Welchman and E. Zambelli (2017) "Gender,
Intersectionality and Youth Engagement".
Working Paper 24. London: School of Oriental and
African Studies.

Seneviratne, D. (2017) *Youth Mainstreaming
in Development Planning*. London:
Commonwealth Secretariat.

Thibodeau, D., A. Farah and N. Wafula (2018) "A Report
on Meaningful Youth Engagement in Political
Parties". CYC.

Tisdall, E. (2014) *Children and Young People's
Participation and Its Transformative Potential*.
Basingstoke: Palgrave Macmillan.

WEF (World Economic Forum) (2020) *Global Gender
Gap Report 2020*. Geneva: WEF.

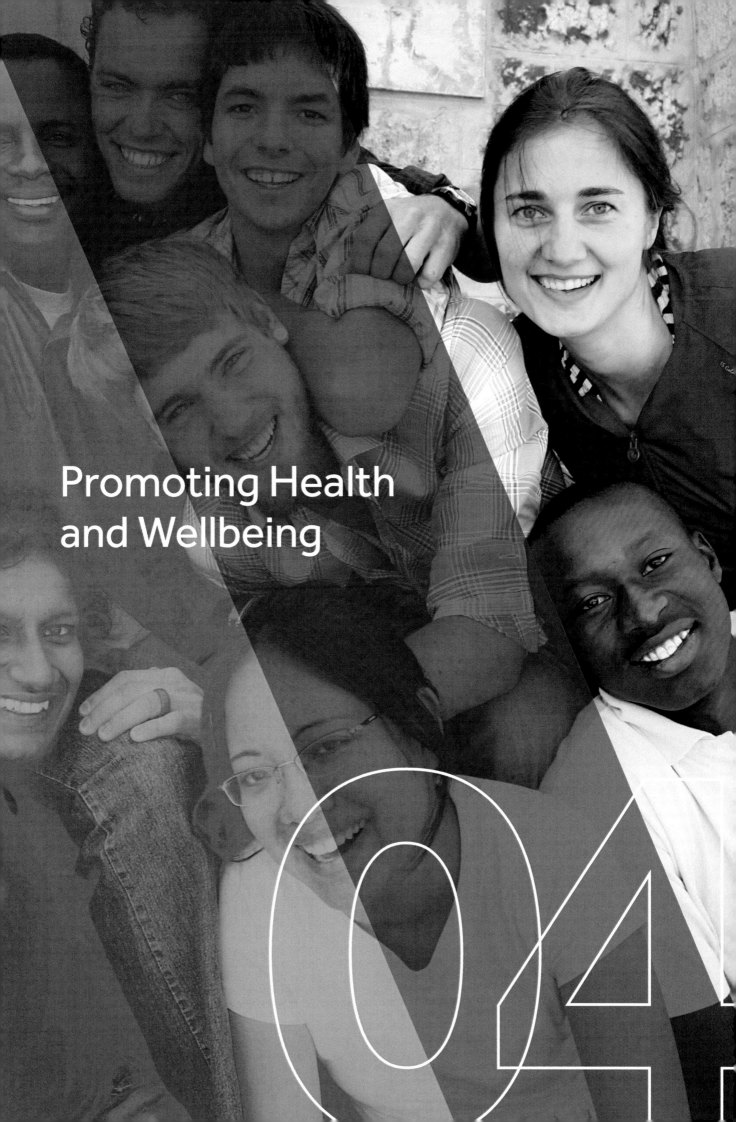

Promoting Health
and Wellbeing

04

Chapter 4

Promoting Health and Wellbeing

Without a doubt, health and wellbeing have been the priority for public policy and individual action in the past year. Longstanding investments in health and wellbeing have been partially responsible for the universally good progress on youth health and wellbeing, as suggested by the results of the 2020 Youth Development Index (YDI). At the same time, the COVID-19 pandemic, and the attendant socio-economic restrictions, threaten the gains made in the past decade.

Youth advocacy on health and wellbeing, including by the Commonwealth Youth Health Network (CYHN), highlights the need for priority attention to promoting sexual and reproductive health rights and good mental health, reducing non-communicable diseases and achieving health equity through universal health care policies. The World Health Organization (WHO, 2021) reminds us that, in 2019, over 1.5 million adolescents and young adults aged 10–24 years died, or nearly 5,000 every day. Injuries (including road traffic injuries and drowning), violence, self-harm and maternal conditions continue to be the leading causes of death among adolescents and young adults. In this chapter, we focus on policies and programmes that can be used to address two of these difficult areas: mental health challenges and road traffic fatalities. We also highlight the Commonwealth #YouthTakingCharge of health and wellbeing in their communities, as a way of inspiring action towards attaining Sustainable Development Goal (SDG) 3: to ensure healthy lives and promote wellbeing for all.

4.1 Promoting good mental health

Although the 2020 YDI shows generally positive global performance in the *Health and Wellbeing* domain, there was a slight decline over the 2010-2018 period in terms of global average indicator scores for years of life lost to mental disorders. Mental health has gained even greater significance since the COVID-19 pandemic. Restrictions have led to greater isolation among young people, including because of disruptions in schooling and employment and the prohibition of social, political and civic gatherings.

4.1.1 Mental health legislation

The updating of mental health legislation and policy, using rights-based frameworks, must remain a priority. A review of legislation in 45 Commonwealth countries demonstrated the need for greater alignment with the Convention on the Rights of Persons with Disabilities (CRPD), including the rights to informed consent to treatment, community-based care and family or care-giver involvement, and protection of vulnerable groups, including young people (as minors), women and those from minority groups (Pathare and Sagade, 2013).

The report showed that in only 11 per cent of states reviewed was mental health care treated as an priority equal to physical health care. In only 29 per cent of member states reviewed were persons with mental disorders given the right to

be informed of their rights when receiving mental health care or treatment. While laws in 24 per cent of member countries contained provisions promoting community care, no legislation met all the criteria to be rated as fully promoting community care and deinstitutionalisation. Mental health laws in most Commonwealth countries provide very little protection to minors and children. Laws in only two countries restrict involuntary admission of minors with mental health problems, and only three countries ban irreversible treatments on children. Across the Commonwealth, the participation of users of mental health services in the formulation of mental health policy, legislation development and service planning is not mandated in law.

In light of the significant concerns about youth mental health, Commonwealth member countries should embark on reform of mental health legislation to meet their obligations under international human rights treaties, in particular the CRPD. Updated legislation should introduce provisions to promote people taking their own decisions about their care with help from others (supported decision-making), the protection of youth rights, community-based services and the involvement of service users and care-givers in the reform process.

4.1.2 Community-based mental health promotion

Community-based solutions are important to rights-based mental health promotion. Innovative and youth-friendly programmes are being implemented around the world that are yielding positive outcomes for participants and their families and communities. We share here the results of one such initiative from the perspective of the implementers.

Guest Contributor

The Wave Alliance: Community-Based Mental Health Through Surfing

Tim Conibear of Waves for Change and Sallu Kamuskay and Margaedah Michaella Samai of the Messeh Leone Trust with the Wave Alliance Sierra Leone

Even before the COVID-19 pandemic, mental health was becoming better understood and prioritised as a development outcome, especially for vulnerable youth and young adults. Now, as the world emerges from over 12 months of lockdown, solutions for scalable, evidence-based and youth-friendly mental health interventions are paramount. Waves for Change's Wave Alliance is one such example. This contribution discusses the genesis of the Wave Alliance programme and its application across 11 countries, and looks at a case study of the Wave Alliance at five beaches in Freetown, Sierra Leone.

Waves for Change is a South African non-profit organisation founded in 2010. It grew out of voluntary weekend surfing sessions run at one local beach in Cape Town. The surfing sessions, run by caring and passionate young adults from Masiphumelele township, ran every Saturday and engaged a regular community of 30 young people. Early research into the effect of the surfing sessions highlighted the valuable psycho-social support that was otherwise unavailable to the participants. Regular connection to caring adults generated a sense of physical and emotional safety. Participation in surfing boosted confidence and taught simple transferable life skills to cope with adversity. Participation in surfing was also found to create a sense of respite from stress.

With an understanding that the key to growing Waves for Change lay in mobilising more passionate youth coaches, the team worked between 2010 and 2018 with local universities and mental health practitioners to refine a coach training programme, pragmatic remote evaluation tools and a codified curriculum to leverage the social and emotional learning offered by participation in surfing. As of March 2021, Waves for Change employs 55 youth mentors along the coast of South Africa, who offer "Surf Therapy" sessions to 2,000 vulnerable youth weekly, referred by a community of social workers, psychologists, local clinics and other outpatient facilities. Common outcomes, as measured by evaluations, include improved emotional regulation, social skills, attention and wellbeing.

In 2018, Waves for Change decided to move beyond direct service delivery and to begin testing methodologies for community-based mental health services, and to encourage systemic change on a broader scale through an initiative called the Wave Alliance. The Wave Alliance is a global network of youth organisations operating on coastlines worldwide. The majority of partners are new to the surfing world and bring surfing to their coastlines for the first time. The Alliance offers a combination of face-to-face training in Cape Town, open access to Waves for Change's evidence-based training, curriculum and evaluation tools, and online programme and evaluation support from Waves for Change programme experts and evaluation consultants from Edinburgh Napier University. To date, the Wave Alliance has trained a total of 17 partner organisations from 11 countries worldwide.

In November 2018, the Wave Alliance project was connected with the Messeh Leone Trust, a registered non-profit organisation in Sierra Leone committed to engaging and empowering young people, women and local communities to build a healthier, safer and better world. In partnership with the Messeh Leone Trust, five youth and community development organisations from Freetown applied and were recruited to complete Wave Alliance training in Cape Town. These organisations – the

Children at Tokeh Beach learn about empathy and communication using a simple water safety drill

Moseray Fadika Trust Foundation, Young Leaders-Sierra Leone, United Sierra Leone, Pipul Pikin Charitable Foundation and Job Opportunities for Youths – joined a representative of Messeh Leone Trust for a two-week training with Waves for Change and Edinburgh Napier University. The training focused on understanding the psycho-social needs of vulnerable young people, identifying and understanding the core ingredients of impactful youth development programmes and designing a pilot Surf Therapy programme for 100 young people from five Freetown beaches.

Waves for Change, Messeh Leone Trust, Edinburgh Napier University and representatives from five Sierra Leone youth organisations at training in Cape Town

Guest Contributor

Sallu Kamuskay presenting at the Cape Town training workshop

The team on the beach in Cape Town

Through funding support from Comic Relief and the Swedish Postcode Lottery, administered by Waves for Change, and support from the Messeh Leone Trust, a Surf Therapy pilot project – Wave Alliance Sierra Leone – was successfully launched. Following the training in Cape Town, the five organisations returned to Freetown and undertook community sensitisation outreach. In each instance, local authorities granted permission to the organisations to use local beaches and land to create safe

spaces from which to base their on-going work. The organisations recruited and trained local community members to assist in the delivery of the Surf Therapy pilot projects, ensuring increased local ownership of the project and its on-going sustainability.

Between November of 2019 and April of 2020, each of the five community organisations delivered a weekly Surf Therapy session to a total community of 100 young people across five Sierra Leone beaches. Each session combined learning

Surfers with the Moseray Fadika Trust Foundation

Surfers with the Moseray Fadika Trust Foundation

to surf with evidence-based social/emotional learning activities. Participants received a snack after each session. Coaches also conducted regular home visits to better understand the home environment of each surfer. Surfing equipment was provided by Waves for Change with additional transport and food provided by the Messeh Leone Trust.

The primary outcomes of the programme are well documented in a pilot evaluation, executed with Jamie Marshall of Edinburgh Napier University and being presented to the government and other agencies, such as the Ministry of Social Welfare, the Ministry of Gender and Children's Affairs, the Ministry of Youth and Sport, the Ministry of Education, the Ministry of Health, the Ministry of Lands and Country Planning, the Ministry of Tourism and Cultural Affairs, the National Tourist Board and the Children's Forum Network. The pilot evaluation data shows statistically significant improvements to youth wellbeing.

To measure improvements to wellbeing, the Stirling Children's Wellbeing Scale, the Short Edinburgh Warwick Mental Wellbeing Scale and other WHO wellbeing scales were tested through pre- and post-Therapy surveys supported by interviews with parents and participants. Figure 4.1 shows the improvements across four of the Sierra Leone sites along with results from pilots in other countries. Wellbeing scores have been converted into a percentage measure to allow for ease of comparison between the varied wellbeing scales that were utilised across the different sites.

At one Sierra Leone site, a forced change of location disrupted the pilot, resulting in data fidelity and consistency challenges, which may be responsible for

Guest Contributor

Figure 4.1 Changes in youth wellbeing after Surf Therapy in select Wave Alliance locations

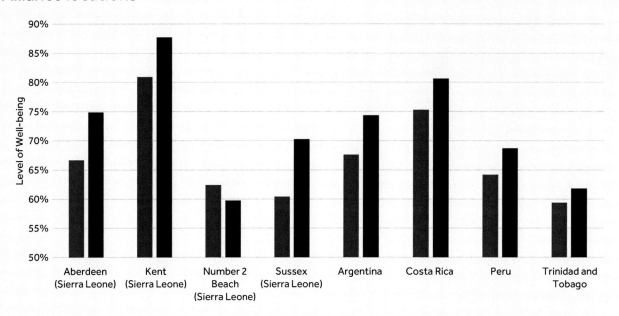

a slight reduction in wellbeing, albeit one that is statistically insignificant. The evaluation provided valuable learnings for the site and all other sites. Through these learnings, the issues faced at pilot stage were addressed and preliminary data from a second cohort of participants at the above-mentioned location shows a positive impact on wellbeing.

Overall, the pilot in Sierra Leone built people's confidence, connections to caring peers and skills to identify emotions and cope with stress. These skills are applied both at the home and in the community. Young people reported feeling healthier, happier and less stressed. This influenced their behaviour at home, school and in the community, where children were more engaged (school), less violent (community) and more helpful (home). These outcomes are consistent with more traditional forms of therapy that aim to boost personal wellbeing and closeness to others and develop skills to regulate behaviour.

Sallu Kamuskay, Coordinator of the Wave Alliance in Sierra Leone, said, "Our sport/Surf Therapy

programme provides young people with the opportunity to practise new behaviours and coping skills that can improve the way they deal with the impact of stress. It combines the natural benefits of sport/surfing with intentional, evidence-based activities proven to help young people build protective personal relationships, identify emotions and cope with change (stress). Sport/surfing has been proven to increase confidence and self-esteem and to provide respite from stress."

Messeh Leone, President of the Messeh Leone Trust, said, "At Wave Alliance, we know we cannot change the situation that our children live in, but we can give young people and local communities the tools to cope more effectively with the challenges they face every day. The Wave Alliance sport/Surf Therapy contributes directly to the United Nations SDGs 3, 5 and 11. The programme seeks to improve wellbeing (SDG 3) including health and mental health, provide access to safe and inclusive spaces (SDG 11) and contribute to overcoming gender/cultural norms (SDG 5)."

As of April 2021, The Wave Alliance in Sierra Leone is strong. Weekly sessions still take place on weekdays, a total of 25 community coaches have now been trained and a total of 100 children engage weekly. The hope is to secure funding to train more partners along the Sierra Leone coastline, and to host a regional training for more West African partners in the 2022/23 year. There are also plans to expand and replicate the programme in other Commonwealth countries.

Wave Alliance representatives with Messeh Leone and officials from the Ministry of Tourism and National Tourist Board presenting their findings

4.2 Reducing road traffic injuries

The second policy priority addressed in this chapter is that of reducing road traffic injuries. Though not measured by the 2020 YDI, road traffic crashes have been the leading cause of death among young people between 15 and 29 years old for over a decade. The issue was described as a "road safety crisis" by young people from 74 countries who met in Stockholm in 2020. The Global Youth Statement on Road Safety (2020) calls for immediate action to address weaknesses in global mobility systems and calls for investment in a Global Youth Coalition for Road Safety, committed to modelling safe road behaviour and supporting evidence-based solutions that will save lives.

Global stakeholders, including Commonwealth member countries, are called on to:

1. Undertake reform of legislation speaking to mental health care and service provisions to better align them with international provisions for rights-based service delivery;

2. Make road safety a priority for health and wellbeing and invest in the Global Youth Coalition for Road Safety and monitoring progress in reducing fatalities and injuries at key Commonwealth ministerial meetings;

3. Recognise and support young people who implement community-based solutions to promote good health.

In the next section, the Towards Zero Foundation and YOURS - Youth for Road Safety – help us better understand the risk factors for youth mortality through traffic crashes and the recommended actions for change.

Guest Contributor

The Greatest Health Threat for Young People: Road Traffic Injuries

The Towards Zero Foundation and Youth for Road Safety (YOURS)

No child should have to fear the walk to school and no parent should have to worry about the safety of their children as they play outside around their house. No young person should have their hopes for a future cut short. Everyone has the right to be safe on our roads, especially the most vulnerable in our communities: our children and young people. Sadly, thousands are killed on their way to or from school, losing their lives while walking to their daily classes or trying to earn an income for their family. And with them, many dreams and hopes are being ended on the world's roads every day before they can be realised. Unfortunately, the road traffic environment that many young people are growing up in is both unsafe and unsustainable, and road traffic injury is the leading global cause of death for children and young people aged 5–29 years (WHO, 2018). This is an especially major challenge for the Commonwealth, where over 60 per cent of the population of member countries is aged under 30. Road traffic injury is a significant public health issue, and represents the greatest health threat facing youth, one that Commonwealth countries need to address urgently to secure the safety and future of our young people. To do this, road safety needs to be made a priority and youth must be engaged as a part of the solution.

The global challenge of road traffic crashes: What the data tells us

Road trauma is one of the biggest public health challenges in the world and is the eighth leading cause of death globally (WHO, 2018). Tragically, road traffic injuries are reaching crisis proportions globally, and over 1.35 million people are killed and many millions more seriously injured every year (ibid.). Road trauma does not affect everyone equally, with inequalities seen between world regions and a death rate three times higher in low-income countries compared with high-income countries (ibid.). Many of the countries most affected are within the Commonwealth region, and road trauma has adverse impacts on the most vulnerable in our communities and on our roads.

Road crashes kill more youth globally than any other public health concern (WHO, 2018). Every year in Commonwealth countries, over 500,000 people are killed in road crashes and millions more are seriously injured (ibid.). Road safety in countries of the Commonwealth is diverse (see Figure 4.2). Fatality rates in road crashes per 100,000 population range from 3 to above 35 (CRSI, 2019). Unfortunately, in nearly all Commonwealth countries, fatality and injury rates are rising rather than falling, and trends are likely to continue beyond the COVID-19 pandemic.

Road traffic injuries and the SDGs

For a long time, road injury prevention was overlooked as an issue related to sustainable development. Fortunately, this has changed recently: road safety is now recognised as a major issue in public health as well as sustainable development. Significantly, road injury prevention has been included in the United Nations 2030 Agenda for Sustainable Development ("Agenda 2030"). The SDGs for good health and wellbeing and for sustainable cities and communities both refer to road safety and have specific targets for road injury prevention (United Nations, 2015):

- Target 3.6: By 2020, halve the number of global deaths and injuries from road traffic accidents.

- Target 11.2: By 2030, provide access to safe, affordable, accessible and sustainable transport systems for all, improving road safety, notably by expanding public transport, with special

Guest Contributor

Figure 4.2 Road traffic death rates in 45 Commonwealth countries with reportable data

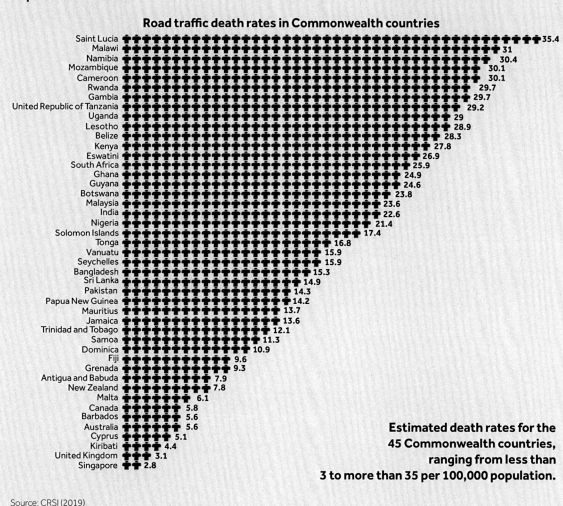

Road traffic death rates in Commonwealth countries

Country	Rate
Saint Lucia	35.4
Malawi	31
Namibia	30.4
Mozambique	30.1
Cameroon	30.1
Rwanda	29.7
Gambia	29.7
United Republic of Tanzania	29.2
Uganda	29
Lesotho	28.9
Belize	28.3
Kenya	27.8
Eswatini	26.9
South Africa	25.9
Ghana	24.9
Guyana	24.6
Botswana	23.8
Malaysia	23.6
India	22.6
Nigeria	21.4
Solomon Islands	17.4
Tonga	16.8
Vanuatu	15.9
Seychelles	15.9
Bangladesh	15.3
Sri Lanka	14.9
Pakistan	14.3
Papua New Guinea	14.2
Mauritius	13.7
Jamaica	13.6
Trinidad and Tobago	12.1
Samoa	11.3
Dominica	10.9
Fiji	9.6
Grenada	9.3
Antigua and Babuda	7.9
New Zealand	7.8
Malta	6.1
Canada	5.8
Barbados	5.6
Australia	5.6
Cyprus	5.1
Kiribati	4.4
United Kingdom	3.1
Singapore	2.8

Estimated death rates for the 45 Commonwealth countries, ranging from less than 3 to more than 35 per 100,000 population.

Source: CRSI (2019)

attention to the needs of those in vulnerable situations, women, children, people with disabilities and older people.

These important commitments are, of course, integrated with other transport-related SDGs to improve air quality, reduce carbon emissions and encourage more sustainable forms of human mobility.

The importance of improving road safety was further reinforced at the Third Global Ministerial Conference on Road Safety, held in February 2020. The outcome of this conference was the adoption of the Stockholm Declaration, which connects road safety to implementation of the 2030 Agenda and includes a call for a new target to reduce road

deaths by at least 50 per cent by 2030 (Third Global Ministerial Conference on Road Safety, 2020).

Importantly, in September 2020, the United Nations General Assembly adopted a new resolution, on Improving Global Road Safety (United Nations, 2020). This "proclaims the period 2021-2030 as the Second Decade of Action for Road Safety, with a goal of reducing road traffic deaths and injuries by at least 50 per cent from 2021 to 2030..."

Together, these represent the strongest-ever mandates globally for countries to commit to and invest in preventing further tragedies on our roads, and its success requires strong leadership at all levels. For Commonwealth countries to meet the 2030 target, there is an urgent need to mobilise further actions in road safety. If the current road mortality trend continues in the Commonwealth, few countries are projected to halve the mortality rate between 2017 and 2030 (CRSI 2019). On the contrary, an increase in the rate is projected in 12 countries (see Figure 4.3), highlighting the need for greater commitments and actions to reduce road trauma.

A threat to sustainable development for all – especially youth

In addition to the tragic loss of lives and health, road trauma also results in huge social and economic losses that could be significantly reduced in all Commonwealth countries. According to the World Bank (2018), on average a 10 per cent reduction in road traffic deaths raises per capita real gross domestic product by 3.6 per cent over a 24-year horizon. Without a priority focus on improving road safety, this will pose a significant threat to youth and sustainable development.

A lack of road safety or unsafe roads has impacts not only in terms of road trauma but also on other areas of public health. When conditions are unsafe, people are less likely to walk, cycle or use public transportation, leading to inactivity, and this has a bearing on other risk factors for non-communicable diseases and leading causes of death such as cardiovascular diseases, diabetes and obesity. Improving road safety will not only have a direct effect on road trauma but will also contribute to reducing the overall burden of other preventable deaths (WHO, 2018).

The United Nations' aim to substantially reduce road traffic deaths and serious injuries is one part of a series of efforts to make our transport systems more sustainable. Population growth, rapid urbanisation and rising levels of motorisation generate inter-related social and environmental problems. This is recognised in the SDGs, which simultaneously aim to tackle climate change, air pollution and road injury.

There is strong potential for youth action for road safety, for example by supporting the safe routes to school campaign of the Child Health & Mobility Initiative,[1] better road design and speed enforcement to protect vulnerable road users, and effective road safety education and training. Such initiatives are also closely linked to other priorities in sustainable transport, such as improving air quality, reducing carbon emissions and promoting healthy lifestyles. Neglect of these issues is estimated to result in 500,000 young lives being cut short each year.[2]

The high number of people killed and seriously injured in road crashes each year is not just a statistic. Behind each number is a person, a family, a friend, a community and a story of how life can change in an instant for many. Road crashes are not inevitable but are both predictable and preventable, and there are known solutions to the issue. However, across the Commonwealth the level of road deaths remains unacceptably high, and urgent action is required to prevent the further loss of life and health, especially for young people, who are the most at risk.

Faces behind the figures

The following stories are sourced from the publication "Faces behind the Figures: Voices of Road Traffic Crash Victims and Their Families" (WHO and ASIRT, 2007).

Abdul Rehman Tipu (Pakistan)

Tipu was the youngest of a family of six and much loved by his family. On a motorcycle with a friend, an overtaking car coming from the opposite direction hit them. Tipu and his friend were both seriously hurt and sustained head injuries and fractured legs. Tipu remained in the intensive care unit and was unconscious till his last breath. He was 18 years old. His friend received multiple operations and remained in hospital for some time but his condition improved. Family members and friends of Tipu were in shock and grieved over the loss of their most loved and caring member. Tipu was a hope for their better future. Friends and neighbours will remember his warm-heartedness and his fondness for making new friends, and his family will miss him always.

Grace Mbuli Kithiki (Kenya)

Grace was travelling in cargo in the back of an overloaded lorry in Kenya when the vehicle overturned and rolled over more than three times. She knew it was not a safe way to travel but it was the only option available. There were no seatbelts and the road was rough and narrow. Six passengers

Guest Contributor

Figure 4.3 Estimated and projected road mortality rate for 2017 and 2030 for selected Commonwealth countries

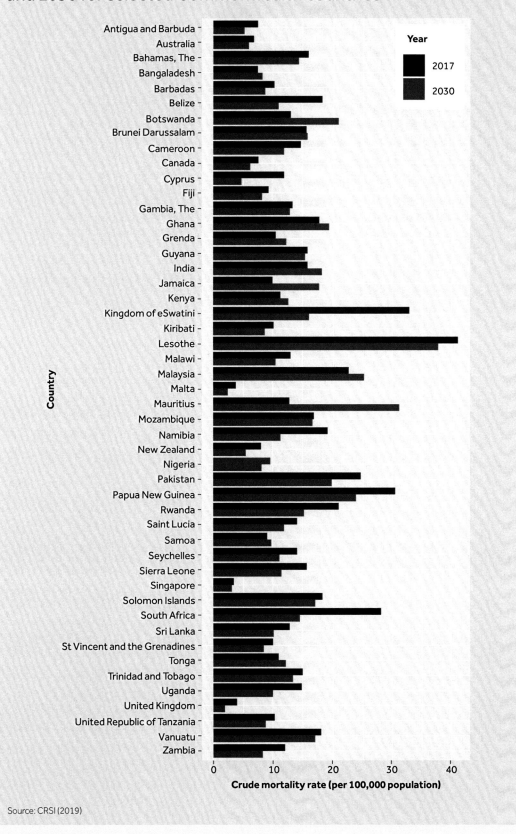

Source: CRSI (2019)

were killed and several others were maimed. Grace suffered serious injuries and spent three months in hospital before moving to a rehabilitation centre. She is now in a wheelchair with severe back pain and discomfort. Grace's life has changed significantly: she was once able to walk and now cannot. She does not know how long she will be in the wheelchair for. She tries to stay cheerful but it is difficult for her to remember what her life used to be before the crash.

Mansoor Chaudhry (UK)

Mansoor was a well-loved, gifted and beautiful person with his whole life ahead of him. He was travelling on his motorcycle when a driver crossed a junction against the red lights and collided with him, causing him horrific injuries. Mansoor was transported to a hospital by air ambulance but unfortunately did not survive. He was 26 years old. His death shattered his family and changed their lives irrevocably. His sister misses him more and more each day and his mother, Brigitte, is no longer able to continue in her profession. At the time of Mansoor's death, Brigitte did not realise the huge scale of road deaths and injuries. She has since become a campaigner for justice, not only for her son but also for all innocent road crash victims, and has set up RoadPeace to support victims of road crashes and work towards reducing road trauma.

Youth advocating for greater participation and change

Youth are a growing and significant proportion of target beneficiaries of road safety policies, as well as an underutilised resource as initiators and implementers of road safety policies and interventions. There is a strong case for meaningful youth participation in road safety in line with the Commonwealth Youth mission to "engage and recognise young people." When decisions or road safety programmes are being designed, or when policies are being developed that concern young people, youth have the fundamental right to co-decide on these issues (United Nations, 1990). Active youth participation also creates stronger policy outcomes for this unique demographic of society. Young people can and should meaningfully participate in all stages of decision-making in road safety, especially on policies designed for

youth, where they exist. Young people have a role to play during the development, implementation and evaluation of road safety initiatives and it is crucial to ensure that road safety initiatives foster meaningful participation with youth that avoid manipulation, decoration and tokenism (Hart, 1992). Young people have a massive opportunity to improve the road safety reality through active engagement and to stimulate positive road safety change as beneficiaries, partners and leaders across the Commonwealth, and, by doing so, to champion the next generation of leaders in road safety. This will result in policies that are more responsive and ensure ownership, buy-in and active participation from future generations. Youth want their needs, ideas, skills and opinions to be taken into account and they hope that this will be the last generation facing this global mobility crisis. And they want their boundless potential to be harnessed and to be a part of the solution. The voices of youth must be heard and they must be empowered to take action as change agents and role models to their peers.

Claiming space at the decision-making table

The youth of the world are saying enough is enough to their peers dying on the world's roads and are claiming their space for safe mobility. To help accelerate the youth movement, 167 young delegates, representing 74 countries across the 7 world regions, attended the Second World Youth Assembly for Road Safety,[3] held in Stockholm on 18 February 2020, initiated by YOURS[4] and co-sponsored by WHO. The goal of the Assembly was to mobilise and inspire global youth leaders and community champions to take action for road safety, and to empower young people and push for meaningful youth engagement on designing, implementing and evaluating a safe mobility system.

It is here that youth adopted the Global Youth Statement for Road Safety, which was rooted in Youth Consultations that had taken place all across the world, in which young people held discussions and debates and answered important questions about how safe they feel on the roads. The Global Youth Statement expresses clearly that the reality youth face is badly designed systems that put the

Guest Contributor

priority of cars first and people second. Going to school, to work or to visit friends is a daily risk for many young people. The Global Youth Statement demands the following from leaders:

- Roads that do not kill our dreams;

- Education for every road user;

- Established and enforced safe speed limits;

- No more death-trap cars;

- Safe and sustainable transport;

- Appropriate safety laws and the political will to enforce them;

- Quick and efficient post-crash care.

A Global Youth Coalition,[5] spearheaded by YOURS, has been created to capture this momentum and steer it towards global and local action. This represents a coalition of hundreds of committed young leaders and youth-led non-governmental organisations (NGOs) from diverse backgrounds, topics of focus, sectors and approaches. Youth are claiming a seat at the decision-making table and taking active steps in better policy design, sustainable urban planning, deeply rooted local community initiatives and the championing of innovative creative ideas to mobility issues. They are already raising awareness, advocating and acting as change agents of their communities towards a safer and healthier future and are calling on decision-makers and stakeholders to join and support them. The Coalition offers young leaders resources, skills, partnerships and opportunities to take their ideas to the next level and maximise impact through global and local actions.

Road safety youth leaders advocating for change

Alex Ayub (Kenya)

"The dream of every young person in Africa is to learn as much they can through education and exposure, in order to make a difference in their communities. As such, every day, a young person wakes up, pumps up and gears up to go out there and face the world with a bold face. The difference between where they stay and where they get an education is marked by a long path – a dangerous road! Many who leave their households in search

of livelihood or an education come back home with serious injuries while others just never get back home. This is the sad reality of millions of young African children and youth.

"The fight against injuries and deaths caused by road traffic crashes is not a one-sided one – it needs collaboration and collective efforts. It is a collective responsibility, not only between road users but also with greater efforts on leadership and policy influence. With proper legislation and enforcement around road use, incidences on our roads could greatly be reduced. To achieve this, we need targeted advocacy, political goodwill and buy–in from the decision-makers and policy influencers. This is why road safety is important to me. To fight and advocate for roads that lead youth towards their dreams and not their deaths."

Alex Ayub is the National Youth Officer for the Kenya Red Cross and is on the Youth Advisory Board of the Global Youth Coalition for Road Safety

Oliva Nalwadda (Uganda)

"In 2013, I was a victim of a motor accident on my way to the university examination hall. The emotional, physical and economic impact it had on me and my family steered a voice of action towards creating safer roads. Roads are the most used mode of transport, yet road safety is barely on the agenda of governments, much less on the international priority agendas. This ignites my passion and desire to drive it to the priority list of key local and international actors.

"Children and youth are the biggest victims of traffic crashes; however, little effort is made to engage us in design, implementation and evaluation of road safety-related policies, frameworks and programmes. Even sadder is the fact that less effort is made to bring road safety onto global youth and adolescent health agendas, despite the statistics. Road safety requires global action and solidarity and the Commonwealth Youth Forum is one of such platforms where voices of youth can be collectively amplified for a common cause. I desire to be part of this global cohort of young leaders working to address global issues, and activating change through participation in decision-making, community action and youth-led accountability and advocacy. I want to represent road safety at the youth forum to reignite a state of urgency for road safety among the youth and other key stakeholders."

Oliva Nalwadda is a Country Coordinator at Norweigan Association of Disabled, Founder of Uzima Ari Uganda, and is on the Youth Advisory Board of the Global Youth Coalition for Road Safety

What needs to be done in the Commonwealth?

Road traffic injuries have a devasting impact on those directly involved as well as an extensive ripple effect on those left behind and in the community. The Commonwealth can play a leading role in tackling this tragic waste of lives and damage to health. To ensure that this happens, it is essential that safe and sustainable transport be included as a key item on all Commonwealth agendas, such as at the Commonwealth Youth Forum, the Commonwealth Youth Ministers Meeting and the Commonwealth Heads of Government Meeting.

Working with young people directly is a crucial part of the road safety equation, and this can be facilitated through a peer-to-peer methodology and the "three-lens" approach to youth involvement in road safety adapted by YOURS. This sees young people as beneficiaries, partners and leaders in road safety, building engagement and participation from a foundational base through empowerment, skills development and investment. An example can be seen in the Belize Youth Capacity Development Programme.[6]

To assist Commonwealth countries to prioritise road safety and further commit to road injury prevention, the CRSI,[7] a programme by the Towards Zero Foundation,[8] has developed a framework for road injury prevention in Commonwealth countries, aiming to halve deaths and serious injuries from road crashes by 2030 and implement the actions needed to avoid a decade of predictable and preventable death and serious injury on the roads of Commonwealth countries. The CRSI has brought together a distinguished panel of road safety experts to prepare a report of recommendations for Commonwealth countries (CRSI, 2019). Building on established Commonwealth commitments to youth, health and the SDGs, the CRSI highlights the importance of:

- Setting a Commonwealth target to halve road deaths and serious injuries by 2030;

- Prioritising road safety as a key focus issue for child and youth;

- Adopting the Safe System Approach to road injury prevention in high-, middle- and low-income Commonwealth countries;

- Promoting good governance and road safety;

- Promoting workplace road safety;

- Building multi-sector Commonwealth partnerships for road safety;

- Integrating road safety within the SDGs.

The expert panel report features 10 key recommendations for Commonwealth countries, including one especially on young people:

Recommendation 4: Reducing Road Trauma of Children and Young People

That the Commonwealth adopt as a priority to address road trauma for children and young people, the leading cause of death for people aged 5–29 years old.

The CRSI is working with the Global Youth Coalition for Road Safety to ensure the voice of young people on the topic of road safety is included in policy decisions that will affect their future, and adoption of the 10 key recommendations of the CRSI by Commonwealth countries will be a great first step in the right direction. Young people themselves have described their reality, demands and commitments to promoting safe and sustainable mobility in the Global Youth Statement. Stakeholders are encouraged to use this document as an anchor point to start conversations and dialogue with young people in their countries and communities.

COVID-19 and road trauma prevention

COVID-19 has had a significant impact on all facets of life and brought the world to a literal stand-still. It has affected the way people move and their choice of transport. Now more than ever, more needs to be done to increase safety on our roads. Hospitals

Guest Contributor

around the world are at breaking point coping with COVID-19, and do not need the extra pressure from road traffic crashes. Ensuring the safety of people on the road will save lives and health not only directly but also indirectly, by alleviating the burden on our health system, allowing resources to be directed to other areas such as COVID-19. While the world has been on lockdown, traffic volume has decreased, but there is evidence of an increase in speed (Katrakazas et al., 2020), increasing the risk of road injuries and thus a flow on pressure to health care systems that are already struggling to cope. This highlights that, while countries focus their efforts on combating COVID-19, and rightly so, countries also cannot afford to lessen their efforts in addressing road trauma as it can add an unnecessary burden to an already overloaded health care system.

As we consider recovery post-COVID, it becomes even more pressing for countries not to neglect road safety. With recovery, there will likely be a corresponding increase in traffic volumes and thus exposure to road traffic injuries. There are already indications of a greater use of personal vehicles and less use of public transport, as well as an increase in walking and cycling (European Commission, 2020). To encourage people to walk and cycle, some cities have implemented infrastructure changes, such as converting streets for priority pedestrian and bicyclist access, widened cycle lanes and mass roll-out of cycle lanes, as well as a lowering of speed limits for greater safety (European Transport Safety Council, 2020). As these transport changes are made to allow for better social distancing, careful consideration must be given to how to do so safely without increasing the risk of road traffic injury.

While COVID-19 has brought many industries and events to a halt, young people have illustrated their resilience and adaptability to continue their work in tackling road trauma. The Global Youth Coalition for Road Safety was launched in July 2020, in the midst of many national lockdowns globally. And it has grown significantly, with more than 250 youth members globally, by taking action online through capacity development, awareness campaigns and global coordination.

While COVID-19 is understandably the public health priority at the moment, road trauma has not disappeared, and countries need to act quickly to also curb this predictable and preventable public health concern during COVID-19 but also beyond.

Conclusion

Road traffic injury is the number one public health issue facing our youth population yet there is not sufficient urgency to reverse this trend. Too many young lives have been lost on the world's roads, and we cannot afford to lose another decade to inaction. Youth are shouting, "Enough is enough" of their peers dying on the world's roads and are demanding greater leadership and a radical change. There must be a paradigm shift in seeing young people as assets in road safety action and not "problem road users" that need to be managed. Young people must be approached as equal partners who can help shape and implement road safety policy and be drivers of road safety change as leaders in communities all around the world. Together with greater commitment, investment and leadership from youth and leaders alike, we can secure the safety and future of young people for generations to come in the Commonwealth.

4.3 Youth taking charge of health and wellbeing

All over the world, young people are taking steps to take charge of their own health, care for others in their communities and innovate for healthy change. The Commonwealth Youth Awards provide a way to recognise exceptional youth contributions. In 2021, the overall winner of the Awards – the Commonwealth Young Person of the Year – was recognised for an innovation that has changed the health care landscape in rural Bangladesh. Other young leaders, including an African finalist encouraging blood donation as well as 11 exceptional young people recognised for their responses to the COVID-19 pandemic, are also highlighted in this chapter.

4.3.1 Commonwealth Young Person of the Year

Faysal Islam is a young entrepreneur who is taking charge of ensuring that no one is left behind in the pursuit of SDG3 on good health and wellbeing. Emergency medical services are not readily accessible to the 105 million people living in rural areas of Bangladesh. In fact, for every 88,000 people there is only 1 ambulance, many of which are not fully functional or suitable to narrow rural roads. Through Safewheel, the social enterprise he co-founded with his friends, Faysal is providing fast and affordable emergency medical services to these rural communities. He and his team designed a mini three-wheeled ambulance, well suited to rural conditions, which costs 10 per cent of a conventional ambulance. With full-time paramedics on board, along with a driver equipped with basic emergency response training, Safewheel provides services at half the cost and three times faster, on average, than other ambulance services. The current fleet of 10 mini ambulances has already attended to over 1,000 persons in 150 villages, including children, pregnant women and elderly people. Faysal and his

team continue to monitor the impact of this social enterprise, working to make it a profitable venture that can be quickly scaled up across Bangladesh and other developing countries. They have recently developed a system which allows people to compare prices online to find the most affordable diagnostic test services and medicines.

4.3.2 Redsplash Kenya, encouraging blood donations

Abdulrehman Alwy is taking charge of good health and wellbeing though Redsplash Kenya, which he co-founded in 2019 with a friend whose mother had lost her life because of a blood shortage. The organisation creates awareness of the importance of voluntary blood donations and tackles misinformation around donating. According to WHO standards, Kenya needs at least 1 million blood donations annually but collects only round 164,765 units - less than 20 per cent of what is required. Women and children use 60 per cent of donated blood and are the most affected by blood shortage. Redsplash hosts educational blood drives with youth-friendly activities that have attracted new donors and operates an online app for donor registration and sending out emergency appeals. The app was useful in 2020 when blood drives could not be held, to keep relationships with past donors and encourage repeat donations. Over 80 per cent of those in the app database contributed to boosting the blood supply in 2020. The initiative has already served over 5,000 patients in need, recruited over 3,000 blood donors, partnered with over 20 hospitals and recruited hundreds of volunteers to support its campaigns.

4.3.3 COVID-19 Heroes

Since the start of the COVID-19 pandemic, many young people have taken the initiative to support their communities to develop healthy and empowering responses to the crisis. The 2021 Commonwealth Youth Awards highlighted 11 exceptional young people who went above and beyond. They are our Commonwealth Youth COVID-19 Heroes, who are positive lights in the pandemic.

Vedika Agarwal (India)

Vedika is Founder of Yein Udaan, an NGO supporting marginalised families in rural Indian communities. During the lockdown, Yein Udaan distributed food supplies equivalent to over 216,000 meals, sanitation supplies to over 3,000 families and educational kits to over 400 students and launched a virtual learning programme in 6 community libraries. The organisation has also worked with doctors to create informative posters in regional languages to tackle health misinformation.

Bilal Amjad (Pakistan)

Bilal is Founder of InstaCare, which launched a response unit to provide free online medical consultations to communities in Pakistan during the pandemic. Over 300 doctors have provided over 10,000 consultations through the platform. InstaCare has also partnered with private institutions, including universities and hospitals, to provide telemedicine services to the public.

Alexia Hilbertidou (New Zealand)

Alexia is Founder of GirlBoss New Zealand, which empowers and equips young women to develop leadership and entrepreneurial skills. During the pandemic, Alexia launched GirlBoss Edge – a virtual career accelerator giving over 1,000 women access to 1:1 mentorship and career skills masterclasses, particularly Indigenous, Pasifika, low-income and rural women.

Dr Isaac Olufadewa (Nigeria)

Isaac is Founder of Slum and Rural Health Initiative (SRHIN). The SRHIN COVID-19 Project has translated COVID-19 health messages from WHO into more than 100 languages, reaching over 1.5 million people. Isaac also launched an Artificial Intelligence-driven app and chatbot offering thousands of young people access to comprehensive sexual and mental health information.

Dr Camir Ricketts (Jamaica)

Camir is Founder of MindsOf Initiative, a programme that increases young people's access to career mentorship and S.T.E.A.M (science, technology, engineering, art and maths) training opportunities. Camir co-launched an online app helping 100,000 people find their nearest COVID-19 testing sites and raised US$4,000 in funds to purchase devices and mobile data for students affected by the pandemic.

Sukhmeet Singh Sachal (Canada)

Sukhmeet is Co-Founder of Translations 4 Our Nations, an initiative that works with indigenous community members to create medically accurate and culturally relevant COVID-19 information in indigenous languages. The programme has recruited over 140 indigenous translators to translate public health policy information into over 45 languages, reaching over 45,000 indigenous people.

Momin Saqib (UK)

In March 2020, Momin launched One Million Meals, an emergency response to the COVID-19 crisis. Led by volunteers, the programme has provided over 100,000 meals and beverages in over 200 locations to frontline key workers, National Health Service staff, homeless people and vulnerable families affected by the pandemic, including through 47 hospitals, trusts and food banks.

Kritz and Bianca Sciessere – Australia

Kritz and Bianca are Founders of The Big Sister Experience, a social enterprise that provides online mentorship to empower young women and girls by building their life skills. During the pandemic, the programme has focused on face-to-face and online workshops to support over 5,000 young girls dealing with isolation and as they return to on-campus learning.

Brent Alexander Scotland – Antigua and Barbuda

Brent is President of the Halo Foundation Generation Y, a national youth body supporting and empowering young people. The foundation funds monthly groceries for vulnerable persons and provides a support network to elderly communities isolated during the pandemic. It has also hosted youth events on character-building and mental health and suicide awareness.

Natalie Robi Tingo – Kenya

Natalie is Founder of Msichana Empowerment Kuria, an organisation combating gender-based violence and female genital mutilation and empowering girls and women in Kenya. During the pandemic, the organisation set up a menstrual care bank to support menstrual health care for 2,000 girls in rural and urban slums, and a community-based cash transfer programme to allow over 400 marginalised girls and young women to access vital funds and support.

Endnotes

1   https://www.childhealthinitiative.org/

2   https://www.mystreet.org/

3   www.wyaroadsafety.org

4   http://www.youthforroadsafety.org

5   www.claimingourspace.org

6   http://www.youthforroadsafety.org/our-work/ workshops/belize

7   https://www.commonwealthrsi.org

8   http://www.towardszerofoundation.org

References

CRSI (Commonwealth Road Safety Initiative) (2019) *Commonwealth Expert Panel Report Putting Road Safety on the Commonwealth Agenda*. London: CRSI. https://issuu.com/commonwealthrsi/docs/ commonwealth_expert_panel_report

European Commission (2020) "Road Safety Measures in the COVID Transitional Era – Common High

Level Group Principles as We Exit the Crisis". https://ec.europa.eu/transport/road_safety/ road-safety-measures-covid-transitional-era-common-high-level-group-principles-we-exit-crisis_en

European Transport Safety Council (2020) "COVID-19: Cities Adapting Road Infrastructure and Speed Limits to Enable Safer Cycling and Walking". 20 April. https://etsc.eu/covid-19-cities-adapting-road-infrastructure-and-speed-limits-to-enable-safer-cycling-and-walking/

Hart, R. (1992) "Children's Participation: From Tokenism to Citizenship". Innocenti Essay 4. New York: UNICEF.

Katrakazas, C., E. Michelaraki, M. Sekadakis and G. Yannis (2020) "A Descriptive Analysis of the Effect of the COVID-19 Pandemic on Driving Behaviour and Road Safety". *Transportation Research Interdisciplinary Perspectives* **7**: 100186.

Pathare, S. and J. Sagade (2013) *Mental Health: A Legislative Framework to Empower, Protect and Care: A Review of Mental Health Legislation in Commonwealth Member States*. London: Commonwealth Health Professions Alliance and Commonwealth Foundation.

Third Global Ministerial Conference on Road Safety (2020) "Stockholm Declaration". https:// www.roadsafetysweden.com/contentassets/ b37f0951c837443eb9661668d5be439e/ stockholm-declaration-english.pdf

United Nations (1990) *United Nations Convention on the Rights of the Child*. New York: United Nations.

United Nations (2015) *Transforming Our World: The 2030 Agenda for Sustainable Development*. New York: United Nations.

United Nations (2020) "74th General Assembly Resolution: 'Improving Global Road Safety'" A/74/L.86, 31 August. https://www.un.org/ pga/74/2020/08/31/improving-global-road-safety/

WHO (World Health Organization) (2018) *Global Status Report on Road Safety 2018*. Geneva: WHO.

WHO (2021) "Adolescent and Young Adult Health". 18 January. https://www.who.int/news-room/ fact-sheets/detail/adolescents-health-risks-and-solutions

WHO (World Health Organization) and ASIRT (Association for Safe International Road Travel) (2007) "Faces behind the Figures: Voices of Road Crash Victims and Their Families". https://apps.who.int/iris/bitstream/ handle/10665/43548/9241594640_eng.pdf;jsess ionid=B2B19101C4C3DCD913690B165C51590B ?sequence=1

World Bank (2018) "Road Deaths and Injuries Hold Back Economic Growth in Developing Countries". Press Release, 9 January. https://www.worldbank. org/en/news/press-release/2018/01/09/ road-deaths-and-injuries-hold-back-economic-growth-in-developing-countries

YOURS (Youth for Road Safety) (2020) "Youth Leading the Charge for Road Safety. 'Challenges'". Annual Report 2019. www.youthforroadsafety.org/uploads/ tekstblok/yours_annual_report_2019_comp.pdf

The Contribution of Sport to the SDGs: Youth Development Perspectives

05

Chapter 5

The Contribution of Sport to the SDGs: Youth Development Perspectives

As discussed in Chapter 2, there is a strong conceptual overlap between the Youth Development Index (YDI) and the Sustainable Development Goals (SDGs) that pertain to youth, especially with the inclusion of the new domains on Peace and Security and Equality and Inclusion in the 2020 YDI. There is a particularly strong relationship with SDG 3, SDG 4, SDG 7 and SDG 16.

However, there are still areas of development that the YDI does not yet capture that also significantly contribute to the attainment of the SDGs. Sport and physical recreation – activities in which young people participate heavily and from which they benefit significantly – is one such area that requires new tools to support monitoring progress.

This chapter, led by the Sport for Development and Peace team,[1] outlines a new initiative of the Commonwealth Secretariat that encourages the global adoption of indicators to measure and maximise the contributions that sport, physical education and physical activity can make to sustainable development.

5.1 Sport and youth development

Sport is a powerful tool that, if used correctly, can positively affect the lives of young people. It is widely recognised for teaching life skills, including social and emotional skills as well as values and attitudes

that frame socially responsible citizenship, and there is significant research establishing sport as an environment for youth development and leadership (Schulenkorf et al., 2016).

"Sport teaches values and attitudes that frame socially responsible citizenship."

Previous Commonwealth publications have detailed evidence-based approaches and policy options to support the contribution of sport to the SDGs (Lindsey and Chapman, 2017). This has been further advanced by global policy frameworks such as the Kazan Action Plan, the United Nations Action Plan on Sport for Development and Peace, the Global Action Plan on Physical Activity and a multitude of institutional strategies on sport and sustainable development.

Despite this knowledge, and despite numerous sport-based programmes positively influencing change across the Commonwealth, there continues to exist a lack of systematic data gathered on the role of sport as a development tool. This in turn has impacts regarding the inclusion of sport as part of social development

policies, and continues a prolonged cycle of reduced investment in sport-based programmes. To help break this cycle and highlight the contribution of sport to sustainable development, the Commonwealth Secretariat has advanced an initiative to develop and implement common global indicators for measuring and maximising the contribution of sport to the SDGs.

5.2 Sport and Agenda 2030

The potential of sport-based approaches to contribute to wide-ranging development outcomes has been acknowledged across international policy declarations, most significantly in the 2030 Agenda for Sustainable Development. This recognises sport as an "important enabler to achieving the Sustainable Development Goals."

While sport, physical education and physical activity can enable a myriad of development outcomes, there is a need for effective management to ensure these outcomes are realised. This requires targeted, well-designed policies, resource availability, and effective monitoring and evaluation of activities within the sport and physical activity ecosystem to contribute to the achievement of specific SDG targets. At the Third Open-Ended Working Group (OEWG) Meeting on Model Indicators on Sport and SDGs, Commonwealth Secretary-General the Rt. Hon Patricia Scotland said that, "While there is no denying the power of sport, it is extremely hard to realise the potential of sport, physical activity and physical education, unless we can effectively measure the impact of these assets, and then take effective decisions to maximise them" (Commonwealth Secretariat, 2020).

To deliver the Sport and SDG Indicators, a global steering group was formed in 2018, comprising

representatives from the United Nations Educational, Scientific and Cultural Organization, the United Nations Department of Social and Economic Affairs, the International Olympic Committee (IOC) and the International Paralympic Committee (IPC), leading member states, sector experts and the Commonwealth Youth Sport for Development and Peace Network (CYSDP). The development process has been spearheaded and coordinated by the Commonwealth Secretariat.

An iterative approach has guided this development process, involving the phased development, testing and revision of model indicators and associated tools. This has included the mapping of existing data or development of new results frameworks by over 15 member countries and institutions and the provision of detailed feedback through an OEWG Meeting held annually since 2018. The latest OEWG Meeting, in 2020, had over 200 registered attendees from across government, sport, business and academic communities.

The final indicator bank and the Sport and SDG Indicators toolkit are available on the Commonwealth Secretariat website.[2] The next step in this project is to drive the scaled adoption of the indicators and to ensure the data gathered drive evidence-based decisions and investment in sport as a development tool.

The early signs are extremely encouraging, with evidence emerging for the contributions of sport, physical activity and physical education in youth development across the Commonwealth, particularly on the basis of indicators focused on Health and Wellbeing, Education, Employment and Peace and

Security. This chapter outlines how sport's contribution in each of these four areas may be measured.

5.3 SDG 4: Quality education

Sport and physical education have specific roles to play in achieving targets under SDG 4. High-quality physical education is essential to young people's development of physical literacy,[3] which has been shown to improve cognitive skills, mental health, social skills and physical health across lifespans (Roetert et al., 2018).

Sport-based activities have been shown to be valuable in attracting those who have been disengaged from education, enhancing wider educational outcomes in line with SDG target 4.1 to ensure that all girls and boys complete free, equitable and quality primary and secondary education leading to relevant and effective learning outcomes. Similarly, there is a growing body of evidence highlighting correlations between the time spent under moderate-vigorous intensity physical activity and academic performance (Booth et al., 2014).

The focus of SDG target 4.5 on inclusion and equality highlights the need to make physical education and sport-based activities accessible by all, and also the need to enhance the potential contribution that such activities can make to engage particular groups in both formal and informal education. Likewise, SDG target 4.7 focuses on ensuring that all learners acquire the knowledge and skills needed to promote sustainable development, including aspects such as knowledge of human rights, gender equality, promotion of peace and global citizenship. It is vital to ensure physical education curricula and teacher qualifications are aligned with these principles.

To ensure this, the Sport and SDG Indicators have been developed in alignment with the UNESCO Quality Physical Education (QPE) Guidelines and data-gathering processes. Data on the following indicators in Table 5.1 will assist in gauging and supporting Commonwealth governments to maximise the contributions physical education is making to important education outcomes.

5.4 SDG 8: Decent work and economic growth

The International Labour Organization (ILO) has identified that young people, and especially young women, around the globe have been significantly affected by a "prolonged job crisis", which the COVID-19 pandemic has exacerbated (ILO, 2020a). Globally, the youth unemployment rate has been estimated at 13.6 per cent, with regional rates as high as 30 per cent in Northern Africa (ILO, 2020b). Since the onset of the COVID-19 pandemic, it is estimated that one in six young people have stopped working altogether, with working hours among employed youth also falling by nearly two hours a day. Youth unemployment and underemployment are especially acute in low-income and developing regions, where problems with the quality, stability and regularity of work are recognised (ILO, 2020a). Young women report greater loss in productivity than do young men.

The sport sector has a significant role to play in driving global employment. According to the European Commission (2018), sport sustains 5.67 million employees, equivalent to a 2.72 per cent share in total employment. Sport is an "employment-intensive economic activity, which generates a greater share in employment than GDP [gross domestic product]" (Kokolakakis et al., 2020).

Research has also shown significant over-representation of young people employed within the sport sector delivering potential benefits in line with SDG target 8.6 on lowering the rate of youth not in employment, education or training globally. For example, in the EU, 35 per cent of persons employed in the sport sector in 2019 were aged 15–29 years old (Eurostat, 2020). This is over twice the average level of representation of young people in total employment

Table 5.1 Sport and Education indicators

#	Indicator	SDG alignment
4	% of (i) primary and (ii) secondary schools reporting implementation of the minimum number of physical education minutes (120 minutes per week in primary school; 180 minutes per week in secondary school)	SDG 3.4.1 SDG 4.1
11	% of schools reporting physical education specialist teachers in (i) primary and (ii) secondary schools	SDG 4.7
12	% of schools reporting full/partial implementation of quality physical education as defined by UNESCO's QPE Guidelines	SDG 4.7

Table 5.2 Sport and Economic Employment indicators

#	Indicator	SDG alignment
7	% contribution of (i) sports activities and amusement and recreation sector and (ii) sport, exercise and active recreation to GDP • Drawing on: System of National Accounts 2008	SDG 8.1 SDG 8.2
8	% of workforce within the sport, fitness and active recreation sector • Drawing on: International Standard Classification of Occupations (ISCO-08) • Disaggregated by age, gender, education level and disability	SDG 8.5 SDG 8.6
9	% of population who volunteer in sport • Drawing on: International Classification of Activities for Time-Use Statistics (2016) • Disaggregated by gender, age, education level and disability	SDG 8.3 SDG 8.6

figures. Involvement in sport and sport volunteering has also been shown to increase social capital, which can provide employment opportunities later in life (Davies et al., 2016).

In recognition of this valuable attribute of the sport sector, the Government of Namibia has identified sport sector development as a key objective in its National Development Plan (NDP). In recognition of the power of sport to empower people and communities, NDP Goal 5 outlines a desire to increase sport sector employment contributions from 0.2 per cent in 2014 to 2 per cent in 2022 (Republic of Namibia, 2017). The Government of Namibia is in the process of adopting the Sport and SGD Indicators to further monitor, evaluate and report on sport's contribution to national development.

Further indicators relating to the economic and employment contributions sport can make under SDG 8 include those in Table 5.2.

5.5 SDG 16: Peace, justice and strong institutions

SDG 16 focuses on the promotion of peaceful and inclusive societies for sustainable development, providing access to justice for all and building effective, accountable and inclusive institutions at all levels. Participation in well-designed sport-based programmes can have large impacts in terms of the reduction of crime and violence. It is also vital that the sector's institutions live up to the standards set out under this Goal in relation to justice and the rule of law (SDG target 16.3), transparency (SDG target 16.6), representative and participatory decision-making (SDG

target 16.7) and promotion of non-discretionary laws and policies (SDG target 16.B).

Likewise, it is important to ensure the integrity of sport is upheld in order to make it possible to effectively deliver development benefits. This includes addressing aspects such as crime and corruption, doping in sport and manipulation of sporting competitions (SDG target 16.4; SDG target 16.5) and the need to protect human rights and combat abuse and all forms of violence in sport (SDG target 16.2). This, of course, has direct implications for youth as the primary participants and consumers of sport worldwide.

5.5.1 Safeguarding children and youth in sport

While engagement in sport has well-noted positive benefits for hundreds of millions of children and youth worldwide, for some children it can bring experiences of abuse and other forms of non-accidental violence. The research into the topic is limited but sheds disturbing insights into the dimensions of violence against children in sport, including retroactive studies indicating 75 per cent of participants experiencing emotional/psychological abuse as child athletes and 29 per cent reporting experiencing sexual harassment, 24 per cent physical abuse and 3 per cent sexual abuse (Alexander et al., 2011).

There has been recent development of specific policies and procedures to protect the rights of participants and children in particular in sport by both state and sport organisations. The Sport and SDG Indicators initiative focuses on national-level actions to monitor the development and implementation of these policies,

Table 5.3 Sport and Safeguarding indicators

#	Indicator	SDG alignment
14	% funded national sport bodies/member organisations that have adopted formal policies (with procedures) to (i) safeguard children and (ii) prevent violence against women	SDG 5.2 SDG 16.2
15	% of (i) presidents, (ii) board members and (iii) CEO/secretary-general post-holders in national sport bodies/member organisations who are female	SDG 5.5 SDG 16.7
18	% funded national sport bodies/member organisations that have adopted formal policies (with procedures) to (i) protect the rights of athletes, spectators, workers and other groups involved, (ii) strengthen measures against the manipulation of sports competitions and (iii) ensure an adequate anti-doping policy framework, its implementation and effective compliance measures, to protect the integrity of sport	SDG 16.4 SDG 16.5 SDG 16.6
19	# of (i) athletes, (ii) coaches/officials and (iii) management/board members in funded national sport bodies/member organisations who were trained in the last year in (a) governance and sport integrity, (b) safeguarding children, youth and vulnerable groups, (c) prevention of violence against women and girls and (d) promoting sustainable development	SDG 16.3 SDG 16.6 SDG 16.10
20	% funded national sport bodies/member organisations with a nominated focal point to (i) co-ordinate child safeguarding and protection and (ii) prevention of violence against women and girls	SDG 16.2

centring on the existence of policies, nominated focal points within institutions and monitoring the delivery of training on related topics.

This data will be vital to ensure children and youth are effectively safeguarded in sport and to enhance the level of access and representation across the sector for greater inclusion. Examples of indicators from the sport and SDG framework that could help with monitoring progress on safeguarding young people in the sector include those outlined in Table 5.3.

5.5.2 Sport and crime reduction

Beyond the focus on the measurement of institutional factors within the sport system, it is also vital to capture and advocate for the valuable contributions the sector makes to specific communities or target groups. There is growing recognition of the role of sport in promoting tolerance, reducing crime and encouraging peace in line with, for example, SDG target 16.1 to "significantly reduce all forms of violence and related deaths globally."

Sport can provide an environment for bringing groups together to engage in dialogue and share experiences, which, when properly managed and delivered in tandem with other interventions, can lead to mutual understanding and reduced tensions (Dudfield and Dingwall-Smith, 2016). Similarly, participation in sport

can provide access to pro-social networks, support structures and positive role models, and offering opportunities to gain new experiences.

Sport programmes have been shown to deliver benefits including enhanced mental health (Woods et al., 2017), diverting youth from deviancy by providing an alternative outlet (Zuckerman, 1991; Nichols, 2007) and promoting social development outcomes, learning and other life skills (Goudas and Giannoudis, 2008; Holt et al., 2009; Ehsani et al., 2012; Ekholm, 2013; McMahon and Belur, 2013).

The Sport and SDG Indicators put forward a conceptual framework to capture the different results delivered by sport-based programmes. This approach recognises that there is a need to support sporting bodies, sport for development organisations and networks, and civil society actors to align, maximise and coherently communicate their contribution to targeted SDGs while also creating coherence between programmatic activity and national and international development priorities.

The approach involves categorising results or changes based on the depth of outcomes (connect, improve, transform) and type of outcomes (e.g. knowledge and understanding, attitudes and behaviour, skills, personal circumstance) achieved by people and communities to which sport-based programmes, projects and events

Table 5.4 Sport and Community Social Cohesion indicators

#	Indicator	SDG alignment
25	**Depth of impact** **Connect:** # reached **Improve:** # reporting programme contributed to improvement in life/community **Transform:** # reporting programme delivered enduring change in circumstance	Dependent on programme theory
26	**Type of impact** **Awareness/knowledge:** # reporting improved awareness, knowledge or understanding **Self-efficacy:** # reporting improved self-efficacy **Attitude/behaviour:** # reporting changes in attitude and behaviour owing to the programme **Skills/effectiveness:** # demonstrating improved non-sport skills, competencies or personal effectiveness **Wellbeing:** # reporting programme contributed to improved subjective wellbeing **Quality of life:** # reporting programme contributed to improved quality of life	Dependent on programme theory
27	**Social return on investment** Value of the social impact delivered by the programme, sector or event in a country or community	Dependent on programme theory

have contributed. This allows for articulation of a broad range of results under a common framework. The indicators in Table 5.4 could be helpful in monitoring progress in knowledge, attitudes and behaviours that promote social cohesion and peace.

Across programmes focused on sport for crime reduction, sport has been shown to provide a return of €5.02 for every €1 invested, through savings related to reductions in crime, truancy and ill-health (Ecroys, 2013). This significant contribution has seen recognition from member governments of the power of sport to reduce crime and promote peace. The National Sport for Development and Peace Strategy of Sierra Leone, for example, outlines a targeted, cross-sector approach for delivering sport programmes in localities experiencing higher crime rates (Mustafa, 2016).

In Jamaica, Fight For Peace (an international sport for development organisation) and the Ministry of National Security have collaborated on the delivery of martial arts and boxing programmes with a focus on education and personal development, including employability, youth support and leadership programming in crime-affected communities. Programme monitoring and evaluation reports outline various prosocial pro-peace benefits of participation while also showing that 80 per cent of surveyed participants reported thinking more carefully about the consequences of their actions and 79 per cent became more accepting of people who were different to them (Fight for Peace, 2019). In the UK, among participants in its London Boxing and Martial Arts Academy who had previously reported carrying a weapon or being involved in a crime, 71 per cent indicated they felt less likely to commit a crime and 73 per cent said they were less likely to carry a weapon after completing the programme (Fight for Peace, 2017). Figure 5.1 shows other benefits among these UK participants.

5.6 SDG 3: Good health and wellbeing

Physical inactivity is one of the four key risk factors for premature mortality from non-communicable diseases, the leading cause of mortality in the world, responsible for 48 per cent of deaths in low- and middle-income countries. While the socio-economic impact of COVID-19 has been widespread, this has

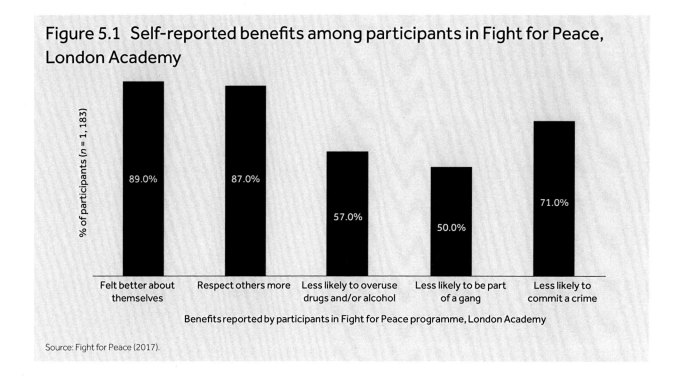

Figure 5.1 Self-reported benefits among participants in Fight for Peace, London Academy

Source: Fight for Peace (2017).

been particularly acute for certain stakeholder groups, including young people.[4] A key factor affecting physical, mental and psychosocial health and wellbeing has involved movement restrictions caused by widespread lockdowns, which have resulted in home confinement, consequently disrupting access to education, socialisation and physical activity (Singh et al., 2020). This impact has been more pronounced for young people with disabilities (Theis et al., 2021).

The pandemic has limited participation in normal daily activities, travel and access to many forms of exercise (e.g. gyms have been closed and group gatherings banned, with increased social distancing recommended). A Lancet Psychiatry study, which analysed data from over 1.2 million people between 2011 and 2015, found that, compared with people who reported doing no exercise, people who exercised reported 1.5 fewer days of poor mental health each month – a reduction of 43.2 per cent (that is, 2 days of poor mental health for people who exercised compared with 3.4 days for people who did not exercise) (Chekroud et al., 2018).

As we look to build back better after the pandemic, increased investment to prioritise physical activity is a low-cost, high-impact tool in overcoming this threat. Sport plays an important role in contributing to this physical activity and physical literacy for an active life, thus contributing to lifelong resilience. In order to secure this investment, however, it is key to actively

demonstrate the value of the sport sector with regard to key development priorities including health.

The World Health Organization Guidelines recommend children and youth aged 5–17 accumulate at least 60 minutes of moderate- to vigorous-intensity physical activity daily (WHO, 2020). Figure 5.2 shows that, across six regions, less than 20 per cent of adolescents are sufficiently physically active or meeting the recommended thresholds. In addition, adolescent girls are less active than adolescent boys.

As noted, sport plays a role in driving this physical activity and work is underway to establish common measures for the frequency of different types of physical activity. As shown in Table 5.5. below, there are key sport participation indictors which provide useful baselines to measure sector contributions to health and well-being over time.

5.7 Conclusions and recommendations

The Sport and SDG Indicators have been designed for use by national governments, sport and non-sport institutions to establish a common language for monitoring, evaluating and reporting the contributions made by sport, physical education and physical activity. Eighty-seven per cent of stakeholders from the government, non-government and sport sectors, surveyed at the Third OEWG Meeting in December

Figure 5.2 Share of adolescent population sufficiently physically active by region

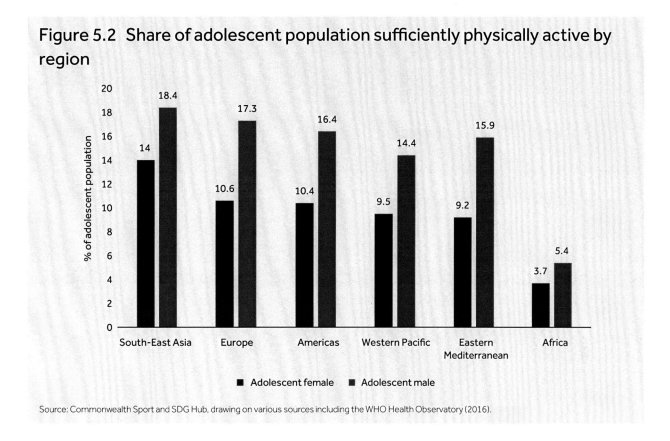

Source: Commonwealth Sport and SDG Hub, drawing on various sources including the WHO Health Observatory (2016).

2020, rated the indicator initiative as either very or extremely valuable.

Alignment with international policy frameworks and existing datasets is an important design feature to further drive coherence and reduce the monitoring burden of governments and sport stakeholders.

Establishing these consistent measures and enhanced global and local datasets on the contribution of sport, physical education and physical activity to the SDGs provides governments, sporting bodies and other groups with information for evidence-based decision-making on where and how to invest in and implement

sport-based policies and programmes. Ninety per cent of surveyed stakeholders agreed or strongly agreed that the Sport and SDG Indicators would help mobilise resources to use sport as a development tool.

Among national governments that have adopted these indicators, we are already observing enhanced cross-governmental and multi-stakeholder support for sport-based initiatives. This is a necessary precursor for enhanced investment in sport as a development tool based on the credible linkage of sport programmes and policies to non-sport national development plans, regional priorities and the SDGs.

Table 5.5 Sport and Physical Activity indictors

#	Indicator	SDG alignment
2	% of (i) adult and (ii) adolescent population sufficiently physically active	SDG 3.4.1
	• Drawing on: WHO Global Health Observatory – prevalence of insufficient physical activity among adults	
	• Disaggregated by gender, age, disability and education level	
3	% of population who participate once a week in sport and exercise	SDG 3.4.1
	• Drawing on: International Classification of Activities for Time–Use Statistics 2016	
	• Disaggregated by gender, age, disability and education level	

Sport, physical activity and physical education are valuable tools for advancing youth development. When deployed effectively and intentionally they can have significant impacts on youth development, in particular driving specific outcomes linked to the YDI, such as youth employment, health outcomes, and delivering peaceful and just societies.

The focus of the Sport and SDG Indicators initiative now moves to driving scaled adoption of the common indicators and generating detailed datasets on how sport, physical activity and physical education are contributing to the SDGs, adding to the global understanding and evidence base for the role of sport in youth development in particular. As the Commonwealth Secretary-General has noted, "We now have ten years to achieve the SDGs. Time is running out, and now, we must implement these tools to empower sport, physical education and physical activity to truly realise their potential" (Commonwealth Secretariat, 2020a).

Endnotes

1   Michael Armstrong and Saurabh Mishra prepared this analysis.

2   https://thecommonwealth.org/ measuring-contribution-sport-sustainable-development-goals

3   Physical literacy is "the motivation, confidence, physical competence, knowledge and understanding to value and take responsibility for engagement in physical activities for life" (Roetert et al., 2018)

4   https://pjp-eu.coe.int/en/web/youth-partnership/ covid-19-impact-on-the-youth-sector

References

Alexander, K., A. Stafford and R. Lewis (2011) "The Experiences of Children Participating in Organised Sport in the UK". Main Report. Edinburgh: University of Edinburgh/NSPCC Centre for UK-Wide Learning in Child Protection.

Booth, J.N., S.D. Leary, C. Joinson, A.R. Ness et al (2014) "Associations between Objectively Measured Physical Activity and Academic Attainment in Adolescents from a UK Cohort". *British Journal of Sports Medicine* **48**(3): 265–270.

Chekroud, S.R, R. Gueorguieva, A.B. Zheutlin, M. Paulus et al (2018) "Association between Physical Exercise and Mental Health in 1·2 Million Individuals in the USA between 2011 and 2015: A Cross-Sectional Study". *The Lancet* **5**(9): 739–746.

Commonwealth Secretariat (2020) "The 3rd Open-Ended Working Group Meeting: Model Indicators on Sport and SDGs". 11 December. https://thecommonwealth.org/media/news/3rd-open-ended-working-group-meeting-model-indicators-sport-and-sdgs#:~:text=The%20 3rd%20Meeting%20of%20the,and%20 UNDESA%20as%20meeting%20hosts

Davies, L., P. Taylor, G. Ramchandani and L. Christy (2016) *Social Return on Investment in Sport: A Participation-Wide Model for England.* Sheffield: SIRC.

Dudfield, O. and M. Dingwall-Smith (2016), *Sport for Development and Peace and the 2030 Agenda for Sustainable Development Analysis Report.* London: Commonwealth Secretariat.

Ecroys (2013) *Sport Scores: The Costs and Benefits of Sport for Crime Reduction.* Laureus Sport for Good Foundation.

Ehsani, M., A. Dehnavi and A. Heidary (2012) "The Influence of Sport and Recreation upon Crime Reduction: A Literature Review". *International Journal of Academic Research in Business and Social Sciences* **2**(6): 98–104.

Ekholm, D. (2013) "Sport and Crime Prevention: Individuality and Transferability in Research". *Journal of Sport for Development* **1**(2): 1–12.

European Commission (2018) "Study on the Economic Impact of Sport through Sport Satellite Accounts". Brussels: Directorate-General Education and Culture.

Eurostat (2020) "Employment in Sport". May. https://ec.europa.eu/eurostat/statistics-explained/index.php/Employment_in_sport#C2.A0.25_of_workers_in_sport_employment_are_aged_15.E2.80.9329(accessed 14 April 2021).

Fight for Peace (2019) "Annual Report". https://fightforpeace.net/wp-content/uploads/2015/06/Annual-Report-2019.pdf

Fight for Peace (2017) "Annual Report". https://fightforpeace.net/wp-content/uploads/2015/06/Fight-for-Peace-Annual-Report-2017-low-res-1.pdf

Goudas, M. and G. Giannoudis (2008) "A Team-Sports-Based Life-Skills Program in a Physical Education Context". *Learning and Instruction* **18**(6): 528–536.

Holt, N.L., K.A. Tamminen, L.N. Tink and D.E. Black (2009) "An Interpretive Analysis of Life Skills Associated with Sport Participation". *Qualitative Research in Sport and Exercise* **1**(2): 160–175.

ILO (International Labour Organization) (2020a) *Youth and COVID-19: Impact on Jobs, Education, Rights and Mental Well-being*. Geneva: ILO.

ILO (2020b) *Global Employment Trends for Youth: Technology and the Future of Jobs*. Geneva: ILO.

Kokolakakis, T., L. Edmondson, S.P. Kung and R. Storey (2020) *Resourcing the Sustainability and Recovery of the Sport Sector during the Coronavirus Pandemic*. London: Commonwealth Secretariat.

Lindsey, I. and T. Chapman (2017) *Enhancing the Contribution of Sport to the SDGs*. London: Commonwealth Secretariat.

McMahon, S. and J. Belur (2013) *Sports-Based Programmes and Reducing Youth Violence and Crime*. London: Project Oracle Children and Youth Evidence Hub.

Mustufa, M. (2016) "Sierra Leone's National Sports for Development and Peace Strategy". Case Study submitted for the Eighth Commonwealth Sports Ministers Meeting.

Nichols, G. (2007) *Sport and Crime Reduction: The Role of Sports in Tackling Youth Crime*. London: Routledge.

Republic of Namibia (2017) "The Fifth National Development Plan 2017/18 – 2021/22: Working Together Towards Prosperity". Windhoek: National Planning Commission.

Roetert, E.P., T.S. Ellenbecker and D. Kriellaars (2018) "Physical Literacy: Why Should We Embrace This Construct?" *British Journal of Sports Medicine* **52**(20): 1291–1292.

Schulenkorf, N., E. Sherry and K. Rowe (2016), "Sport for Development: An Integrated Literature Review". *Journal of Sport Management* **30**: 22–39.

Singh, S., D. Roy, K. Sinha, S. Parveen et al (2020) "Impact of COVID-19 and Lockdown on Mental Health of Children and Adolescents: A Narrative Review with Recommendations". *Psychiatry Research* 293.

Theis, N., N. Campbell, J. De Leeuw, M. Ownen and K. Schenke (2021) "The Effects of COVID-19 Restrictions on Physical Activity and Mental Health of Children and Young Adults with Physical and/or Intellectual Disabilities". *Disability Health* 101064.

Woods, D., G. Breslin and D. Hassan (2017) "Positive Collateral Damage or Purposeful Design: How Sport-Based Interventions Impact the Psychological Well-Being of People in Prison". *Mental Health and Physical Activity* **13**: 152–162.

WHO (World Health Organization) (2020) "Physical Activity". 26 November. https://www.who.int/news-room/fact-sheets/detail/physical-activity

Zuckerman, M. (1991) "Sensation Seeking: The Balance between Risk and Reward", in Lipsitt, L. and L. Mitnick (eds) *Self Regulatory Behavior and Risk Taking: Causes and Consequences*. Norwood, NJ: v

Education, Training and the Future of Work

06

Chapter 6

Education, Training and the Future of Work

6.1 Introduction

Young people are often the focus of most human capital development policies and programmes around the world. Investments in education, training and employment schemes represent significant investments in young people. However, how do policies and programmes need to shift so as to fully equip young people for a changing world and society?

This chapter explores this question by drawing on two guest contributions that offer perspectives on preparing young people for the world of work. The first contribution proposes reimagining work in a way that will secure decent work for young people in the context of an increasingly digitalised economy. The second reflects on the experiences of a network of employers that has built partnerships to support skills development for young people, including in response to the disruptions of the COVID-19 pandemic. We also highlight three youth awardees who are creating positive change in the education and training spheres.

Guest Contributor

Youth Education and Employment in the Digital Economy

Swartz and Krish Chetty, Human Sciences Research Council, South Africa

Decent work, digitisation and disruption

Key development goals for young people have included access to education, improving completion rates, minimising the gender gap in educational attainment and keeping a watchful eye on those neither in educational institutions nor in employment. Also of importance has been the potential of well-educated, healthy, youthful populations, especially in developing countries, to bring about increased prosperity for their countries – the so-called "demographic dividend" resulting from the "youth bulge." At the 2018 Commonwealth Heads of Government Meeting, it was agreed to provide the opportunity for at least 12 years of quality education and learning for girls and boys by 2030, by investing in skilled motivated and supportive teachers, educational facilities, and focusing on education reforms.

While these remain key commitments, more recently a focus on the world of work, after formal education, has emerged. This is especially geared towards the future of work for young people, given the technological digitisation underway, and of course the disruption caused by the ongoing global COVID-19 pandemic. What advocates have remained adamant about, and rightly so, is the need for decent and dignified work – how it should be defined and measured, the need to include those frequently marginalised and where to find new opportunities for a growing global population.

This contribution reviews Youth Development Index (YDI) trends given the digitisation of work and its impact on how jobs are valued in a post-COVID world. In describing the application of what we call "a refracted economies framework," we connect the decent work and digital inclusion agendas for young people. We further show how this framework supports the aspirations of young people and increases their ability to navigate disruption.

The disruption caused by the COVID-19 pandemic

COVID-19 has of course caused untold disruption to livelihoods, as communities and countries have locked down, closing businesses and limiting people's movement. The pandemic has also offered opportunities to reflect upon which occupations are essential for countries and communities' continued operation and survival. Formerly marginalised and low-paid professions have become highly valued for their essential service. The pandemic has fast-tracked our reliance on digital communication, business and retail technologies, and centred the need for pervasive digitisation (Kramer and Kramer, 2020; Shin et al., 2020; Sirt, 2020). As our online meetings have soared, so our need to be physically present across international borders has diminished. Those who are "digital natives" have been able to "work from anywhere" – but, for those who are not, the rapid transition has exposed our economies' stark digital divide (Lee, 2020; van Deursen, 2020).

The "digital natives" indicator

This divide is neatly portrayed in the 2020 YDI's digital natives indicator, which measures young people's skills and online engagement. In 2013, young people in a developed nation such as Canada (90 per cent) scored 10 times higher than those in a developing country such as Uganda (9 per cent), exposing the stark differences across the Commonwealth. In countries like Uganda, weaknesses in digital access, experience and skills contribute to comparatively poor education performance and higher unemployment levels

Guest Contributor

among young people (S4YE, 2018; Steele, 2020). These inequalities are likely to widen without targeted digitisation interventions. The YDI's digital natives indicator shines a spotlight on areas that require the greatest and most urgent intervention (Baimuratova and Dolgova, 2018; Chetty et al., 2018). Such a chasm between young people in developing and developed nations is less visible if one concentrates on general development indicators such as literacy. As the YDI shows, general literacy in the Commonwealth's developing countries ranges between 85 and 98 per cent. These are much more acceptable than the digital skill and online engagement rates, as described through the digital natives indicator.

Without a doubt, this indicator demands that attention be given in development priorities towards digital concerns in a post-COVID world. As the world's dependency on the digital economy deepens, a nation's digital capital, inclusive of its digital competencies and resources, will prove to carry similar weight in determining young people's employability (Digital Work Research, 2018, Ragnedda and Ruiu, 2020). Like other capitals, digital capital drives social mobility, providing opportunities to access networks, institutions and livelihoods.

Youth unemployment rates and disruption

Global unemployment rates for young people average at around 14 per cent, with young women disproportionately affected. In the Global South, unemployment rates are highest in Latin America, North Africa and pockets of Southern Africa, and lowest in Asian countries (Elder and Rojas, 2015). Furthermore, according to the United Nations (2018), those young people in the Global South who are employed are mainly to be found in the informal economy (roughly 60 per cent), without social protections such as unemployment insurance, sick leave, safety regulations or decent wages (ILO, 2018). These jobs are also mainly to be found in traditional economic sectors, such as agriculture, rather than in modern economic sectors, such as information and communication technology (ICT) (ILO, 2013).

It is important to note that both informal and formal workers can be employers of others, be employees, work alone for their own account or work in a family business. The International Labour Organization (ILO) classifies any family members working in a business without a formal contract as informal workers. These definitions are important since there has been an increasing divide between formal and informal work, so-called skilled vs. unskilled, salaried vs. entrepreneurial, permanent vs. gig, sustainable vs. unsustainable – with the former valorised and the latter vilified by both young people and the adults who guide them. Similarly, many of these descriptors are viewed as static binaries instead of as being ends of a spectrum along which one can move. These binaries obscure definitions of, opportunities for, and hindrances to decent and dignified work.

The Decent Work agenda

Promoting decent and dignified work is the ILO's core policy, placing people at the centre of development. The Decent Work agenda lies at the heart of the United Nations' sustainable and inclusive growth strategy and is encapsulated within Sustainable Development Goal (SDG) 8 on decent work and economic growth. The ILO describes decent work in the context of human aspirations, arguing in favour of equality, fair incomes, job security, social protection, opportunities for development and freedom to participate in decision-making (ILO, 2005). This agenda has gained prominence since it was found that human aspirations were becoming increasingly eroded in several professions. In contrast, a, hopeful and fulfilling working environment not only was a laudable moral aim but also boosted economic productivity.

As countries attempt to achieve the 2030 SDG targets, there is a need to redesign how labour structures are organised to ensure the principles of decent work are embedded in our international economic system. For instance, the ILO's International Standard Classification of Occupations (ISCO), adopted in 2008, refers to "non-standard forms" of work (ILO, 2017). This broad term does not distinguish between informal

work that is temporary, task-based, part-time or self-employed (ILO, 2016). The framework, which is used to quantify occupation and employment trends, effectively excludes a large portion of the workforce from labour statistics, impeding a government's ability to respond to emerging trends of precariousness, unemployment or under-employment (Schmid, 2010; OECD, 2020).

Furthermore, the ISCO framework is unresponsive to the needs of workers and governments – particularly the demand for work to adhere to principles of decency, and to measure the drivers of un- and under-employment (Sengenberger, 2011). During 2020, such a framework could have helped quantify occupations providing essential services during the global pandemic but traditionally underappreciated. Often, it was the essential worker who assumed the greatest risks during the lockdown but who received the least social protection (Szpejna and Kennedy, 2020). In this instance, our current ILO data collection framework denies us an opportunity to define the scale of these experiences.

To return decency to work is to recognise the dignity inherent in the jobs people perform (Liszcz, 2017). One way to achieve this is to reimagine work and reclassify how it is described. This addresses the imperative for work to be decent, but has the added bonus of presenting an opportunity to think about disruption (through technology or pandemic) and digitisation across a broader range of possibilities than previously imagined.

Reimagining work through a new prism

In our recent work, we have proposed a potential framework to replace the traditional occupational classification system. Using an extended metaphor of light passing through a prism, we describe a refracted economies framework, with colour-coded descriptions of various occupations, professions and sectors, that has the potential to ignite young people's imagination with regard to opportunities for decent work, work with dignity, new forms of work and work in contexts of disruption. Such a framework does not distinguish binaries of formality and informality, skilled and unskilled, etc. but rather describes livelihoods based on their contribution to human development along a wide spectrum. Historically, the status of all professions is not recognised equitably. The doctor and the domestic worker both make valued contributions to society but, under our current employment classification frameworks, the doctor is recognised while the cleaner remains invisible. They both could be said to form part of "the helping professions" or what we term "the lavender economy".

We are not the first to label clusters of jobs or professions with a label of a particular colour. Many of us have heard of "the green economy" (Stroebel,

Guest Contributor

2015) – work that conserves the environment and produces sustainable energy – or "the blue economy" (Keen et al., 2018) – work utilising water resources. Some may have heard of "the orange economy" (Restrepo and Marquez, 2013) – work in the creative, cultural and leisure activities (sport, music, drama, art and film, for example). But what if we extended this characterisation to include other colours such as "the lavender economy" – those in the helping and caring professions, including the medical doctor, the dog walker and the domestic worker in the same category? What about "the yellow economy" – work in the public service and for social good, including that done by both civil servants and community workers?

The list could be extended to include "the bronze economy" (industries that both cultivate and extract), "the silver economy" (those that manufacture, distribute and retail goods), "the teal economy" (jobs that develop, operate and maintain infrastructure); "the gold economy" (management of finance and assets) and "the platinum economy" (jobs that develop – rather than just use – information technology). Arguably, the list could also include "the red economy" – jobs that are criminal in nature, such as trading in illicit goods or services – and "the invisible economy" – work that goes unrecognised such as that done by women in the home or community.

Ultimately, it does not matter what names we give to each element of our taxonomy. Rather, what matters is that it allows us to develop an extensive map of the many industries, occupations, sectors and spaces in which young people might develop a livelihood. We also believe that characterising work in a new way, and in a way that traverses the usual boundaries, serves to engage young people to think differently about possible opportunities for their lives. A key aim is to broaden young people's imagination beyond professions that have conventionally been held in high esteem, and to inspire them to dream and strategise for a wide variety of jobs that are currently available and might emerge, and to do so at various stages of their lives. It also addresses the valorised-vilified problem described earlier whereby jobs are seen as static and in opposition to each other rather than as on a spectrum, between the two ends of which movement is possible in gradual increments.

Collecting disparate hierarchically esteemed work into common economies makes it possible to embark on any livelihood with a sense of pride and self-esteem. For example, an unpaid home-based care-giver living in poor conditions, working in the informal sector, is not recognised in the standard occupation classification system. However, this worker has developed skills and offers a valuable service to the recipients of their care. The care-giver operates within the lavender economy, dedicated to helping and caring, in the same segment grouping as doctors and social workers. This structure opens new pathways for the erstwhile informal or unrecognised care-giver's career trajectory and is vital for young people who wish to determine their career opportunities.

A taxonomy also expands what it might mean to be an entrepreneur and shows how entrepreneurship could operate in multiple ways in each of the spheres described above. Young people should imagine the possibilities of being an orange economy entrepreneur as much as of being a gold or blue economy entrepreneur. By doing so, more young people may both attempt and succeed at innovation. By mapping these career pathways, we can answer the call from young people participating in the G20's Youth 20 Summit in 2020. This group was particularly concerned by workplace and labour disruptions resulting from COVID-19 and technology-induced changes, and they seek clear pathways for young people to find productive jobs (Y20, 2020).

Redesigning work with a digital future in mind

Every sector within the economy is susceptible to technological change. The COVID-19 pandemic has proven how quickly traditional business models can change. For instance, the hospitality industry has been forced to redefine its business model in the face of stringent lockdown regulations. Restaurants able to integrate into online platforms have been able to serve customers through food delivery systems, while those that ignored the change struggled to remain open in 2020 (Deloitte, 2020). Successful businesses have managed to integrate technology into their business model. The same is true for all employers.

Table 6.1 New work opportunities based on technological advancement

Refracted economy	Type of jobs	Examples of technology-based work opportunities
Orange	Creative, cultural and leisure activities	3-D printed designs Non-fungible tokens Online market places
Green	Energy and environmental conservation	Solar and wind energy installations Recycling through smart tagging
Blue	Utilising water resources	Coastal tourism promoted through platforms Sustainable sourcing and sales of seafood
Lavender	Helping and caring	On-demand platform work
Yellow	Social sector and public service	Educational technologies Blockchain
Bronze	Cultivation and extraction	Smart farming through Internet of Things (IoT) applications
Silver	Manufacturing, distribution and consumption	Online retail
Teal	Developing, operating and maintaining infrastructure	IoT applications linked to construction projects
Gold	Managing finance and assets	FinTech applications
Platinum	Information technology	X-tech (new innovations)
Red	Criminal pursuits	Cybercrime
Invisible	Unrecognised work	Electronic human rights abuse reporting

Frye (2019) calls for innovative thinking to respond to the impact of technological change on the labour market. The refracted economies framework provides an innovative basis to conceptualise the economy, given its economic segmentation and recognition of each profession's fluid characteristics. Table 6.1 describes a few examples of new work opportunities that have emerged from recent technology advancements, which young people may feel are worth pursuing in future. Depending on one's digital capital, many of these new jobs become accessible (Bannykh, 2020). Furthermore, technology also helps provide care-givers and other informal workers with new opportunities to find work by connecting them with potential employers/clients.

A new paradigm for career guidance

None of this new imagining of pathways and opportunities will be possible without a redesigned approach to career guidance in schools, higher education institutions and community-based youth development programmes. We already know

that career guidance has the potential to improve young people's job prospects (Veal and Dunbar, 2018), but if we want young people's vision of the future of work to expand then career guidance must change. The G20's Youth Summit resolution includes a recommendation for governments to invest in online career navigation and mentoring hubs, using technology to broadly mediate career guidance across borders (Y20, 2020). In the Caribbean, the International Youth Foundation found that career guidance was particularly valuable for impoverished youth, who must overcome several social barriers before accessing a productive job. The Centre for Adolescent Renewal and Care found that, with several non-directive inputs from multidisciplinary career counsellors, young people were more likely to develop their own opinion about a suitable path (International Youth Foundation, 2013). Luken (2019) further notes that, often, guidance counsellors unintentionally introduce their personal biases when advising students. This almost always closes rather than expands possibilities for young people, especially when there is a generational divide between the counsellor who

Guest Contributor

only has experience in traditional job classifications and the young person thinking about the future of work in a new technologically disrupted paradigm. Luken (2019) argues that the sector is overdue for a paradigm overhaul that recognises recent innovations and disruptions in the working world, with its associated redefinition of jobs.

The refracted economies framework offers such a paradigm shift for career guidance. Opportunities in each refracted economy can be identified and anticipated, and pathways mapped out, despite ever-moving terrain. Career progressions can be described, not using the antiquated metaphor of a ladder but by thinking about a journey. Included in this journey is a commitment to life-long learning and to adaptability to disruption and change. These trends require a new cadre of specialised contemporary career guidance workers (OECD, 2019) who understand the labour market's changing dynamics. Critical too, is the ability to understand and communicate (and anticipate) how ICT usage articulates with each work opportunity in every refracted economy (Jayaram et al., 2013). The refracted economies framework provides career guidance specialists with a basis to plot potential career paths within a specific economy. Assuming the worker can develop a base of transferrable knowledge about a particular refracted economy, career guidance specialists can identify the logical career paths a worker could follow. The counsellor could also advise the student about appropriate training to improve their employment chances. They could also easily introduce conversations about dignity and decency into colour-coded economies that include a wide array of livelihoods like doctor and domestic worker (lavender); basket weaver and rock star (orange); waste picker and solar cell manufacturer (green); youth worker and parliamentarian (yellow); and construction worker and civil engineer (teal).

Ensuring integrated digital training in a post-COVID world

The influence of the COVID-19 pandemic on society has emphasised the centrality of digital skills in the workplace. The pandemic could accelerate the use of technology in the workplace, rapidly redefining jobs (Chernoff and Warman, 2017). All

segments of the economy could experience a form of digital disruption. Digital skills are essential because they can be transferable to a new context, where the technology is in use. The Organisation for Economic Co-operation and Development (OECD) recommends that training programmes integrate ICT skills into their curricula, as these are necessary skills and tools for learning. Access to digital infrastructure must be supplemented with appropriate training to ensure students learn how to apply the tools in multiple contexts (OECD, 2016).

Workers will require transferable skills that can be applied in different contexts. Basic digital literacy provides a worker with the ability to transition between jobs, as they have the means to use their digital skills in a new context (Beblavý et al., 2016). The European Commission has found that 90 per cent of workplaces in Europe now require basic digital skills. It recommends expanding digital awareness, digital skills and access to technology programmes to respond to these changes. There is also a call to address the digital divide to ensure equality of opportunities (European Commission, 2017). A key point common in studies is that workers must apply their domain-specific skills using ICT tools. Beyond acquiring digital skills, digital capital and other capital forms are vital for young people to achieve their aspirations. These capitals are vital for developing agency, helping young people advance from their current states of adversity to realise equalised opportunities as they enter the labour market (Swartz, 2021).

Beyond digital skills and capital, the general skills relevant to each thematic segment of the economy must be identified across all refracted economies. These skills will be transferable, allowing people to move between jobs. They must include familiarity with and access to various platforms, and the ability to navigate basic and changing forms of electronic communication and transactions. The European Commission differentiates between basic skills, generic skills, key skills/competencies/qualifications and employability skills (European Commission, 2011). All will require attention. The YDI introduces an interesting comparative indicator that contrasts young people's experiences – those not in any education, employment and training

(NEET) in developed and developing countries. Training develops basic, generic and key skills, which is crucial in securing formal work opportunities. For example, in the UK and Australia between 2010 and 2018, the NEET indicator decreased by between 21 and 23 per cent. In contrast, in developing countries like Uganda and Ghana, the NEET indicator rose by between 130 and 175 per cent. This trend emphasises the difficulties developing countries experience in growing their skills base.

Given how crucial these skills are, this trend suggests that developing countries require some support in implementing training programmes. In future, the YDI would benefit from disaggregated skills indicators that distinguish between basic and generic skills levels. Such data could help assess how prepared the workforce is to transfer their skills across knowledge domains along the spectrum of a refracted economies framework; and in so doing to move into increasingly dignified and decent work.

Guest Contributor

Lessons Learnt from Apprenticeship Programmes

The Global Apprenticeship Network

The GAN is a global, business-driven alliance through which private sector companies, employer federations, international organisations and thought leaders work together to shape agile and responsive workforce development using work-based learning as a key driver. It seeks to influence by leveraging the expertise of its founding partners, the International Organisation of Employers (IOE), the ILO, the OECD and Business at OECD (BIAC), and the practical experience of our company members.

We build knowledge and inspire action by sharing real-world examples of effective work-based learning approaches that are being implemented by companies large and small across diverse sectors around the globe. Together with our members and partners, we implement initiatives that help remove barriers and create opportunities for work-based learning in 16 countries around the world, where the GAN has networks. We facilitate dialogue on promising and tested approaches related to work-based learning and apprenticeships by companies and governments.

Our work focuses on four key pillars:

1. Policy advocacy and analysis to create and shape enabling policy frameworks at a global and local level;

2. Amplifying the private sector voice in the space of employment and education;

3. Thought leadership, based on active project implementation; and

4. Peer-to-peer learning between networks, members and partner organisations to ensure innovation and to close the jobs and skills mismatch.

Responses to COVID-19 and beyond

The importance of the GAN's strategic focus is amplified by the current disruptions being caused by COVID-19. The crisis has renewed and strengthened the need for a private sector-led skilling and employment-linked initiative that gave rise to the GAN's inception in 2013.

The extensive disruptions over the past year have emphasised the need for agile workforces with skills that can respond to changes in the world of work, as well as for an urgent response to the disruptive effects on youth employment opportunities. The GAN's value-added has been demonstrated: as a unique organisation that convenes public and private sector partners to drive evidence-based action, our members and partners have responded rapidly to the challenges and opportunities that the changing times are presenting.

A focus has been on the creation of enabling environments to take the world through COVID-19 and beyond, built on collaboration, an openness to learning (even among business leaders and policy-makers) and recognition that the current systems need to be updated to respond to effective fundamental shifts in the labour market.

Our projects

In 2016, GAN Global received a grant from the US Department of Labor (USDOL) to implement a project entitled "Promoting Apprenticeship as a Path for Youth Employment in Argentina, Costa Rica, and Kenya through GAN National Networks." The project was primarily designed to create sustainable GAN Networks in Argentina, Costa Rica and Kenya to promote work-based learning (WBL) opportunities for vulnerable and marginalised

youth in these three countries, as a complement to other USDOL-funded projects promoting youth employment. The direct beneficiaries were businesses and institutions involved in advocacy for and the creation of WBL programmes. USDOL project funds contributed directly to the development of GAN Argentina and its mandate, which includes research, capacity-building and policy advocacy.

The Labour Integration Programme in Buenos Aires, Argentina

In 2019, GAN Argentina funded a study to evaluate the Labour Integration Programme (PIL) implemented by the Centre for Entrepreneurship and Labour Development (CEDEL) of the Government of the Autonomous City of Buenos Aires, in Argentina. The PIL involved a series of actions to improve employment possibilities for Villa 31 neighbourhood residents by connecting them to formal employment opportunities within local companies. It provided residents with essential training to facilitate their employment search process (Job Orientation Workshop, Transfer of Learning (TOL)) while also approaching formally established companies operating in areas relatively close to neighbourhood residents in order to assess their labour demands and connect job-seekers with available opportunities.

The goal of the study was to evaluate the programme and generate information to reinforce the training, inclusion and monitoring processes of populations participating in employment promotion activities in deprived neighbourhoods. The study sought to understand the benefits for participating

companies, based on the experience with CEDEL, along with the perceptions, experiences and reviews of the neighbourhood residents who had participated in the PIL. The results also contributed to a practical guide that contains recommendations for replicating and implementing a labour inclusion project that will be applicable to other contexts.

Between July 2018 and June 2019, a total of 1,692 people approached CEDEL with the aim of obtaining formal employment unrelated to the construction sector. Their socio-demographic profiles were heterogeneous; however, women and young people dominated. Only half of those who approached the project completed the TOL workshop, and significant differences were observed according to their level of education: the higher the participant's level of education, the higher the TOL completion rate.

Of those who completed the TOL, approximately 16 per cent obtained formal employment within two months. This percentage was higher among men than women (20 per cent vs. 13 per cent), among those who had completed secondary education (17 per cent vs. 10 per cent) and among Argentinean nationals (15 per cent for Argentineans vs. 10 per cent for Peruvians).

Guest Contributor

An important factor to take into account, given its influence on CEDEL's programme, is that this study was carried out at a time of economic stagnation and low levels of employment in Argentina. In other words, the general economic context did not favour employment promotion programmes or policies. Thus, the recruitment that took place was aimed predominantly at placing participants in temporary positions (substitutions, absences, specific workforce needs).

Companies and participants alike rated their experience with CEDEL highly. For companies, the particular aspects that stood out regarding their experience with the programme were the following: (i) the fact that the workers lived near the workplace improved accessibility; (ii) the training given to the workers improved their soft skills; (iii) CEDEL's policy of following up with workers placed in positions improved retention and quality; and (iv) the contact with CEDEL was direct and smooth, and CEDEL was willing to provide support.

An important aspect of the programme was that the individuals implementing it for CEDEL had previous work experience within human resource departments in private companies. This had provided them with a clearer understanding of the logic and methods of the recruitment process. Furthermore, it facilitated interactions with companies based on both personal knowledge and professional trust.

Neighbourhood participants valued the following aspects of the programme:

- The training they received during the TOL improved their skills and their understanding of expectations in a formal work setting.

- The job interview advice was helpful even in their independent job searches.

- The mentoring and support they received from the work team was beneficial.

Another significant positive aspect participants highlighted was that their experience with CEDEL had provided them with opportunities to interview for positions in formal private companies and government offices (and, in some cases, to become employed by these entities). These individuals believed that, without CEDEL's support, connections and implicit endorsement of job-seekers in the programme, they would have experienced difficulties accessing these opportunities, and might not even have been considered owing to the discrimination surrounding the employment of Villa 31 inhabitants.

For similar programmes in the future, companies expressed the following:

- The need for more refined calibration between the profiles requested by the companies and those proposed by the programme;

- The relevance of providing more advanced training in soft skills; and

- The need to include more local companies in the programme in order to increase employment rates.

Programme participants identified the following aspects for improvement in the future:

- Further training geared towards specific job roles;

- Greater control and/or reliable information regarding the working conditions being offered by the companies (a significant number of participants did not agree with the working conditions and wages); and

- Support for dealing with the frustration caused by unsuccessful interviews.

Digital skilling project funded by Microsoft Philanthropies

Since August 2020, in alignment with Microsoft and LinkedIn's recommendations for an inclusive economic recovery from the effects of the pandemic, and as part of its Global Skilling Initiative, the GAN has received funding for the Skills for Employability project promoting the digital skilling of the most underserved groups in Australia, Colombia and New Zealand, with a special focus on girls and women.

Our initiative seeks to offer access to digital skilling for 2,500 people with the promotion and uptake of the Microsoft learning tools made available for free. Where possible, we will build the capacities of identified select groups by forging meaningful and solid partnerships with relevant local stakeholders. Out of the total 2,500 beneficiaries, the GAN has committed to 50 per cent female representation, with more disaggregated data for targets in each of the project countries.

To date, the project teams at GAN Global and the country networks have focused on creating a strong understanding of project country contexts through the finalisation of two main research activities:

- 16 GAN Network situational assessments: The situational assessments focus on unpacking the skills development frameworks, particularly looking at vocational education and apprenticeship training-related initiatives in each country. The documents also reflect an analysis of the WBL situation in each of the countries where the GAN counts on the presence and operations of the GAN Networks. The analysis of the skills landscape ensures that projects can be tailored to the needs of the local policy context as well as the very specific labour market demands.

- Project country digital skills assessments (GAN Australia, GAN Colombia, GAN New Zealand/ GAN Global with a supporting role): All three project countries have finalised a research process aimed at producing comprehensive, practical national analyses that help in determining the existing supply of a digitally skilled cohort at national level, assessing skills demand from the industry, identifying skills gaps and developing recommendations and possible approaches to address future digital skills requirements and ensure equal access and training opportunities for all.

Key findings from Australia and New Zealand are as follows:

- Social inclusion should be a consideration for all stakeholders working across initiatives to expand and enhance access to digital technology, and for those delivering skills training. Evaluation of programmes and the rollout of technology should specifically reference the effects on disadvantaged groups (Australia).

- Foundation-level digital skills training must be delivered in accessible formats for those without basic digital skills; online training is appropriate only once a baseline of skills has been developed. In general, there is a need for digital skills to be contextualised to specific roles that can be achieved through greater nuance in the design of training for digital competency development (Australia).

- Digital skills training can exist within both formal qualifications and non-accredited training. Government digital skilling policy should create an ecosystem in which training providers can implement new models of qualification and accreditation (Australia).

- Systemic barriers in education have exacerbated the lack of formal or systematic "earn and learn" options in the sector. This could be resolved through the current vocational education reforms but will equally critically rely on employer engagement and behaviour change (New Zealand).

- Given the multi-year nature of most post-secondary qualifications, there will always be a time lag between what is learnt and what is applied in industry. Therefore, to support lifelong learning and improve skills matching, enterprise partners must help with the work readiness of graduates and reskill those already in the workforce or who have been excluded in the past for whatever reason (New Zealand).

Policy recommendations

It is clear from the work done by GAN Global to date that there are several policy actions that countries can take to address the issue of workforce development, WBL and inclusive vocational education strategies:

- Strategies can be developed that focus on accelerating workforce inclusion, particularly in response to the impact (positive and negative) of trends related to the Future of Work.

Guest Contributor

- Alignment needs to be ensured between skills development and vocational education and training policy and the needs of the labour market. Policies must consider current needs as well as anticipating future skills trends.

- Policy-makers need to ensure that labour market policies, along with developments in education and training frameworks, address the long-term impact of COVID-19 on socioeconomic systems.

6.2 Youth taking charge of Education

Three finalists in the 2021 Commonwealth Youth Awards were recognised for work that contributes to the attainment of SDG 4 on quality education. We highlight their work here to encourage and give inspiration to plans to further invest in youth-led initiatives.

Siena Castellon from the UK is Founder of Neurodiversity Celebration Week, an initiative designed to encourage schools and colleges to change the way they perceive autistic students and students with learning differences. In addition to providing practical advice on overcoming challenges at school, the programme provides free resources to help teachers better support neurodiverse students. The 2020 programme reached over 850 schools and more than 500,000 students across the world, and the online mentoring programme currently has over 1,000 global subscribers.

Taahir Bulbulia from Barbados is Founder of the Sports Science Society, a student-based organisation that promotes the holistic benefits of sport and provides mentorship to at-risk youth on mental health, sports law and drug prevention. The programme has trained 30 volunteers across 10 organisations and reached 500 young people in the Caribbean region, particularly helping tackle bullying and mental health issues.

Dawsher Charles is taking charge through Survival Scholars, a project she founded in Trinidad and Tobago that promotes self-care, good mental health and wellbeing among at-risk and disadvantaged youth through workshops on social and emotional learning skills, the arts and storytelling. The project has reached over 6,000 young people and parents and equipped youths with stressor coping mechanisms for school and life, particularly during the COVID-19 pandemic.

References

Baimuratova, L. and O. Dolgova (2018) "Digital Literacy for the Economy of the Future". https://nafi.ru/upload/iblock/8f0/8f019c7e455b141dd16f56a1a926bdd0.pdf

Bannykh, G. (2020) "Digital Capital and the Labor Market: Factors of Mutual Influence". *Advances in Economics, Business and Management Research* **128**: 2946–2953.

Beblavý, M., B. Fabo and K. Lenaerts (2016) "Demand for Digital Skills in the US Labour Market: The IT Skills Pyramid". CEPS Special Report 154. https://papers.ssrn.com/sol3/papers.cfm?abstract_id=3047102

Chernoff, A. W. and C. Warman (2017) "COVID-19 and Implications for Automation". Working Paper 27249. Boston, MA: NBER.

Chetty, K., Q. Liu, G. Nozibele, J. Jaya et al (2018) "Bridging the Digital Divide: Measuring Digital Literacy". *Economics E-Journal* **12**(23). http://www.economics-ejournal.org/economics/journalarticles/2018-23

Deloitte (2020) "The Future of Hospitality – Uncovering Opportunities to Recover and Thrive in the New Normal". https://www2.deloitte.com/content/dam/Deloitte/ca/Documents/consumer-industrial-products/ca-future-of-hospitality-pov-aoda-en.pdf

Digital Work Research (2018) "The Digital Workplace Skills Framework Ensuring the Workforce Is Ready to Work Digitally". https://digitalworkresearch.com/wp-content/uploads/2018/08/The-Digital-Workplace-Skills-Framework-final.pdf

Elder, S. and G. Rojas (2015). *Global employment trends for youth 2015: Scaling up investments in decent jobs for youth*. Geneva, Switzerland: International Labour Organization.

European Commission (2011) *Transferability of Skills across Economic Sectors*. Brussels: European Commission.

European Commission (2017) *ICT for Work: Digital Skills in the Workplace*. Brussels: European Commission.

Frye, I. (2019) Jobless and Hopeless: Drastic Times Call for Drastic Measures, Studies in Poverty and Inequality Institute, 17 May. https://spii.org.za/jobless-and-hopeless-drastic-times-call-for-drastic-measures/

ILO (International Labour Organization) (2005) "Youth: Pathways to Decent Work – Promoting Youth Employment – Tackling the Challenge". International Labour Conference, 93rd Session, Geneva. https://www.ilo.org/youthmakingithappen/PDF/rep-vi_en.pdf

ILO (2013). *Global employment trends for youth: A generation at risk*. Geneva: ILO. https://www.ilo.org/wcmsp5/groups/public/---dgreports/---dcomm/documents/publication/wcms_212423.pdf

ILO (2016) *Non-Standard Employment around the world – Understanding Challenges, Shaping Prospects*. Geneva: ILO.

ILO (2017) *Global Employment Trends for Youth 2017 – Paths to a Better Working Future*. Geneva: ILO.

ILO (2018). *Women and men in the informal economy: A statistical picture (Third edition)*. Geneva: ILO. https://www.ilo.org/global/publications/books/WCMS_626831/lang--en/index.htm

International Youth Foundation (2013) "Preparing Youth for the 21st Century Workplace". Career Guidance Case Study. Baltimore: International Youth Foundation.

Jayaram, S., T. Hill and D. Plaut (2013) *Training Models for Employment in the Digital Economy*. Washington, DC: R4D.

Keen, M., A. Schwarz and L. Wini-Simeon (2018) "Towards Defining the Blue Economy: Practical Lessons from Pacific Ocean Governance". *Marine Policy* **88**: 333–341.

Kramer, A. and K. Z. Kramer (2020) "The Potential Impact of the Covid-19 Pandemic on Occupational Status, Work from Home, and Occupational Mobility". *Journal of Vocational Behavior* **119**: 1–4.

Lee, N. T. (2020) "What the Coronavirus Reveals about the Digital Divide between Schools and Communities". Brookings blog, 17 March. www.brookings.edu/blog/techtank/2020/03/17/what-the-coronavirus-reveals-about-the-digital-divide-between-schools-and-communities/

Liszcz, T. (2017) "Human Work: A Commodity or an Ethical Value". *Ethnolinguistic* **28**(59): 63–84.

Luken, T. (2019) "Problems in Career Counselling". CareerWise by Ceric. https://careerwise.ceric.ca/2019/10/23/big-problems-in-career-counselling-and-a-possible-way-out/#.YILPIRMzYb1

OECD (Organisation for Economic Co-operation and Development) (2016) "Skills and Jobs in the Digital Economy", in *A Digital Economy Toolkit*. Paris: OECD, 269–297.

OECD (2019) *OECD Employment Outlook 2019*. Paris: OECD.

OECD (2020) *Tackling Coronavirus (COVID-19): Contributing to a Global Effort. Distributional Risks Associated with Non-Standard Work: Stylised Facts and Policy Considerations*. Paris: OECD.

Ragnedda, M. and M. L. Ruiu (2020) "Defining Digital Capital", in *Digital Capital*, 9–38. https://doi.org/10.1108/978-1-83909-550-420201002

Restrepo, F. and I. Marquez (2013) *The Orange Economy: An Infinite Opportunity*. Washington, DC: Inter-American Development Bank.

Schmid, G. (2010) "Non-Standard Employment and Labour Force Participation: A Comparative View of the Recent Development in Europe". Discussion Paper 5087. Bonn: IZA.

Sengenberger, W. (2011) *Beyond the Measurement of Unemployment and Underemployment: The Case for Extending and Amending Labour Market Statistics*. Geneva: ILO.

Shin, M., S. Li and X. Cheng (2020) "The Asian Tech Industry's Coronavirus Response: Now and the Future". Bain and Company, 17 March. https://www.bain.com/insights/asia-tech-industry-responds-to-coronavirus/

Sirt, T. (2020) "Coronavirus Forces Digital Transformation in Business World". Daily Sabah, 20 March. https://www.dailysabah.com/business/tech/coronavirus-forces-digital-transformation-in-business-world

S4YE (Solutions for Youth Employment) (2018) *Digital Jobs for Youth : Young Women in the Digital Economy*. Washington, DC: World Bank.

Steele, C. (2020) "The Impacts of Digital Divide". Digital Divide Council, 20 September. www.digitaldividecouncil.com/the-impacts-of-digital-divide/

Stroebel, M. (2015) "Tourism and the Green Economy: Inspiring or Averting Change?" *Third World Quarterly* **36** (12): 2225–2243.

Swartz, S. (2021) "Navigational Capacities for Southern Youth in Adverse Contexts", forthcoming in Swartz, S. et al (eds) *The Oxford Handbook of Global South Youth Studies*. New York: Oxford Scholarship.

Szpejna, M. and A. Kennedy (2020) "Mitigating the Employment and Social Effects of the COVID-19 Pandemic". EMPL in Focus. Brussels European Parliament.

UN (United Nations) (2018). World Youth Report. New York: United Nations. https://www.un.org/development/desa/youth/wp-content/uploads/sites/21/2018/12/WorldYouthReport-2030Agenda.pdf

Van Deursen, A. J. A. M. (2020) "Digital Inequality during a Pandemic: Quantitative Study of Differences in COVID-19-Related Internet Uses and Outcomes among the General Population". *Journal of Medical Internet Research* **22**(8): 1–13.

Veal, K. and M. Dunbar (2018) "How Career Guidance Can Improve Job Prospects for Young People". Development Asia, 10 January. https://development.asia/explainer/how-career-guidance-can-improve-job-prospects-young-people

Y20 (Youth 20) (2020) "Y20 Summit 2020 Communiqué". Al Khobar, 17 October. https://reports.youth20saudi.org/Y20_Communique.pdf

Opportunities for Youth in the Digital Economy

07

Chapter 7

Opportunities for Youth in the Digital Economy

Digital engagement and its connection to the world of work have increased in relevance in the past year, especially for young people. The recent period, associated with increasing levels of remote working as a result of the COVID-19 pandemic, has also revealed significant information and communication technology (ICT)-related inequalities across the global. The 2020 Youth Development Index (YDI) has acknowledged these trends and highlighted the significance of digital skills to positive youth development. The difference between the scores on the 2020 YDI digital natives indicator for the 10 highest- and the 10 lowest-ranked countries was substantial.

At the same time, it has been difficult to fully measure progress in young people's digital skills and engagement over time, since scores on digital natives in the YDI have remained constant (at just under 0.4 for the global score), because of the lack of globally comparable time series data. In addition, reliance on a single indicator is insufficient to guide discussion on challenges and opportunities for young people in the digital economy. This chapter, therefore, seeks to broaden the discussion by highlighting the ways in which young people are engaging in the digital economy and proposing features of an enabling environment required to sustain continued positive youth engagement in this sphere.

7.1 Building the policy foundation for young people to meaningfully participate in the digital economy[1]

Youth today are learning and entering the workforce at a time of significant change. The world is entering the Fourth Industrial Revolution, whose capacity for change and disruption is unlike that of any of the industrial revolutions before it. While each industrial revolution has fundamentally changed the world and each has been technology-based – the first used water and steam for mechanisation, the second saw the development of electricity and the rise of mass production and the third witnessed the development of electronics and computing for automation - the fourth is blurring the distinction between the digital and physical worlds. The result is that, although the technologies are at the core of the Fourth Industrial Revolution, it is the scope, speed and scale of the changes that set this revolution apart and are marking out for young people an entirely different world to that experienced by previous generations.

At the core of this change is the digitalisation of the economic system. As an ecosystem, the policies needed for the digital economy are broad. However, they can be divided into three broad policy areas. The first include digital enablers, such as digital

infrastructure, e-government, digital innovation, digital skills, digital financial services, data governance and digital trust. The second entail the sectoral digital policies that examine digital transformation in specific sectors such as trade, agriculture and fisheries. Finally, there are cross-sectoral policies and strategies, such as national development strategies and energy, financial and business environment policies, all of which act as precursors to successful delivery of any digital economy strategy.

The transition to digital economies presents new opportunities and threats. It has the potential to solve some of humanity's greatest challenges. At the same time, significant risk emerges if appropriate policy interventions are not put in place. Some risk assessments have identified youth disillusionment as one of the major societal short-term global risks, ranking not very far from climate, disease and livelihood risks (WEF, 2021). This risk arises from the danger that the Fourth Industrial Revolution will break the social contract and that future generations will not have the same opportunities for prosperity as those available to previous generations.

"Transition to digital economies has the potential to solve some of humanity's greatest challenges."

The dangers posed by this risk are heightened by the already precarious livelihoods of many young people. Although, globally, young people account for 40 per cent of the population, they account for 66 per cent of the global poor (World Bank, 2020). To prevent the Fourth Industrial Revolution from perpetuating or worsening these inequalities, youth-specific interventions that address their shared challenges are needed. Policy-makers should address three areas in particular.

7.1.1 The differential impact of the digital divide on different youth

First, policy-makers should consider how to ensure that no young person is left behind. COVID-19 has accelerated the use of digital technologies across both developed and emerging economies. However, at the same time, it has compounded existing inequalities. Prior to the pandemic, only half of the global population was online, and within this there were wide differences according to age, gender and location. These are the digital divides. They exist across several factors such as young vs old, male vs female, urban vs rural, living in a developing vs a developed economy.

On the most basic level, the data shows that young people have a high level of access to the internet. Within the Commonwealth, in line with global trends, young people aged between 15 and 25 are the most digitally connected demographic, with 67 per cent having access to the internet (Commonwealth Secretariat, 2020). However, policy-makers have to be careful not to then say that this is an area where interventions are not needed for young people. The data identifies only one characteristic – access to internet – but digital divide factors can nevertheless work together to compound disadvantage. So, for example, a young person in a rural area may have less access than older people within cities within that same country. The lesson for policy-makers is to avoid the assumption that young people are "digital natives."

The experience of youth will not be monolithic. As the YDI shows, less than 40 per cent of youth can be considered digital natives measured by internet use of five years or more.

It is particularly important when designing interventions to avoid assumptions of capacities and capabilities that will serve to reinforce this disenfranchisement. To avoid this, countries need to develop granular interventions for their youth populations, separating programmes targeted at different divides: (i) those with no access, (ii) those with access but with no use, (iii) those with use who are operating at a rudimentary level and (iv) digital natives. The latter can be used as a resource to train the former. Rwanda's Digital Ambassador Programme (DAP) is a good case study of such an approach (see Box 7.1).

7.1.2 Transitioning to lifelong skilling

Second, policy-makers should take targeted steps to provide youth with the opportunity to acquire future-relevant skills. An open question is what the world of work will look like in the coming decades, given the impact of technologies. It is clear that much change is taking place. Previous projections by the Commonwealth Secretariat have shown that, across the Commonwealth, 50,000 jobs will have to be

created daily to absorb the youth who are entering the workforce (Commonwealth Secretariat, 2020).

COVID-19 has ramped up the urgency of the need for a policy response that enables the development of future-ready skills. As Figure 7.1 shows, COVID-19 has disproportionately affected the livelihoods of young people, as more young people have become unemployed, or, more commonly, have stopped looking for work or delayed the start to their search for work. Building on the lessons from the 2008/09 global financial crisis, interventions are needed to ensure that the career prospects of these young people are not permanent damaged.

According to one approach, 85 per cent of the jobs available in the next decade have not yet been invented (Institute for the Future, 2017). As high as this seems, the experience of the past decade has shown the unexpected new occupations that technology can create. A decade ago, full-time jobs as YouTuber, influencer, social media manager, big data architect, crypto currency trader and Uber driver did not exist. Five years ago, blockchain analysis and machine learning engineering were nascent fields. In some cases, new jobs are the natural extension of a current field. In others, they represent a quantum leap from existing practices. Looking ahead 10 years, some

Box 7.1 Enhancing digital skills: Rwanda's Digital Ambassador Programme

The DAP aims to increase the digital literacy of 5 million Rwandans. It leverages young people and their knowledge of both technology and their communities so they can act as levers of change. These youth ambassadors provide trainings on basic digital literacy targeting those with low or no experience using the internet, as well as training on how to use e-government services. The programme also upskills Ambassadors by providing training on both hard and soft digital skills.

Several key features of the programme hold lessons for policy-makers considering similar interventions. First is that the programme sits within a clear and coherent policy ecosystem. The DAP is an implementation component of the national digital skills framework, the Digital Talent Policy, which itself sits within Rwanda's overall national digital transformation framework, the Smart Rwanda Master Plan. The lesson here lies in the importance of considering policies in a holistic manner.

Second, the programme leverages existing capabilities among the sub-category of young people who are more likely to be digital natives. Additionally, the programme is designed in a way that is responsive to sub-national conditions. The Ambassadors are from, and deployed at, the local level. This ensures that the training is as relevant as possible to community circumstances.

Finally, the programme embeds a gender balance in its Ambassadors: there is a 50-50 balance of women and men trainers in the proof of concept phase. This conscious decision by the Government of Rwanda has had follow-on impacts on results in terms of both female beneficiaries - 60 per cent of women entrepreneurs reported business expansion and improved profits – and their families – 58 per cent of women reported improved family outcomes.

Source: Digital Opportunity Trust (2019).

Figure 7.1 COVID-induced employment losses by sex and age as a share of the labour force

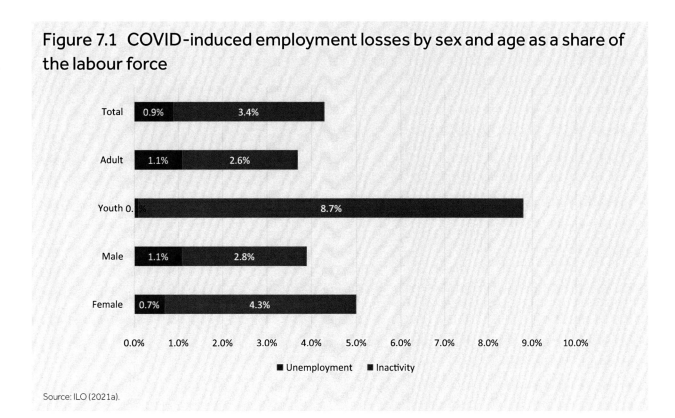

Source: ILO (2021a).

of these very new jobs may themselves already be replaced through automation. The challenge for both youth and policy-makers is not to prepare for one ideal job but to focus on the core skills that can be used across several jobs. These core skills will have to be identified on a national basis in light of the industries and value chains in which a country has positioned itself or is seeking to position itself.

Given the pace of change, policy-makers need to put an ecosystem in place that can manage these transitions. The ecosystem has to be designed so as to support constant transitions across jobs and fields. Supporting these transitions can make use of both monetary and non-monetary tools. On the monetary side, in the ideal scenario, governments would be able to provide financial support to bridge these transition gaps, such as through redefining the thresholds for unemployment support and subsidies to engage in lifelong learning during transitions, where the fiscal space exists.

However, again, as we have seen during the economic response to the COVID-19 pandemic, not all countries have the necessary fiscal space to provide this. In such instances, the non-monetary tools are even more important. Governments can support the transition by undertaking some straightforward interventions. So, for example, encouraging adoption of standardised

definitions of tasks that can be adopted across different jobs in different industries would increase the transferability of skills. Workers would know which skills prepare them for which range of jobs; in transition periods, this will help them identify the next job path or alternatively the skills gaps that they can undertake training for in that period to prepare them for the next job.

The pandemic has created differential experiences based on the nature of occupation. Remote working has been the preserve of workers in specific types of jobs where performance is not required in a specific place. Recent analysis of remote work during the pandemic confirms this: it shows that it is specific occupations - finance and insurance; management; professional, scientific and technical services – that have the highest potential for remote work without productivity loss (McKinsey Global Institute, 2020). Conversely, construction accommodation and food services and agriculture show the lowest potential for efficient remote work. However, it is not the case that it is only low-wage jobs that cannot be done remotely. The important caveat is in some human sciences, such as research and development (R&D) and health care.

At the moment, the challenge from automation is not that it is replacing entire jobs. A reliable estimate is that less than 5 per cent of current jobs are fully automatable (McKinsey Global Institute, 2017). These jobs involve repetitive physical work, and include factory jobs and customer interaction-based jobs such as food service work and office support. More difficult to replace entirely are creatives, technology professionals, teachers and care providers. To respond to this, what is taught and how it is taught need to change. Online safety skills are necessary and can be taught through, for example, digital citizenship programmes. Beyond this, there is a need to rebalance the thinking around education – on the kinds of subjects taught and the importance of methods of thinking vis-à-vis knowledge acquisition.

7.1.3 An innovation ecosystem to capture the value of young people's creations

Finally, digital natives and those youth who are online and have the appropriate digital skills will still need to be supported by an ecosystem that can help them innovate, turn that innovation into a viable business and be able to be rewarded for such innovation. The two core new business models in the digital economy - the sharing economy and the platform economy - are being driven disproportionately by youth as content creators or platform users. The relationship between youth and platforms is best expressed as this duality - platforms provide a broader social universe that allows

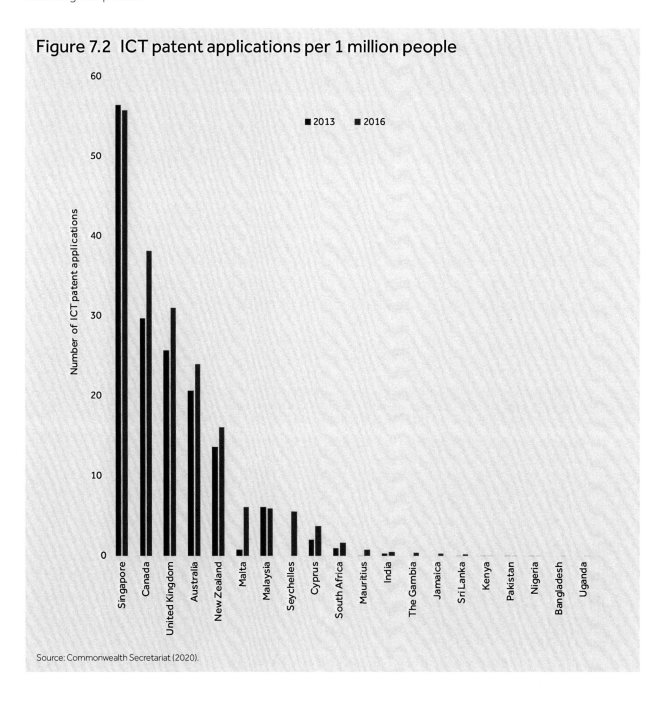

Figure 7.2 ICT patent applications per 1 million people

Source: Commonwealth Secretariat (2020).

for creation, collaboration, knowledge generation and awareness on a global scale while, at the same time, by virtue of the business models of platforms, the economic value that young people gain may not be commensurate with their role of creators and consumers.

There is a perception that the digital economy has widened the opportunity for individuals to become successful revenue-generating creators. Some youth in this category display remarkable skill and long-term planning, such as those who invest in accumulating followers whom they in turn monetise for advertisement and endorsement revenue. However, this, too, is subject to the intersectionality of the divides: it is overwhelmingly young people from developed countries who have been able to do this, and only in limited numbers. For instance, only 3 per cent of YouTube channels generate 90 per cent of total views capturing the commensurate share of creator revenue (Bärtl, 2018).

A key policy intervention for policy-makers will involve undertaking targeted interventions that help young

people capture and retain value. In Commonwealth countries, this is simply not taking place. Using ICT-related patent applications as a measure of current digital innovation, for economies where data is available, knowledge generation for which patent protection is sought is very low.

However, current patents are the result of years of prior R&D. To understand future paths, current R&D spending can act as a proxy of future innovation. Even here, however, the trendlines in the Commonwealth are not encouraging. As Figure 7.3 shows, for the 21 Commonwealth economies for which there is data between 2014 and 2016, more than half fell below the global average. More concerning was that R&D spending actually contracted over the period in five economies - India, Mozambique, Pakistan, Sri Lanka and Uganda.

To solve this problem, it is important to identify the priority levers for innovation policy that enable the digital economy. A key element of this is to align research with the needs of the digital economy. This will involve closer collaboration between education and

Figure 7.3 R&D expenditure as a share of gross domestic product

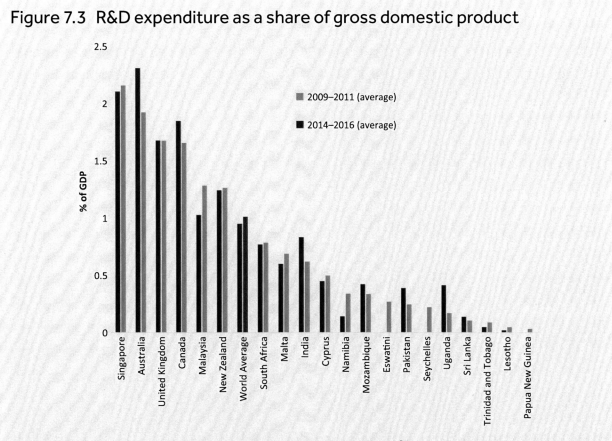

Source: Authors' calculations based on World Bank data. No 2009-2011 data was available for Eswatini, Seychelles and Papua New Guinea. Commonwealth Secretariat (2020).

industry, so as to develop innovation ecosystems and an entrepreneurial culture.

By focusing policy interventions on these three areas – digital divides, lifelong skilling and the innovation ecosystem – policy-makers can provide a foundation that, when combined with sectoral interventions, can provide young people with an ecosystem in which to maximise their potential. This will position them to take advantage of the opportunities and to be prepared for the risks involved in the changing employment and entrepreneurship environment being brought about by the Fourth Industrial Revolution.

7.2 Youth experiences in the digital economy

In this section, we learn from the experiences of young people working in the platform economy about the kinds of policies that governments and the private sector can implement to support their success. Caribou Digital's participatory video project has provided a space for young people to share their stories and lessons. In addition, Generation Unlimited's Youth Marketplace offers an example of ways to connect youth to opportunities for up-skilling, employment and making social contributions

Guest Contributor

Youth and the Platform Economy

Grace Natabaalo, Research Lead at Caribou Digital

Young people around the world increasingly rely on digital tools to find and perform paid work. Globally, the majority of people currently engaged in digital work are below the age of 35 (ILO, 2021b). This section highlights four ways policy-makers and the private sector can help the next generation prosper in the emerging digital workplace.

The section draws on the stories of 11 young people from Uganda, Nigeria, Kenya and Ghana who use digital platforms to find and do work (referred to as "platform workers and sellers"). The participants recorded themselves in a self-shot video storytelling project initiated by Caribou Digital, conducted with the support of the Mastercard Foundation between October and November 2020.[2] These platform workers and sellers, including motorcycle taxi drivers, e-commerce sellers and on-demand labourers, share the real challenges and opportunities of platform work in the age of COVID-19.

A lack of benefits and social protection

Young people are proactively leveraging the new digital platforms by upskilling, diversifying their incomes and capitalising on their social media networks to reach new markets and to weather the pandemic.

Despite the impressive uptick in use of digital platforms for work, many young people using them still lack access to credit or health insurance that could guarantee income security.

For example, Mary (24) uses Facebook to find customers for her mushrooms and strawberry business in Kenya. She also runs a YouTube channel, sharing tips on good farming practices. The COVID-19 lockdown in Kenya meant she had to sell the mushrooms at a lower price while the cost of transport and critical farming materials both shot up. "It was very stressful, especially

thinking about how you do not have the money and you do not even have the capacity to borrow," she said.

Mary needed a loan but her entire business was not profitable enough to secure a loan of even 100,000 shillings (US$900). Although not available in Kenya presently, a credit product offered by Indian FinTech company Avail Finance could have helped Mary. During the worst of the pandemic, Avail offered Indian gig workers loans that included a repayment holiday (Tiwary, 2020).

Some digital platforms can facilitate loans to their platform workers. Sabina (29), a carpenter on freelance platform Lynk in Kenya, has access to micro-credit through the platform but it is not in a portable form. This means she cannot use her credit score generated on Lynk when applying for a new loan on a different platform. A portable loan system would also help those working simultaneously across multiple digital platforms.

The Kenyan company Qhala (2020) is already exploring a flexible benefits platform for gig workers that would allow for health insurance, retirement, savings plans, discounted memberships, product financing and other portable benefits. Policy-makers should find ways to simplify the existing regulations governing worker benefits so digital workers can easily transfer their packages between platforms.

Few asset loan programmes are tailored to the platform economy

The Kenyan government has created the Ajira programme to empower young people to find opportunities and succeed in online freelancing.[3] This programme can be replicated in other countries along with parallel programmes to provide young people with favourable credit to kick-start their freelance careers. Any loans should be pinned to the purchase of assets like laptops, motorcycles or cars and other job tools like training.

Based in the Ghanaian city of Accra, David (28) saw an advertisement by SolarTaxi, a ride-hailing platform that was looking to hire drivers. He applied immediately because he could not find a job and did not have the capital to start his own business. SolarTaxi gave David a loan in the form of a motorbike and enabled him to start earning a living. He signed up to two other delivery platforms for extra income.

Even Uber has spotted opportunities to expand its reach in the burgeoning digital world. The global ride-hailing app partnered with Nigerian flexible car ownership company Moove to provide all Uber driver-partners with short- and long-term access to vehicles (Lukhanyu, 2020). These kinds of arrangements, if well structured, and if they have backing from governments, can help more young people access the right assets needed to do the work.

Women are often unsafe while working on digital platforms

Women face unique challenges in platform work, such as child care constraints, gender discrimination and threats to their personal safety while working. A good example is the booming ride-hailing sector in underemployed parts of Africa where most drivers and riders are male. Gender expectations and safety concerns keep women from joining this sector.

Dathive (31) is one of only two female motorcycle taxi drivers on Uganda's SafeBoda ride-hailing platform. She joined SafeBoda with the support of a motorcycle loan from the company after various other ventures failed, including a mobile money business, a restaurant and a fashion boutique. Dathive said the SafeBoda platform had proactively promoted her as a female driver to help her earn the trust of customers in a country with restrictive gender norms. Working for SafeBoda also gives Dathive a sense of security because the platform can track both her and the rider in case of any incident, she says. But, for her personal safety, Dathive she says she does not work late hours.

Similar to Dathive, Sabina's move into carpentry was possible because of a collaboration between Lynk and BuildHer, a social enterprise equipping Kenyan women with vocational and life skills. In addition to helping hone her carpentry skills, Lynk provides Sabina with a monthly stipend and access to micro-credit.

Again, large platform companies like Bolt are taking steps to include more women in the ride-hailing sector. Bolt announced recently that it would trial a "women for women" ride-hailing service in South Africa to hopefully solve some of key safety concerns for females in the sector.

Mothers doing work on platforms struggle

The International Labour Organization (ILO) (2021b) found that about 23 per cent of women who performed online work had children under the age of six years. Of the five female participants in our video storytelling project, three are single mothers who, in their efforts to continue earning an income, also have to contend with the effects of school closures and lack of outside help owing to social distancing rules. For example, Gloria, 31, a social commerce seller in Uganda, said it was a struggle to combine child care and work. "I was homeschooling, running the business and making sure meals are prepared," she said. Mary says she struggles to balance her responsibilities as a mother and her commitment to her YouTube followers.

Studies of women freelancers find that extra household responsibilities, including child care, prevent women from taking on as many hours as men (Gray and Suri, 2019). To help encourage more females to benefit from freelancing, governments should incentivise platforms to introduce more flexible working hours for women freelancers with child care responsibilities.

Not just digital skills: Young people need skills for a digital age

The technical, digital and soft skills needed to thrive on digital platforms may come naturally to some, but for others success requires a bit of extra training. Platforms recognise this need and invest in training initiatives for workers on their platforms, providing them with skills that can be used on and off the platforms (Donner et al., 2020).

For example, when Dathive signed up as a new driver, SafeBoda provided her with digital skills training and financial literacy. Sabina receives on-going carpentry training set up by Lynk. And David was trained by SolarTaxi on how to use the app and how to manage his finances.

Digital skills are the foundation of the platform economy. However, a broad set of "skills for a digital age" must include soft skills, coding, social media and e-commerce selling, digital marketing, data analytics and much more (Donner, 2020). Those responsible for measuring whether the younger generation is ready to enter this new digital world must update their own definitions of skills to include all the above. Upskilling initiatives can be scaled up through partnerships between governments, development agencies and platforms, and must be made available at all levels of education.

Conclusion: Create the enabling environment

The benefits of digital labour markets are enormous but they also introduce new tensions, contradictions, trade-offs and complexities. Many countries have created enabling environments for such platforms to thrive but must give more attention to the welfare of the platform workers and sellers. Governments and platforms can work together to update regulatory guidelines on worker benefits, access to micro-loans, safety and representation of women and ways to upskill gig workers. Youth economic empowerment on digital platforms depends on ensuring the work is fulfilling and dignified for all genders (see Mastercard Foundation, 2021).

Platform work, as one of the more prominent (and disruptive) elements of a larger digital transformation, is, rightly, a focus of debate and policy exploration. For example, the ILO's framework on decent work is a good guide for policy-makers, development partners and platforms. No one will be affected more by these shifts than youth - after all, they are the ones who will live in the future of work emerging now. For that reason, the experiences, challenges and successes of young people, around the world (but perhaps illustrated by these 11), are a critical part of this on-going endeavour to make a digital economy that works for everyone.

7.3 Youth taking charge of Employment and Opportunity

Three finalists in the 2021 Commonwealth Youth Awards demonstrate how young people are taking charge in creating employment opportunities for others, including through the use of digital tools. They are each working on initiatives that will contribute to the attainment of Sustainable Development Goal 1 on reducing poverty and Sustainable Development Goal 9 on industry, innovation and infrastructure.

Syed Ommer Amer from Pakistan is the founder of Daastan, a modern book publishing company and go-to platform for global authors. The company uses a social enterprise model to support authors to monetise their time, content and skills through online training and workshops. Daastan has supported 10,000 authors from 17 countries and helped publish over 300 titles.

Jubilanté Joanna Cutting from Guyana is the founder of the Guyana Animation Network, which raises awareness and advocates for youth opportunities

and skills training in digital media, animation and the STEM (science, technology, engineering and maths) subjects. The programme includes Digital Summer Camps, a Girls in ICT initiative and mentorship support. It has trained over 300 young people in ICT and entrepreneurship and supported critical online training in business marketing and digital skills.

Bradley Heslop from the UK is Co-Founder of WSV Global, an organisation that develops community business solutions to social needs affecting communities living on less than US$5 a day. These solutions, packaged as franchises, work to provide a range of vital products and services including addressing menstrual hygiene challenges, access to solar energy and recycling waste into fertiliser. WSV Global has helped support over 40,000 vulnerable people and helped over 250 entrepreneurs scale their work and income.

Guest Contributor

The Youth Agency Marketplace (Yoma): Designed by youth and led by youth

Guest Contribution by Generation Unlimited

Generation Unlimited (GenU) believes that preparing youth for today for the skills mismatch and emerging jobs is key for their participation in the digital economy. To this effect GenU and partners (UNICEF, GIZ and Botnar) are working with youth to create value for themselves. The Youth Agency Marketplace (Yoma) is a digital ecosystem platform where youth grow, learn and thrive through engaging in social impact initiatives and are linked to skilling and economic opportunities. Initiatives on the platform align with the SDGs, creating a vibrant youth marketplace for skills, digital profiles, employment and entrepreneurship.

Yoma offers the opportunity for public and private partner organisations to reach and interact with youth to support and tap their potential. As youth engage in the opportunities offered by Yoma, their active involvement and skills acquired is recorded on a verifiable digital CV with certified credentials using blockchain technology. Their efforts are further rewarded and incentivised with the platform's digital currency (ZLTO), a digital token, that can be spent in the Yoma marketplace to purchase goods and services. Yoma onboards local partners to provide opportunities to youth on the platform; namely, through three categories; Grow (experiential learning, individualised pathways), Impact (impact tasks and volunteering), and Thrive (entrepreneurship, employment opportunities).

Yoma originated from a small group of African youth who issued a challenge to find a way to focus the digital innovation landscape on the needs of youth, to navigate complex and disjointed skilling opportunities and find ways to identify 'diamonds in

the rough'. This is based on the premise that "talent is universal, opportunities are not". To identify these diamonds in the rough, Yoma is focusing on verifiable skills acquired through non-formal learning and social impact to elevate the profile of youth and demonstrate their potential.

Yoma also supports participation of vulnerable youth in the digital economy, such as those on the move, female and internally displaced. Innovative ways of combining online and offline engagements are being piloted to offer pathways to coding careers together with the South African NGO, Umuzi, training youth for digital roles at leading employers.

During the pandemic, Yoma launched a COVID-19 social impact challenge where over 80,000 young people participated to design solutions in support of their communities. Many of the innovative solutions received prizes related to the digital economy, such as free digital learning and online market applications to enable continued skilling and income generation during the pandemic.

GenU and Yoma partners plan to expand Yoma to 3 million by the end of 2022 through youth engagements, the creation of 1.5 million individualised learning pathways, and matching youth with 500,000 job opportunities.

Youth can join Yoma at https://www.yoma.world/. Interested partner organisations can visit https://www.yoma.foundation/ or contact GenU's Yoma Ecosystem and Partnerships Lead, Wesley Furrow at wfurrow@unicef.org for more information on how they can join forces with Yoma, provide opportunities, support outreach, promotion and funding

Endnotes

1   This analysis has been prepared by Kirk Haywood, Adviser, Regulatory Framework and Connectivity Agenda in the Trade, Oceans and Natural Resources Directorate of the Commonwealth Secretariat

2   https://www.platformlivelihoods.com/covid-19-video-project/. While the Mastercard Foundation funded the COVID-19 Video Storytelling – Platform Livelihoods work, the thoughts in this guest article are those of the author and Caribou Digital.

3   https://ajiradigital.go.ke/online_work

References

Bärtl, M. (2018) "YouTube Channels, Uploads and Views: A Statistical Analysis of the Past 10 Years". *Convergence: The International Journal of Research into New Media Technologies* 24(1): 16–32.

Commonwealth Secretariat (2020) *State of the Digital Economy Report*. London: Commonwealth Secretariat.

Digital Opportunity Trust (2019) "Digital Ambassador Program Proof of Concept". Final Evaluation. Kigali: Ministry of ICT and Innovation.

Donner, J. (2020) "1600+ Ways to Teach 'Skills in the Digital Age'". Caribou Digital, 30 March. https://medium.com/caribou-digital/1600-ways-to-teach-skills-in-the-digital-age-69cb061b6e59

Donner, J., M. Dean, J. Osborn and A. Schiff (2020) "Platform-Led Transformational Upskilling: How Marketplace Platforms Can Transform Emerging Markets by Investing in Skills Development". Farnham: Caribou Digital Publishing.

Gray, M. L. and S. Suri (2019) *Ghost Work: How to Stop Silicon Valley from Building a New Global Underclass*. Boston, MA: Houghton Mifflin Harcourt.

ILO (International Labour Organization) (2021a) "ILO Monitor: COVID-19 and the World of Work". Seventh Edition, 25 January. Geneva: ILO.

ILO (2021b) *World Employment and Social Outlook. The Role of Digital Labour Platforms in Transforming the World of Work*. Geneva: ILO.

Institute for the Future (2017) "Technologies' Impact On Society & Work In 2030 The next era of Human Machine Partnerships". Report for Dell Technologies https://www.delltechnologies.com/content/dam/delltechnologies/assets/perspectives/2030/pdf/SR1940_IFTFforDellTechnologies_Human-Machine_070517_readerhigh-res.pdf

Lukhanyu, M. (2020) "Uber Partners Moove to Increase Vehicle Ownership for Its Drivers in Africa". TechMoran. https://techmoran.com/2020/07/14/uber-partners-nigerias-moove-to-increase-vehicle-ownership-for-its-drivers/

Mastercard Foundation (2021) "Mastercard Foundation Launches 10-Year Plan to Enable 3 Million Young People in Uganda to Access Dignified Work". 23 July. https://mastercardfdn.org/mastercard-foundation-launches-10-year-plan-to-enable-3-million-young-people-in-uganda-to-access-dignified-work/

McKinsey Global Institute (2017) "Jobs Lost, Jobs Gained: Workforce Transitions in a Time of Automation". December. https://www.mckinsey.com/~/media/McKinsey/Industries/Public%20and%20Social%20Sector/Our%20Insights/What%20the%20future%20of%20work%20will%20mean%20for%20jobs%20skills%20and%20wages/MGI-Jobs-Lost-Jobs-Gained-Executive-summary-December-6-2017.pdf

McKinsey Global Institute (2020) "What's Next for Remote Work: An Analysis of 2000 Tasks, 800 Jobs and Nine Countries". 23 November. https://www.mckinsey.com/featured-insights/future-of-work/whats-next-for-remote-work-an-analysis-of-2000-tasks-800-jobs-and-nine-countries

Qhala (2020) "Perks.gg: Flexible, Affordable, Portable Social Safety Nets for Gig Workers". 16 November. https://medium.com/qhalahq/perks-gg-flexible-affordable-portable-social-safety-nets-for-gig-workers-9b7ad8bde85d

Tiwary, T. (2020) "Fintech Company Avail Finance Rolls out Loan Programme for Gig Economy Workers". Techcircle, 2 April. https://www.techcircle.in/2020/04/02/fintech-company-avail-finance-rolls-out-loan-programme-for-gig-economy-workers

WEF (World Economic Forum) (2021) *The Global Risks Report 2021*. Geneva: WEF.

World Bank (2020) *Poverty and Shared Prosperity 2020: Reversals of Fortune*. Washington, DC: World Bank.

Youth Promoting Equality and Inclusion

08

Chapter 8

Youth Promoting Equality and Inclusion

The inclusion of a new domain on Equality and Inclusion in the 2020 Youth Development Index (YDI) prompts reflection on the differential experiences of various groups of young people in the pursuit of the Sustainable Development Goals (SDGs). The trends over the 2010–2018 period are encouraging in relation to economic marginalisation and socio-economic gender parity. Gender parity in safety and security was more or less flat over the decade, with significantly more young men than young women around the world reporting that they felt safe in their communities. The gender gap in feelings of safety is widest in the world's most peaceful countries, indicating that gains in peacefulness have, thus far, accrued disproportionately to men.

We know, however, that, since the advent of the COVID-19 pandemic, young women have been disproportionately affected by loss of employment and education disruption – new trends that threaten the progress over the past decade. There is a need for continued focus on these issues, as discussed in Chapters 6, 7 and 11, as well as on differential impacts on other groups of young people like those with disabilities – an issue that will be addressed in Chapter 9.

This short chapter celebrates the positive trends up to 2018 by focusing on the work of young people who have been #TakingCharge of equality and inclusion through their own initiatives. These examples are shared to inspire investment in further change. The chapter also includes a reflection from a young advocate on what remains to be done to achieve gender equality.

8.1 Youth taking charge of Equality

All over the world, young people are taking steps to create opportunities for those in their communities to experience economic empowerment, gender equality and justice. In this chapter, we highlight the work of five Commonwealth Youth Award (CYA) 2021 recipients who are taking charge of reversing inequality and creating opportunities.

8.1.1 Promoting gender equality

Wadi Ben-Hirki founded the Wadi Ben-Hirki Foundation to champion the empowerment of less privileged, disadvantaged and marginalised groups in Nigeria. Her vision is of "a world where no woman or child is left behind and everyone has a fighting chance." In this regard, the foundation's work includes a focus on fighting for girls to live and thrive and to reverse perceptions of them as wives or property. The CYA recognised the Wadi Ben-Hirki Foundation was recognised for its work on empowering women and girls. In particular, the foundation has donated food and education materials to Boko Haram victims and other internally displaced persons, led campaigns against child marriage and sexual violence and provided safe spaces for vulnerable girls and women. These projects have together changed the lives of thousands across Nigeria.

Through the **Street to School** initiative, over 1,100 teachers have received training to improve learning among vulnerable young people for over 7,000 students, who have also received new educational materials. The training includes innovative approaches, including engaging students through radio schooling and boosting the computer literacy of teachers and students. In northern Nigeria, the **Girls Not Wives** initiative has sought to break the cycle of child marriage and gender-based violence by conducting over 100 awareness-raising programmes, which has changed outcomes for more than 500 girls. The foundation has also engaged women and girls in empowerment workshops through the **SHEROES i**nitiative, which seeks to build leadership skills in women and girls.

Through initiatives like these, Wadi Ben-Hirki has demonstrated that young people, working at community level, have impressive reach and are able to deliver relevant and innovative support to those most in need.

Shanal Sivan is Founder and Producer of Jazbaat, Fiji's biggest digital storytelling platform for women. Shanal developed an online platform that has become the vehicle for a video talk show series – Stories of Hope – which features the stories of women from diverse backgrounds who are heroes in their communities, at work and in their personal lives.

Jazbaat, which means "emotions" in Fiji Hindi, acknowledges the roles of these powerful women, who have not shied away from challenging situations in life, who have broken stereotypes and come out more powerful than ever before. The platform has reached over 300,000 women and helped tackle sensitive and important issues including domestic violence, online harassment, body shaming and support to children with special needs and who face barriers to education and employment.

8.1.2 Peace and social justice

Diego Armando Aparicio was a European finalist in the 2021 CYA, acknowledged for founding Queer Wave, the first LGBTQ+ film festival in Cyprus, designed to tackle stigma and promote a more inclusive society through art and cinema. The COVID-19 pandemic resulted in Pride celebrations being cancelled in Cyprus and so Diego and his team decided to provide a way for people who were feeling isolated to celebrate diversity and togetherness. The first edition of the festival was an online screening in August 2020 of 25 films, from 5 continents, which was attended by over 1,200 individuals. The online event united audiences from both ethnic communities in Cyprus, in a context where travel between the two sides of the country was restricted as a COVID-19 safety measure. Queer Wave has helped connect new audiences and raise important issues around social and gender inequalities in order to foster inclusivity and peace-building across divided communities.

8.1.3 Decent work for people with disabilities

Alina Alam is Founder of Mitti Café, a chain of cafés that provides experiential training and employment to adults with physical, intellectual and psychiatric disabilities in India. Today, there are 8 permanent cafes in 3 cities in India, employing 116 staff members with disabilities.

The organisation's outreach initiative also helps create awareness about inclusion and disability rights. Alina and her team believe that awareness about inclusion is the key to shifting perceptions about disability and ensuring that people with disabilities obtain access to equal opportunities in employment, based on their talent, and that they also attain access to safer and inclusive workspaces that enable them to work alongside their peers with pride and dignity. Parents of people with disabilities, particularly mothers, also receive training to help them become more economically empowered.

Although the Mitti Cafés have had to shut down during periods of COVID-19 lockdown, the social enterprise has pivoted to provide meals to frontline and essential workers though the Mitti Karuna (Compassion) Meals – No Hunger Campaign. Mitti Cafés have trained over 850 persons with disabilities and served over 5 million meals to vulnerable communities and homeless groups, including 1.3 million during the COVID-19 pandemic.

8.1.4 Inclusive emergency response

Maselina Iuta is the regional winner of the 2021 CYA for the Pacific. She is Project Assistant and Founding Member of the Deaf Association of Samoa, an organisation that advocates for the development of inclusive opportunities, policies and legislation for deaf and hearing-impaired persons. She has worked, through the association, and in partnership with the Government of Samoa, to ensure that there has been inclusive messaging from state organisations during the state of emergency and response to COVID-19. In fact, thanks to the efforts of the association, the prime minister's address on COVID-19, four times per week, has been interpreted into sign language. This is the first time this has been done. Maselina also provided interpretation for the Samoan prime minister's broadcast during International Week of the Deaf in 2020. With her award, Maselina will continue her support for deaf-led advocacy, services and programmes in Samoa and ensure that responses to the pandemic continue to be inclusive and accessible to persons who are deaf and hard of hearing.

8.2 Supporting youth-led initiatives

These few examples of youth taking charge of equality demonstrate the importance of partnership with youth and investment in their youth-led initiatives. Their work continues to inspire and change the circumstances of not just young people but everyone in their communities and countries. In many cases, their work requires bold steps to break down political, economic, social and generational barriers that have excluded some young people from accessing important opportunities. Partnerships with community, local government and federal actors have helped support the success of the initiatives.

Guest Contributor

"We are the Generation Equality"

Guest Contribution by Vivian Onano, Founder and Director of the Leading Light Initiative

2021 has been a monumental year for Gender Equality as world leaders, civil society organisations and youth advocates came together to commemorate 26 years since the Beijing Women's Forum. The Generation Equality Forum highlighted a myriad of issues that are still holding women and girls back, and provided an opportunity for governments, corporates, and civil society organisations to make bold and ambitious commitments towards making gender equality a reality for all. Young women and girls were not left out of these important discussions, they were at the centre, even virtually, given that most of them could not travel to Mexico or France due to COVID-19 restrictions.

The COVID-19 pandemic has affected women and girls disproportionately and exacerbated the inequalities that have been persistent in our communities. According to the 2020 Global Education Monitoring Report, since the signing of the monumental Beijing Declaration and Platform for Action in 1995, we have seen 180 million more girls enrolled in school. And more girls are staying in school and graduating than ever before. Despite this progress, there is an ongoing fear that some of these gains will be undone by the ongoing pandemic. It is estimated that another 20 million girls may never go back to school post-pandemic. Since the schools' closure in 2020 to curb the spread of the COVID-19 virus, there have been reported cases of increased teenage pregnancies, gender-based violence, child labour, among many other issues that are facing young women and girls during this pandemic. As a result of these challenges, many girls may find it difficult to resume school or have normal lives once we are past this pandemic. Access to safe and quality education is imperative to us achieving gender equality; with education, the girls are informed, skilled, aware, and able to make choices and contribute to the socio-economic development of their communities and countries. Education is a basic human right that no child should be denied access to. In a few weeks, the governments of Kenya and the UK in collaboration with the Global Partnership for Education will be hosting the Global Education Summit to rally governments to increase their investments towards education and to ensure that girls can stay in school. This Summit is very timely to urge our leaders to ensure that girls can go back to school, and the necessary resources are in place to support their re-entry. It is only an educated nation that can be well equipped and prepared to tackle future pandemics, eradicate poverty, achieve gender equality, and curb climate change.

Achieving gender equality is everyone's business and there is no demographic that has taken on this issue more seriously than the young people. It's been very encouraging to even see young men and boys being vocal on the issue and playing a major advocacy role in their communities. Men and boys are our allies on this journey and their voices and actions are just as important. It is true that young people are taking charge of their future and are no longer waiting for solutions to be brought to them. In Tanzania, Flaviana Matata of Flaviana Matata Foundation realised that many young girls were lacking proper menstrual hygiene products during their menses, and this affected their education. As an entrepreneur and philanthropist, she invested in the production of ethical sanitary towels through her company Lavy and partnered with her Foundation to distribute sanitary towels to marginalised girls to help curb period poverty and ensure that girls can manage their menstruation hygienically, safely, and without shame. Through this initiative, Flaviana can provide sanitary towels to 2,000 young girls every month, and in addition, teach them about proper menstrual hygiene as part of the broader sexual and reproductive health and rights curriculum. A biological cycle like menstruation can determine whether a girl stays in school or not. Initiatives like the one managed by Flaviana will ensure that girls stay in school and continue to play an active role in their learning.

Young leaders such as Bina Maseno from Kenya, have realized that without women leaders taking up political offices, there will be slow progress towards achieving gender equality. Women political representation is imperative to ensure that laws and legislations are put in place that help protect the rights of women to achieve their full potential by having access to opportunities. Bina has taken it upon herself to ensure that many young women are involved in political processes, and they fully understand the important role that they are playing to bring change. Through her organization, Badili Africa, they merge beauty with civic dialogues for political awareness and involvement with governance and democratic processes. As a result of their work, they nurture and strengthen the leadership capacities of women and girls by

encouraging and providing safe spaces that enable grassroots women to organize as leaders and to demand accountability and inclusion in decision-making processes.

Young people's involvement in achieving gender equality is critical, and they need to be supported with the resources and provided with a seat at the decision-making table. Young people are at the forefront demanding accountability from our leaders, and they need to be listened to because the world needs the youthful energy and sense of urgency to deliver on their promises when it comes to achieving gender equality. The passion, innovation, and determination of young people should be fully harnessed if we are to achieve the development goals and create a world where every individual can fully maximize their potential. Young people are the Generation Equality, and they are ready to be part of the change and make gender equality a reality in our generation.

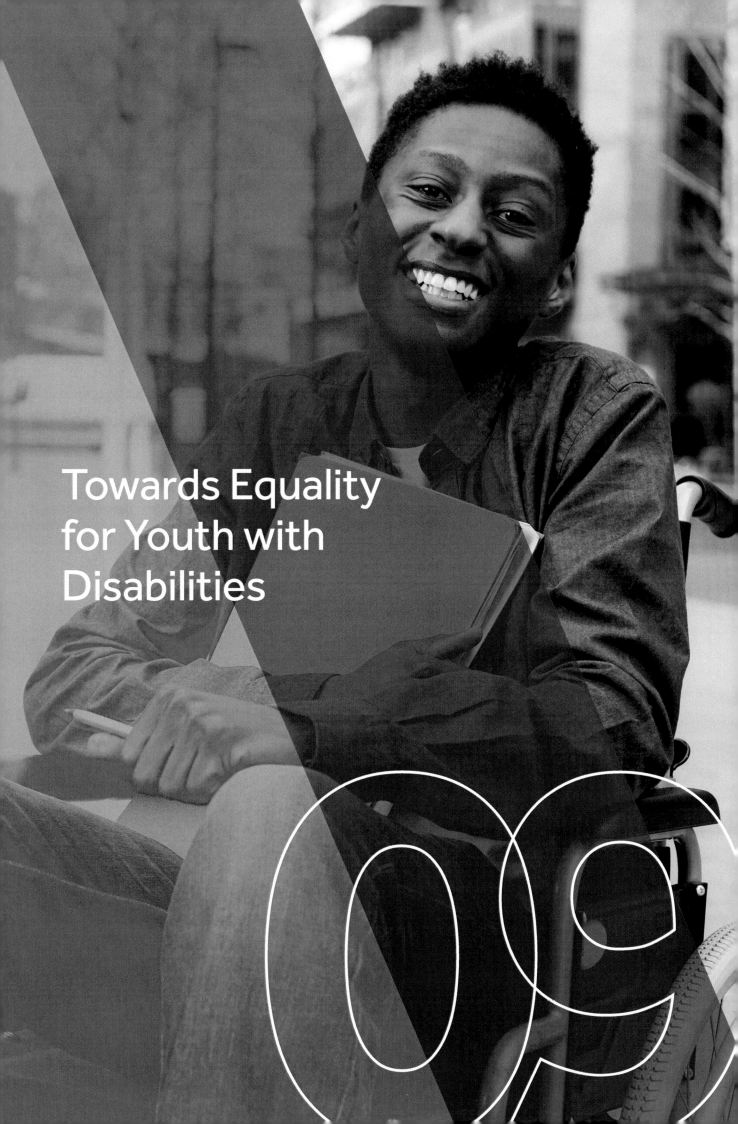

Towards Equality for Youth with Disabilities

09

Chapter 9

Towards Equality for Youth with Disabilities

The inclusion of a new domain in the 2020 Youth Development Index (YDI) on Equality and Inclusion prompts reflection on differential experiences and needs among young people and an exploration of which groups may be left behind in pursuit of the Sustainable Development Goals (SDGs). This chapter examines high-quality data from around the world on the situation of young people with disabilities on two areas of the YDI – education and employment – and also considers the context of the COVID-19 pandemic as a cross-cutting theme. This chapter has been prepared by Leonard Cheshire, which is a leading inclusive development agency, working to improve the lives of persons with disabilities in developing countries across the globe. Leonard Cheshire focuses on inclusion and participation, working to achieve this in a range of ways in 16 countries across Asia and Africa.

The chapter cites quantitative data captured from Leonard Cheshire's Disability Data Portal, as well as qualitative individual case studies and testimonies. Both data sources provide a strong evidence base to reflect the realities of youth with disabilities across the world. Inconsistent and poor-quality data hampers the progress of youth with disabilities. That is why in 2018 Leonard Cheshire created the Disability Data Portal. Through this portal, persons with disabilities are empowered with data to demand change within their countries.

The data captured shows that millions of youth with disabilities are still being left behind. If the global community is to deliver on its commitment to "leave no one behind" (UNCDP, 2018), policy-makers must ensure youth with disabilities are central to development processes in terms of policy development, monitoring and implementation. This chapter includes key policy recommendations that ensure youth with disabilities are included in all efforts to improve the lives of young people globally.

Leonard Cheshire

Guest Contributor

A Message from Equality Advocates and Citizen Reporters

Yohana Kibe and Maria Njeri, Leonard Cheshire, 2030 and Counting citizen reporters, Kenya

We are living in a world where the most important weapon in the fight for equality is information.

Having data about youth with disabilities takes us one step closer to understanding what we go through and how it can be addressed. Good decisions are evidence-based, and the existence of data on disability can translate into better policies for us.

Despite facing similar challenges to our non-disabled peers, youth with disabilities seldom have their perspectives sought and remain under-represented. Our needs are often lumped together; there is a lack of emphasis on our unique perspective.

We became citizen reporters on Leonard Cheshire's 2030 and Counting data project to draw attention to the realities for youth and children with disabilities in Kenya.

We have heard time and again that stigma and discrimination contribute to inequalities in accessing health, education, employment and opportunities.

The SDGs and the United Nations Convention on the Rights of Persons with Disabilities (CRPD) are global frameworks that, if implemented fully by countries around the world, would eradicate most of the challenges facing youth with disabilities. Yet the data is often lacking, and therefore our concerns are not seen as a priority.

We welcome the disability chapter of the YDI Report as an important part of this process.

Equality will be beneficial not only for youth with disabilities, to help them achieve the full extent of their potential, but also in the development and economic growth of nations, particularly at such a challenging time as we are now facing, as the world responds to the COVID-19 pandemic.

More than 60 per cent of the Commonwealth are under the age of 30. The Commonwealth member countries have a fantastic opportunity to harness the power of all young people, including youth with disabilities, to build strong, productive and inclusive communities. And that starts with data.

9.1 Introduction

> **"Education is one of the keys to success for everyone whether you have a disability or not."** Michael, Kenya
>
> **"People with disabilities have to work harder than non-disabled people to get their foot on the career ladder."** Rudith, Zambia

Leonard Cheshire recognises youth with disabilities as actors in development and empowers them to raise their voices. This chapter combines government- and citizen-generated data, both qualitative and quantitative, bringing to the fore the personal stories behind the statistics and the value of youth-led processes in doing so. As Table 9.1 indicates, this analysis focuses on four disability data indicators related to two of the seven YDI domains.[1]

Youth with disabilities face additional challenges during times of crisis. Given the additional barriers facing persons with disabilities in relation to receiving education and securing and retaining employment, it is likely they will be among the hardest hit by the impacts of the COVID-19 pandemic. Findings from Leonard Cheshire's youth-led action research provide insights into how youth with disabilities have experienced the pandemic. The project gathered the views of over 500 youth with disabilities from India, Indonesia, Kenya, South Sudan and Zambia. Those youth perspectives in relation to education, employment and data availability have been included throughout the chapter.

9.2 The data context

Estimates suggest there are around 220 million youth with disabilities worldwide. Nearly 80 per cent of these live in lower- and middle-income countries (Groce, 2003). Youth with disabilities are still among the most marginalised and poorest of the world's youth (Groce, 2004). They are routinely excluded from most educational, economic, social and cultural opportunities.

Global disability data collection has progressed considerably in recent years, catalysed by the adoption of the widely ratified CRPD in 2006 and the 2030 Agenda for Sustainable Development in 2015, both of which include requirements for disability data disaggregation.

The CRPD introduces an explicit obligation on governments to consult with persons with disabilities when developing policies and legislation that affects them. Article 7 demands the provision of disability- and age-appropriate assistance to ensure children with disabilities can exercise the right to be heard and taken seriously.

Out of the 17 SDGs, there are 5 goals and 7 targets that specifically mention persons with disabilities.[1] There are 20 youth-specific targets spread over 6 SDGs.[2] However, a lack of data regarding the situation makes it hard to identify the key issues youth with disabilities are facing and to effectively advocate for change. Despite recent progress, challenges in the collection and use of disability data remain. Data that is collected is not always made available, often for political reasons. These limitations make it difficult to use this data fully to improve the inclusion of persons with disabilities at national level or to provide a comprehensive global picture of progress and gaps.

To address some of these challenges, Leonard Cheshire, in collaboration with UK Aid, launched the Disability Data Portal at the Global Disability Summit in 2018. This is a data-sharing platform that aims to provide a growing body of disability data that can be easily accessed and analysed. It currently captures data on 48 countries, providing a snapshot of the situation of persons with disabilities globally. It collates pre-

Table 9.1 Youth Development Index and Disability Data Portal indicators

	YDI indicators	Disability Data Portal indicators
Education	% of people who can both read and write with understanding of a short simple statement about their everyday life, ages 15–24	Proportion of population in a given age group achieving at least a fixed level of proficiency in functional literacy skills, by sex (below 25 years)
Education	Ratio of total secondary school enrolment to the population of the age group that officially corresponds to the level of education shown	Secondary school completion rate
Employment & Opportunity	% of young people who are not in education, employment or training (NEET)	Proportion of youth (aged 15–24) not in education, employment and training

Box 9.1 Examples of disability-inclusive data projects

There are many examples of disability-inclusive data projects that aim to address these inequalities. Below is a small snapshot of work from across the Commonwealth.

2030 and Counting is Leonard Cheshire's global initiative to connect youth with disabilities in Kenya and Zambia to the development of their country through data collection. Youth with disabilities, alongside organisations of persons with disabilities, are trained as "citizen reporters" to lead on the collection of qualitative data, in the form of stories highlighting their own experiences and those of their peers. The project breaks down barriers of participation for pan-disability groups of youth with disabilities to contribute to the collection of youth-specific disability data. This in turn has supported improved trend analysis for stronger global influencing and advocacy. In addition, it has supported leadership development for youth with disabilities to engage in public life.

The **Commonwealth Children and Youth Disability Network (CCYDN)** was launched by Include Me TOO in 2019 with the aim of increasing access to platforms designed to help youth with disabilities influence positive change on issues that matter to them. The CCYDN sought the authentic voices of children and youth with disabilities on many issues they faced and how they wished to be included and represented. These children and youth also shared the commitments they would wish to see in a charter to support their rights, inclusion, independence, equality, dignity and dreams. This led to the Global Disability Children and Young People's Charter and its 12 commitments, which reinforce the provisions of the CRPD, the United Nations Convention on the Rights of the Child and the SDGs. For more see includemetoo.org.uk/ccydn/

Restless Development's **Ewakisi Project** focused on the integration of young persons living with disabilities in mainstream education and economic systems in Karamoja in northern Uganda. The project worked with local communities, educational institutions, the private sector, local government and development actors to increase their awareness and strengthen disability inclusion in their work. Restless Development supported a team of 10 community youth researchers, 50 per cent of whom were young persons with disabilities, to conduct youth-led research on the economic and educational exclusion of young persons living with disabilities. Government, private sector and development partners acted on the evidence and insights the young people generated. The project resulted in a 20 per cent increase in the number of people with a positive attitude towards persons with disabilities.

existing sources of population-level data that could be disaggregated by disability, with data gathered primarily from censuses and demographic and health surveys (DHS), as well as some other national household surveys. For more about the data portal, please visit www.disabilitydataportal.com

9.3 Education

9.3.1 Vanessa's story

Vanessa Achieng lives in Kisumu town, Kenya. When she was three years old, her parents became aware that she had hearing problems. They felt very worried about her situation. The people around her thought she was pretending or was just being rude and ignoring them.

When Vanessa started primary school, she experienced a lot of negative attitudes. Her teachers were annoyed with her as they felt she did not want to pay attention in class. Her classmates would call her names and bully her because of her hearing problems. The problems persisted and her performance at school started to decline. Her parents were thinking about transferring her to another school, but before doing so they took her for an assessment at the Educational Assessment and Rehabilitation Centre. The centre's officials confirmed that Vanessa had a hearing impairment and would need an assistive device to help her hear.

They also advised her parents to enrol her at Nyamasaria Primary School, which is one of the schools taking part in Leonard Cheshire's Girls' Education Challenge project in Kenya. Vanessa joined the project in 2014 and the first step was to make sure she obtained a hearing aid, which assisted her hearing ability. She could now hear well and respond without much effort. This greatly boosted her academic performance and her social interaction with her peers.

In 2019, when Vanessa was 13, she completed her primary-level education in the same primary school and scored 340 marks out of 500 in her final exams – one of the top marks in her class. As a result, she managed to receive a scholarship that will cover the costs of her secondary education from Equity Bank, through their Elimu Bora scholarship scheme. This scheme provides scholarships for students in Kenya with financial needs who display academic excellence.

"My advice to other students with disability is to work hard in order to achieve their goals. I have a disability, but I am also working hard and am pretty sure that, given the right support, I can achieve the same goals as my peers without disability and even surpass them."

9.3.2 Inequalities in education

The available data shows us that young people with disabilities are less likely to complete secondary school, have lower literacy rates.

School completion

Figure 9.1 shows that, in general, youth with disabilities are less likely to complete secondary education than youth without disabilities. In the 42 countries that could produce data, an average of just 19.2 per cent of youth with disabilities complete secondary school (see Table 9.2)Table 9.3. This statistic corresponds to a gap of 12.2 percentage points when considering completion rates for youth without disabilities (31.4 per cent). Of the 17 Commonwealth countries that could produce this indicator, the gap is 8.1 percentage points (compared with 14.9 percentage points for the 25 non-Commonwealth countries).

Literacy

When we consider literacy, we again see disparities. Considering the 28 countries that could produce data on functional literacy levels, Figure 9.2 shows that an average of 53.9 per cent of persons with disabilities below the age of 25 displayed functional literacy skills. This statistic corresponds to 73 per cent when we consider persons without disabilities, leading to a gap of 19.1 percentage points between the two groups. Of

the 10 Commonwealth countries that could produce this indicator, the gap is 14.4 percentage points, compared with 21.3 percentage points for the 18 non-Commonwealth countries.

Every child has the right to a quality education. The CRPD recognises the right to inclusive education for all (Article 24). To meet the SDGs by 2030, the international community needs to prioritise inclusive education to build a more inclusive and equitable society (Leonard Cheshire, 2019).

Only when classrooms, schools and education systems are designed to meet the needs of a diversity of learners can we hope to realise the goal of inclusive and equitable quality education for youth with disabilities (Leonard Cheshire, World Bank and Inclusion International, 2019).

"Many parents of children with disabilities have nothing to do. They have no money at all. They can't send children back to school with this situation they are in. If they fail to get enough to eat how will they afford taking children to school?" **COVID-19 survey respondent, Zambia**

"The government introduced the distant learning programmes as part of the COVID-19 national response strategy, which focuses mainly on radio. Youth with hearing impairments are far more excluded. We are not getting it [education] like others although we used to attend the same school". **COVID-19 survey respondent, South Sudan**

9.4 Employment and opportunity
9.4.1 Julius' story

Figure 9.1 Secondary school completion rates for youth with and without disabilities

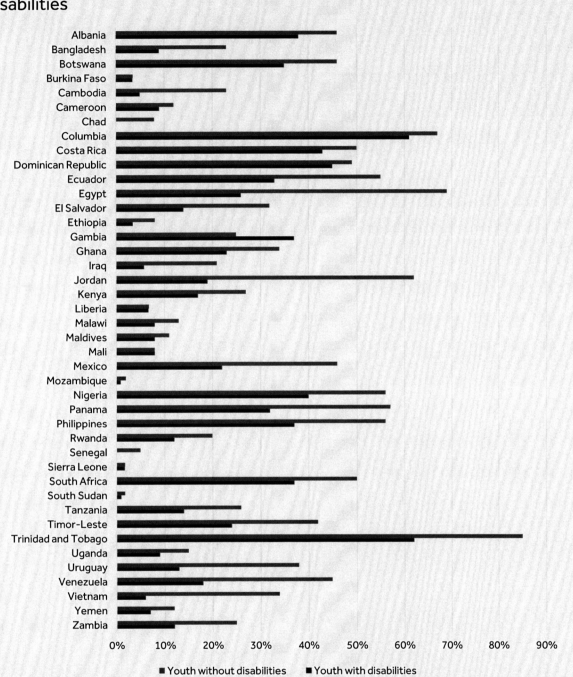

■ Youth without disabilities   ■ Youth with disabilities

Note: This indicator could be produced for 42 countries. Calculation follows the methodology recommended by the United Nations Educational, Scientific and Cultural Organization, which defines the school completion rate as the percentage of people aged three to five years above the intended age for the last grade of each level of education who have completed that grade. The available datasets from the 42 countries provided us with the 2 variables required for the calculation of educational attainment – that is, individuals' age and a variable that allows us to identify whether or not children have completed primary or secondary education.

Table 9.2 Average secondary school completion rates (Commonwealth vs. non-Commonwealth countries)

	Youth with disabilities	Youth without disabilities
All 42 countries	19.2%	31.4%
17 Commonwealth countries	19.7%	27.8%
25 non-Commonwealth countries	18.9%	33.8%

Table 9.3 Proportion of population in a given age group achieving at least a fixed level of proficiency in functional literacy skills below 25 years (Commonwealth vs. non-Commonwealth countries)

	Youth with disabilities	Youth without disabilities[3]
All 28 countries	53.9%	73%
10 Commonwealth countries	51.4%	65.8%
18 non-Commonwealth countries	55.3%	76.6%

Asiga Julius is 23 years old and lives in a village in Moyo district, Uganda. Julius was born with a learning disability and at the age of two his mother disappeared. He is one of eight children; they were originally nine but his twin brother, James, sadly passed away when he was just five.

Julius's father was left caring for the family alone. The children were enrolled at school but Julius had to drop out in Primary 4 because his teachers did not understand how to support him. Stuck at home, he was completely reliant on his father. Then they heard about Leonard Cheshire's Livelihoods project, which is supporting persons with disabilities into paid employment, and things started to change.

Once Julius had been registered, he was medically assessed and given mental health support and careers training. After taking an interest in business skills, he joined a training group where he met lots of other budding entrepreneurs. For six months they received training and then each member was given a loan by Leonard Cheshire to help set up their own business.

Julius was keen to start his own poultry-keeping business and took out a loan from the group. Using the money, he constructed a breeding house and bought two turkeys. The business is growing and he now has 20 turkeys. There is a ready market for Julius's poultry and, with the income he raises, Julius can meet his own basic needs and pay for his younger sisters' school fees.

9.4.2 Inequalities in employment

Analysis based on Figure 9.3 shows that an average of 39.3 per cent of persons with disabilities who are aged from 15 to 24 years old are not in education, employment or training. This statistic corresponds to 22.1 per cent when we consider persons without disabilities, leading to a gap of 17.2 percentage points between the two groups. Of the 17 Commonwealth countries that could produce this indicator, the gap is 12.6 percentage points compared with 20 percentage points for non-Commonwealth countries (see Table 9.4).

Existing data tells us youth with disabilities are more likely to experience adverse socio-economic outcomes than youth without disabilities (Mitra et al., 2013). Leonard Cheshire believes in putting youth with disabilities at the heart of social and economic development and recognises that policy-makers must prioritise inclusive education to give youth with disabilities greater access to secure livelihoods.

The situation facing youth with disabilities has become even starker following the COVID-19 pandemic. Findings from the survey illustrate this. "Due to COVID-19, my employer had to retrench some people and since I am disabled I was the first employee the company retrenched. They thought I was not very productive." **COVID-19 survey respondent, Kenya**

9.5 Conclusion and recommendations

Youth with disabilities face the same issues as their peers without disabilities but often have opportunities denied owing to negative attitudes, discrimination and barriers to access. Disparities in education and

Figure 9.2 Proportion of population in a given age group achieving at least a fixed level of proficiency in functional literacy skills (below 25 years)

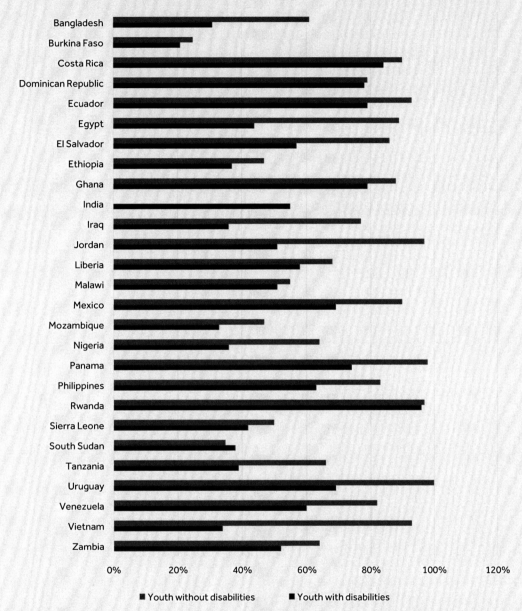

■ Youth without disabilities   ■ Youth with disabilities

Note: In censuses, the variable LIT identifies literacy as the ability to read and write in any language. Emphasis is put on both reading and writing skills, so that a person will be considered illiterate if she/he can read but not write. In DHS, literacy is captured by the variables V155 (female sample) and MV155 (male sample). V155 indicates whether a respondent who attended primary schooling can read a whole or part of a sentence shown. Individuals who attended secondary education or higher education are coded as literate as well as those who could read a whole sentence.

employment are more pronounced in youth with disabilities, and it is critical that national governments support decent work and education for all, in line with SDGs 4 and 8 and Articles 24 and 27 of the CRPD.

During the 2030 and Counting project, strong views emerged from youth with disabilities on how their

governments and other duty-bearers could address the issues they raised. These voices have formed the backbone of the policy recommendations made here.

National governments must adopt anti-discrimination legislation to ensure equal access to education, employment and full participation in society for

Figure 9.3 Proportion of youth (aged 15–24 years) not in education, employment or training

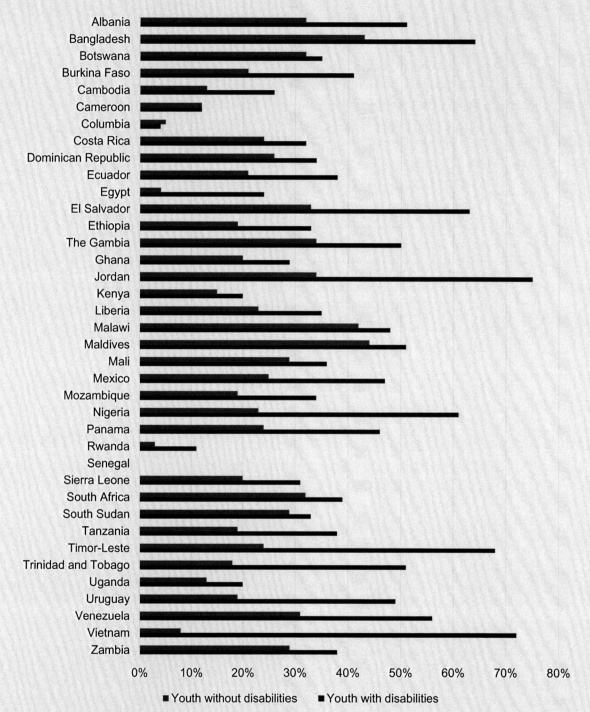

This indicator could be produced for 38 countries. In our analysis, this indicator is measured by the proportion of youth who neither attend school nor work. For countries where the estimate was calculating using census data, both unemployed and inactive people constitute the group of non-workers.

Table 9.4 Average proportion of 15–24 year olds not in education, employment or training (Commonwealth vs. non-Commonwealth countries)

	Youth with disabilities	Youth without disabilities
All 38 countries	39.3%	22.1%
17 Commonwealth countries	37.2%	24.6%
21 non-Commonwealth countries	41.1%	21.1%

youth with disabilities. But policy-makers must also implement sector-specific interventions to break down the life cycle of disability-based marginalisation experienced by youth with disabilities and to ensure their rights are fulfilled. Youth organisations and youth with disabilities need to be at the heart of the planning and implementation of these policies, and not the mere recipients.

Specifically, we recommend:

Education

Countries need to invest in education systems that remove the barriers limiting the participation and achievement of youth with disabilities. In particular, countries need to:

- Develop inclusive curricula that can break down barriers facing children with disabilities in the classroom, and support teachers with training and pedagogical tools to help every learner achieve their full potential;

- Invest in additional resources to provide teachers with specialised training, ensure schools are physically accessible and provide children with specially designed learning materials to realise their potential.

"What I hope is there should be seminars for all the teachers, not just 'special education' teachers, on how to include students with disabilities. They will benefit not only the persons with disabilities but also the whole school and community." **Leonard Cheshire youth with disability advocate, Zambia**

Employment

To ensure youth with disabilities can access and retain employment, national governments must:

- Adopt policies and targets to reduce the unemployment gap between persons with disabilities and their non-disabled peers;

- Create incentives so that employers are encouraged to hire youth with disabilities and make it mandatory for companies to report on the number of youth with disabilities they employ.

"Employees who have disabilities should be treated equally when it comes to promotion and other activities involved at the workplace. We should be given a chance to prove our strength and worth." **Leonard Cheshire youth with disability advocate, the Philippines**

Data

When it comes to advocacy, it is essential that youth with disabilities have access to high-quality data. That way, we can improve public knowledge and awareness of the rights of persons with disabilities. Measuring progress on youth with disabilities requires strong and comprehensive datasets. This means that countries must:

- Adopt data collection models that allow for better comparability across countries. The widely used Washington Group Questions provide a standardised methodology and enable internationally comparable data collection, providing a baseline on SDG and CRPD implementation;

- Disaggregate all national indicators by disability in line with Article 31 of the CRPD to enable the collection of statistics and data to create and implement policies that fulfil the rights of persons with disabilities.

"Disability must be made a priority. Collaborating with disability institutions to record data on disabilities is the best solution." **COVID-19 survey respondent, Indonesia**

COVID-19 response

Youth with disabilities face additional challenges during times of crisis across a range of issues, including education, employment and access to information. This means countries must:

- Ensure that education and employment opportunities in response to the pandemic consider the needs and are inclusive of youth with disabilities;

- Ensure youth with disabilities are fully included in consultations and policy responses to the pandemic.

Endnotes

1   SDG 4 on quality education – 4.5, 4.a; SDG 8 on decent work and economic growth – 8.5; SDG 10 on reduced inequalities – 10.2; SDG 11 on inclusive cities and communities – 11.2, 11.7; and SDG 17 on data collection and monitoring of the SDGs – 17.18.

2   SDG 2 (hunger), SDG 4 (education), SDG 5 (gender equality), SDG 8 (decent work), SDG 10 (inequality) and SDG 13 (climate change).

3   There was no data available for persons without disabilities in India therefore the data is drawn from 27 countries rather than 28.

References

Groce, N.E. (2003) "HIV/AIDS and People with Disability". *The Lancet* **361**(9367): 1401–1402.

Groce, N.E. (2004) "Adolescents and Youth with Disabilities: Issues and Challenges". *Asia Pacific Disability Rehabilitation Journal* **15**(2): 13–32.

Leonard Cheshire (2019) "Inclusive Education for Persons with Disabilities – Are We Making Progress?" Background Paper prepared for the International Forum on Inclusion and Equity in Education – Every Learner Matters, Cali, 11–13 September.

Leonard Cheshire, World Bank and Inclusion International (2019) "Every Learner Matters – Unpacking the Learning Crisis for Children with Disabilities". Washington, DC: World Bank.

Mitra, S., A. Posarac and B. Vick (2013) "Disability and Poverty in Developing Countries: A Multidimensional Study" *World Development* **41**: 1–18.

UNCDP (United Nations Committee for Development Policy) (2018) "Leaving No One Behind". https://sustainabledevelopment.un.org/content/documents/2754713_July_PM_2._Leaving_no_one_behind_Summary_from_UN_Committee_for_Development_Policy.pdf

Responding to the Climate Crisis

10

Chapter 10

Responding to the Climate Crisis

The inclusion of the Index for Risk Management (INFORM) score in the 2020 Youth Development Index (YDI) allows us to account for climate change-related risks to young people living around the world. However, the available measures of risk must be considered alongside the priorities that young people have in relation to addressing the climate crisis, and must explore ways in which youth can be mainstreamed in policy and programmatic response. This chapter offers two interesting perspectives on this issue. The first explores the challenges and opportunities for youth mainstreaming and inclusion in member country commitments under the United Nations Framework Convention on Climate Change (UNFCCC) and the second reflects on the experiences of young people with respect to participation and inclusion in decision-making.

10.1 Mainstreaming youth in climate action[1]

10.1.1 Climate change impact

Environmental degradation, in addition to the escalating impacts of climate change, poses significant multi-sectoral threats to lives and livelihoods across the world. While the Paris Agreement was a key milestone in addressing these issues, it has become clear that the target of limiting global temperature rise to 1.5°C by the end of the century is becoming increasingly difficult to meet in the absence of more ambitious national climate action plans and significant changes

in all emission sectors. The latest UNFCCC Nationally Determined Contribution (NDC) Synthesis Report, released in February 2021, has clearly shown that greater ambition is needed from member countries if they are to meet these targets of the Paris Agreement.

Particularly in developing countries, there is still a need to further scale up levels of implementation, in order to avoid falling behind with managing climate risks. While there are positive trends, the latest United Nations Environment Programme (UNEP) Adaptation Gap Report also highlights that the scale of adaptation progress at the national level is insufficient, and tracking progress remains a challenge (UNEP, 2021). This creates a real risk that adaptation costs will increase at a quicker rate than adaptation-oriented finance, potentially leading to increasing climate risk levels, even if emissions are reduced and global warming is limited to 1.5–2°C above pre-industrial temperatures.

Overcoming the existential threat of climate change requires the co-operation and involvement of all segments of society, with young people playing a central role, given that they are poised to experience the most severe impacts of climate change, based on current trends and projections. In light of this, there have been increasing global calls for the mainstreaming of youth in climate action, to ensure they have an opportunity to contribute to devising and implementing climate policies and programmes. Ensuring young people are central to this process will assist in guiding national and multinational development in a manner that prioritises sustainability.

10.1.2 Challenges to mainstreaming youth in climate action

The integration of gender and youth into climate change initiatives is fundamental in building resilience in an equitable manner, as these groups are often at a greater disadvantage from the impacts of climate change and are often underrepresented in decision-making. Recognising the increased vulnerability of young people to the impacts of climate change, there has been a global thrust, particularly following the 21st session of the Conference of the Parties (COP21) to the UNFCCC, towards their inclusion and participation in the climate process. While the Paris Agreement does not specifically mention young people, it does highlight the need to respect and consider the right to intergenerational equity in all actions by parties in addressing climate change. However, there are several barriers to progress on integration that can ensure such equity. These significant barriers to youth mainstreaming are outlined here.

Limited access to climate information

First, all citizens, particularly vulnerable groups, must have the ability and capacity to access and interpret climate data and information to ensure a greater level of awareness and to inform appropriate mitigation and adaptation responses. Young people, as a demographic that is particularly vulnerable to the impacts of climate change, often do not have such access, or are not equipped with the necessary tools to facilitate ease of understanding of environmental issues.

Whether this problem stems from the governmental or the multilateral level, these limits on ease of access, and the lack of attention to outlining the issues in a youth-friendly manner, pose a major hindrance to young people with regard to effectively advocating and mobilising others towards advancing climate action.

Limited capacity to access resources and scale up climate initiatives

Within the Commonwealth and globally, there are various youth-led climate resilience initiatives across different various sectors, such as water, land management, ocean and biodiversity conservation. However, these innovative projects are often on a very limited scale. In spite of significant expansion potential, the initiatives are constrained by youth inability to access finance and/or technical support to facilitate growth. In many cases, the primary issue lies not necessarily in availability of financing, but rather youth leaders or entrepreneurs having the requisite fundraising and grant-making skills or collateral and equity requirements to access such support facilities.

Absence/limited national policies for direct youth engagement

Young people often call for greater inclusion within decision-making processes but have found that they are only partially engaged. The absence of legislative frameworks and national policies that mandate the involvement and consideration of youth input is, in many countries, a significant contributor to exclusion.

"Young people often call for greater inclusion within decision-making processes."

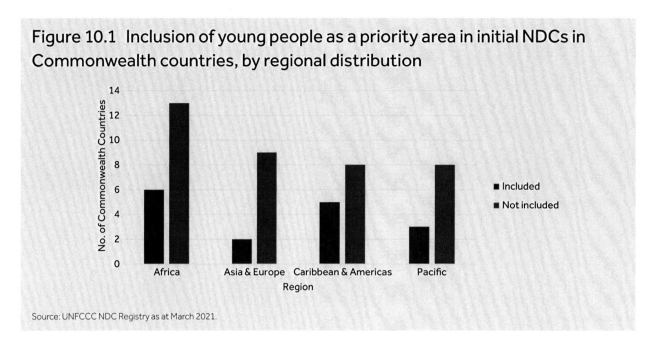

Figure 10.1   Inclusion of young people as a priority area in initial NDCs in Commonwealth countries, by regional distribution

Source: UNFCCC NDC Registry as at March 2021.

For instance, while many member countries have established National Climate Change Committees sanctioned by government, meaningful youth participation is limited. It is therefore crucial that young people have a permanent seat within such spaces to ensure they can provide input within the national climate change policy and programme development process.

Inclusion in Nationally Determined Contributions

Central to the Paris Agreement are the NDCs, in which countries outline their specific climate targets. In the first round of NDC submissions, about 40 percent of all NDCs made direct reference to children or youth. This has steadily improved, with roughly 75 percent of updated submissions thus far now prioritising youth as at November 2020 (UNDP, 2020). With more countries expected to submit new or revised NDCs ahead of COP26, which will take place in November 2021, this is opportune time to address this critical gap in many of the climate strategies regarding the role of young people in meaningfully participating in both climate policy-making and implementation, given that they continue to face a myriad of challenges in this regard.

From the Commonwealth perspective, it is evident, as Figure 10.1 shows, that there is still room for increased focus on young people in the initial NDCs of member countries. In every region, the number of countries that make no direct mention of youth in their climate targets is greater than the number of countries that have included them. While this by no means serves as a full indication of the level of in-country youth engagement in climate action, prioritising such in the NDCs will play a

critical role in ensuring the formal participation of young people within the NDC implementation process.

Given that a minority – 30 per cent – of member countries make specific mention of youth in the initial NDCs, as Figure 10.2 shows, there is significant scope for improvement – and several countries are still due to submit their revised NDCs ahead of COP26. At 31 March 2021, only 18 of the 54 Commonwealth member countries have submitted their new or revised NDCs. However, among those countries, a positive trend of increasing youth inclusion is emerging. Of these 18, 44 percent have included a focus on young people, which marks a 14 percent increase on the rate of inclusion in the initial submissions for the Commonwealth (Figure 10.3).

Figure 10.2   Commonwealth countries that have included young people as a priority area in their initial NDCs (%)

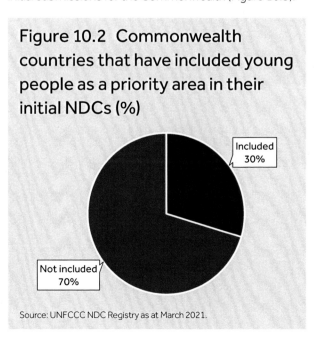

Source: UNFCCC NDC Registry as at March 2021.

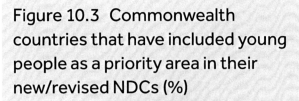

Figure 10.3 Commonwealth countries that have included young people as a priority area in their new/revised NDCs (%)

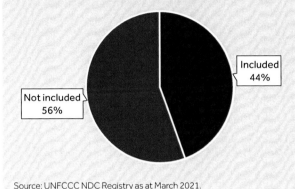

Included 44%

Not included 56%

Source: UNFCCC NDC Registry as at March 2021.

Such improvements therefore serve as a positive indication of progress being made in mainstreaming youth in the climate process by governments. Nonetheless, the Commonwealth Secretariat recognises that gaps still exist and, through its country-driven support on enhancing and fast-tracking NDC progress, will continue to place emphasis on overcoming these barriers and advance greater inclusion of young people in such processes.

10.1.3 Youth climate change policy priorities

Climate change has in recent years become an issue of great concern for youth from across the Commonwealth and globally. Because of this increasing risk, young people are becoming more involved and vocal in outlining their priority areas of focus to governments and relevant stakeholders within the environmental space. Based on consultations held with young people in developing its Youth Engagement Plan, the NDC Partnership highlighted four priority areas for youth inclusion. These are reviewed below.

Education, training and capacity development

Looking beyond the formal inclusion of climate change education within the established school system, priority must be placed on the provision of specialised and context-specific training and capacity development programmes for young people who are active within the environmental space. This is particularly critical for youth in the Global South. Against the background of efforts towards "building back better" within the

context of a post-pandemic green recovery, youth organisations require capacity to mobilise resources, to develop and utilise various youth engagement tools and facilities and to conduct regular research, analysis and knowledge-sharing that can support national and regional recovery efforts. The Commonwealth is, for instance, supporting Cambridge University in advancing a Climate Policy Boot Camp, which seeks to introduce systems thinking into a participatory policy consultation process.

The training must be context-specific to speak to the direct needs and situation of each member country, thereby setting the framework for more effective results.

Disaster risk reduction and resilience

Youth have great potential to drive disaster risk reduction and resilience-building efforts. While disaster effects on children and young people are often key considerations in disaster risk reduction planning, young people should also be seen as assets in designing and developing early warning systems as well as other mitigation actions.

The April 2021 International Union for Conservation of Nature (IUCN) Global Youth Summit has highlighted the growing involvement and contribution of young people around the globe in nature conservation and climate movements. Moreover, nature-based solutions (NbS) such as coral reefs and forest conservation practices are useful in helping communities prepare for, deal with and recover from direct and indirect impacts of natural disasters. In relation to natural disasters, ecosystems can act as a natural buffer, while also conserving biodiversity and improving soil and water conditions, thereby strengthening the overall resilience of citizens. Therefore, a continued increase in youth participation in guiding NbS will be critical in driving global nature restoration efforts within this United Nations Decade of Ecosystem Restoration (2021-2030).

The Commonwealth Secretariat through the proposed Living Lands Charter will contribute towards co-ordinated action on advancing NbS as key, cost-effective options to address climate, biodiversity and land degradation issues, while also delivering socio-economic benefits and reducing climate hazards in climatically vulnerable countries. Within the implementation process of the Charter, five action groups,[2] which will co-ordinate implementation, provide an ideal platform for young people to actively be involved in advancing NbS in member countries.

Employment

> "*It is crucial that young people become active players within the green economy.*"

The COVID-19 pandemic has exacerbated existing employment challenges facing young people around the globe, with further emerging challenges expected within the post-COVID era. As part of global efforts to build back better, there will be increased emphasis on advancing a green recovery, with green jobs a central component of this transition.

It is therefore crucial that young people position themselves to be active players within the green economy as employers and employees. National and multilateral agencies should stand ready to embrace this transition, providing the necessary support, particularly to youth-led interventions that will catalyse global climate and economic recovery efforts.

Research and innovation

The dynamic nature of the threats posed by climate change to lives and livelihoods means that there is always a need to develop, assess and enhance solutions to meet the diverse changes. Young people from across the Commonwealth have demonstrated the ability to develop high-impact solutions to meet our environmental challenges. The examples shared in Section 10.3 of this chapter on #YouthTakingCharge of environment and climate change represent but a few illustrations of youth innovation and contribution.

Research and development must be central in our efforts towards achieving the Sustainable Development Goals, in particular SDG 13 on climate action. Such approaches will set the basis for the utilisation in climate resilience efforts of emerging technologies for which young people are developing the relevant expertise. The Climate Change Section of the Commonwealth Secretariat has, for instance, embraced the need to support and incorporate innovations within its programme of support to member countries, by exploring the use of blockchain technology, remote sensing technologies and, potentially, artificial intelligence in climate financing.

Public–private sector partnerships can play a significant role in driving the level of youth-led research and innovation necessary to create meaningful environmental impact. There is a growing thrust towards, for example, governments exploring with development banks in facilitating the provision of more accessible financing facilities for youth-led climate research projects.

10.1.4 Commonwealth Climate Change Programme and youth engagement

The Commonwealth has a demonstrated track record in assisting and supporting its member countries to address and deal with the adverse impacts of climate change. In addition to influencing international policies, mechanisms and rules to be more responsive to the development needs of climate change-vulnerable countries, the Secretariat places a great emphasis on facilitating the capacity development of member countries to access climate finance – providing assistance to enable member countries to enhance and implement their NDCs as part of the Paris Agreement.

Young people (under 30 years) constitute more than 60 percent of the Commonwealth population and are therefore seen as key stakeholders in the development process. The Commonwealth's mandate on youth empowerment emphasises meaningful access to development and policy processes, as a critical way of ensuring that young people's unique perspectives and ideas are heard and included in decision-making.

The Commonwealth Youth Climate Change Network (CYCN), for instance, was established in 2009 as a platform for enhancing the capacity of young people to effectively advocate and facilitate action aimed at addressing climate change and other environmental issues. The CYCN plays a critical role in advocating within governments, international agencies and global spaces such as COPs to the UNFCCC, ensuring that the voices of youth are heard and considered in the development of climate policies.

The Climate Change Section is placing an increased focus on mainstreaming youth in the climate change space, ensuring they are empowered to effectively engage in climate change mitigation and adaptation efforts at all levels. In this regard, working together with the Youth Division and its affiliate Youth Climate Change Network in the lead-up to COP26, the section seeks to facilitate and ensure greater formal inclusion of Commonwealth youth in NDCs and their implementation. Throughout this process, the Secretariat will place emphasis on encouraging member countries to recognise the key role of young people as stakeholders in supporting the attainment of Paris Agreement targets and to prioritise youth in the NDC process. This engagement also involves utilising the convening power of the Commonwealth as a platform to help showcase youth-led climate change interventions to facilitate potential scaling-up of such initiatives within the margins of COP26 and associated events.

Moreover, the flagship initiative of the Climate Change Programme – the Commonwealth Climate Finance Access Hub (CCFAH), which deploys climate finance experts in government departments – is a key vehicle of assistance to member countries in developing grant applications, strengthening climate change policy and building capacity. In an effort to mainstream the involvement of youth in climate action, there is now a greater focus on the inclusion of youth and gender within the work programme of these climate finance advisers. Furthermore, as the CYCN expands with the establishment of chapters in member countries, a mapping of CCFAH advisers alongside CYCN chapters is being conducted to better tailor direct in-country youth in climate action support.

The Secretariat will continue to leverage partnerships and build on synergies in a continued thrust to enhance programmes of support in response to the needs of member countries, contributing to their ability to deliver on their climate change policies and NDCs in an inclusive manner.

Recommendations

Young people have a critical role to play across all phases of NDCs, from development and enhancement to implementation. Formalising the inclusion of young people in climate action, particularly within the formal UNFCCC processes, will play a critical role in advancing and catalysing climate action in member countries. Also, within the context of the COVID-19 green recovery efforts, it is therefore important that:

Youth

- Place emphasis on mobilising young people, particularly from the Global South, in improving their understanding of the direct climate change impacts and their role in contributing to resilience efforts;

- Capitalise on existing small grants facilities such as the Global Environment Facility Small Grants Programme, through multi stakeholder partnerships to support accessibility, in advancing community-based climate change mitigation and adaptation actions to support national efforts.

Member countries

- Member countries fully recognise the importance and formally commit to engaging youth in the development, implementation, monitoring and evaluation of climate change policies and programmes through formal legal frameworks, including addressing these within NDCs;

- Ensure the inclusion of young people in sectoral adaptation planning, particularly in small island developing states (SIDS), thereby ensuring the inclusion of diverse youth in environmental development planning, while also taking into account gender and ethnic considerations in line with Article 7 of the Paris Agreement;

- In line with Article 11 of the Paris Agreement, facilitate capacity-building of young people as partners in resilience efforts, ensuring their skill development and providing the technical support necessary to enhance access to climate finance and to scale up youth-led climate action initiatives;

- Prioritise NbS as a cost-effective tool to accelerate climate action while also ensuring its inclusion in climate change negotiation, financing and action.

International organisations

- Prioritise and enhance dedicated financing facilities to support youth-led climate change research and innovation, which will facilitate the integration of emerging technologies and methodologies in national and regional resilience efforts. This can help address existing gaps such as data limitations for climate finance in developing countries;

- Continue to utilise their convening power in providing a platform for knowledge-sharing among young people, while also bringing forth their solutions with potential for scaling-up.

Guest Contributor

Youth and Climate Change: An Inter-generational Injustice Worsened

Angelique Pouponneau, Chief Executive Officer of the Seychelles' Conservation and Climate Adaptation Trust[3]

Born to existential and debt crises: A reality for today's youth and future generations

Generally, it seemed we were heading in the right direction, and 2020 was set to be a year of hope. The countries of the world intended to set a new target for global marine protection, to raise climate ambition through revised national climate plans; finally, we would have had a legally binding instrument that would reverse years of *laissez-faire* on two-thirds of the planet – that is, the high seas. Some targets under SDG 14 had matured and were providing an opportunity for us to see what had gone wrong and why we had not been successful.

Then, the pandemic struck, and decades of work and progress were eroded with one contagious cough. A youthful world waited for hope – but instead now faces even higher youth unemployment, limited prospects and the risk of inheriting an economic crisis of epic proportions; and all the while a climate crisis looms. Faced with an existential threat and a debt crisis spiralling out of control, young people remain on the side-lines of governance and marginalised from decision-making processes at national, regional and international levels.

Years lost, debts gained

COVID-19 is confining young people to their homes. Many children and youth are going months without access to education, and some are experiencing a clear reduction in the quality of education. The internet is perceived to be the solution, yet the challenges of access to electrification, let alone the internet, are well known. Others have had their access to educational progression delayed as scholarships dwindle. School leavers and university graduates apply for jobs without success, either because posts have closed as businesses shrink or shut their doors or because preference is given to others who are now unemployed but have experience. A sense of hopelessness is rising across a generation while the older generation takes decisions, alone, whose impacts the youth will automatically inherit.

With little time committed to planning and innovation, many governments have found that incurring more debt is the only way to finance the recovery. Officials from global financial institutions fly across the world to provide "expert" advice and incur new debts that no one at the table will ever have to contribute to paying. The sharp increase in debt accumulated by governments to fund the recovery of COVID-19 will undoubtedly mean that today's youth, anyone born today and at least two generations to follow will inherit huge amounts of financial obligation.

The existential threat

Threatening the lives of young people is not only the debt burden but also the existential threat of climate change. In 2015, countries submitted their climate plans in line with the Paris Agreement, stating commitment to achieving global goals, including to keep temperature rise to below 1.5°C above pre-industrial levels. However, work is not on the right trajectory; instead, reports are indicating a 3.2°C rise in temperature. At the less than 3.2°C scenario, normality will mean facing an existential threat for small island states. Of the world's 38 SIDS, 25 are Commonwealth member countries. This means that some our Commonwealth family may cease to be above sea level and droves of people, including large proportions of young people, will be forcefully displaced. The only hope is that the revised climate plans will close the emissions gap. However, the first synthesis report of the United Nations Climate Secretariat, based on the submission of 48 revised climate plans, indicates that they fall significantly short of meeting the 45 per cent reduction in total CO_2 emissions from 2010 to keep warming below 1.5°C. The combined emissions cut is at only 3 per cent.

Perhaps it is no surprise. The responsibility for developing these five-, ten- or twenty-five-year plans lies in the hands of a few people in decision-making positions, assisted by international organisations. Some countries applaud efforts to consult young people; other countries see these documents as too high level for youth. Nonetheless, consulted or not, youth will automatically inherit these plans. However, it has often been seen that, when youth are part of the process very early on, they are likely to have a sense of ownership of such documents, and to lead the changes and plans that have been agreed. These revised climate plans thus provide a key opportunity to make decisions and plans that ensure intergenerational equity and protect the human rights of citizens, especially the future of youth. Meanwhile, there are calls to bridge the gap between the street activism of millions of young people and the negotiation table, which would be helped through the inclusion of youth in developing NDCs.

Today, decisions are taken by those aged 55 and above, and it is their deliberations that will decide the fate and lives of the children and youth of today. Current decision-making outcomes will decide whether the youth of today will be grappling with collapsed ecosystems, a crippled economy and a lack of alternatives, or whether they will have an opportunity to escape these scientific predictions and be able to look back and think that decisions were taken in their best interests. As things stand, youth are preparing themselves for the former – a dire future.

Since the last Commonwealth Heads of Government Meeting (CHOGM), the catastrophic effects of a changing climate have already been felt, with these extreme weather events predicted to be the new normal. We have seen more people affected by such events in the Commonwealth. For example, people have lost their lives to more intense and prolonged heat waves in India; Nigeria has seen the displacement of more than 500,000 people following severe flooding; and Hurricane Dorian, a Category 5 hurricane, has ravaged The Bahamas. Cyclones Idai and Kenneth in Mozambique, Zimbabwe and Malawi affected 3 million people, including 1.5 million children (under the age of 18) (UNICEF, 2019). Unfortunately, youth-disaggregated data is unavailable or difficult to find when assessing the impacts of such disasters on young people. Such disasters also lead to economic losses and distress, in particular in least developed countries (LDCs) and SIDS, with the impacts felt in communities for many years.

While such events catch the attention of the media, and humanitarian assistance is flown in, slow-onset events caused by climate change, such as the warming and acidification of the ocean, causing the collapse of coral reefs or the rise of sea levels, do not receive the same focus. Small states in the Commonwealth are particularly vulnerable as these events undermine the food security of the local population, endanger the livelihoods of people dependent on tourism and, in fact, pose a threat to their existence. Inaction today could lead to statelessness and undermine all our efforts to achieve the SDGs.

Born to debt and an existential threat – it is unfair but the one way not to further aggravate this double injustice lies in the way governments choose to recover. Debt financing for COVID-19 recovery should go towards a low-carbon green or blue recovery. That is, this should be used as an opportunity to invest in renewable energy to meet energy needs, to create jobs that are environmentally friendly and to invest in green and blue solutions. In doing so, at least the future is less bleak than if the same fossil fuel-driven investments are made, with the same excuse that this is how it has always been done.

In spite of all of this, youth are forging a pathway to build a secure and resilient future, using COVID-19 as an opportunity for regeneration, to rethink and rebuild in a more resilient society.

Guest Contributor

Youth priorities

Faced with existential threats and an increasing debt burden, young people are invested in building a future that ensures their survival. They have prioritised education, green or blue entrepreneurship, climate finance, and civic and political participation as avenues to transform their realities into a resilient future.

Education

Education is critical to the transition to green development. In 2015, the Commonwealth had already developed a set of recommendations for governments to ensure climate change was addressed in formal and non-formal education. However, so far, in most Commonwealth countries, climate change remains only informally included in the curriculum. Without an initial investment in the education on sustainability and climate change, youth will not be in a position to transform their reality. Education should be engaged as a mechanism to develop a workforce with the skills and knowledge to power green growth.

Blue and green entrepreneurship

Efforts to address climate change are often seen as the work of well-meaning activists and not-for-profits calling to save the world. Absent from such efforts to provide climate solutions has been the private sector. Blue/green enterprises represent an opportunity to solve a global challenge while generating revenue. However, kick-starting such enterprises is not easy. Seed capital is required, especially for young people unable to secure the guarantees for bank loans. At a time when resources seem limited, many are asking how to finance such initiatives. Governments have an opportunity to ensure a blue/green recovery by re-channelling investments and subsidies that currently go to fossil fuel industries towards clean energy sources and to youth innovation and entrepreneurship. Outstanding innovations have been seen across all regions of the Commonwealth, as shown in Section 10.3 of this chapter. In addition, we can take note of:

- **Brian Kakembo**, 2020 Commonwealth Young Person of the Year, from Uganda, is transforming biodegradable plastics and organic waste into eco-friendly charcoal briquettes. Through education, Brian empowers his community to generate bio-gas and recycle non-bio-waste products. He has successfully empowered 800 women and youth.

- **Bobby Siarani**, the 2018 Commonwealth youth awardee from Solomon Islands, seeks to convert organic waste to bio-gas and to solve the major problem of the absence of cooking gas in Solomon Islands. He has now expanded his project to provide clean energy to hundreds of people in the rural areas of Solomon Islands.

- **Jonathan Barcant** from Trinidad and Tobago, a civil engineer, has founded the Vetivier Education and Empowerment Project, a cost-effective bio-engineering scheme to build climate change resilience. The scheme delivers a penetrating root system to stabilise land, preventing erosion and slowing down water run-off. This is a proven powerful tool to build resilience against climate change.

Climate finance

Many developing countries have expressed disappointment that a preference for mitigation projects over adaptation projects persists in the Green Climate Fund. Countries have been calling for attainment of a 50:50 balance in funding allocations between adaptation and mitigation. And yet, adapting to the impacts of climate change is costly, and finance is scarce because adaptation action seldom generates revenue. Nevertheless, failing to mitigate and adapt means we will reach the tipping point – where we reach the limit to adaptation. That is, loss and damage. This is where ecosystems are collapsing beyond rehabilitation, human mobility across borders is the norm and both sudden and slow-onset events are very frequent. There is no funding stream to support such circumstances and, although some think this is many years away, it is not. We saw all the Barbudans displaced in one event!

Young people know what is required to resolve many of the issues facing them today but are seldom included in the planning, designing and evaluation phases of climate change projects. As a result, projects fail to meet the needs of youth or to include innovation. In 2019, the Japanese minister responsible for the environment called for the Green Climate Fund (GCF) to invest in technological climate initiatives undertaken by youth (IISD, 2019). Young people are also calling on governments to make structures such as the GCF and the Adaptation Fund more accessible, including for youth. At this point in time, though, youth are unable to access these financing opportunities. The lack of finance channelled to youth means that greener solutions and blue and green businesses cannot be scaled up to provide the transformational change that is required. Such efforts thus remain small in scale. If funds are made available, they are not made accessible to youth organisations, as these often have limited experience in writing elaborate project applications.[4]

Case profile: The Youth Climate Lab

YCL, a Canada-based but global non-profit organisation that accelerates youth-led policy, projects and businesses was founded by Dominique Souris of Canada and Ana Gonzales Guerro of Mexico to support and scale youth-led climate solutions. YCL designs youth-inclusive climate financing tools and cohorts that build the capacity of young people to co-create ideas, strengthen their impact and increase their ability to access finance. Since its inception in 2017, it has supported over 47 early-stage youth-led climate solutions. As it continues to increase its portfolio, YCL is focused on addressing the systemic barriers that limit youth access to resources. It is designing new projects to catalyse youth-responsive financing by convening funders and partners to develop and facilitate innovative financing mechanisms to build the capacity of young climate leaders and entrepreneurs and help them scale their transformative ideas.

Political inclusion

Disillusioned by their realities, young people are reacting in a mixed way to political processes; in some instances, young people are actively being deprived of their ability to participate in public office or political processes.

While for many countries the delegation attending climate negotiations has an average age of 60, some Commonwealth member countries have shown their willingness to give young people some responsibility by allowing them to participate officially in the meetings of the UNFCCC. **Lia Nicholson**, a Queen's Young Leader, is one such youth, who advises and assists the Government of Antigua and Barbuda to develop policies to address the threats of climate change. Lia is described as a climate finance expert with significant experience in implementing solutions in the community and helping secure funds for implementation.

Dominique and Angelique co-ordinate the Seychelles Support Team (SST), a group of young people from around the world who are trained in responding to the priorities of small island nations and negotiating on the international stage. The group is badged by the Government of Seychelles, to provide support to Seychelles and ensure that all speeches delivered by the minister encompass the voices of young people. At COP24, the Seychelles delegation benefited from over 618 hours research and synthesis provided by SST members, while the latter gained access to the full extent of the negotiations as Party delegates, spoke with thought leaders on climate policy and formed connections around the world. Meaningful participation in negotiations means full understanding, access and ability to contribute to policy outcomes. To this end, SST members produced summaries of changes in negotiating text that Alliance of Small Island States co-ordinators for adaptation were able to use in co-ordination meetings. Team members distilled notes from negotiating sessions down to key issues and red and pink lines crossed. The summaries allowed Seychelles to keep informed about key developments on cross-cutting issues, such as loss and damage, across all negotiating streams in a way that would be otherwise impossible given the size of the delegation.

This initiative is supported by the Prep4COP initiative led by the CYCN, which prepares youth from across the Commonwealth to become effective climate change advocates.

Recommendations from a young CEO

It is clear that young people are not mere bystanders but active nation-builders and will be instrumental in ensuring that the future is

Guest Contributor

equitable, safe and habitable. It is still of utmost importance that governments provide the space and opportunities to make this possible by:

- Creating platforms where young people can engage directly with decision-makers at all levels of governance and be part of decision-making;

- Making finance, multilateral, regional or national funds available and accessible to youth. This should include technical support and capacity-building, as available through the CCFAH;

- Taking bold steps such as removing subsidies for fossil fuel companies and re-channelling these to renewable and clean energy and supporting green/blue enterprises;

- Planning for an economic recovery that is sustainable and does not simply push debt obligations to future generations;

- Taking bold and ambitious climate actions both nationally and internationally.

10.2 Youth taking charge of the Environment and Climate

In addition to the cases highlighted by Angelique Pouponneau in her perspective piece, we highlight here recent finalists of the 2021 Commonwealth Youth Awards who are implementing interesting initiatives to protect the environment and respond to climate change.

Ellenor McIntosh from the UK is taking charge of protecting the environment by creating products that will help achieve SDG 6 on clean water and sanitation. Ellenor is the Co-Founder and Inventor of Twipes, a flushable, biodegradable wet wipe made of wood pulp. Through the production and sales of Twipes, the company aims to reduce the environmental damage caused by traditional wet wipes. The product has been sold to restaurants, gyms and hotel chains across the UK and a percentage of the business profits is donated to creating clean water systems in Uganda.

Jeremiah Thoronka is taking charge of the environment and climate change by contributing to the attainment of SDG 7 on affordable and clean energy. Jeremiah is the founder of Optim Energy, a company that harnesses solar energy through innovative technology to create affordable, accessible and clean power for communities

in Sierra Leone. The project has helped power over 150 households and 15 schools in Sierra Leone at minimal cost, has benefited over 10,000 people and provides best practice training on energy efficiency and conservation to the younger generation

Nawa Joe Silishebo is taking charge of the environment by engaging young people to achieve SDG 8 on decent work and economic growth. Nawa is the Co-Founder of the Young Emerging Farmers Initiative, which promotes and empowers young people in agribusiness and climate change action through skills training, fundraising and outreach programmes in Zambia. The initiative has reached over 500,000 young people across 10 Zambian provinces in rural and urban areas and helped train 5,000 youths in agribusiness, including connecting over 100 "agri-preneurs" to financial support and markets.

Mogesh Sababathy is contributing to sustaining life below water (SDG 14). He is Co-Founder of Project Ocean Hope, a youth-led group that aims to raise the visibility of ocean issues and environmental conservation through campaigns and youth leadership training. The group has also run educational community projects to reduce littering and unsustainable fishing practices, and an ocean literacy webinar series on waste management, reaching over 10,000 individuals across 15 countries.

Bevon Chadel Charles is from Grenada and is taking charge through agriculture, which will reduce hunger in the Caribbean (SDG 2) and contribute to employment and sustainability. Bevon founded Akata Farms, which aims to create sustainable farms and livelihoods across the Caribbean through climate-smart agriculture. The farms operate across 100 acres providing fresh, quality goods in person and online, and the organisation provides peer-to-peer mentorship to young people, particularly women, looking to start businesses in agriculture.

'Ilaisaane Lolohea Manu from Tonga is creating employment opportunities for young people while taking care of the environment through sustainable fashion. 'Ilaisaane is a National Youth Advocate and Programme Administrator & Community Liaison Officer for GO GREEN!, a youth-led community initiative creating employment opportunities through entrepreneurship and mentorship support. The programme also provides affordable, sustainable fashion as well as encouraging fashion and design talent and ethical recycling. The programme has

engaged over 1,000 people through community-led outreach initiatives, provided basic work skills to hundreds of volunteers and repurposed over 1,000 pieces of clothing.

Endnotes

1   This analysis has been led by the Climate Change Section of the Commonwealth Secretariat and prepared by Jevanic Henry.

2   The Action Groups focus on 1. Climate Resilient Agriculture for Food Security 2. Soil and Water Conservation and Management 3. Sustainable Green Cover and Biodiversity 4. Carbon Neutral and Climate Resilient Livestock Rearing and Animal Husbandry 5. Indigenous Peoples and Climate Resilient Development.

3   Appointed at the age of 28, Angelique Pouponneau, former Executive Member of the Commonwealth Youth Council, now heads up a multi-million-dollar trust fund, the Seychelles' Conservation and Climate Adaptation Trust (SeyCCAT). Within her first year in office, she had moved SeyCCAT's grants portfolio from 7 per cent (US$7,400) of grants channelled to youth to 30 per cent (over $300,000) providing finance for youth-driven climate and ocean initiatives.

4   The Secretariat notes that it is equally important to provide capacity-building and technical assistance to young people in support of their access to financing and effective project implementation. The CCFAH has been supporting these types of capacity-building projects.

References

IISD (International Institute for Sustainable Development) (2019) "GCF Presents First Replenishment to Increase Climate Finance for Most Vulnerable". 19 December. https://sdg.iisd.org/news/gcf-presents-first-replenishment-to-increase-climate-finance-for-most-vulnerable/

UNDP (United Nations Development Programme) (2020) *Climate Promise Progress Report Special Edition on NDCs and Inclusivity*. New York: UNDP.

UNEP (United Nations Environment Programme) (2021) "Executive Summary", in Adaptation Gap Report 2020. Nairobi: UNEP.

UNICEF (United Nations Children's Fund) (2019) "Cyclone Idai Response". 27 March. https://www.unicef.org/press-releases/cyclone-idai-more-15-million-children-urgently-need-assistance-across-mozambique

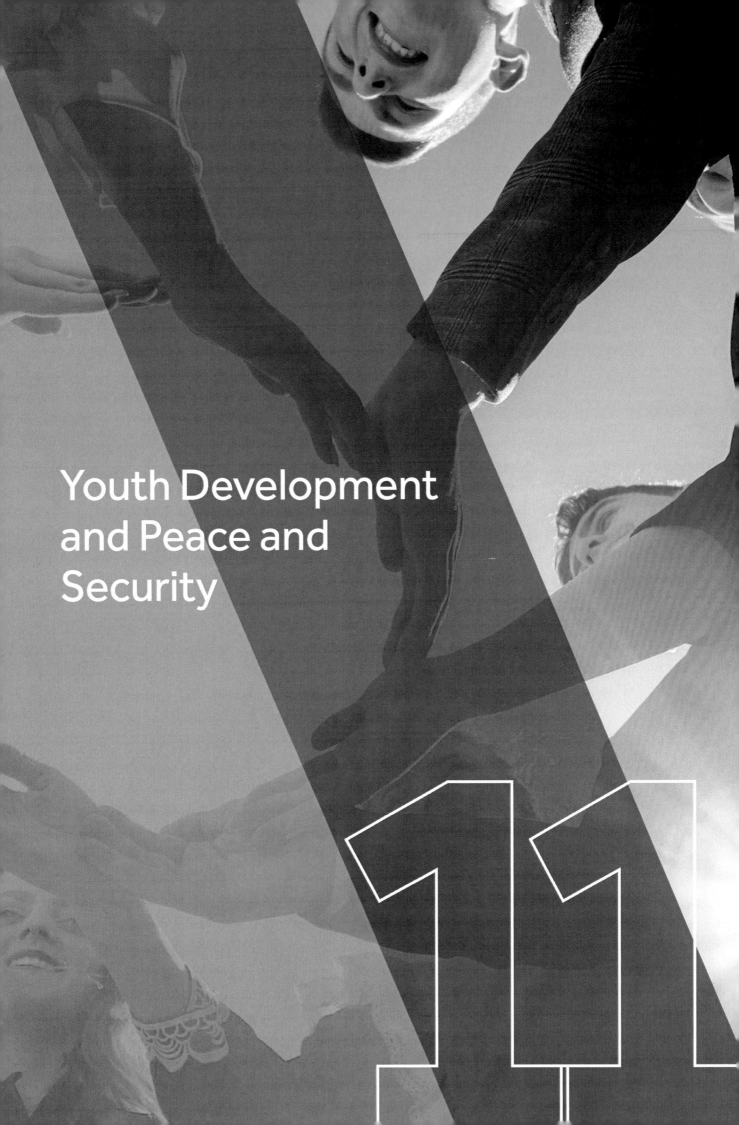

Youth Development and Peace and Security

11

Chapter 11

Youth Development and Peace and Security

The year 2020 marks the fifth anniversary of the adoption of UN Security Council Resolution 2250 (UNSCR 2250), which initiated a global agenda on Youth, Peace and Security (YPS) based on five key pillars to address the security needs of young people and recognising their positive role in promoting peace and security in the world. The agenda was acknowledged and endorsed by the Commonwealth Heads of Government Meeting in 2018. The anniversary calls for reflection on the progress that has been made on the main elements of the agenda - participation, protection, prevention, partnerships, and disengagement and reintegration.

This chapter seeks to reflect on progress on the advancement of the YPS Agenda in two ways. First, it highlights innovative initiatives that have been designed and implemented since the adoption of the resolution and in response to the recommendations of the Global Progress Study on YPS: "The Missing Peace." Second, it reflects on the potential to strengthen data for use in monitoring progress in this area. The 2020 YDI includes, for the first time, indicators that assess the effects of interpersonal violence, conflict, terrorism, and humanitarian crisis and disaster on young people. As a newly included domain, Peace and Security has the potential for refinement, and this chapter discusses proposals for related indicators that could be considered in the future.

Guest Contributor

#Youth4Peace – Changing Faces of Leadership in Peace and Security

Lakshita Saji Prelis, Co-Chair of the Global Coalition on Youth Peace and Security and Director of Children and Youth Programs at Search for Common Ground

One in four youth are directly affected by armed conflict or violence. Across Africa, Asia and the Middle East, the median age is in the teens or 20s. Young people constitute a broad heterogeneous group with multiple and intersecting identities in relation to gender, sexual orientation, skin colour, ethnic origin, religion, disability, status as a refugee, migrant or internally displaced person, rural or suburban background, and educational background.

They are now experiencing the intersection of several crises, including the COVID-19 pandemic; systemic marginalisation, such as racism, class divides and sectarian conflicts, that fuels massive inequities; climate change; exclusionary politics that benefit the elite and well connected at the expense of the majority; and an unemployment crisis that is characterised by limited opportunities and low and steadily declining wages.

In the face of these unprecedented and historic challenges, young people are woven in an interconnected global network, leading trans-local lives and organising powerful social movements that transcend national boundaries. Evidence from around the world clearly shows how young people are effectively preventing violence, and how their voices continue to represent the resistance needed against the exclusionary systems that divide and deprioritise the needs of young people both today and tomorrow (Simpson, 2018; Search for Common Ground, 2019).

Overview of the YPS Agenda

Young people have been contributing to peace for millennia. Their work received international political recognition first in 2015 with the adoption of UNSCR 2250, followed by UNSCR 2419 (in 2018) and UNSCR 2535 (in 2020). With the adoption of these historic resolutions, the YPS Agenda brought a paradigm shift to peace-building, humanitarian action and sustainable development by recognising young people as critical actors and urging the integration of their specific needs into peace processes and humanitarian action. Commonwealth Youth Ministers were early adopters of this agenda when they first endorsed the Guiding Principles for Young People's Participation in Peacebuilding in 2015, a key milestone that shaped UNSCR (Search for Common Ground, 2015). The United States House of Representatives has now also introduced legislation to further support this agenda that improves how the US Government supports young people in shaping the country's foreign policy (United States Congress, 2020).

Over the past six years, several milestones have been achieved in the implementation of the YPS Agenda. A global coalition of over a 100 UN agencies, inter-governmental bodies, international civil society and youth-led groups, donors and scholars has come together to co-shape the agenda.[1] In addition, inspired by these global shifts in narrative, young people have forged their own paths locally by forming a growing number of national YPS coalitions to work collaboratively and inter-generationally with various national and international stakeholders in their countries. The YPS Agenda encourages the international community and national actors to ask a new question. Beyond focusing on why young people join armed groups, this represents an effort to understand *Why are most youth peaceful?* This question is at the heart of the prevention agenda. It focuses on working with young people and communities to address the underlying causes of violence and exclusion.

Guest Contributor

Progress on the Agenda

Four formative documents have been produced to ground the YPS Agenda and showcase how young people address the underlying causes of violent conflict, thereby contributing to prevention. They are the following.

- "The Missing Peace: The Independent Progress Study on Youth, Peace and Security" (Simpson, 2018) was the first comprehensive study on the positive contributions of youth, inspired by the new question Why are most youth peaceful? It describes how youth-led peace work is often proactive, pre-emptive and preventive.

- Responding to UNSCR 2419, the Global Policy Paper "We Are Here: An Integrated Approach to Youth Inclusive Peace Processes" (Altiok and Grizelj, 2019) illustrates the political agency of youth as positive forces for peace, via their contributions to previously closed and top-down peace processes. It also shows how the inclusion of young people during all phases of peace processes increases the sustainability of agreements.

- The UN Secretary-General produced the first official progress report on YPS in March 2020. While recognising positive contributions to the agenda, the Secretary-General also identified key challenges that needed to be addressed. These include enduring structural barriers that limit the participation of young people and their capacity to influence decision-making; violations of their human rights; and insufficient investment in facilitating their inclusion and empowerment (UN Secretary-General, 2020).

- Subsequently, the African Union (AU) Continental Framework for Youth, Peace and Security and its "Study on the Roles and Contributions of Youth to Peace and Security in Africa" have further strengthened the YPS agenda, guiding responses on the continent (AU, 2020a; 2020b).

As the YPS agenda gains more attention, three parallel and complementary efforts will underpin the next decade of work: (i) shaping a set of positive social norms about youth; (ii) strengthening institutional commitments to partner with youth to address the compounded and complex challenges faced by countries; and (iii) developing a new marketplace for sustaining peace locally, nationally, regionally and globally. To succeed, a new generation of YPS practice must be founded in the institutional and individual collaboration in pursuit of collective impact at the national, regional and international levels. The new collaborative practice is developing in the following five areas.

Political buy-in and strengthening the enabling environment for YPS

In 2022, the Governments of Finland, Qatar and Colombia will co-host a high-level conference in Doha, Qatar. At that event, Heads of State and Government will gather alongside leaders from international organisations, civil society actors and youth leaders from countries that have majority youth populations, experiences of armed conflict and violence and active formal peace processes. The conference will launch (i) guidance for governments on how to develop and sustain national YPS strategies and actions and (ii) a five-year strategic roadmap for collaboratively developing and strengthening the field of youth inclusive peace processes. This is in response to UNSCR 2419 and UNSCR 2535. The process is co-led by Search for Common Ground (Search) and the UN Secretary-General's Envoy on Youth (on behalf of the UN) in partnership with members of the Global Coalition on Youth, Peace and Security and the Mediation Support Units of the UN, the EU, the AU and sub-regional organisations.

Strengthening youth leadership for change

To move beyond the traditional, top-down style of youth-focused programming often implemented in the peace-building field, Search and the United Network of Young Peacebuilders (UNOY) have developed a holistic support model called Youth 360.[2] Youth 360 creates a new partnership dynamic through a facilitated youth-led, adult-supported process whereby youth groups gain access to funding, technical support and decision-making power. This model has been developed in close collaboration with the UN Alliance of Civilizations and the UN Peacebuilding Fund. The Youth 360 approach includes collaborative context analysis, participatory grant-making, mentorship and capacity development workshops. In 2020, Search and UNOY piloted this approach with over 500 youth groups. Initial findings indicate that it has been highly successful in transforming traditional power dynamics that have limited the role of young people, while also helping youth lead change in their own contexts.

Measuring the social return on investment in youth-led peace-building

An SROI study will help quantify the impact of youth-led peace-building-oriented efforts on their peers, their communities, various national and local institutions, and the private sector. The analysis could serve as a basis for funding and investment decisions; communicating impact and financial results to stakeholders; and ensuring long-term accountability to young people. The SROI methodology forges a collective new understanding among stakeholders on how to assess impact. Currently, a proof of concept approach is being developed to pilot the methodology. The pilot is intended to provide an empirical evidence base on the impact of youth-led peace-building efforts, with a view to better informing broader decisions about investments and programming by policy-makers, donors, international non-governmental organisations and youth themselves. The lead research team conducting the SROI analysis will be supported by an Expert Advisory Group convened by Search. This group includes experts from the Commonwealth Secretariat, the World Bank, the AU Youth Peace & Security Division, the Alliance for Peacebuilding, the US Agency for International Development (USAID), the UN Peacebuilding Support Office and UNOY peace-builders.

Strengthening investments in youth leadership for peace

Lack of adequate financial resources for youth is a profound impediment to achievement of the Sustainable Development Goals and peace-building. For approximately 65 per cent of youth-led peace-building groups, the annual operating budget is below US$10,000. To meet this challenge, "The Missing Peace" made the case for "allocating US$1.8 billion, representing an investment of US$1 per young person, by 2025 for the 10th anniversary of resolution 2250." The UN's Peacebuilding Fund

has taken proactive measures to support young people's critical contributions to peace-building at the local and national levels through the annual Youth Promotion Initiative. Between 2016 and 2019, the Peacebuilding Fund invested a total of $57.2 million through the initiative. The EU and USAID have also increased their investments to support young peace-builders. Unfortunately, barriers remain that prevent some young peace-builders from accessing funding through these formal channels, further disenfranchising them. In this context, Search and UNOY launched an independent global YPS Fund in March 2021 that intends to disrupt traditional funding models by (i) ensuring young people are co-owners and co-investors of the fund, (ii) moving from a transactional short-term relationship to a long-term collaborative decision-making model and (iii) adopting the Youth 360 approach to support youth leadership and capacity as a foundational pillar of the fund to ensure that organisations at varying levels of capacity can access support.[3]

Protection and safeguarding of young peace-builders and young human rights defenders

The protection pillar of UNSCR 2250 is a central tenet of the YPS Agenda. Yet young people are facing a multitude of protection-related threats and challenges. The UN Secretary-General notes continuing threats to and human rights violations against young peace-builders and human rights defenders. Throughout the COVID-19 pandemic of 2020 and 2021, the lack of effective protection mechanisms has become very visible, especially for those who have organised peaceful protests. Many notable non-violent protests and social movements, led by young people, have been faced with threats, intimidation, violence and even murder. These movements include Fridays for Future, Black Lives Matter, #EndSARS and the democracy movement in Myanmar, known locally as the Spring Revolution. Search has partnered with the Office of the UN Secretary-General's Envoy on Youth to co-lead a working group with over 60 members to develop guidance on strengthening protection and safeguarding measures for young people, as part of the Global Coalition's mandate. Based on existing research, the working group

Guest Contributor

has identified the following categories and types of protection challenges faced by young peace-builders around the world.

- **Political:** Targeted persecution, disabling environment and exclusion;

- **Physical:** Violence, torture, abuse and imprisonment;

- **Financial:** Adult dependence and lack of accessible funds;

- **Gendered:** Gender-based violence, cultural stigma and exclusion on the basis of gender;

- **Legal:** Restrictive legislation and policies, including on freedom of assembly and lawsuits;

- **Sociocultural:** Stereotyping, pressure and stigmatisation;

- **Psychosocial:** Mental health disorders, post-traumatic stress disorder, intimidation and age-based health disparities;

- **Digital:** Online harassment, censorship, surveillance and violation of privacy.

Overall, what is clear is that a majority of young people are targeted simply because of their young age and their activism. It is important to note that these threats do not happen in isolation, but rather in cumulative, and complex, ways, often overlapping and transforming from one to another.

Recommendations on the way forward for practice

In 2020, the COVID-19 pandemic disrupted the lives of young people worldwide. Traditional rituals of going to school, graduating, going to places of employment and visiting places of worship all stopped as countries locked down to stop the spread of a virus that does not discriminate based on religion or nationality, but that has had a devastating impact on the poor globally. This quickly became a defining cultural and political moment for young people globally, while exposing the deepest cracks in our social, political, economic and health systems. Recovery will take decades. This defining moment could be embraced as an opportunity for governments and civil society to rewrite a new social contract in partnership with young people.

To do this well, it is critical to transform the systems that reinforce exclusion by addressing the structural barriers limiting meaningful youth inclusion and participation at the community and national levels. Based on this, key recommendations are to:

- Appoint Youth Advisers at the highest level of government decision-making and within key government bodies;

- Adopt an inclusive approach to develop national YPS strategies and actions in partnership with young people;

- Reimagine what the next generation of mediation processes could look like and engage young people in the process of developing an inclusive national infrastructure for peace to address the root causes of conflict and exclusion;

- Support, strengthen and embrace young people's non-violent movements and protests as a key foundation within the infrastructure for peace;

- Financially invest in youth civic engagement and participation.

11.1 Towards quantifying progress[4]

The five pillars of UNSCR 2250 – participation, protection, prevention, partnerships, and disengagement and reintegration – are vital to the provision of an enabling environment for youth to actively participate in transitioning to and sustaining peace. Under each pillar, UNSCR 2250 describes in more detail the focus area as well as what actions need to be taken, and by whom, to ensure progress is made on the pillar; however, to date, there has been little attempt to systematically quantify such progress. More broadly, there is a lack of systemic or sufficient data to understand the role of youth in building more peaceful societies. For example, in 2017, the Institute for Economics & Peace (IEP) found that there was insufficient data available to measure, globally, the number of youth:

- Engaged in armed conflict or organised violence;

- Engaged in direct peace-making, peacekeeping or peace-building activities;

- Killed or injured by armed conflict (including psychological injury);

- Unable to attend work or school because of armed conflict.

The YDI 2020 includes a Peace and Security dimension for the first time since its inception in 2010, and this domain is designed to capture the degree to which young people can live in safety and pursue their goals without the risk of violence. In essence, this domain and its component indicators try to capture to some degree the progress being made on YPS, and represent a first step in filling the data void to track progress on UNSCR 2250. But more can be done.

The previous section has outlined some of the progress made on the YPS Agenda to date as well as proposals for measuring the SROI of youth-led peace-building initiatives. Additional UNSCRs 2419 (2018) and 2535 (2020) add particular requirements with regard to advancing the agenda related to youth participation in negotiating and implementing peace agreements as well as in humanitarian responses, including post-conflict reconstruction and climate and public health emergencies. Among other things, UNSCR 2535 reaffirms the obligation to protect human rights and calls for equal access to justice, as well as protecting the civic and political space in which youth activists operate. Perhaps most significantly from an operational perspective, UNSCR 2535 calls for biennial reporting from the UN Secretary-General to the UN Security Council (UNSC) on progress in implementation of all three resolutions 2250, 2419 and 2535.

Against this background, this section discusses each of the five pillars of UNSCR 2250 – further reaffirmed by UNSCR 2419 and UNSCR 2535 – and presents some relevant indicators that currently exist as well as suggesting indicators to be collected that could more accurately track progress on these five specific pillars. In doing so, this section looks to build on "The Missing Peace" and the UN Secretary-General's Report on Youth and Peace and Security.

11.2 Pillar 1: Participation

Participation as defined in UNSCR 2250 refers to increasing the representation of youth in decision-making at all levels for the prevention and resolution of conflict, and in negotiating and implementing peace agreements.

Participation combats exclusion and promotes social integration as well as youth development by giving young people a stake in their society. Young people's participation in their community's political life shows the extent to which they are empowered and engaged in the political process. In addition, stronger intergenerational bonds are formed when young people are given a say in the development of their community. Because young people often constitute the majority population in many countries transitioning from conflict and with ongoing peace processes, youth participation in peace-making, and the representation of youth interests, is not only a demographic necessity but also a democratic imperative (Altiok and Grizelj, 2019).

Participation in peace processes

The need for meaningful participation of youth in peace processes is reaffirmed in UNSCR 2419 and UNSCR 2535, the latter of which recognises that "their marginalization is detrimental to building a sustainable peace." UNSCR 2250 and The Missing Peace define youth participation and representation in peace processes as multi-layered – participation "in the room," "around the room" and "outside the room." Ideal indicators to measure each of these components systematically might include the following:

- "Inside the room": Proportion of young people on negotiating teams or delegations; proportion of youth people who are observers to negotiations;

- "Around the room": Presence of youth delegations or committees at national dialogues; numbers of youth engaged in ceasefire monitoring; presence of youth-specific policies in peace agreements;

- "Outside the room": Numbers of youth civil society organisations or youth involved in civil society organisations campaigning for and working on peace-related matters.

However, currently, quantitative data to track these indicators over time in a globally comparable manner is lacking, and efforts should be made to rectify this. Having said that, there is certainly anecdotal evidence that youth are becoming increasingly engaged in peace processes. For example, youth played a critical role in Colombia's 2016 peace settlement, and the Syrian Youth Council continues to play an important role advocating for youth issues in any sort of ceasefire or peace settlement to be reached in the ongoing conflict there (UN Secretary-General, 2020).

Youth issue representation in peace agreements

There is one publicly available data source on peace agreements, the Peace Agreements Database available at peaceagreements.org. This specifies the degree to which signed peace agreements incorporate youth considerations and policies. This allows an initial assessment of progress being made on the theoretical representation of youth issues in peace agreements.

The database codes all peace agreements signed between 1990 and 2020, and captures whether each agreement holds references to youth rights, and the veracity of these references. Each agreement is scored on a 0–3 scale; a score of 0 indicates no mention of youth and youth rights, a 1 indicates a rhetorical mention of youth rights, a 2 indicates the agreement contains some provisions concerning youth and a 3 indicates the agreement has substantial and substantive provisions for youth rights. Based on this data, we can conclude that there is a long way to go in terms of youth representation: of the 1,868 agreements that took place between 1990 and 2020, the majority (83 per cent) make no mention of youth or youth rights. Figure 3.1 shows the distribution of peace agreements by level of youth issue representation.

There has been no clear improvement on this indicator over time either, but rather some year-on-year variation in terms of the youth issue contents of peace agreements, even since UNSCR 2250 was implemented in 2016, as Figure 11.2 shows.

In a regional breakdown, while there is regional variation in the extent to which youth issues are represented in

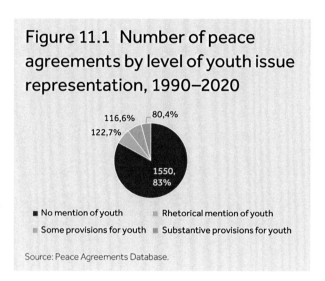

Figure 11.1 Number of peace agreements by level of youth issue representation, 1990–2020

Source: Peace Agreements Database.

peace agreements, there has been no distinct regional improvement since UNSCR 2250 was implemented. As Figure 3.3 shows, Europe and Eurasia has the highest proportion of peace agreements with no mention of youth or youth issues, looking at the 1990–2020 time period.

Participation in governance, political processes and civil society

As the 2020 UN Secretary General's-report on the status of the YPS Agenda states, "young people's participation and representation in political processes contribute to successful peacebuilding, yet their participation therein remains extremely low."

So what exactly is the state of youth participation and representation in political processes? The Political and Civic Participation domain of the YDI allows us to draw some conclusions on the extent to which youth are active in political life and civil society. As the results section of this YDI Report has shown, the Political and Civic Participation domain is the only one to have deteriorated globally over the past decade, with 102 countries deteriorating while 79 countries improved. This is a potentially concerning trend: if youth are not engaged overall in the political environment or processes, even in countries that are potentially more peaceful, it may be harder to include them in specific peace-making processes themselves (UN Secretary-General, 2020). The good news is that some regions have shown signs of improvements, in particular sub-Saharan Africa, which has improved its score by 5 per cent, and ranks second in terms of regions on this domain.

Unpacking this YDI domain further, of all the indicators to deteriorate, perhaps the most concerning is the "Voice

Figure 11.2 Number of peace agreements by level of youth issue representation, 1990–2020

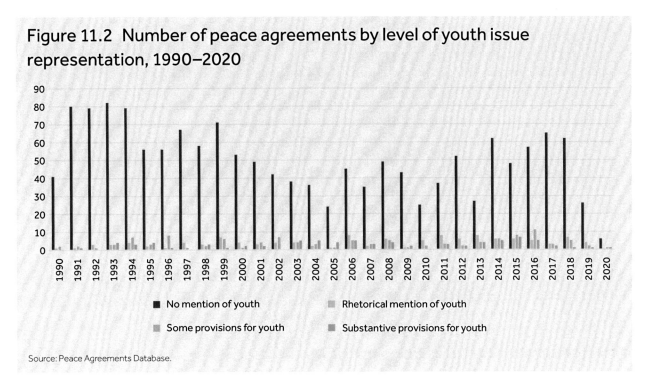

- No mention of youth
- Rhetorical mention of youth
- Some provisions for youth
- Substantive provisions for youth

Source: Peace Agreements Database.

an opinion to an official" indicator, which has declined globally by an average of 3 per cent over the past decade. This could be related to the fact that youth feel less comfortable or inclined to get involved in activism or the political process. This finding also corresponds to global trends in youth voter turnout; a global survey in 2016 showed that, on average, youth voter turnout was 43 per cent in national elections, as compared with 63 per cent for non-youth (IDEA, 2016). A more recent analysis of youth voter turnout in 24 countries shows that the

turnout gap between youth (registered voters aged 18–29) and non-youth ranges from 1 to 20 per cent, with youth turnout highest in Sweden, at 86 per cent, and lowest in Switzerland, at 33 per cent (Symonds, 2020).

On participation in formal political institutions, the Inter-Parliamentary Union database includes an indicator for the percentage of MPs in each country's lower house (or unicameral system) who are under the age of 30. This data shows that youth participation is

Figure 11.3. Peace agreements and percentage with no mention of youth issues by region, 1990–2020

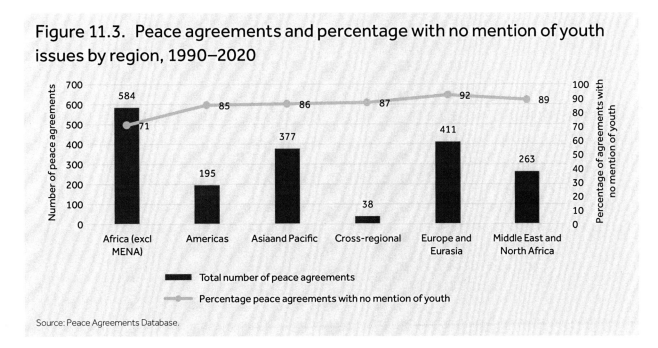

- Total number of peace agreements
- Percentage peace agreements with no mention of youth

Source: Peace Agreements Database.

very low on average globally but there has been some progress since 2012. In 2012, the average percentage of MPs under 30 in a national legislature was just 1.35 per cent. By 2016 this had increased to 2.5 per cent, and by 2020 to 3.2 per cent. In 2012, 29 per cent of 49 national parliaments assessed had no MPs under the age of 30. In 2016 this share was 25 per cent of 118 national parliaments, and in 2020 19 per cent of the 93 parliaments assessed.

The top five countries in terms of youthful MPs in parliament in 2020 were Norway (13.61 per cent), Armenia (12.12 per cent), San Marino (11.67 per cent), Ecuador (10.95 per cent), and The Gambia (10.34 per cent). Figure 11.4 shows the top five improvers between 2016 and 2020, with wide regional representation.

To systematically assess progress being made on the extent to which youth participate in governance, political processes and civil society, the following is a list of non-exhaustive data that it will be critical to collect and analyse:

- Time-series data on youth voter turnout, by country;

- Time-series data on youth representation in all branches of government, by country;

- Time-series data on youth-focused and -led registered civil society organisations, by country;

Youth participation in humanitarian action

UNSCR 2535 explicitly recognises the pivotal role that youth play in the planning, design and execution of humanitarian activities in conflict and post-conflict settings, as well as in preparation for and in response to climate and public health emergencies (para. 10). The emphasis on youth participation in humanitarian action builds on the Compact for Young People in Humanitarian Action, which was launched at the World Humanitarian Summit in Istanbul in 2016. As of 2018, more than 50 humanitarian agencies had signed on to the compact (Engel and Stefanik, 2018), which consists of five actions, with Action 2 focusing on participation. The 2018 progress report details many anecdotal cases of organisations putting youth front and centre of humanitarian responses, including in the Ebola crisis in Sierra Leone in 2014/15 and in the aftermath of Hurricane Matthew in Haiti in 2016 (ibid.). However, no systemic data exists on the extent to which youth are participating in humanitarian action, perhaps partly because actions are siloed across countries, regions and organisations.

The UN Office for the Coordination of Humanitarian Affairs (OCHA) is responsible for the Who Does What, Where and When database, which collects information on humanitarian actors in crises responses, and classifies which sector they work in, as well as where and on which specific projects. Using this as a starting point, each organisation that is represented in the database could also self-report indicators such as "Percentage of employees or volunteers that are youth."

11.3 Pillar 2: Protection

UNSCR 2250 refers specifically to the obligation of all parties involved in conflict to protect youth from all forms of sexual and gender-based violence (SGBV), as well as ensuring the protection of the human rights of youth within their territory. It reaffirms these calls to actions and further urges member states to "protect youth from violence in armed conflict and urges all parties to eliminate all forms of sexual and gender-based violence as well as human trafficking" (para. 4).

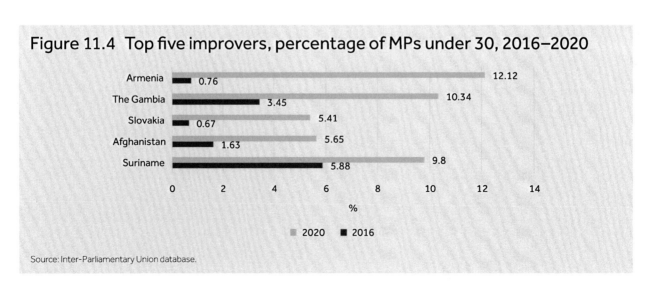

Figure 11.4 Top five improvers, percentage of MPs under 30, 2016–2020

Armenia: 0.76 (2016), 12.12 (2020)
The Gambia: 3.45 (2016), 10.34 (2020)
Slovakia: 0.67 (2016), 5.41 (2020)
Afghanistan: 1.63 (2016), 5.65 (2020)
Suriname: 5.88 (2016), 9.8 (2020)

■ 2020 ■ 2016

Source: Inter-Parliamentary Union database.

Figure 11.5 Share of peace agreements with clear provisions for the protection of women and girls by region, 2015–2020

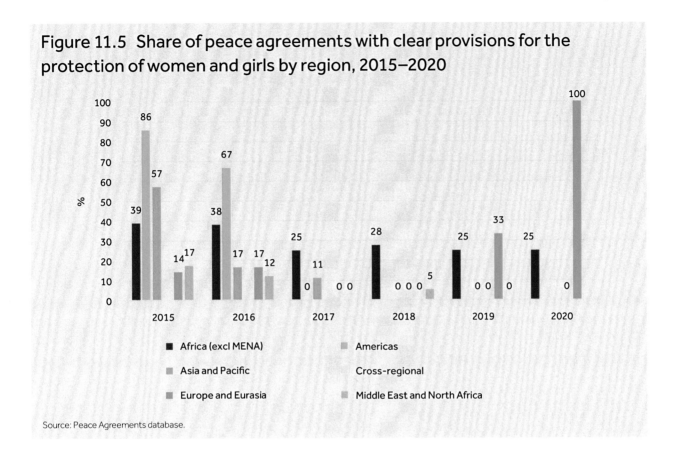

Source: Peace Agreements database.

Sexual and gender-based violence

Globally comprehensive systemic data on the prevalence of SGBV does not currently exist. Best estimates from the World Health Organization (WHO) as of 2017, however, put the prevalence of SGBV at an astounding level, with 35 per cent of women worldwide having experienced either physical and/or sexual intimate partner violence or non-partner sexual violence in their lifetime (WHO, 2017). Furthermore, UN Women estimates that, globally, approximately 15 million girls aged 15–19 have experienced forced sexual intercourse or other sexual acts at some point in their life (UN Women, 2020) Although there is an evidence gap in terms of numbers and rates of SGBV, initial research from several countries, including the UK, the US and China, suggests that the COVID-19 pandemic in 2020 has also led to an increase in domestic violence and SGBV (WHO, 2020). In conflict settings, SGBV is thought to have an even higher prevalence, and is often used as a distinct tactic by warring parties. A 2019 report by the UN Secretary-General on Conflict-Related Sexual Violence found that sexual violence "continues as part of the broader strategy of conflict and that women and girls are significantly affected." SGBV perpetrated by both state and non-state actors is used to displace communities and seize contested

lands, and as a means of repression, control and terror. In the 19 countries included in the analysis for which verified cases of sexual violence were recorded, 50 parties were involved, of which 37 were non-state actors such as local militias and criminal groups (ibid.). OCHA estimates that one in five internally displaced or refugee women living in humanitarian crisis and armed conflict have experienced sexual violence, and that less than 1 per cent of global humanitarian funding is being spent on SGBV prevention and response activities (OCHA, 2019).

One dataset on the prevalence of sexual violence in armed conflict, which coded conflict events between 1989 and 2009, found that, of the total 51,893 conflict events, 2.2 per cent had massive prevalence of sexual violence, 9.3 per cent had high prevalence and 29.6 per cent had some prevalence. Data showed that prevalence was highest in conflict events occurring in Africa, where 6.4 per cent of all conflict events during the time period involved massive prevalence of sexual violence – compared with 1.1 per cent in Asia and 0 per cent in the Americas and Europe.[5] This same data extrapolated to include the years up to 2015 suggested that 1.4 per cent of all conflict actors active between 2010 and 2015 inflicted massive prevalence of sexual violence in the conflicts in which they were engaged.[6]

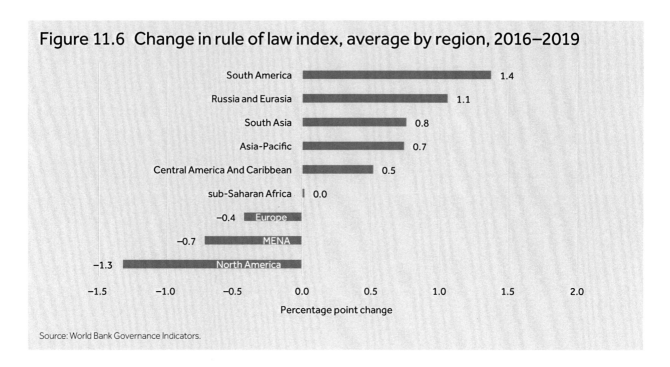

Figure 11.6 Change in rule of law index, average by region, 2016–2019

Source: World Bank Governance Indicators.

Protections for women and girls in peace agreements

While accurate data on the extent of SGBV globally and in conflict settings does not exist, we can look to data on the extent of protections afforded to women and girls codified in peace agreements to glean progress being made in transitions to peace. In the Peace Agreements database, the variable "GeWom" assesses whether any of the peace agreement provisions are specifically addressing women, their inclusion and their rights. This includes references to girls, widows, mothers, sexual violence (or forms thereof), gender violence, UNSC 1325 or the Convention on the Elimination of All Forms of Discrimination Against Women (CEDAW) and lactating women.[7] It is coded as 1 if there are references to women and girls and 0 otherwise. While by no means a perfect measure, as it does not account for provisions for men and boys and looks only at the obligations on paper rather than the situation on the ground, this can nonetheless provide a starting point.

Data going back to 1990 shows that, in the 1,868 peace agreements coded, less than 20 per cent (371) make any explicit reference to women and girls in their provisions, and there have been no significant gains made over the past decade in this respect. There is regional variation in the extent to which provisions exist in peace agreements for women and girls, with those signed between parties in conflict in sub-Saharan Africa showing the highest proportion (29 per cent since 1990) and those signed between parties in Europe and Eurasia the lowest (only 11 per cent since 1990).

Since UNSCR 2250 was adopted in December 2015, we have not seen any consistent improvement in peace agreement provisions for women and girls, except in the Europe and Eurasia region, which saw an increase from only 14 per cent of agreements in 2015 to 100 per cent of agreements in 2020 having these provisions, as seen in Figure 11.5.

To note, since 2016, Organisation for Economic Co-operation and Development (OECD) Development Assistance Committee (DAC) donors have explicitly allocated and disbursed official development assistance (ODA) funding for a category of activities titled "Ending Violence against Women and Girls." Between 2016 and 2018, over US$747 million (constant 2018 US$) was disbursed in this sector across developing countries (OECD.Stat 2021). This comprises 0.12 per cent of total ODA disbursed over this period, and indicates that member states are acting on UNSCR 2250, UNSCR 2419 and UNSCR 2535 by funding activities explicitly aimed at gender-based violence.

Human rights protections

UNSCR 2535 details the necessary human rights protections expected of member states and reaffirms obligations to respect, promote and protect these rights and fundamental freedoms and ensure equal access to justice, preserving the integrity of the rule of law (para. 2)

The World Bank Governance Indicators track progress on several aspects of governance, including Rule of

Law to 2019. This indicator "captures perceptions of the extent to which agents have confidence in and abide by the rules of society, and in particular the quality of contract enforcement, property rights, the police, and the courts, as well as the likelihood of crime and violence."[8] The scoring can be interpreted as a percentile ranging from 0 to 100 per cent, with higher values indicating more rule of law. Analysing this data over the decade from 2010 to 2019 shows little change at the global level, with an average score of around 50 per cent. However, a regional breakdown reveals stark differences in performance, with the Central American average improving by 7 percentage points over the decade at the same time as the sub-Saharan African average deteriorated by 3 percentage points. Examining changes since 2016 when UNSCR 2250 was implemented, Figure 11.6 shows the regional variation on improvements on the Rule of Law Index. While six of nine regions improved or stayed static, Europe, the Middle East and North Africa (MENA) and North America deteriorated on this score.

For countries in conflict and transitioning to peace, protections on human rights can be explicitly codified in peace agreements. The Peace Agreements database covers explicit provisions on commitment to Human Rights (HrGen) or to protections of civilians (ProtCiv). Only 29 per cent of all agreements signed between 1990 and 2020 had human rights provisions, with a high of 39 per cent in sub-Saharan Africa. Since 2015,

the global proportion has been even lower, at only 19 per cent of all agreements. An even smaller proportion of agreements have explicit provisions for protecting civilians, with only 5 per cent of all 1,861 agreements signed since 1990, with marginally more since 2015 – at 6.5 per cent.

11.4 Pillar 3: Prevention and Pillar 4: Partnerships

The prevention pillar refers to member states' obligations to provide an enabling environment for youth to implement violence prevention activities and build social cohesion. The partnerships pillar calls for increased support from member states, be it political, financial, technical or logistical, to allow for youth to participate in peace efforts, including partnering with local communities and non-governmental organisations to counter the violent extremist narrative.

Long-term prevention of conflict and violent extremism necessarily means addressing the underlying root drivers of conflict, which can include structural and institutional inequalities, corruption, discrimination and exclusion. The 2020 UN Secretary-General's Report notes that partnerships are key to ensuring a successful preventative agenda, but also that awareness of the importance of prevention, partnerships and the role of youth in peace-building

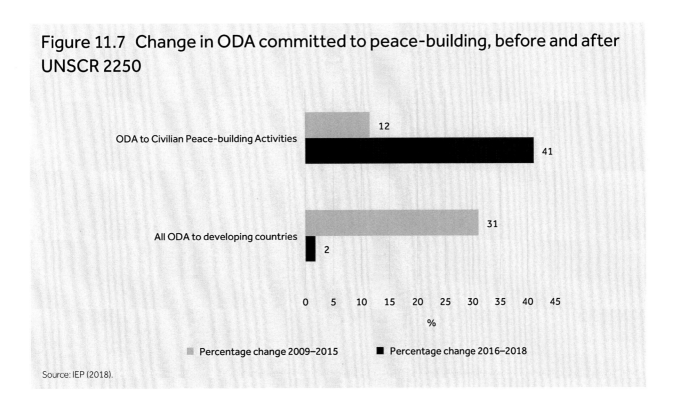

Figure 11.7 Change in ODA committed to peace-building, before and after UNSCR 2250

ODA to Civilian Peace-building Activities: 12, 41
All ODA to developing countries: 31, 2

Percentage change 2009–2015
Percentage change 2016–2018

Source: IEP (2018).

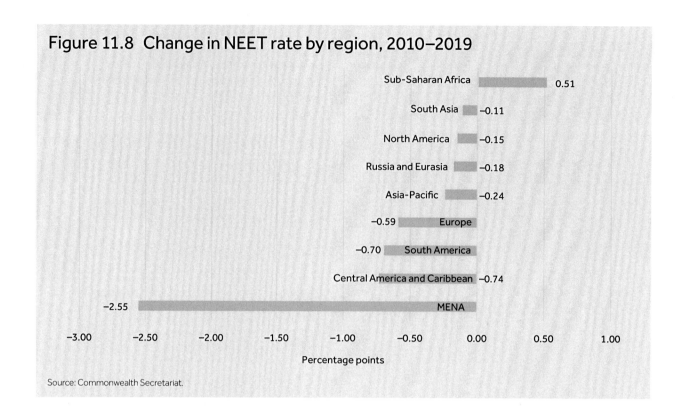

Figure 11.8 Change in NEET rate by region, 2010–2019

Source: Commonwealth Secretariat.

"still needs to be translated into concrete actions, including national level measures, institutional priorities and dedicated funding."

While a systemic globally comparable measure of prevention activities or partnerships is difficult to distil, we can look to the ODA funding priorities of OECD DAC donors to analyse whether funding allocations reflect the components of the five pillars highlighted in UNSCR 2250. Without ODA, most conflict-affected countries cannot implement programming for the YPS Agenda.

The OECD Creditor Reporting System (CRS) shows the flow of ODA at a sectoral level from 2009 to 2018, and thus we can analyse funding for civilian-led peace-building and conflict prevention activities over the past decade and since the passing of UNSCR 2250.

Funding for civilian peace-building, conflict prevention and resolution

A study by the IEP in 2017 on the cost-effectiveness of peace-building calculated that the cost-effectiveness ratio of peace-building at approximately 1:16, indicating that, if countries currently in conflict increased or received levels of peace-building funding to appropriate levels estimated by this model, then for every US$1 invested now the cost of conflict would be reduced by $16 in the long run. In 10-year forward projections from 2016, it is estimated that $2.94 trillion in direct and

indirect losses from conflict would be saved. The same study notes, however, that, to achieve this outcome, an approximate doubling of peace-building expenditure toward the 31 most fragile and conflict-affected nations of the world would be required (IEP, 2018).

Examining funding data, since 2009 total gross disbursements from all DAC donors allocated to civilian peace-building, conflict prevention and resolution activities in developing countries[9] have remained fairly constant as a share of total ODA gross disbursements, hovering around 1 per cent. The absolute amount allocated to civilian peace-building over the decade has increased by 76 per cent, from US$1.58 billion (constant 2018 US$) to $2.78 billion. An examination of the period before the passing of UNSCR 2250 and after – that is, dividing the timeframe into the years 2009–2015 and then 2016–2018 – shows that, after UNSCR 2250 was passed, the share of ODA allocated to peace-building activities increased substantially more than total ODA disbursements, as seen in Figure 3.7. In addition, the proportion of ODA going to peace-building activities has grown slowly but consistently since 2016, from 1.03 per cent (of $1.9 billion) to 1.42 per cent (of 1.95 billion). This could indicate that DAC donors have made progress on actualising verbal and written commitments to providing an enabling environment for peace-building activities.

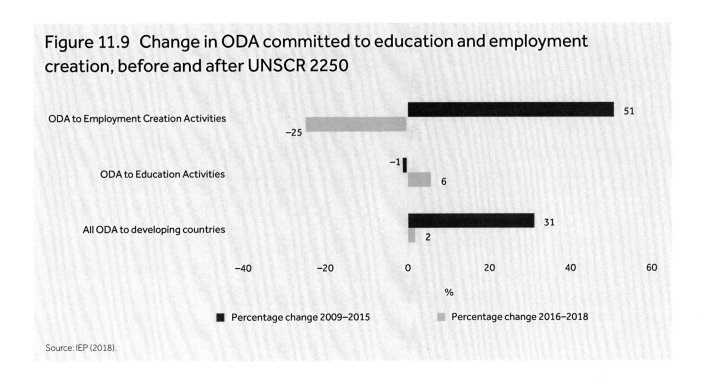

Figure 11.9 Change in ODA committed to education and employment creation, before and after UNSCR 2250

Source: IEP (2018).

11.5 Pillar 5: Disengagement and reintegration

The resolution calls for disarmament, demobilisation and reintegration activities to account for the needs of youth affected by armed conflict, including gender-sensitive youth employment opportunities, as well as investing in up-skilling youth through relevant educational opportunities.

The YDI Employment and Opportunity domain measures structural and institutional factors that give youth opportunities to engage in productive income-generating activities and therefore an ability to aspire toward and reach economic and livelihood goals. Results from the YDI show that this domain improved globally by 3 per cent between 2010 and 2018, with each of the nine regions in the world showing an improvement. The range of improvement across the nine regions is quite varied, however, from a high of over 8 per cent in North America to just over 2 per cent in sub-Saharan Africa. Moreover, improvements have been driven by metrics of financial inclusion rather than by any significant improvement in employment metrics.

In fact, as Figure 3.8 shows, over the long term, the not in education, employment or training (NEET) rate has decreased only marginally in most regions, and in sub-Saharan Africa it actually increased between 2010 and 2019. This coincides with an increase in conflict fatalities on the African continent since 2010, both in absolute numbers and as a rate per million population,

as internal conflict proliferates and the numbers of violent extremist actors operating in the region multiply (Cilliers, 2018). This suggests there is much work to be done in addressing opportunities for young people, in particularly conflict-affected areas.

The disengagement and reintegration pillar calls for efforts by all member states, not just conflicted-affected states, to address education and employment opportunities for youth. It may thus be useful to look at OECD DAC donor member states' commitments to this pillar by looking again at ODA funding allocations. Using the OECD's CRS, the details of disbursements to education and employment creation and activities can be assessed.

Between 2009 and 2018, DAC donors disbursed US$1.65 trillion to developing countries across all sectors. Of this total, 7.4 per cent was allocated to education and 0.43 per cent to employment creation. Since UNSCR 2250, the share of ODA allocated to educational activities has increased but the share allocated to employment creation activities has decreased, as seen in Figure 3.9.

11.6 Conclusion on the way forward for data

This chapter has examined the progress that has been made around the world on implementing UNSCR 2250 and the follow on resolutions UNSCR 2419 and UNSCR 2535. Five pillars are outlined in UNSCR 2250 and built-upon in the follow-on resolutions: participation, protection, partnerships, prevention, and disengagement and reintegration. Although there are few perfect indicators currently available to track each of these pillars in a globally systemic way, each pillar has lent itself to some form of quantification using both the YDI components and other data sources.

The chapter finds that progress has been mixed. Since the implementation of UNSCR 2250, there has been progress made on youth participation in governance institutions such as parliaments, as well as in humanitarian action. Globally, improvements have also been seen in the rule of law and donor funding commitments to peace-building activities and educational activities. At the same time, there have been no significant improvements in youth representation in peace agreements, or in protections for women and girls or human rights. In addition, employment opportunities have not improved significantly since 2016.

The chapter has suggested indicators that would be useful to collect and track for each pillar in order to be able to give a complete picture of progress that is comparable across countries and time. In particular, data on involvement in peace negotiations and humanitarian action, as well as on SGBV, will be critical.

Endnotes

1   https://www.youth4peace.info/About_GCYPS

2   https://www.sfcg.org/youth-360/

3   https://www.sfcg.org/the-youth-peace-and-security-fund/

4   The proposals for quantitative measurement of YPS have been prepared with the support of the Institute for Economics & Peace (IEP).

5   https://www.prio.org/Data/Armed-Conflict/GEO-SVAC/

6   http://www.sexualviolencedata.org/dataset/

7   This variable is GeWom; Geocoded SVAC Dataset (GEO-SVAC) version 1.0.

8   http://info.worldbank.org/governance/wgi/Home/Documents#wgiOverTime

9   This the OECD DAC donor definition of developing countries, and the full list of these countries can be found at www.stats.oecd.org

References

AU (African Union) (2020a) Continental Framework for Youth, Peace and Security. Addis Ababa: AU.

AU (2020b) Study on the Roles and Contributions of Youth to Peace and Security in Africa. Addis Ababa: AU.

Altiok, A. and I. Grizelj (2019) "We Are Here: An Integrated Approach to Youth Inclusive Peace Processes". Global Policy Paper. Global Coalition on Youth, Peace and Security. https://www.youth4peace.info/node/348

Cilliers, J. (2018) Violence in Africa. Trends, Drivers, and Prospects 2023. Pretoria: Institute for Security Studies.

Engel, D. and M. Stefanik (2018) Compact for Young People in Humanitarian Action. Progress Report. New York: UNFPA.

IEP (Institute for Economics & Peace) (2018) "Measuring Peacebuilding Cost-Effectiveness". Sydney: IEP.

IDEA (2016) "Annual Outcome Report 2016". https://www.idea.int/about-us/annual-reports

OCHA (UN Office for the Coordination of Humanitarian Affairs) (2019) "Gender-Based Violence: A Closer Look at the Numbers". 19 May. https://www.unocha.org/story/gender-based-violence-closer-look-numbers

Search for Common Ground (2015), "Guiding Principles in Young People's Participation in Peacebuilding". https://www.sfcg.org/guidingprinciples/

Search for Common Ground (2019) "Evidence from Around the World: Youth Peace and Security – A Summary of 'The Missing Peace: Independent Progress Study on Youth, Peace, and Security'". September. https://www.sfcg.org/youth-peace-security-act/YPS_Case_Statement_October_2019.pdf

Simpson, G. (2018) The Missing Peace: Independent Progress Study on Youth, Peace and Security. New York: UNFPA and PBSO.

Symonds, A. (2020) "Why Don't Young People Vote, and What Can Be Done About It?" The New York Times, 8 October. https://www.nytimes.com/2020/10/08/upshot/youth-voting-2020-election.html

UN Secretary-General (2019) "Report of the United Nations Secretary-General on Conflict Related Sexual Violence". 29 March. www. un.org/sexualviolenceinconflict/wp-content/ uploads/2019/04/report/s-2019-280/Annual-report-2018.pdf

UN Secretary-General (2020) *First Report of the UN Secretary General on Youth and Peace and Security*. 2 March. https://undocs.org/en/S/2020/167

UN Women (2020) "Facts and figures: Ending Violence against Women". https://www.unwomen.org/en/ what-we-do/ending-violence-against-women/ facts-and-figures

United States Congress (2020) "H.R.6174 – Youth, Peace, and Security Act of 2020 116th Congress (2019–2020)". https://www.congress.gov/ bill/116th-congress/house-bill/6174

WHO (World Health Organization) (2017) "Violence against Women". Factsheet, 29 November.

WHO (2020) "COVID-19 and Violence against Women: What the Health Sector/System Can Do". 7 April. Geneva: WHO.

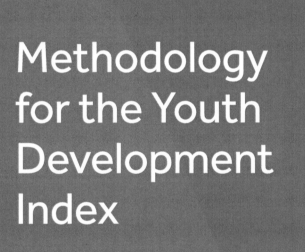

Methodology
for the Youth
Development
Index

Annex 1

Methodology for the Youth Development Index

In constructing an index like the YDI, disparate datasets are aggregated to capture a broader concept, such as youth development. These datasets are incommensurable by themselves but complement each other in capturing the broader, multifaceted concept. A number of procedural steps are involved in taking raw country data and combining it into a composite index. The general index construct process has the following stages:

- Sourcing and collating raw data;

- Filling and imputing data gaps;

- Banding;

- Weighting;

- Aggregating into an index.

This annex outlines the process of constructing the 2020 YDI.

A1.1 Sourcing and collecting raw data

The YDI is designed to measure youth development based on six domains:

- Health and Wellbeing

- Education

- Employment and Opportunity

- Equality and Inclusion

- Political and Civic Participation

- Peace and Security

These domains, and the indicators within each domain, were decided upon through consultation with the YDI Expert Panel. To capture youth development within each country across all domains, 27 indicators were sourced. Table A1.1 gives the domains, indicators and their sources.

A1.2 Improvements to 2016 Youth Development Index indicators

As data has continued to improve in quality and accessibility since the last YDI was published in 2016, the domains and indicators in the 2020 YDI have been updated according to the outcomes of a scoping study for improved data, conducted in June of 2019 by IEP, and reviewed by the Secretariat and the YDI Expert Panel in early 2020. Changes to domains and indicators are summarised below.

A1.2.1 Health and Wellbeing

In the process of developing the 2020 YDI, the expert panel reviewed the *Health and Wellbeing* domain at length. A similar approach has been taken here as for the *Equality and Opportunity* domain: the conceptual basis for the domain creates room to improve the specific indicators as better data becomes available.

Table A1.1 2020 YDI domains and indicators

Domain	Indicator	Definition	Source
Health & Wellbeing	Mortality rate	Deaths from all causes, ages 15–29	IHME, GBD
	HIV rate	HIV rate, ages 15–24	UNAIDS estimates
	Self-harm	YLL from self-harm, ages 15–29	IHME GBD
	Mental health	YLL from mental disorders, ages 15–29	IHME GBD
	Drug abuse	YLL from drug use disorders, ages 15–29	IHME GBD
	Alcohol abuse	YLL from alcohol use disorders, ages 15–29	IHME GBD
	Tobacco consumption	Tobacco smokers, % of ages 15–29	IHME GBD
Education	Literacy rate	Literacy rate, youth total, % of ages 15–24	UNESCO Institute for Statistics
	School completion	Lower secondary completion rate, total, % of country-specific age group	UNESCO Institute for Statistics
	Digital natives	Five or more years' experience using the internet, % of ages 15–29	ITU
Employment & Opportunity	NEET	NEET youth, % of ages 15–24	ILO
	Underemployment	Time-related underemployment, ages 15–24	ILO modelled estimates
	Adolescent fertility rate	Adolescent fertility rate, births per 1,000 women ages 15–19	United Nations Population Division, World Population Prospects
	Account	Respondents who report having an account (by themselves or together with someone else) at a bank or other financial institution or report using mobile money in the past 12 months, % ages 15–24	World Bank Global Findex Database
Equality & Inclusion	Gender parity in NEET	Distance from parity between percentages of NEET young women and NEET young men, ages 15–24	UNDESA Global SDG Indicators Database, IEP calculations
	Gender parity in safety and security	Distance from parity between percentages of young women and young men who report feeling safe walking alone in their neighbourhood at night	GWP, IEP calculations
	Gender parity in literacy	Literacy rate, youth, ages 15–24, GPI	UNESCO Institute for Statistics
	Early marriage	Women first married by age 18, % of women ages 20–24	Country surveys collected by the World Bank and OECD
	Economic marginalisation	Population percentage classified as extremely poor (< US$ 1.90 PPP) or moderately poor (>= US$ 1.90 and < US$ 3.20 PPP), ages 15–24	ILO modelled estimates

(Continued)

Domain	Indicator	Definition	Source
Political & Civic Participation	**Youth policy score**	Scores on youth policy and legislation, public institutions, youth representation, and public budget and spending	Youth Policy Labs, IEP calculation
	Voiced opinion to an official	Responding that they have voiced their opinion to an official in the past 30 days, % ages 15–29	GWP
	Volunteered time	Responding that they have volunteered time in the past 30 days, % ages 15–29	GWP
	Recognition for community improvement	Responding "agree" or "strongly agree' with the statement "In the last 12 months, you have received recognition for helping to improve the city or area where you live," % ages 15–29	GWP
Peace & Security	**Internal peace score**	Composite score for domestic peace and safety and security	IEP Global Peace Index
	Interpersonal violence	YLL from interpersonal violence, ages 15–29	IHME GBD
	Conflict and terrorism	YLL from armed conflict and terrorism, ages 15–29	IHME GBD
	INFORM score	Risk of humanitarian crisis and disaster, including climate change related risks	EU INFORM

The Secretariat and the YDI Expert Panel recommended that the domain have four indicators:

- Physical health, proxied by communicable diseases;

- Mental health, proxied by self-harm and suicide;

- Wellbeing behaviours, proxied by drug, alcohol and tobacco use YLL;

- Youth mortality.

It was recommended that the proxy for physical health (communicable diseases) include prevalence of both HIV and STIs. However, it has not been possible to find a comprehensive global dataset on STIs, hence this indicator is left out of the final index.

Similarly, it was recommended that the index capture the social harm caused by non-communicable diseases, which often develop based on habits formed in youth. The wellbeing behaviours indicators capture this reality as best as possible with the currently available data, while indicators of a healthy diet and participation in sport and physical activity can be incorporated as global data improves.

These changes reflect a conceptual improvement to the domain vis-à-vis the 2016 YDI, and result in some changes to the particular included indicators.

Physical health and youth mortality are measured in the same way. The *HIV rate* indicator has been maintained, and is calculated by averaging prevalence rates of HIV among females and males aged 15–24 (the best available data). The *youth mortality* indicator has also been maintained, and is calculated as the average rate of youth deaths per 100,000 young people across the three age cohorts provided in the GBD data: ages 15–19, 20–24 and 25–29.

The mental health metrics have been expanded to include the *self-harm* indicator alongside the *mental health* indicator, reflecting the fact that self-harm is the third leading cause of death for all adolescents, and the second leading cause of death for young women (UNICEF, 2019). Both are measured in terms of YLL.

The prevalence of tobacco use among youth has been added as a behavioural health indicator alongside *drug abuse* and *alcohol abuse*, both of which are maintained from the previous YDI.

Finally, the GWP *Global Wellbeing Index* indicator has been removed both because the time series of available data ended in 2015 and to reduce collinearity in the index.

A1.2.2 Education

The *literacy rate* and *digital natives* indicators remain the same in the 2020 YDI as in the 2016 iteration; however. the *school completion* indicator replaces *enrolment in secondary education* as a more concrete measure of educational outcomes. The YDI Expert Panel advised that some countries experience substantial gaps between secondary school enrolment and completion, thus a measure of completion was necessary as an important indicator of youth development progress.

A1.2.3 Employment and Opportunity

The *NEET* and *adolescent fertility rate* indicators remain the same as in the 2016 YDI. The *youth unemployment ratio* (the ratio of young people who are unemployed compared with the adult population) has been removed for lack of up-to-date data. IEP has replaced it with *youth underemployment*, which captures whether young people are achieving their full potential, able to make significant contributions to society and likely to have economic security. The later indicator was recommended to IEP by ILO as a robust measure of whether the economy is providing adequate opportunity for young people, and as an appropriate metric for comparing across developing and developed economies.

IEP has also expanded the *accounts* indicator in the 2020 YDI to include the use of mobile money. The updated dataset measures the percentage of youth who report having an account (by themselves or together with someone else) at a bank or other financial institution and/or report using mobile money in the past 12 months.

A1.2.4 Equality and Inclusion

The *Equality and Inclusion* domain was newly developed for the 2020 YDI. The goal of this domain is to capture the degree to which various groups of young people are enjoying equal opportunities in society. In the 2020 YDI, this domain is included with scalability in mind. As global data on a broader set of inclusion issues becomes available – such as data measuring the experiences of young people with different abilities – those indicators can be incorporated into the Global YDI. The domain also serves as a placeholder for important metrics in national and regional YDIs. For example, a country-level YDI might include here indicators that measure locally relevant inclusion issues, such as the experiences of youth from different ethnic groups, which cannot be comparably measured across countries.

Based on the data available at the time of writing, the *Equality and Inclusion* domain captures economic inclusion using the *economic marginalisation* indicator and gender equality across four indicators.[1] Each of the included gender indicators captures a different aspect of the ways in which opportunity may be limited for one group or the other: education (*parity in literacy rates*), employment (*parity in unemployment*), safety (*parity in feeling* safe) and the opportunity to pursue a future of one's own choosing (*early marriage*). The three parity indicators measure gaps between female and male youth experiences and opportunities. Hence, disparities favouring young males are evaluated as being as harmful to youth development as disparities favouring young females, although the later are less frequent.

The *early marriage* indicator is not able to measure parity because data is available only for female youth marriages. The World Bank Early Marriage dataset, of young women aged 20–24 who were first married at age 18, is the primary dataset used for this indicator. However, it does not include OECD countries. Therefore, OECD Statistics on Early Marriage for the year 2014 have been used to impute values for OECD countries. The two datasets are not identical: the OECD data reports the percentage of females aged 15–19 years who are or ever have been married, whereas the World Bank data reports the percentage of women aged 20–24 who were first married by age 18. However, the datasets are considered comparable enough to provide a reasonable imputation for the OECD countries that are missing from the World Bank dataset. This imputation potentially penalises the OECD countries, as the OECD statistics include more years for youth marriage compared with the World Bank data. However, the actual values for the OECD countries are much lower than with any other imputation method (such as the global average), thus negating this issue.

It should be noted that the Early Marriage OECD data is available only for the year 2014. Hence, the value for OECD countries is kept constant across the time series, whereas the World Bank dataset covers the full time series, 2010–2018, for most countries.

It has not been possible to locate a similar dataset to impute values for OECD countries for the *parity in literacy rate* indicator, as the OECD does not provide gender-disaggregated data on youth literacy rates. OECD countries have, therefore, been assigned a value of 0, equivalent to parity in literacy rates, as several studies indicate that male and female literacy rates are close to parity in OECD countries (Andersen et al., 2011; United Nations, 2013). An OECD Education Working Paper by Borognovi et al. (2018) highlights that a gender gap in literacy exists during childhood and youth, peaking at age 15, in OECD countries. However, the same paper (p. 13) finds that the gender gap is close to non-existent at age 27 for OECD countries, supporting the assumption that male and female youth in the OECD enter adulthood with the same opportunities.

For each of the three parity indicators (*parity in unemployment, parity in feeling safe* and *parity in literacy rates*), the value is calculated as the absolute value of distance from parity. For example, if female literacy rates and male literacy rates are 100 per cent and 90 per cent, respectively, the indicator value would be 0.1. The results, therefore, do not differentiate between disparity that favours young men compared with disparity that favours young women. The indicators simply assess disparity in general as being problematic for youth development.

A1.2.5 Political and Civic Participation

Upon review of data limitations regarding youth participation, and in concert with the methodological choices made at the country and regional level, it was recommended that the previous two Civic and Political Participation domains be condensed into a single domain. The YDI Expert Panel considered the distinct concepts of "political participation" and "civic participation" limiting, and somewhat of a false dichotomy, and these indicators suffer the greatest data limitations.

Accordingly, the Political Participation and Civic Participation domains have been compressed into one single domain with the following four indicators:

- Voiced opinion to an official;

- Youth policy;

- Volunteered time;

- Recognition for community improvement.

The choice of indicators was informed by data availability (especially up-to-date data), expert review, and the results of a PCA performed by IEP.

IEP has calculated an improved *youth policy* score. Previous iterations of the YDI simply awarded countries a point value based on the existence of either a draft or a completed policy that addresses youth. In the 2020 YDI, scores have been updated to reflect the existence of the policy as well as the existence of a public institution, representation for young people and a budget allocated for youth programming.

Based on the Youth Policy Lab's data, the calculation of each Youth Policy Score weighs four criteria equally:

1. Policy and Legislation: Is there a national youth policy?

2. Public Institutions: Is there a governmental authority (ministry, department or office) that is primarily responsible for youth?

3. Youth and Representation: Does the country have a national youth organisation/association (council, platform, body)?

4. Budget and Spending: Is there a budget allocated to the governmental authority (ministry, department or office) that is primarily responsible for youth and/or youth programming?

Each country is granted one point per criteria, resulting in a score between 0 and 4, with 0 indicating that the country does not have any youth policy, formal institution and representation or budgets specifically for youth development, and 4 indicating that a country meets all these conditions. The data is current as of 2014 and, given the lack of time series data available for this or any other youth policy indicator, each country's score is held constant for each year of the YDI times series (2010–2018 inclusive).

A1.2.6 Peace and Security

Peace and Security is also a new domain in the 2020 YDI, designed to capture the degree to which young people can live in safety and pursue their goals without the risk of violence. The domain consists of two individual-level indicators and two macro-level indicators that assess the "enabling environment" for youth peace and security. Data from the GBD database allows for the inclusion of YLL among youth as a consequence *of interpersonal violence* and *terrorism and violent conflict*. The *internal peace* score from IEP's GPI and the EU's INFORM risk score measure, respectively, the current levels of conflict and violence for society at large and the country's risk of disaster and humanitarian crisis. These macro-level indicators capture the context in which young people will face challenges as a generation, including those induced by climate change.

The *conflict and terrorism* and *interpersonal violence* indicators are calculated as the average of YLLs for three age categories (15-19, 20-24 and 25-29).

A1.3 Data limitations

A1.3.1 Overall limitations

The global YDI relies on existing datasets from a variety of sources to measure each of its key concepts. For the most part, high-quality data is available from global organisations and the YDI represents the leading effort to bring together a diverse set of relevant datasets. However, the international community still has room for improvement in measuring the experiences of young people. IEP encountered the following data limitations in developing the 2020 YDI:

- Complete country coverage for all indicators; for example, some datasets include most but not all of the 2020 YDI countries;

- Complete time series coverage for all indicators; for example, some datasets do not cover all years from 2010 to 2018;

- Age group variations; for example, some data covers 15–24 year olds and others cover 15–29 year olds; and

- Availability of viable data for a variety of political participation, health and inclusion indicators.

In developing the 2020 YDI methodology, IEP addressed these challenges in a variety of ways. In all cases, the best available data was used. IEP's 2019 scoping study included a literature review identifying the key aspects of youth development that were unmeasured in the 2016 index. This review identified possibilities for new concepts, which were then incorporated into the index.

The study also identified a list of possible data sources for each of the 2020 YDI domains. In some cases, data was entirely unavailable. These conceptual data limitations are outlined in Chapter 1 of this report. Of the available indicators, many were of limited usefulness owing to factors such as a skewed distribution or general lack of variance. Indicators with either too little variation between countries or uni- or bi-modal distributions (i.e. most countries have the same very good or very bad score) contribute little to a cross-country index and as a result were not included.

Statistical tests were performed to determine the veracity and suitability of each indicator, and the best options were reviewed by the YDI expert panel. Expert panel feedback was incorporated in order to make it possible to make the best choices between imperfect datasets.

Section A1.3.1 explains the imputation methods that were used to fill gaps in country and time-series

coverage. Where datasets were not available to measure exactly the age range of 15–29 for each indicator, alternative age ranges were used. Many of the YDI indicators measure smaller age cohorts; in these cases, the available data for a subset of youth should be considered a proxy for the experiences of the wider age group. On the other hand, some datasets provide individual measures for several cohorts within the YDI age range. In these cases, the average of the age cohorts was used.

Lastly, in one instance, IEP developed an improved indicator by creating a new dataset on youth policy, detailed further in Section A.1.2.5. This process helped counter some of the persistent data availability limitations in the *Civic and Political Participation* domain.

A1.3.2 Imputations

The 2020 YDI's methodology has been designed to be in line with other prominent global development indices, and substantial effort has been made to populate the index with the best available country data. However, a major challenge to developing a harmonised composite index lies in attempting to overcome the paucity of consistent and comprehensive data across very diverse countries around the world. Data varies significantly not just in demographic and geographic terms but also with regard to socio-economic characteristics, which can often affect data collection and quality. Meanwhile, consistent and comprehensive datasets covering youth development remain scarce. Data availability has been a challenge particularly for the *Equality and Inclusion* and the *Political and Civic Participation* domains. Constructing the 2020 YDI has, therefore, highlighted gaps in youth development data and the need for further improvement in data collection.

The issue of data gaps is a common challenge to creating an index. The OECD recommends a number of statistical techniques for dealing with data imputation to fill in data gaps (OECD et al., 2008). Table A1.2 lists the approaches used in the 2020 YDI. Using a combination of these techniques, the YDI represents the use of the best possible data without an overly complex methodology.

Figure A1.1 compares the proportion of the data in the index that has been imputed, showing that 90.87 per cent of country-indicator pairs included in the 2020 YDI are based on existing country data between 2010 and 2018, while 9.13 per cent of the data in the index has been imputed.

While the YDI makes use of the best available data to estimate the level of youth development globally, caution must be exercised in interpreting the results. For example, one of the key findings in this report is that, on average, youth development improved globally between 2010 and 2018. This should be interpreted as follows: "Given the availability of information for each year, the evidence suggests that youth development has improved between 2010 and 2018."

This is particularly true for countries for which a large share of the data has been imputed. Effort was made in the design of the methodology to include as many Commonwealth countries as possible, resulting in high imputation thresholds in some places. Countries with at least 50 per cent of the needed data were included in the index. Table A1.3 gives data availability by country, indicating for which countries data coverage is near-complete and for which additional data is needed.

The scarcity of complete global data highlights that collecting more and better age-disaggregated data must be made a priority to further understand country-specific and global trends in youth development.

A1.4 The banding process

In order to aggregate the incommensurable indicators, all indicators have been banded (normalised). This means each indicator is scaled to a score ranging between 0 and 1, relative to the initial global range. Appropriate minimum and maximum values are, therefore, chosen for each indicator so that any values below the minimum are assigned 0 and values above the maximum are assigned 1. All other values are scaled between 0 and 1, equivalent to their position in the original minimum-maximum range. Depending on the nature of the data, the banding process can take slightly different forms.

For example, for the *literacy rate* indicator, a higher score reflects a more desirable situation. Therefore, in this case, the banding process has assigned the largest data point a value of 1. Conversely, the lowest data point in the indicator has been assigned a value of 0, while all other data are scaled relative to these two points. This process is referred to as forward banding. On the other hand, a lower score in the *mortality* indicator reflects a more desirable situation. In this case, the data are reverse banded, so the lowest value is assigned 1 while the highest is assigned 0.

Therefore, for year y, a forward banded score is calculated for indicator i by Equation 1. A reverse banded score is calculated using Equation 2.

$$Banded_i = \frac{\text{Country indicator value in year } y_i - Minimum\ cutoff_i}{Maximum\ cutoff_i - Minimum\ cutoff_i} \quad (1)$$

$$Reverse\ Banded_i = 1 - \frac{\text{Country indicator value in year } y_i - Minimum\ cutoff_i}{Maximum\ cutoff_i - Minimum\ cutoff_i} \quad (2)$$

An integral part of the banding process is to set appropriate minimum and maximum cut-off values for the banded scores. Some data has a normal distribution and, therefore, outliers can be easily defined as those greater than three standard deviations from the mean. However, other datasets do not follow the bell-curved distribution trend. A number of considerations are, therefore, essential in choosing the appropriate technique: the nature of the data, the distribution, the purpose of the index, the information to be conveyed and so on. When investigating global datasets for the 2020 YDI, very few can be classified as having a normal distribution. The presence of outliers defines the variance, skewing both the minimum and the maximum values. To account for this, IEP has set minimum and maximum banding values to safeguard that outliers do not influence results too heavily. These upper and lower limits have either been decided on normatively or calculated using a common definition of outliers as being data points that lie outside of 1.5 times the interquartile range from the second and third quartiles of the distribution. Table A1.4 outlines the data distribution and bands for each indicator.

A1.5 Weighting indicators and domains

Table A1.5 shows the indicators and respective weights applied in the 2020 YDI. The YDI assigns a higher weighting to three domains; *Health and Wellbeing, Education* and *Employment and Opportunity*, 22 per cent each, as these domains are considered key to youth development and data quality and availability are higher here. *Equality and Inclusion* is weighted at 14 per cent, while *Political and Civic Participation* and *Peace and Security* are both weighted at 10 per cent each.

Within each domain, indicators are weighted by their relative importance to the other indicators in the

Table A1.2 Data imputation methods applied in the 2020 YDI

Imputation method	Description	Application in the 2020 YDI
Time series imputation	Replace missing values using linear interpolation	The YDI uses this method when at least two data points exist in a time series for an indicator-country pair, to estimate data for unreported years. Similarly, when only one year of data is available for all countries, the values for that year are used for all years in the index.
Cold deck imputation	Replace the missing value with a value from another source	The YDI uses this method when additional country statistics are available to fill in gaps.
Hot deck imputation	Replace the missing value with a KNN imputation. KNN is an algorithm that is useful for matching a point with its closest k neighbours in a multidimensional space. It can be used for data that is continuous, discrete, ordinal and categorical, which makes it particularly useful for dealing with missing data. The NI fills in data gaps using the five most similar countries to impute a value.	The YDI uses this method for data that is not available for all countries.

respective domain. In some instances, indicators are weighted equally, indicating that they together comprise the core features of the respective domain and are equally essential. Across the three core domains, which comprise 66 per cent of the overall index, three indicators are considered primary:

mortality rate, literacy rate and *NEET*. These primary indicators are weighted slightly higher than others in the index and they therefore have a big impact on domain scores. In some cases, they grant countries a more pronounced domain score, regardless of their overall rank in the YDI.

Figure A1.1 Proportion of imputed and available data for the 2020 YDI, 2010–2018

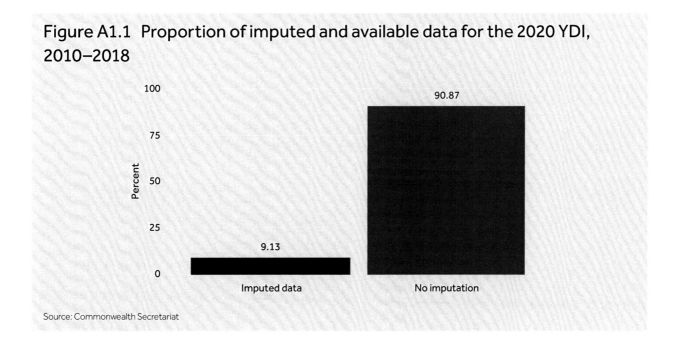

Source: Commonwealth Secretariat

Table A1.3 Data availability for YDI countries, in ascending order of imputed data/descending order of real data

Country	Imputed data (%)	Real data (%)
Angola	0	100
Burundi	0	100
Benin	0	100
Bangladesh	0	100
Belarus	0	100
Bolivia	0	100
Chile	0	100
Cameroon	0	100
Colombia	0	100
Costa Rica	0	100
Dominican Republic	0	100
Algeria	0	100
Ecuador	0	100
Egypt	0	100
Ethiopia	0	100
Ghana	0	100
Guinea	0	100
Guatemala	0	100
Honduras	0	100
Indonesia	0	100
Cambodia	0	100
Liberia	0	100
Sri Lanka	0	100
Madagascar	0	100
Mexico	0	100
Mali	0	100
Myanmar	0	100
Montenegro	0	100
Mongolia	0	100
Mauritania	0	100
Niger	0	100
Nigeria	0	100
Nicaragua	0	100
Nepal	0	100
Pakistan	0	100
Panama	0	100
Peru	0	100
Paraguay	0	100
Rwanda	0	100
Senegal	0	100
Sierra Leone	0	100

(Continued)

Country	Imputed data (%)	Real data (%)
El Salvador	0	100
Serbia	0	100
Togo	0	100
Thailand	0	100
Tajikistan	0	100
Tunisia	0	100
Uganda	0	100
Uruguay	0	100
Yemen	0	100
South Africa	0	100
Zambia	0	100
Zimbabwe	0	100
Albania	3.7	96.3
Argentina	3.7	96.3
Armenia	3.7	96.3
Bosnia and Herzegovina	3.7	96.3
Brazil	3.7	96.3
Botswana	3.7	96.3
Democratic Republic of Congo	3.7	96.3
Spain	3.7	96.3
Estonia	3.7	96.3
Georgia	3.7	96.3
Hungary	3.7	96.3
India	3.7	96.3
Iran	3.7	96.3
Iraq	3.7	96.3
Italy	3.7	96.3
Kazakhstan	3.7	96.3
Kenya	3.7	96.3
Lebanon	3.7	96.3
Latvia	3.7	96.3
Macedonia	3.7	96.3
Philippines	3.7	96.3
Sudan	3.7	96.3
Singapore	3.7	96.3
Trinidad and Tobago	3.7	96.3
Turkey	3.7	96.3
Ukraine	3.7	96.3
Vietnam	3.7	96.3
Afghanistan	7.41	92.59
United Arab Emirates	7.41	92.59
Burkina Faso	7.41	92.59
Bhutan	7.41	92.59
Switzerland	7.41	92.59

(Continued)

Country	Imputed data (%)	Real data (%)
Côte d'Ivoire	7.41	92.59
Republic of Congo	7.41	92.59
Comoros	7.41	92.59
Germany	7.41	92.59
Denmark	7.41	92.59
Finland	7.41	92.59
France	7.41	92.59
Greece	7.41	92.59
Croatia	7.41	92.59
Haiti	7.41	92.59
Ireland	7.41	92.59
Jamaica	7.41	92.59
Jordan	7.41	92.59
Kyrgyz Republic	7.41	92.59
Laos	7.41	92.59
Lithuania	7.41	92.59
Morocco	7.41	92.59
Moldova	7.41	92.59
Mauritius	7.41	92.59
Malawi	7.41	92.59
Malaysia	7.41	92.59
Norway	7.41	92.59
Poland	7.41	92.59
Portugal	7.41	92.59
Qatar	7.41	92.59
Romania	7.41	92.59
Saudi Arabia	7.41	92.59
Slovakia	7.41	92.59
Slovenia	7.41	92.59
Chad	7.41	92.59
Tanzania	7.41	92.59
Australia	11.11	88.89
Austria	11.11	88.89
Azerbaijan	11.11	88.89
Belgium	11.11	88.89
Bulgaria	11.11	88.89
Belize	11.11	88.89
Central African Republic	11.11	88.89
Cyprus	11.11	88.89
Czech Republic	11.11	88.89
Gabon	11.11	88.89
The Gambia	11.11	88.89
Guyana	11.11	88.89
Iceland	11.11	88.89

(Continued)

Country	Imputed data (%)	Real data (%)
Israel	11.11	88.89
Japan	11.11	88.89
Kuwait	11.11	88.89
Lesotho	11.11	88.89
Luxembourg	11.11	88.89
Mozambique	11.11	88.89
Namibia	11.11	88.89
Netherlands	11.11	88.89
New Zealand	11.11	88.89
Palestine	11.11	88.89
Russia	11.11	88.89
Sweden	11.11	88.89
Swaziland	11.11	88.89
Syria	11.11	88.89
Venezuela	11.11	88.89
Canada	14.81	85.19
China	14.81	85.19
Cuba	14.81	85.19
United Kingdom	14.81	85.19
Libya	14.81	85.19
Maldives	14.81	85.19
Malta	14.81	85.19
South Sudan	14.81	85.19
Turkmenistan	14.81	85.19
United States of America	14.81	85.19
Uzbekistan	14.81	85.19
Bahrain	18.52	81.48
South Korea	18.52	81.48
Papua New Guinea	18.52	81.48
Somalia	18.52	81.48
Suriname	18.52	81.48
Djibouti	22.22	77.78
Oman	22.22	77.78
Timor-Leste	22.22	77.78
Eritrea	25.93	74.07
Guinea-Bissau	25.93	74.07
Equatorial Guinea	25.93	74.07
Barbados	29.63	70.37
Fiji	29.63	70.37
Samoa	29.63	70.37
Brunei	33.33	66.67
Cabo Verde	33.33	66.67
Vanuatu	33.33	66.67
Solomon Islands	37.04	62.96

(Continued)

Country	Imputed data (%)	Real data (%)
Tonga	37.04	62.96
São Tomé and Príncipe	40.74	59.26
Taiwan	40.74	59.26
Bahamas	44.44	55.56
Grenada	44.44	55.56
Saint Lucia	44.44	55.56
Kiribati	48.15	51.85
Seychelles	48.15	51.85

With the addition of new domains to the 2020 YDI to better represent current development issues, weightings have been realigned and country rankings in this iteration of the YDI have changed as a consequence. The only time series comparison recommended by IEP is, therefore, to use this iteration across the years provided, 2010-2018.

A1.6 YDI aggregation and calculation

Once the data has been banded and weights have been assigned, the final stage is to multiply each banded indicator with its corresponding weight and to add each country's performance to arrive at an overall YDI score. Final scores are calculated by combining scores for the six individual domains into the overall YDI score, as Figure A1.2 demonstrates.

Table A1.4 Banding limits for the 2020 YDI

Domain	Indicator	Minimum	Maximum	Mean	Standard deviation	Lower band	Upper band
Health & Wellbeing	Alcohol abuse*	2.29	769.52	44.34	77.39	2.49	66.29
	Mortality rate	23.72	16,540.28	174.77	266.15	0	250
	Drug abuse	4.57	1,183.54	87.61	112.49	0	500
	HIV rate*	0.10	17.70	0.95	2.09	0.1	0.725
	Mental health	0.00	10.94	0.50	1.14	0	4
	Tobacco consumption	0.01	0.52	0.15	0.09	0	1
	Self-harm	91.30	12,074.07	774.75	789.56	0	5,000
Education	Digital natives	0.60	99.60	38.65	32.41	0	100
	Literacy rate	13.14	100.00	84.09	15.56	0	100
	School completion*	0.24	141.88	61.04	29.59	10.5	113.82
Employment & Opportunity	Account	0.00	1.00	0.45	0.29	0	1
	Adolescent fertility rate	0.28	232.48	77.06	52.43	0	250
	NEET	0.06	79.17	17.20	8.75	0	100
	Underemployment	0.06	8,668.10	208.03	660.11	0.07	433.21
Equality & Inclusion	Economic marginalisation*	0.00	0.99	0.34	0.32	0	0.91
	Gender parity in literacy	0.00	0.76	0.09	0.11	0	1
	Gender parity in NEET*	0.00	55.00	8.12	9.81	0	32.56
	Gender parity in safety and security	0.00	0.39	0.13	0.07	0	1
	Early marriage	0.00	83.50	26.94	17.91	0	100
Political & Civic Participation	Recognition for community improvement	0.00	0.40	0.10	0.07	0	1
	Voiced opinion to an official	0.01	0.51	0.17	0.08	0	1
	Volunteered time	0.02	0.66	0.20	0.10	0	1
	Youth policy score	0.00	4.00	2.71	1.07	0	4
Peace & Security	Conflict and terrorism*	0.00	1,054,908	588.65	14,576.05	0	32,615
	INFORM score	0.50	9.30	3.81	1.74	0	10
	Internal peace score	1.09	4.45	2.39	0.64	1	5
	Interpersonal violence	20.76	12,377.72	781.99	1,184.74	20.91	1601.5

* Upper and lower bands calculated at 1.5 times the interquartile range from the second and third quartiles of the distribution.

Table A1.5 Weights used in the 2020 YDI

Domain	Domain weight	Indicator	Indicator weight
Health & Wellbeing	22%	Mortality rate	10%
		HIV rate	2%
		Self-harm	2%
		Mental health	2%
		Drug abuse	2%
		Alcohol abuse	2%
		Tobacco consumption	2%
Education	22%	Literacy rate	10%
		School completion	8%
		Digital natives	4%
Employment & Opportunity	22%	NEET	10%
		Underemployment	4%
		Adolescent fertility rate	4%
		Account	4%
Equality & Inclusion	14%	Gender parity in NEET	2.80%
		Gender parity in safety and security	2.80%
		Gender parity in literacy	2.80%
		Early marriage	2.80%
		Economic marginalisation	2.80%
Political & Civic Participation	10%	Youth policy score	2.50%
		Voiced opinion to an official	2.50%
		Volunteered time	2.50%
		Recognition for community improvement	2.50%
Peace & Security	10%	Internal peace score	2.50%
		Interpersonal violence	2.50%
		Conflict and terrorism	2.50%
		INFORM score	2.50%

Figure A1.2 Composition of indicators into domains and the final YDI scores

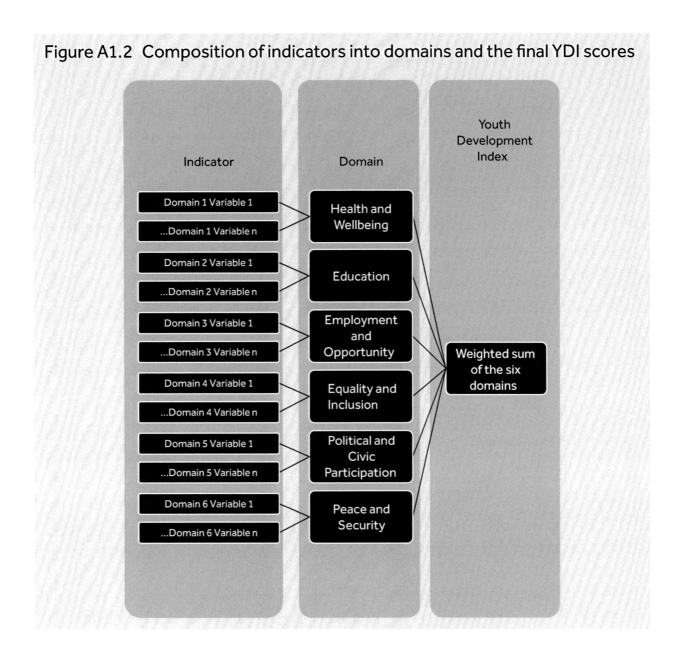

Endnotes

1   Conceptually, this domain purports to measure *gender* equality, but it necessarily uses biological sex as a proxy for gender identity in most cases. Gender refers to an individual's identity, and can be understood via multiple categories, including but not limited to man/boy and woman/girl. Sex refers to the category (male, female or intersex) assigned to the individual at birth, usually based on their anatomy, and may or may not be the same as their gender identity. Recognition of gender categories other than man/boy and woman/girl varies across and within societies, cultures and countries; as a result, relevant datasets for the YDI include only the two most commonly used genders. Furthermore, while individuals may have the option to select their gender identity when responding to surveys, non-self-reported data most often uses biological sex as a proxy for the genders of the persons being counted. More comprehensive data can be collected by capturing sex and gender as distinct variables and allowing individuals more gender categories within which to record their experiences.

References

Andersen, A.M., N. Egelund, T.P. Jensen, M. Krone, L. Lindenskov and J. Mejding (2011) "Forventninger og færdigheder – danske unge i en international sammenhæng". Paris: OECD. https://www.oecd.org/denmark/33684813.pdf

Borognovi, F., A. Choi and M. Paccagnella (2018) "The Evolution of Gender Gaps in Numeracy and Literacy Between Childhood and Adulthood'. Working Paper 184. Paris: OECD.

OECD (Organisation for Economic Co-operation and Development and European Commission) (2008) *Handbook on Constructing Composite Indicators: Methodology and User Guide*. Paris: OECD.

United Nations (2013) *The Millennium Development Goals Report 2013*. New York: United Nations. https://www.un.org/millenniumgoals/pdf/report-2013/mdg-report-2013-english.pdf

UNICEF (United Nations Children's Fund) (2019) *Adolescent Mental Health Matters – A Landscape Analysis of UNICEF's Response and Agenda for Action*. New York: UNICEF.

2020 Youth Development Index Results Tables: Country Rankings and Domain Scores

Annex 2

2020 Youth Development Index Results Tables: Country Rankings and Domain Scores

This annex presents, in detail, the rankings and domain scores for 181 countries in the 2020 Global Youth Development Index (YDI), including 48 of the 54 Commonwealth countries. Tables of global results are provided in formats that allow for identification of countries by level of youth development (Very High, High, Medium and Low) or alphabetically. Readers may also access these results through the 2020 Global YDI Dashboard.

Table A2.1   2020 Global YDI overall and domain scores and ranks[1]

Global rank	Country	YDI Overall score	Education rank	Education score	Employ- ment & Opport- unity rank	Employ- ment & Opport- unity score	Equality & Inclusion rank
Very High Youth Development							
1	Singapore	0.875	4	0.946	1	0.969	13
2	Slovenia	0.866	13	0.929	3	0.965	8
3	Norway	0.862	10	0.93	2	0.968	5
4	Malta	0.859	23	0.913	5	0.953	33
5	Denmark	0.858	7	0.939	6	0.951	14
6	Sweden	0.857	1	0.963	7	0.948	24
7	Switzerland	0.849	17	0.923	11	0.939	32
8	Netherlands	0.848	24	0.91	9	0.942	19
9	Ireland	0.846	26	0.909	17	0.907	4
10	Luxembourg	0.845	24	0.91	4	0.963	1
10	Portugal	0.845	31	0.899	19	0.906	34
12	Austria	0.842	21	0.917	10	0.941	5
13	Belgium	0.839	26	0.909	12	0.934	37
14	Spain	0.833	28	0.906	49	0.814	3
15	Germany	0.831	40	0.879	16	0.911	10
15	Iceland	0.831	14	0.928	28	0.862	24
17	Finland	0.827	5	0.944	8	0.945	30
18	Cyprus	0.825	41	0.874	22	0.886	28
19	New Zealand	0.824	30	0.901	14	0.914	48
20	South Korea	0.821	9	0.932	26	0.867	49
21	Hungary	0.819	33	0.896	30	0.859	54
22	Croatia	0.818	35	0.891	40	0.834	15
23	Italy	0.816	36	0.889	46	0.819	16
23	Japan	0.816	15	0.925	36	0.845	37
25	Israel	0.815	20	0.921	26	0.867	9
25	Slovakia	0.815	37	0.887	32	0.851	26
27	Kuwait	0.814	49	0.847	31	0.855	41
28	Czechia	0.811	31	0.899	41	0.831	34
29	Australia	0.807	29	0.903	61	0.796	46
29	France	0.807	10	0.93	81	0.754	5
31	Latvia	0.805	6	0.941	17	0.907	19
32	Qatar	0.802	88	0.775	14	0.914	30
32	Serbia	0.802	44	0.869	66	0.782	12
34	Greece	0.799	39	0.881	42	0.827	29
34	Lithuania	0.799	10	0.93	21	0.889	10

Country	Equality & Inclusion score	Health & Wellbeing rank	Health & Wellbeing score	Peace & Security rank	Peace & Security score	Political & Civic Participation rank	Political & Civic Participation score
Singapore	0.97	1	0.927	1	0.962	162	0.178
Slovenia	0.977	33	0.818	6	0.94	18	0.388
Norway	0.978	49	0.794	4	0.949	19	0.385
Malta	0.95	18	0.853	33	0.882	11	0.398
Denmark	0.967	24	0.839	3	0.951	102	0.272
Sweden	0.959	43	0.808	11	0.931	64	0.318
Switzerland	0.951	51	0.786	5	0.943	14	0.392
Netherlands	0.962	38	0.813	13	0.929	44	0.342
Ireland	0.98	45	0.805	15	0.918	9	0.405
Luxembourg	0.991	79	0.739	21	0.902	3	0.412
Portugal	0.945	7	0.885	9	0.933	98	0.275
Austria	0.978	81	0.736	8	0.936	8	0.408
Belgium	0.943	38	0.813	22	0.901	58	0.322
Spain	0.985	5	0.901	26	0.898	89	0.288
Germany	0.972	62	0.773	16	0.916	14	0.392
Iceland	0.959	28	0.826	2	0.958	116	0.252
Finland	0.952	104	0.675	6	0.94	36	0.355
Cyprus	0.955	16	0.858	41	0.865	88	0.292
New Zealand	0.93	60	0.777	11	0.931	77	0.308
South Korea	0.928	38	0.813	17	0.912	120	0.248
Hungary	0.918	14	0.863	20	0.903	125	0.24
Croatia	0.966	20	0.845	23	0.9	104	0.27
Italy	0.964	6	0.887	41	0.865	125	0.24
Japan	0.943	35	0.815	14	0.926	139	0.225
Israel	0.974	3	0.906	117	0.631	142	0.222
Slovakia	0.957	32	0.819	23	0.9	91	0.283
Kuwait	0.941	10	0.87	33	0.882	93	0.279
Czechia	0.945	28	0.826	9	0.933	133	0.232
Australia	0.932	56	0.78	25	0.899	3	0.412
France	0.978	46	0.804	29	0.892	45	0.34
Latvia	0.962	99	0.698	37	0.875	142	0.222
Qatar	0.952	11	0.866	19	0.906	168	0.161
Serbia	0.971	9	0.873	46	0.848	113	0.258
Greece	0.953	30	0.822	46	0.848	129	0.235
Lithuania	0.972	103	0.677	32	0.883	118	0.25

(Continued)

Global rank	Country	YDI Overall score	Education rank	Education score	Employ- ment & Opport- unity rank	Employ- ment & Opport- unity score	Equality & Inclusion rank
36	Canada	0.798	21	0.917	20	0.901	21
36	Estonia	0.798	2	0.96	12	0.934	21
36	Poland	0.798	17	0.923	24	0.87	21
39	Maldives	0.794	47	0.857	80	0.755	54
40	United Kingdom	0.793	15	0.925	91	0.731	2
40	Montenegro	0.793	42	0.873	51	0.812	18
42	North Macedonia	0.791	50	0.844	71	0.769	43
43	Romania	0.784	53	0.838	58	0.8	51
44	Bulgaria	0.783	45	0.865	59	0.799	34
45	Chile	0.782	45	0.865	54	0.811	50
High Youth Development							
46	Taiwan	0.78	72	0.807	37	0.844	60
47	Bahrain	0.779	52	0.84	35	0.848	74
47	Barbados	0.779	8	0.936	59	0.799	57
49	Brunei	0.777	17	0.923	69	0.778	46
50	Malaysia	0.775	59	0.83	23	0.881	66
51	Belarus	0.774	54	0.837	38	0.841	16
52	Oman	0.769	62	0.823	48	0.817	63
53	Bosnia and Herzegovina	0.768	69	0.811	70	0.777	27
54	Mauritius	0.766	77	0.795	33	0.85	64
55	Albania	0.764	67	0.816	105	0.706	45
56	United Arab Emirates	0.763	84	0.785	24	0.87	68
57	Saudi Arabia	0.76	33	0.896	39	0.836	89
58	Mongolia	0.758	65	0.819	28	0.862	51
59	Costa Rica	0.75	95	0.762	56	0.806	74
60	Fiji	0.748	63	0.822	51	0.812	109
61	Sri Lanka	0.747	92	0.769	56	0.806	117
62	China	0.745	59	0.83	89	0.734	94
63	Cuba	0.744	79	0.793	77	0.762	84
63	Vietnam	0.744	57	0.833	85	0.741	66
65	United States	0.737	3	0.956	44	0.824	40
66	Armenia	0.736	91	0.771	101	0.716	42
66	Grenada	0.736	43	0.871	108	0.703	70
68	Peru	0.734	48	0.853	117	0.685	79
68	Uruguay	0.734	79	0.793	77	0.762	72
70	Georgia	0.731	70	0.81	103	0.713	86
70	Kazakhstan	0.731	56	0.834	55	0.81	43
72	Samoa	0.728	71	0.808	110	0.701	59
73	Seychelles	0.725	38	0.886	120	0.675	80
73	Turkey	0.725	63	0.822	79	0.76	91

Country	Equality & Inclusion score	Health & Wellbeing rank	Health & Wellbeing score	Peace & Security rank	Peace & Security score	Political & Civic Participation rank	Political & Civic Participation score
Canada	0.96	73	0.742	30	0.891	177	0.115
Estonia	0.96	137	0.568	28	0.896	58	0.322
Poland	0.96	75	0.741	27	0.897	169	0.16
Maldives	0.918	2	0.913	45	0.859	124	0.243
United Kingdom	0.988	67	0.752	18	0.91	45	0.34
Montenegro	0.963	26	0.831	49	0.838	150	0.21
North Macedonia	0.937	11	0.866	50	0.836	75	0.31
Romania	0.919	33	0.818	36	0.877	94	0.277
Bulgaria	0.945	41	0.811	40	0.869	161	0.188
Chile	0.92	47	0.803	61	0.799	98	0.275
Taiwan	0.903	19	0.848	43	0.864	164	0.173
Bahrain	0.877	4	0.903	125	0.594	107	0.265
Barbados	0.912	61	0.776	102	0.696	85	0.293
Brunei	0.932	92	0.714	35	0.878	95	0.276
Malaysia	0.887	86	0.724	48	0.844	74	0.311
Belarus	0.964	96	0.705	51	0.834	64	0.318
Oman	0.898	21	0.843	44	0.861	178	0.108
Bosnia and Herzegovina	0.956	15	0.86	56	0.805	173	0.148
Mauritius	0.892	95	0.709	38	0.874	36	0.355
Albania	0.933	25	0.832	53	0.819	48	0.335
United Arab Emirates	0.885	65	0.756	30	0.891	155	0.198
Saudi Arabia	0.836	35	0.815	132	0.575	118	0.25
Mongolia	0.919	112	0.645	73	0.777	12	0.395
Costa Rica	0.877	48	0.798	101	0.7	25	0.37
Fiji	0.81	85	0.727	67	0.792	36	0.355
Sri Lanka	0.798	58	0.778	72	0.778	12	0.395
China	0.833	31	0.821	64	0.797	122	0.245
Cuba	0.845	23	0.84	82	0.758	132	0.233
Vietnam	0.887	72	0.743	52	0.822	92	0.28
United States	0.942	144	0.538	95	0.716	131	0.234
Armenia	0.94	35	0.815	58	0.803	166	0.17
Grenada	0.881	55	0.782	68	0.791	172	0.149
Peru	0.869	44	0.806	85	0.751	148	0.212
Uruguay	0.878	63	0.77	70	0.786	148	0.212
Georgia	0.842	73	0.742	70	0.786	30	0.362
Kazakhstan	0.937	120	0.621	68	0.791	136	0.227
Samoa	0.905	77	0.74	59	0.802	109	0.264
Seychelles	0.866	67	0.752	66	0.794	171	0.157
Turkey	0.835	21	0.843	155	0.446	80	0.305

(Continued)

Global rank	Country	YDI Overall score	Education rank	Education score	Employment & Opportunity rank	Employment & Opportunity score	Equality & Inclusion rank
75	Jamaica	0.724	86	0.776	47	0.818	86
75	Tonga	0.724	107	0.726	71	0.769	54
77	Bhutan	0.719	118	0.701	92	0.729	108
78	Cape Verde	0.717	106	0.738	111	0.699	58
78	Jordan	0.717	119	0.696	83	0.749	37
80	Saint Lucia	0.716	65	0.819	64	0.785	81
81	Tunisia	0.714	104	0.739	96	0.724	70
82	Russia	0.709	50	0.844	34	0.849	51
83	Moldova	0.706	76	0.799	90	0.732	74
84	Thailand	0.704	95	0.762	42	0.827	72
85	Lebanon	0.701	74	0.804	82	0.752	65
85	Panama	0.701	93	0.767	86	0.74	92
87	Argentina	0.699	61	0.827	156	0.585	78
88	Indonesia	0.696	98	0.758	153	0.588	105
88	Kyrgyzstan	0.696	72	0.807	136	0.633	111
90	Azerbaijan	0.693	90	0.772	131	0.639	62
Medium Youth Development							
91	Bolivia	0.691	101	0.749	74	0.768	111
91	Tajikistan	0.691	82	0.787	124	0.661	121
93	Morocco	0.69	112	0.719	133	0.636	100
94	Algeria	0.689	102	0.743	97	0.721	105
94	Nepal	0.689	111	0.723	143	0.61	122
96	Paraguay	0.687	117	0.703	87	0.739	100
97	Cambodia	0.685	137	0.591	49	0.814	114
98	Uzbekistan	0.681	82	0.787	145	0.606	133
99	Iran	0.677	94	0.766	84	0.744	128
100	Timor-Leste	0.676	126	0.664	94	0.725	126
101	Trinidad and Tobago	0.674	67	0.816	119	0.68	82
102	Nicaragua	0.673	129	0.631	94	0.725	139
103	Ecuador	0.672	75	0.803	112	0.698	98
104	Bahamas, The	0.67	57	0.833	75	0.767	100
105	Dominican Republic	0.668	85	0.783	114	0.695	96
106	São Tomé and Príncipe	0.661	107	0.726	115	0.69	134
107	Ukraine	0.66	81	0.788	45	0.822	60
108	Botswana	0.659	88	0.775	105	0.706	128
108	Palestinian Territories	0.659	78	0.794	174	0.519	74
110	Libya	0.657	104	0.739	62	0.794	94
111	Solomon Islands	0.656	128	0.642	51	0.812	127
112	Turkmenistan	0.653	109	0.725	126	0.658	113

Country	Equality & Inclusion score	Health & Wellbeing rank	Health & Wellbeing score	Peace & Security rank	Peace & Security score	Political & Civic Participation rank	Political & Civic Participation score
Jamaica	0.842	81	0.736	134	0.564	25	0.37
Tonga	0.918	97	0.699	59	0.802	57	0.323
Bhutan	0.811	50	0.793	39	0.87	85	0.293
Cape Verde	0.91	70	0.749	96	0.711	21	0.382
Jordan	0.943	8	0.875	142	0.523	145	0.22
Saint Lucia	0.864	102	0.682	119	0.612	80	0.305
Tunisia	0.881	13	0.865	110	0.657	175	0.13
Russia	0.919	147	0.533	128	0.582	53	0.328
Moldova	0.877	105	0.671	54	0.813	163	0.174
Thailand	0.878	123	0.614	114	0.653	68	0.315
Lebanon	0.888	58	0.778	161	0.402	136	0.227
Panama	0.834	79	0.739	126	0.59	73	0.312
Argentina	0.87	51	0.786	89	0.738	155	0.198
Indonesia	0.814	71	0.746	65	0.795	1	0.425
Kyrgyzstan	0.806	91	0.717	74	0.775	64	0.318
Azerbaijan	0.9	87	0.723	86	0.75	142	0.222
Bolivia	0.806	75	0.741	93	0.724	179	0.088
Tajikistan	0.79	100	0.691	84	0.753	45	0.34
Morocco	0.82	53	0.785	56	0.805	129	0.235
Algeria	0.814	27	0.83	139	0.545	170	0.159
Nepal	0.788	63	0.77	81	0.759	10	0.4
Paraguay	0.82	90	0.719	108	0.662	82	0.3
Cambodia	0.804	94	0.71	86	0.75	58	0.322
Uzbekistan	0.75	84	0.731	55	0.811	95	0.276
Iran	0.763	88	0.722	111	0.656	174	0.132
Timor-Leste	0.769	92	0.714	78	0.763	84	0.294
Trinidad and Tobago	0.862	131	0.586	127	0.589	29	0.365
Nicaragua	0.729	77	0.74	100	0.705	14	0.392
Ecuador	0.824	108	0.655	121	0.606	145	0.22
Bahamas, The	0.82	145	0.536	131	0.578	104	0.27
Dominican Republic	0.832	111	0.646	138	0.548	82	0.3
São Tomé and Príncipe	0.747	122	0.616	75	0.773	67	0.316
Ukraine	0.903	158	0.502	171	0.364	58	0.322
Botswana	0.763	138	0.559	91	0.73	77	0.308
Palestinian Territories	0.877	17	0.857	153	0.471	176	0.118
Libya	0.833	128	0.598	166	0.38	48	0.335
Solomon Islands	0.765	140	0.549	99	0.709	22	0.377
Turkmenistan	0.805	117	0.628	76	0.768	153	0.205

(*Continued*)

Global rank	Country	YDI Overall score	Education rank	Education score	Employment & Opportunity rank	Employment & Opportunity score	Equality & Inclusion rank
113	Colombia	0.646	95	0.762	162	0.563	109
114	Gabon	0.645	139	0.57	65	0.784	88
114	Suriname	0.645	130	0.628	88	0.736	85
116	Brazil	0.637	86	0.776	159	0.568	92
117	Mexico	0.636	55	0.835	159	0.568	124
118	Kiribati	0.635	100	0.75	117	0.685	119
119	Namibia	0.632	121	0.692	76	0.764	83
120	Vanuatu	0.628	134	0.617	66	0.782	89
121	Comoros	0.627	152	0.5	128	0.657	125
122	India	0.626	119	0.696	139	0.618	172
123	Egypt	0.624	109	0.725	167	0.544	103
124	Belize	0.619	122	0.688	102	0.715	131
125	Guyana	0.617	103	0.74	123	0.663	123
126	Bangladesh	0.616	116	0.705	172	0.526	174
127	El Salvador	0.615	115	0.709	122	0.669	130
128	Djibouti	0.612	149	0.506	63	0.788	136
128	Venezuela	0.612	99	0.756	152	0.589	104
130	Myanmar (Burma)	0.61	140	0.565	113	0.696	107
131	Ghana	0.608	123	0.675	159	0.568	118
131	South Africa	0.608	113	0.714	100	0.717	69
133	Philippines	0.603	113	0.714	166	0.549	98
133	Senegal	0.603	163	0.443	135	0.635	167
135	Haiti	0.598	138	0.587	97	0.721	115

Low Youth Development

Global rank	Country	YDI Overall score	Education rank	Education score	Employment & Opportunity rank	Employment & Opportunity score	Equality & Inclusion rank
136	Honduras	0.595	135	0.602	137	0.63	153
136	Laos	0.595	131	0.627	177	0.489	135
138	Sierra Leone	0.58	162	0.447	107	0.705	148
139	Gambia, The	0.577	150	0.503	143	0.61	151
139	Kenya	0.577	123	0.675	126	0.658	140
141	Togo	0.575	146	0.525	68	0.779	144
142	Rwanda	0.574	156	0.495	167	0.544	142
143	Mauritania	0.573	166	0.408	146	0.603	162
144	Papua New Guinea	0.572	154	0.499	71	0.769	115
145	Liberia	0.567	173	0.373	99	0.719	169
146	Equatorial Guinea	0.564	151	0.502	130	0.646	119
147	Guatemala	0.562	132	0.622	138	0.619	167
148	Eritrea	0.559	141	0.555	93	0.728	154
148	Tanzania	0.559	157	0.488	129	0.65	149
150	Burundi	0.557	158	0.482	104	0.712	138
150	Sudan	0.557	143	0.533	163	0.562	155
152	Eswatini	0.553	127	0.652	157	0.581	97

Country	Equality & Inclusion score	Health & Wellbeing rank	Health & Wellbeing score	Peace & Security rank	Peace & Security score	Political & Civic Participation rank	Political & Civic Participation score
Colombia	0.81	81	0.736	152	0.48	68	0.315
Gabon	0.839	133	0.581	88	0.745	104	0.27
Suriname	0.844	126	0.602	98	0.71	128	0.238
Brazil	0.834	115	0.629	140	0.541	58	0.322
Mexico	0.776	106	0.659	154	0.466	98	0.275
Kiribati	0.791	170	0.427	80	0.761	17	0.39
Namibia	0.847	166	0.462	136	0.559	34	0.358
Vanuatu	0.836	168	0.445	83	0.756	85	0.293
Comoros	0.774	69	0.75	90	0.737	115	0.253
India	0.61	101	0.683	106	0.679	51	0.332
Egypt	0.818	54	0.784	149	0.492	179	0.088
Belize	0.753	148	0.529	130	0.58	77	0.308
Guyana	0.779	159	0.498	133	0.566	53	0.328
Bangladesh	0.561	42	0.809	105	0.681	151	0.208
El Salvador	0.756	146	0.534	141	0.526	33	0.36
Djibouti	0.736	114	0.639	122	0.605	134	0.228
Venezuela	0.816	141	0.548	148	0.497	58	0.322
Myanmar (Burma)	0.813	125	0.605	111	0.656	155	0.198
Ghana	0.793	141	0.548	107	0.675	40	0.35
South Africa	0.884	173	0.405	157	0.426	23	0.375
Philippines	0.824	109	0.654	177	0.309	40	0.35
Senegal	0.637	88	0.722	63	0.798	19	0.385
Haiti	0.8	151	0.518	150	0.489	35	0.356
Honduras	0.672	119	0.622	145	0.514	3	0.412
Laos	0.74	109	0.654	78	0.763	116	0.252
Sierra Leone	0.691	161	0.495	61	0.799	3	0.412
Gambia, The	0.678	127	0.601	103	0.688	28	0.367
Kenya	0.723	161	0.495	170	0.365	25	0.37
Togo	0.709	155	0.508	147	0.508	110	0.262
Rwanda	0.716	121	0.618	92	0.729	30	0.362
Mauritania	0.651	57	0.779	111	0.656	145	0.22
Papua New Guinea	0.8	173	0.405	123	0.604	71	0.314
Liberia	0.634	133	0.581	104	0.686	2	0.415
Equatorial Guinea	0.791	163	0.49	77	0.766	167	0.169
Guatemala	0.637	149	0.526	146	0.51	53	0.328
Eritrea	0.67	165	0.467	120	0.609	160	0.191
Tanzania	0.69	135	0.571	116	0.641	134	0.228
Burundi	0.734	151	0.518	151	0.486	89	0.288
Sudan	0.663	65	0.756	162	0.392	164	0.173
Eswatini	0.826	180	0.384	135	0.561	114	0.257

(*Continued*)

Global rank	Country	YDI Overall score	Education rank	Education score	Employment & Opportunity rank	Employment & Opportunity score	Equality & Inclusion rank
153	Syria	0.551	133	0.62	132	0.637	132
154	Zambia	0.548	136	0.596	165	0.551	143
155	Benin	0.547	165	0.41	157	0.581	157
156	Madagascar	0.544	160	0.466	164	0.558	146
157	Uganda	0.534	159	0.479	167	0.544	160
158	Ethiopia	0.529	168	0.4	149	0.591	147
159	Zimbabwe	0.528	125	0.67	178	0.47	151
160	Cameroon	0.527	144	0.529	148	0.596	136
161	Nigeria	0.52	154	0.499	173	0.52	157
162	Pakistan	0.517	152	0.5	146	0.603	165
163	Lesotho	0.511	142	0.539	121	0.67	145
164	Congo - Brazzaville	0.509	146	0.525	140	0.616	140
165	Guinea-Bissau	0.508	171	0.377	108	0.703	164
166	Angola	0.506	167	0.402	151	0.59	163
166	Burkina Faso	0.506	170	0.383	141	0.612	171
168	Guinea	0.5	176	0.302	116	0.687	156
168	Iraq	0.5	169	0.394	154	0.587	150
170	Congo - Kinshasa	0.499	144	0.529	176	0.493	170
171	Malawi	0.484	172	0.375	175	0.514	160
172	Yemen	0.474	148	0.522	171	0.529	180
173	Mozambique	0.46	174	0.37	155	0.586	166
174	Côte d'Ivoire	0.457	164	0.411	179	0.454	173
175	Mali	0.447	177	0.3	170	0.532	175
176	Somalia	0.436	175	0.311	133	0.636	177
177	Niger	0.424	179	0.213	180	0.45	181
178	Afghanistan	0.421	161	0.457	181	0.413	178
178	South Sudan	0.421	178	0.251	141	0.612	159
180	Central African Republic	0.399	180	0.176	125	0.659	176
181	Chad	0.398	181	0.16	149	0.591	179

Country	Equality & Inclusion score	Health & Wellbeing rank	Health & Wellbeing score	Peace & Security rank	Peace & Security score	Political & Civic Participation rank	Political & Civic Participation score
Syria	0.752	157	0.505	172	0.357	136	0.227
Zambia	0.714	170	0.427	96	0.711	75	0.31
Benin	0.655	115	0.629	115	0.652	48	0.335
Madagascar	0.701	113	0.643	144	0.518	98	0.275
Uganda	0.653	150	0.522	118	0.621	7	0.41
Ethiopia	0.695	97	0.699	167	0.377	139	0.225
Zimbabwe	0.678	177	0.399	124	0.603	43	0.345
Cameroon	0.736	167	0.461	158	0.422	53	0.328
Nigeria	0.655	129	0.589	168	0.373	23	0.375
Pakistan	0.64	124	0.61	156	0.438	181	0.06
Lesotho	0.704	181	0.378	164	0.389	122	0.245
Congo - Brazzaville	0.723	175	0.404	160	0.41	102	0.272
Guinea-Bissau	0.641	175	0.404	108	0.662	112	0.259
Angola	0.65	156	0.507	128	0.582	107	0.265
Burkina Faso	0.611	132	0.584	159	0.416	68	0.315
Guinea	0.662	154	0.515	143	0.521	120	0.248
Iraq	0.684	118	0.625	176	0.311	159	0.196
Congo - Kinshasa	0.612	141	0.548	174	0.321	39	0.352
Malawi	0.653	172	0.417	94	0.719	52	0.331
Yemen	0.44	129	0.589	175	0.316	158	0.197
Mozambique	0.639	178	0.392	163	0.39	42	0.348
Côte d'Ivoire	0.568	164	0.475	137	0.555	95	0.276
Mali	0.532	135	0.571	165	0.384	111	0.26
Somalia	0.515	153	0.516	180	0.213	151	0.208
Niger	0.429	106	0.659	169	0.37	30	0.362
Afghanistan	0.509	139	0.556	181	0.142	141	0.223
South Sudan	0.654	169	0.428	179	0.216	125	0.24
Central African Republic	0.52	178	0.392	178	0.25	72	0.313
Chad	0.49	159	0.498	173	0.339	153	0.205

Table A2.2 Global YDI overall scores, 2010–2018 (countries listed alphabetically)

Country	2010	2011	2012	2013	2014	2015	2016	2017	2018
Afghanistan	0.351	0.351	0.362	0.365	0.377	0.382	0.392	0.414	0.421
Albania	0.753	0.755	0.761	0.758	0.753	0.762	0.76	0.755	0.764
Algeria	0.637	0.649	0.693	0.676	0.681	0.683	0.692	0.691	0.689
Angola	0.495	0.509	0.51	0.511	0.516	0.518	0.511	0.507	0.506
Argentina	0.691	0.696	0.693	0.696	0.695	0.702	0.699	0.702	0.699
Armenia	0.684	0.684	0.691	0.695	0.688	0.695	0.694	0.736	0.736
Australia	0.802	0.805	0.811	0.808	0.81	0.807	0.811	0.805	0.807
Austria	0.825	0.83	0.832	0.835	0.841	0.838	0.841	0.84	0.842
Azerbaijan	0.688	0.689	0.696	0.692	0.674	0.677	0.671	0.695	0.693
Bahamas, The	0.667	0.666	0.661	0.662	0.662	0.662	0.667	0.67	0.67
Bahrain	0.785	0.78	0.761	0.774	0.778	0.779	0.8	0.779	0.779
Bangladesh	0.548	0.566	0.582	0.603	0.595	0.595	0.598	0.605	0.616
Barbados	0.769	0.772	0.775	0.777	0.779	0.779	0.779	0.779	0.779
Belarus	0.73	0.715	0.754	0.748	0.754	0.776	0.777	0.777	0.774
Belgium	0.827	0.83	0.83	0.835	0.839	0.843	0.816	0.843	0.839
Belize	0.597	0.624	0.624	0.609	0.611	0.614	0.623	0.619	0.619
Benin	0.511	0.501	0.51	0.512	0.522	0.534	0.534	0.543	0.547
Bhutan	0.681	0.686	0.694	0.698	0.705	0.708	0.713	0.717	0.719
Bolivia	0.68	0.678	0.687	0.693	0.694	0.692	0.697	0.696	0.691
Bosnia & Herzegovina	0.763	0.764	0.76	0.763	0.763	0.746	0.757	0.769	0.768
Botswana	0.611	0.61	0.615	0.628	0.649	0.658	0.657	0.667	0.659
Brazil	0.633	0.633	0.637	0.639	0.642	0.639	0.642	0.637	0.637
Brunei	0.777	0.776	0.778	0.783	0.78	0.778	0.775	0.775	0.777
Bulgaria	0.772	0.776	0.771	0.774	0.773	0.778	0.78	0.783	0.783
Burkina Faso	0.449	0.455	0.452	0.471	0.478	0.483	0.48	0.496	0.506
Burundi	0.502	0.509	0.521	0.533	0.536	0.544	0.553	0.557	0.557
Cambodia	0.646	0.642	0.639	0.658	0.669	0.672	0.674	0.682	0.685
Cameroon	0.513	0.515	0.517	0.521	0.496	0.514	0.522	0.527	0.527
Canada	0.791	0.799	0.798	0.797	0.797	0.798	0.797	0.8	0.798
Cape Verde	0.706	0.715	0.718	0.72	0.72	0.718	0.723	0.726	0.717
Central African Republic	0.396	0.392	0.398	0.385	0.382	0.379	0.384	0.397	0.399
Chad	0.401	0.396	0.403	0.41	0.405	0.391	0.403	0.396	0.398
Chile	0.757	0.762	0.771	0.772	0.779	0.781	0.782	0.785	0.782
China	0.718	0.722	0.726	0.731	0.73	0.735	0.74	0.743	0.745
Colombia	0.602	0.61	0.615	0.608	0.618	0.616	0.634	0.643	0.646
Comoros	0.597	0.585	0.593	0.599	0.609	0.614	0.619	0.624	0.627
Congo - Brazzaville	0.515	0.515	0.516	0.499	0.508	0.531	0.505	0.511	0.509
Congo - Kinshasa	0.447	0.451	0.458	0.469	0.48	0.49	0.498	0.5	0.499
Costa Rica	0.725	0.727	0.741	0.734	0.742	0.737	0.739	0.742	0.75
Côte d'Ivoire	0.431	0.42	0.437	0.439	0.437	0.442	0.442	0.453	0.457
Croatia	0.806	0.814	0.811	0.813	0.813	0.804	0.812	0.817	0.818
Cuba	0.741	0.736	0.741	0.744	0.747	0.744	0.743	0.745	0.744
Cyprus	0.822	0.818	0.818	0.813	0.82	0.822	0.821	0.824	0.825

(Continued)

Country	2010	2011	2012	2013	2014	2015	2016	2017	2018
Czechia	0.806	0.807	0.812	0.814	0.815	0.816	0.817	0.813	0.811
Denmark	0.849	0.845	0.858	0.865	0.863	0.865	0.86	0.862	0.858
Djibouti	0.574	0.609	0.603	0.609	0.597	0.587	0.612	0.61	0.612
Dominican Republic	0.662	0.659	0.662	0.66	0.662	0.666	0.671	0.668	0.668
Ecuador	0.629	0.627	0.638	0.647	0.66	0.668	0.673	0.67	0.672
Egypt	0.621	0.617	0.622	0.613	0.618	0.628	0.624	0.623	0.624
El Salvador	0.601	0.608	0.585	0.589	0.588	0.594	0.615	0.611	0.615
Equatorial Guinea	0.518	0.545	0.539	0.55	0.555	0.556	0.559	0.564	0.564
Eritrea	0.524	0.536	0.583	0.549	0.55	0.543	0.532	0.557	0.559
Estonia	0.757	0.753	0.777	0.791	0.795	0.792	0.799	0.797	0.798
Eswatini, Kingdom of	0.538	0.538	0.538	0.54	0.539	0.541	0.549	0.554	0.553
Ethiopia	0.467	0.474	0.481	0.495	0.515	0.51	0.515	0.529	0.529
Fiji	0.74	0.744	0.744	0.749	0.75	0.749	0.745	0.747	0.748
Finland	0.812	0.815	0.817	0.819	0.821	0.828	0.825	0.825	0.827
France	0.791	0.795	0.804	0.799	0.805	0.774	0.784	0.806	0.807
Gabon	0.594	0.601	0.609	0.617	0.623	0.628	0.64	0.648	0.645
Gambia, The	0.552	0.56	0.541	0.571	0.579	0.586	0.588	0.578	0.577
Georgia	0.683	0.696	0.683	0.691	0.712	0.721	0.723	0.732	0.731
Germany	0.817	0.82	0.825	0.823	0.832	0.829	0.826	0.831	0.831
Ghana	0.6	0.608	0.61	0.62	0.621	0.621	0.616	0.605	0.608
Greece	0.778	0.784	0.783	0.787	0.786	0.792	0.769	0.799	0.799
Grenada	0.734	0.733	0.737	0.737	0.736	0.73	0.734	0.735	0.736
Guatemala	0.541	0.537	0.554	0.567	0.575	0.583	0.579	0.564	0.562
Guinea	0.453	0.452	0.468	0.46	0.483	0.485	0.503	0.494	0.5
Guinea-Bissau	0.504	0.495	0.481	0.506	0.48	0.508	0.508	0.508	0.508
Guyana	0.606	0.603	0.604	0.608	0.611	0.614	0.615	0.616	0.617
Haiti	0.544	0.559	0.567	0.571	0.577	0.581	0.584	0.599	0.598
Honduras	0.58	0.582	0.542	0.539	0.554	0.556	0.597	0.598	0.595
Hungary	0.813	0.815	0.814	0.814	0.818	0.818	0.822	0.826	0.819
Iceland	0.825	0.825	0.828	0.827	0.83	0.829	0.833	0.832	0.831
India	0.527	0.544	0.564	0.579	0.59	0.606	0.613	0.622	0.626
Indonesia	0.636	0.649	0.651	0.658	0.668	0.671	0.692	0.691	0.696
Iran	0.64	0.646	0.671	0.671	0.683	0.686	0.681	0.683	0.677
Iraq	0.506	0.512	0.511	0.505	0.487	0.506	0.506	0.506	0.5
Ireland	0.818	0.814	0.82	0.836	0.839	0.84	0.839	0.845	0.846
Israel	0.781	0.777	0.798	0.816	0.789	0.811	0.806	0.814	0.815
Italy	0.794	0.8	0.806	0.799	0.812	0.811	0.811	0.817	0.816
Jamaica	0.741	0.729	0.723	0.73	0.73	0.727	0.729	0.726	0.724
Japan	0.795	0.794	0.804	0.808	0.808	0.812	0.813	0.817	0.816
Jordan	0.749	0.749	0.748	0.739	0.744	0.739	0.725	0.719	0.717
Kazakhstan	0.675	0.686	0.685	0.718	0.726	0.727	0.736	0.735	0.731
Kenya	0.52	0.525	0.53	0.543	0.554	0.56	0.572	0.576	0.577
Kiribati	0.638	0.638	0.639	0.639	0.639	0.637	0.635	0.636	0.635
Kuwait	0.818	0.812	0.814	0.811	0.811	0.786	0.81	0.814	0.814
Kyrgyzstan	0.643	0.605	0.604	0.669	0.679	0.682	0.692	0.695	0.696
Laos	0.573	0.569	0.574	0.58	0.588	0.592	0.588	0.592	0.595

(Continued)

Country	2010	2011	2012	2013	2014	2015	2016	2017	2018
Latvia	0.79	0.797	0.802	0.805	0.802	0.802	0.8	0.802	0.805
Lebanon	0.727	0.726	0.705	0.702	0.699	0.699	0.703	0.701	0.701
Lesotho	0.507	0.514	0.498	0.52	0.52	0.512	0.526	0.512	0.511
Liberia	0.516	0.504	0.539	0.536	0.511	0.527	0.544	0.567	0.567
Libya	0.721	0.632	0.665	0.673	0.639	0.641	0.643	0.66	0.657
Lithuania	0.766	0.771	0.773	0.773	0.77	0.785	0.794	0.805	0.799
Luxembourg	0.835	0.839	0.844	0.841	0.84	0.838	0.844	0.843	0.845
Madagascar	0.524	0.53	0.537	0.525	0.527	0.531	0.532	0.54	0.544
Malawi	0.462	0.455	0.456	0.463	0.478	0.476	0.477	0.486	0.484
Malaysia	0.764	0.766	0.767	0.757	0.778	0.783	0.781	0.779	0.775
Maldives	0.778	0.778	0.778	0.783	0.781	0.784	0.789	0.794	0.794
Mali	0.448	0.45	0.437	0.434	0.436	0.436	0.431	0.445	0.447
Malta	0.839	0.842	0.846	0.848	0.86	0.854	0.858	0.859	0.859
Mauritania	0.534	0.515	0.536	0.543	0.562	0.565	0.564	0.568	0.573
Mauritius	0.764	0.765	0.761	0.762	0.76	0.758	0.763	0.766	0.766
Mexico	0.628	0.627	0.633	0.642	0.648	0.644	0.644	0.634	0.636
Moldova	0.687	0.69	0.694	0.696	0.694	0.703	0.709	0.711	0.706
Mongolia	0.719	0.741	0.728	0.756	0.761	0.761	0.761	0.761	0.758
Montenegro	0.766	0.765	0.781	0.778	0.781	0.781	0.788	0.795	0.793
Morocco	0.648	0.651	0.671	0.679	0.682	0.689	0.688	0.689	0.69
Mozambique	0.47	0.477	0.477	0.465	0.471	0.48	0.468	0.461	0.46
Myanmar (Burma)	0.552	0.554	0.56	0.57	0.582	0.586	0.59	0.611	0.61
Namibia	0.6	0.602	0.6	0.603	0.604	0.609	0.627	0.634	0.632
Nepal	0.634	0.64	0.655	0.663	0.669	0.667	0.679	0.686	0.689
Netherlands	0.843	0.849	0.847	0.846	0.818	0.848	0.848	0.85	0.848
New Zealand	0.816	0.789	0.821	0.826	0.83	0.827	0.829	0.823	0.824
Nicaragua	0.631	0.636	0.638	0.645	0.648	0.665	0.666	0.673	0.673
Niger	0.416	0.417	0.432	0.424	0.446	0.424	0.424	0.426	0.424
Nigeria	0.512	0.513	0.511	0.509	0.505	0.538	0.517	0.523	0.52
North Macedonia	0.805	0.807	0.787	0.803	0.797	0.794	0.798	0.791	0.791
Norway	0.824	0.818	0.849	0.85	0.852	0.856	0.854	0.863	0.862
Oman	0.762	0.756	0.752	0.753	0.761	0.764	0.767	0.768	0.769
Pakistan	0.481	0.476	0.482	0.485	0.498	0.502	0.504	0.519	0.517
Palestinian Territories	0.631	0.634	0.623	0.639	0.627	0.643	0.646	0.652	0.659
Panama	0.67	0.677	0.687	0.691	0.694	0.697	0.703	0.703	0.701
Papua New Guinea	0.566	0.566	0.566	0.569	0.571	0.573	0.573	0.571	0.572
Paraguay	0.646	0.661	0.659	0.646	0.649	0.656	0.65	0.686	0.687
Peru	0.667	0.673	0.681	0.701	0.709	0.716	0.722	0.732	0.734
Philippines	0.589	0.59	0.593	0.592	0.601	0.602	0.607	0.595	0.603
Poland	0.781	0.777	0.785	0.787	0.789	0.799	0.8	0.801	0.798
Portugal	0.826	0.826	0.831	0.838	0.84	0.843	0.846	0.844	0.845
Qatar	0.793	0.799	0.791	0.782	0.781	0.801	0.809	0.8	0.802
Romania	0.766	0.783	0.77	0.776	0.784	0.782	0.785	0.785	0.784
Russia	0.622	0.643	0.654	0.666	0.672	0.689	0.699	0.706	0.709
Rwanda	0.539	0.557	0.541	0.57	0.576	0.573	0.569	0.574	0.574
Samoa	0.731	0.73	0.728	0.731	0.733	0.735	0.731	0.731	0.728

(Continued)

Country	2010	2011	2012	2013	2014	2015	2016	2017	2018
São Tomé & Príncipe	0.605	0.622	0.638	0.653	0.649	0.653	0.658	0.66	0.661
Saudi Arabia	0.764	0.76	0.767	0.78	0.787	0.765	0.764	0.759	0.76
Senegal	0.543	0.535	0.549	0.554	0.564	0.583	0.584	0.603	0.603
Serbia	0.778	0.784	0.797	0.801	0.81	0.808	0.799	0.796	0.802
Seychelles	0.727	0.725	0.727	0.726	0.726	0.729	0.727	0.724	0.725
Sierra Leone	0.517	0.522	0.532	0.536	0.541	0.542	0.576	0.581	0.58
Singapore	0.867	0.87	0.873	0.877	0.882	0.879	0.88	0.885	0.875
Slovakia	0.805	0.804	0.8	0.797	0.798	0.796	0.807	0.81	0.815
Slovenia	0.871	0.868	0.858	0.853	0.863	0.863	0.861	0.865	0.866
Solomon Islands	0.637	0.641	0.642	0.644	0.645	0.649	0.652	0.655	0.656
Somalia	0.422	0.432	0.426	0.433	0.432	0.434	0.436	0.436	0.436
South Africa	0.59	0.597	0.582	0.607	0.603	0.594	0.608	0.609	0.608
South Korea	0.796	0.82	0.821	0.822	0.832	0.837	0.832	0.826	0.821
South Sudan	0.412	0.41	0.41	0.406	0.413	0.413	0.403	0.42	0.421
Spain	0.805	0.809	0.813	0.818	0.829	0.832	0.83	0.833	0.833
Sri Lanka	0.682	0.733	0.739	0.747	0.75	0.754	0.754	0.754	0.747
St. Lucia	0.727	0.722	0.718	0.714	0.717	0.718	0.719	0.719	0.716
Sudan	0.529	0.53	0.529	0.528	0.533	0.565	0.543	0.555	0.557
Suriname	0.623	0.626	0.63	0.638	0.645	0.65	0.647	0.646	0.645
Sweden	0.843	0.846	0.847	0.849	0.855	0.853	0.v854	0.859	0.857
Switzerland	0.836	0.837	0.839	0.838	0.84	0.846	0.849	0.852	0.849
Syria	0.688	0.633	0.589	0.558	0.544	0.545	0.547	0.552	0.551
Taiwan	0.772	0.77	0.774	0.781	0.779	0.78	0.778	0.78	0.78
Tajikistan	0.64	0.646	0.64	0.664	0.662	0.658	0.686	0.694	0.691
Tanzania	0.51	0.523	0.545	0.543	0.549	0.553	0.557	0.56	0.559
Thailand	0.658	0.662	0.667	0.678	0.681	0.702	0.699	0.702	0.704
Timor-Leste	0.649	0.654	0.653	0.65	0.654	0.661	0.666	0.67	0.676
Togo	0.543	0.543	0.548	0.545	0.554	0.575	0.587	0.572	0.575
Tonga	0.721	0.721	0.721	0.721	0.721	0.722	0.723	0.724	0.724
Trinidad & Tobago	0.66	0.669	0.67	0.669	0.671	0.673	0.674	0.674	0.674
Tunisia	0.73	0.708	0.711	0.688	0.697	0.696	0.705	0.714	0.714
Turkey	0.716	0.715	0.721	0.718	0.733	0.736	0.733	0.73	0.725
Turkmenistan	0.62	0.637	0.626	0.64	0.624	0.65	0.648	0.655	0.653
Uganda	0.49	0.508	0.503	0.518	0.513	0.531	0.515	0.536	0.534
Ukraine	0.736	0.729	0.731	0.726	0.682	0.652	0.656	0.662	0.66
United Arab Emirates	0.735	0.741	0.74	0.749	0.761	0.761	0.763	0.764	0.763
United Kingdom	0.768	0.776	0.78	0.787	0.795	0.793	0.791	0.793	0.793
United States	0.715	0.717	0.733	0.74	0.742	0.743	0.741	0.737	0.737
Uruguay	0.724	0.72	0.722	0.722	0.727	0.731	0.73	0.736	0.734
Uzbekistan	0.646	0.668	0.653	0.679	0.679	0.673	0.681	0.681	0.681
Vanuatu	0.619	0.621	0.623	0.624	0.624	0.624	0.626	0.627	0.628
Venezuela	0.598	0.599	0.597	0.599	0.601	0.609	0.607	0.615	0.612
Vietnam	0.694	0.695	0.699	0.703	0.725	0.735	0.741	0.743	0.744
Yemen	0.515	0.511	0.512	0.517	0.511	0.497	0.468	0.47	0.474
Zambia	0.55	0.54	0.538	0.542	0.541	0.539	0.549	0.55	0.548
Zimbabwe	0.537	0.541	0.525	0.519	0.514	0.515	0.524	0.525	0.528

Table A2.3 2020 Global YDI overall and domain scores and ranks (countries listed alphabetically)

Global Rank	Country	YDI Overall score	Education rank	Education score	Employ- ment & Opport- unity rank	Employ- ment & Opport- unity score	Equality & Inclusion rank
178	Afghanistan	0.421	161	0.457	181	0.413	178
55	Albania	0.764	67	0.816	105	0.706	45
94	Algeria	0.689	102	0.743	97	0.721	105
166	Angola	0.506	167	0.402	151	0.59	163
87	Argentina	0.699	61	0.827	156	0.585	78
66	Armenia	0.736	91	0.771	101	0.716	42
29	Australia	0.807	29	0.903	61	0.796	46
12	Austria	0.842	21	0.917	10	0.941	5
90	Azerbaijan	0.693	90	0.772	131	0.639	62
104	Bahamas, The	0.67	57	0.833	75	0.767	100
47	Bahrain	0.779	52	0.84	35	0.848	74
126	Bangladesh	0.616	116	0.705	172	0.526	174
47	Barbados	0.779	8	0.936	59	0.799	57
51	Belarus	0.774	54	0.837	38	0.841	16
13	Belgium	0.839	26	0.909	12	0.934	37
124	Belize	0.619	122	0.688	102	0.715	131
155	Benin	0.547	165	0.41	157	0.581	157
77	Bhutan	0.719	118	0.701	92	0.729	108
91	Bolivia	0.691	101	0.749	74	0.768	111
53	Bosnia and Herzegovina	0.768	69	0.811	70	0.777	27
108	Botswana	0.659	88	0.775	105	0.706	128
116	Brazil	0.637	86	0.776	159	0.568	92
49	Brunei	0.777	17	0.923	69	0.778	46
44	Bulgaria	0.783	45	0.865	59	0.799	34
166	Burkina Faso	0.506	170	0.383	141	0.612	171
150	Burundi	0.557	158	0.482	104	0.712	138
97	Cambodia	0.685	137	0.591	49	0.814	114
160	Cameroon	0.527	144	0.529	148	0.596	136
36	Canada	0.798	21	0.917	20	0.901	21
78	Cape Verde	0.717	106	0.738	111	0.699	58
180	Central African Republic	0.399	180	0.176	125	0.659	176
181	Chad	0.398	181	0.16	149	0.591	179
45	Chile	0.782	45	0.865	54	0.811	50
62	China	0.745	59	0.83	89	0.734	94
113	Colombia	0.646	95	0.762	162	0.563	109

Country	Equality & Inclusion score	Health & Wellbeing rank	Health & Wellbeing score	Peace & Security rank	Peace & Security score	Political & Civic Parti-cipation rank	Political & Civic Part-icipation score
Afghanistan	0.509	139	0.556	181	0.142	141	0.223
Albania	0.933	25	0.832	53	0.819	48	0.335
Algeria	0.814	27	0.83	139	0.545	170	0.159
Angola	0.65	156	0.507	128	0.582	107	0.265
Argentina	0.87	51	0.786	89	0.738	155	0.198
Armenia	0.94	35	0.815	58	0.803	166	0.17
Australia	0.932	56	0.78	25	0.899	3	0.412
Austria	0.978	81	0.736	8	0.936	8	0.408
Azerbaijan	0.9	87	0.723	86	0.75	142	0.222
Bahamas, The	0.82	145	0.536	131	0.578	104	0.27
Bahrain	0.877	4	0.903	125	0.594	107	0.265
Bangladesh	0.561	42	0.809	105	0.681	151	0.208
Barbados	0.912	61	0.776	102	0.696	85	0.293
Belarus	0.964	96	0.705	51	0.834	64	0.318
Belgium	0.943	38	0.813	22	0.901	58	0.322
Belize	0.753	148	0.529	130	0.58	77	0.308
Benin	0.655	115	0.629	115	0.652	48	0.335
Bhutan	0.811	50	0.793	39	0.87	85	0.293
Bolivia	0.806	75	0.741	93	0.724	179	0.088
Bosnia and Herzegovina	0.956	15	0.86	56	0.805	173	0.148
Botswana	0.763	138	0.559	91	0.73	77	0.308
Brazil	0.834	115	0.629	140	0.541	58	0.322
Brunei	0.932	92	0.714	35	0.878	95	0.276
Bulgaria	0.945	41	0.811	40	0.869	161	0.188
Burkina Faso	0.611	132	0.584	159	0.416	68	0.315
Burundi	0.734	151	0.518	151	0.486	89	0.288
Cambodia	0.804	94	0.71	86	0.75	58	0.322
Cameroon	0.736	167	0.461	158	0.422	53	0.328
Canada	0.96	73	0.742	30	0.891	177	0.115
Cape Verde	0.91	70	0.749	96	0.711	21	0.382
Central African Republic	0.52	178	0.392	178	0.25	72	0.313
Chad	0.49	159	0.498	173	0.339	153	0.205
Chile	0.92	47	0.803	61	0.799	98	0.275
China	0.833	31	0.821	64	0.797	122	0.245
Colombia	0.81	81	0.736	152	0.48	68	0.315

(Continued)

Global Rank	Country	YDI Overall score	Education rank	Education score	Employ- ment & Opport- unity rank	Employ- ment & Opport- unity score	Equality & Inclusion rank
121	Comoros	0.627	152	0.5	128	0.657	125
164	Congo - Brazzaville	0.509	146	0.525	140	0.616	140
170	Congo - Kinshasa	0.499	144	0.529	176	0.493	170
59	Costa Rica	0.75	95	0.762	56	0.806	74
174	Côte d'Ivoire	0.457	164	0.411	179	0.454	173
22	Croatia	0.818	35	0.891	40	0.834	15
63	Cuba	0.744	79	0.793	77	0.762	84
18	Cyprus	0.825	41	0.874	22	0.886	28
28	Czechia	0.811	31	0.899	41	0.831	34
5	Denmark	0.858	7	0.939	6	0.951	14
128	Djibouti	0.612	149	0.506	63	0.788	136
105	Dominican Republic	0.668	85	0.783	114	0.695	96
103	Ecuador	0.672	75	0.803	112	0.698	98
123	Egypt	0.624	109	0.725	167	0.544	103
127	El Salvador	0.615	115	0.709	122	0.669	130
146	Equatorial Guinea	0.564	151	0.502	130	0.646	119
148	Eritrea	0.559	141	0.555	93	0.728	154
36	Estonia	0.798	2	0.96	12	0.934	21
152	Eswatini, Kingdom of	0.553	127	0.652	157	0.581	97
158	Ethiopia	0.529	168	0.4	149	0.591	147
60	Fiji	0.748	63	0.822	51	0.812	109
17	Finland	0.827	5	0.944	8	0.945	30
29	France	0.807	10	0.93	81	0.754	5
114	Gabon	0.645	139	0.57	65	0.784	88
139	Gambia, The	0.577	150	0.503	143	0.61	151
70	Georgia	0.731	70	0.81	103	0.713	86
15	Germany	0.831	40	0.879	16	0.911	10
131	Ghana	0.608	123	0.675	159	0.568	118
34	Greece	0.799	39	0.881	42	0.827	29
66	Grenada	0.736	43	0.871	108	0.703	70
147	Guatemala	0.562	132	0.622	138	0.619	167
168	Guinea	0.5	176	0.302	116	0.687	156
165	Guinea-Bissau	0.508	171	0.377	108	0.703	164
125	Guyana	0.617	103	0.74	123	0.663	123
135	Haiti	0.598	138	0.587	97	0.721	115
136	Honduras	0.595	135	0.602	137	0.63	153
21	Hungary	0.819	33	0.896	30	0.859	54
15	Iceland	0.831	14	0.928	28	0.862	24
122	India	0.626	119	0.696	139	0.618	172

Country	Equality & Inclusion score	Health & Wellbeing rank	Health & Wellbeing score	Peace & Security rank	Peace & Security score	Political & Civic Participation rank	Political & Civic Participation score
Comoros	0.774	69	0.75	90	0.737	115	0.253
Congo - Brazzaville	0.723	175	0.404	160	0.41	102	0.272
Congo - Kinshasa	0.612	141	0.548	174	0.321	39	0.352
Costa Rica	0.877	48	0.798	101	0.7	25	0.37
Côte d'Ivoire	0.568	164	0.475	137	0.555	95	0.276
Croatia	0.966	20	0.845	23	0.9	104	0.27
Cuba	0.845	23	0.84	82	0.758	132	0.233
Cyprus	0.955	16	0.858	41	0.865	88	0.292
Czechia	0.945	28	0.826	9	0.933	133	0.232
Denmark	0.967	24	0.839	3	0.951	102	0.272
Djibouti	0.736	114	0.639	122	0.605	134	0.228
Dominican Republic	0.832	111	0.646	138	0.548	82	0.3
Ecuador	0.824	108	0.655	121	0.606	145	0.22
Egypt	0.818	54	0.784	149	0.492	179	0.088
El Salvador	0.756	146	0.534	141	0.526	33	0.36
Equatorial Guinea	0.791	163	0.49	77	0.766	167	0.169
Eritrea	0.67	165	0.467	120	0.609	160	0.191
Estonia	0.96	137	0.568	28	0.896	58	0.322
Eswatini, Kingdom of	0.826	180	0.384	135	0.561	114	0.257
Ethiopia	0.695	97	0.699	167	0.377	139	0.225
Fiji	0.81	85	0.727	67	0.792	36	0.355
Finland	0.952	104	0.675	6	0.94	36	0.355
France	0.978	46	0.804	29	0.892	45	0.34
Gabon	0.839	133	0.581	88	0.745	104	0.27
Gambia, The	0.678	127	0.601	103	0.688	28	0.367
Georgia	0.842	73	0.742	70	0.786	30	0.362
Germany	0.972	62	0.773	16	0.916	14	0.392
Ghana	0.793	141	0.548	107	0.675	40	0.35
Greece	0.953	30	0.822	46	0.848	129	0.235
Grenada	0.881	55	0.782	68	0.791	172	0.149
Guatemala	0.637	149	0.526	146	0.51	53	0.328
Guinea	0.662	154	0.515	143	0.521	120	0.248
Guinea-Bissau	0.641	175	0.404	108	0.662	112	0.259
Guyana	0.779	159	0.498	133	0.566	53	0.328
Haiti	0.8	151	0.518	150	0.489	35	0.356
Honduras	0.672	119	0.622	145	0.514	3	0.412
Hungary	0.918	14	0.863	20	0.903	125	0.24
Iceland	0.959	28	0.826	2	0.958	116	0.252
India	0.61	101	0.683	106	0.679	51	0.332

(Continued)

Global Rank	Country	YDI Overall score	Education rank	Education score	Employment & Opportunity rank	Employment & Opportunity score	Equality & Inclusion rank	
88	Indonesia	0.696	98	0.758	153	0.588	105	
99	Iran	0.677	94	0.766	84	0.744	128	
168	Iraq	0.5	169	0.394	154	0.587	150	
9	Ireland	0.846	26	0.909	17	0.907	4	
25	Israel	0.815	20	0.921	26	0.867	9	
23	Italy	0.816	36	0.889	46	0.819	16	
75	Jamaica	0.724	86	0.776	47	0.818	86	
23	Japan	0.816	15	0.925	36	0.845	37	
78	Jordan	0.717	119	0.696	83	0.749	37	
70	Kazakhstan	0.731	56	0.834	55	0.81	43	
139	Kenya	0.577	123	0.675	126	0.658	140	
118	Kiribati	0.635	100	0.75	117	0.685	119	
27	Kuwait	0.814	49	0.847	31	0.855	41	
88	Kyrgyzstan	0.696	72	0.807	136	0.633	111	
136	Laos	0.595	131	0.627	177	0.489	135	
31	Latvia	0.805	6	0.941	17	0.907	19	
85	Lebanon	0.701	74	0.804	82	0.752	65	
163	Lesotho	0.511	142	0.539	121	0.67	145	
145	Liberia	0.567	173	0.373	99	0.719	169	
110	Libya	0.657	104	0.739	62	0.794	94	
34	Lithuania	0.799	10	0.93	21	0.889	10	
10	Luxembourg	0.845	24	0.91	4	0.963	1	
156	Madagascar	0.544	160	0.466	164	0.558	146	
171	Malawi	0.484	172	0.375	175	0.514	160	
50	Malaysia	0.775	59	0.83	23	0.881	66	
39	Maldives	0.794	47	0.857	80	0.755	54	
175	Mali	0.447	177	0.3	170	0.532	175	
4	Malta	0.859	23	0.913	5	0.953	33	
143	Mauritania	0.573	166	0.408	146	0.603	162	
54	Mauritius	0.766	77	0.795	33	0.85	64	
117	Mexico	0.636	55	0.835	159	0.568	124	
83	Moldova	0.706	76	0.799	90	0.732	74	
58	Mongolia	0.758	65	0.819	28	0.862	51	
40	Montenegro	0.793	42	0.873	51	0.812	18	
93	Morocco	0.69	112	0.719	133	0.636	100	
173	Mozambique	0.46	174	0.37	155	0.586	166	
130	Myanmar (Burma)	0.61	140	0.565	113	0.696	107	
119	Namibia	0.632	121	0.692	76	0.764	83	
94	Nepal	0.689	111	0.723	143	0.61	122	
8	Netherlands	0.848	24	0.91	9	0.942	19	

Country	Equality & Inclusion score	Health & Wellbeing rank	Health & Wellbeing score	Peace & Security rank	Peace & Security score	Political & Civic Participation rank	Political & Civic Participation score
Indonesia	0.814	71	0.746	65	0.795	1	0.425
Iran	0.763	88	0.722	111	0.656	174	0.132
Iraq	0.684	118	0.625	176	0.311	159	0.196
Ireland	0.98	45	0.805	15	0.918	9	0.405
Israel	0.974	3	0.906	117	0.631	142	0.222
Italy	0.964	6	0.887	41	0.865	125	0.24
Jamaica	0.842	81	0.736	134	0.564	25	0.37
Japan	0.943	35	0.815	14	0.926	139	0.225
Jordan	0.943	8	0.875	142	0.523	145	0.22
Kazakhstan	0.937	120	0.621	68	0.791	136	0.227
Kenya	0.723	161	0.495	170	0.365	25	0.37
Kiribati	0.791	170	0.427	80	0.761	17	0.39
Kuwait	0.941	10	0.87	33	0.882	93	0.279
Kyrgyzstan	0.806	91	0.717	74	0.775	64	0.318
Laos	0.74	109	0.654	78	0.763	116	0.252
Latvia	0.962	99	0.698	37	0.875	142	0.222
Lebanon	0.888	58	0.778	161	0.402	136	0.227
Lesotho	0.704	181	0.378	164	0.389	122	0.245
Liberia	0.634	133	0.581	104	0.686	2	0.415
Libya	0.833	128	0.598	166	0.38	48	0.335
Lithuania	0.972	103	0.677	32	0.883	118	0.25
Luxembourg	0.991	79	0.739	21	0.902	3	0.412
Madagascar	0.701	113	0.643	144	0.518	98	0.275
Malawi	0.653	172	0.417	94	0.719	52	0.331
Malaysia	0.887	86	0.724	48	0.844	74	0.311
Maldives	0.918	2	0.913	45	0.859	124	0.243
Mali	0.532	135	0.571	165	0.384	111	0.26
Malta	0.95	18	0.853	33	0.882	11	0.398
Mauritania	0.651	57	0.779	111	0.656	145	0.22
Mauritius	0.892	95	0.709	38	0.874	36	0.355
Mexico	0.776	106	0.659	154	0.466	98	0.275
Moldova	0.877	105	0.671	54	0.813	163	0.174
Mongolia	0.919	112	0.645	73	0.777	12	0.395
Montenegro	0.963	26	0.831	49	0.838	150	0.21
Morocco	0.82	53	0.785	56	0.805	129	0.235
Mozambique	0.639	178	0.392	163	0.39	42	0.348
Myanmar (Burma)	0.813	125	0.605	111	0.656	155	0.198
Namibia	0.847	166	0.462	136	0.559	34	0.358
Nepal	0.788	63	0.77	81	0.759	10	0.4
Netherlands	0.962	38	0.813	13	0.929	44	0.342

(Continued)

Global Rank	Country	YDI Overall score	Education rank	Education score	Employ- ment & Opport- unity rank	Employ- ment & Opport- unity score	Equality & Inclusion rank
19	New Zealand	0.824	30	0.901	14	0.914	48
102	Nicaragua	0.673	129	0.631	94	0.725	139
177	Niger	0.424	179	0.213	180	0.45	181
161	Nigeria	0.52	154	0.499	173	0.52	157
42	North Macedonia	0.791	50	0.844	71	0.769	43
3	Norway	0.862	10	0.93	2	0.968	5
52	Oman	0.769	62	0.823	48	0.817	63
162	Pakistan	0.517	152	0.5	146	0.603	165
108	Palestinian Territories	0.659	78	0.794	174	0.519	74
85	Panama	0.701	93	0.767	86	0.74	92
144	Papua New Guinea	0.572	154	0.499	71	0.769	115
96	Paraguay	0.687	117	0.703	87	0.739	100
68	Peru	0.734	48	0.853	117	0.685	79
133	Philippines	0.603	113	0.714	166	0.549	98
36	Poland	0.798	17	0.923	24	0.87	21
10	Portugal	0.845	31	0.899	19	0.906	34
32	Qatar	0.802	88	0.775	14	0.914	30
43	Romania	0.784	53	0.838	58	0.8	51
82	Russia	0.709	50	0.844	34	0.849	51
142	Rwanda	0.574	156	0.495	167	0.544	142
80	Saint Lucia	0.716	65	0.819	64	0.785	81
72	Samoa	0.728	71	0.808	110	0.701	59
106	São Tomé and Príncipe	0.661	107	0.726	115	0.69	134
57	Saudi Arabia	0.76	33	0.896	39	0.836	89
133	Senegal	0.603	163	0.443	135	0.635	167
32	Serbia	0.802	44	0.869	66	0.782	12
73	Seychelles	0.725	38	0.886	120	0.675	80
138	Sierra Leone	0.58	162	0.447	107	0.705	148
1	Singapore	0.875	4	0.946	1	0.969	13
25	Slovakia	0.815	37	0.887	32	0.851	26
2	Slovenia	0.866	13	0.929	3	0.965	8
111	Solomon Islands	0.656	128	0.642	51	0.812	127
176	Somalia	0.436	175	0.311	133	0.636	177
131	South Africa	0.608	113	0.714	100	0.717	69
20	South Korea	0.821	9	0.932	26	0.867	49
178	South Sudan	0.421	178	0.251	141	0.612	159
14	Spain	0.833	28	0.906	49	0.814	3

Country	Equality & Inclusion score	Health & Wellbeing rank	Health & Wellbeing score	Peace & Security rank	Peace & Security score	Political & Civic Participation rank	Political & Civic Participation score
New Zealand	0.93	60	0.777	11	0.931	77	0.308
Nicaragua	0.729	77	0.74	100	0.705	14	0.392
Niger	0.429	106	0.659	169	0.37	30	0.362
Nigeria	0.655	129	0.589	168	0.373	23	0.375
North Macedonia	0.937	11	0.866	50	0.836	75	0.31
Norway	0.978	49	0.794	4	0.949	19	0.385
Oman	0.898	21	0.843	44	0.861	178	0.108
Pakistan	0.64	124	0.61	156	0.438	181	0.06
Palestinian Territories	0.877	17	0.857	153	0.471	176	0.118
Panama	0.834	79	0.739	126	0.59	73	0.312
Papua New Guinea	0.8	173	0.405	123	0.604	71	0.314
Paraguay	0.82	90	0.719	108	0.662	82	0.3
Peru	0.869	44	0.806	85	0.751	148	0.212
Philippines	0.824	109	0.654	177	0.309	40	0.35
Poland	0.96	75	0.741	27	0.897	169	0.16
Portugal	0.945	7	0.885	9	0.933	98	0.275
Qatar	0.952	11	0.866	19	0.906	168	0.161
Romania	0.919	33	0.818	36	0.877	94	0.277
Russia	0.919	147	0.533	128	0.582	53	0.328
Rwanda	0.716	121	0.618	92	0.729	30	0.362
Saint Lucia	0.864	102	0.682	119	0.612	80	0.305
Samoa	0.905	77	0.74	59	0.802	109	0.264
São Tomé and Príncipe	0.747	122	0.616	75	0.773	67	0.316
Saudi Arabia	0.836	35	0.815	132	0.575	118	0.25
Senegal	0.637	88	0.722	63	0.798	19	0.385
Serbia	0.971	9	0.873	46	0.848	113	0.258
Seychelles	0.866	67	0.752	66	0.794	171	0.157
Sierra Leone	0.691	161	0.495	61	0.799	3	0.412
Singapore	0.97	1	0.927	1	0.962	162	0.178
Slovakia	0.957	32	0.819	23	0.9	91	0.283
Slovenia	0.977	33	0.818	6	0.94	18	0.388
Solomon Islands	0.765	140	0.549	99	0.709	22	0.377
Somalia	0.515	153	0.516	180	0.213	151	0.208
South Africa	0.884	173	0.405	157	0.426	23	0.375
South Korea	0.928	38	0.813	17	0.912	120	0.248
South Sudan	0.654	169	0.428	179	0.216	125	0.24
Spain	0.985	5	0.901	26	0.898	89	0.288

(*Continued*)

Global Rank	Country	YDI Overall score	Education rank	Education score	Employ- ment & Opport- unity rank	Employ- ment & Opport- unity score	Equality & Inclusion rank
61	Sri Lanka	0.747	92	0.769	56	0.806	117
150	Sudan	0.557	143	0.533	163	0.562	155
114	Suriname	0.645	130	0.628	88	0.736	85
6	Sweden	0.857	1	0.963	7	0.948	24
7	Switzerland	0.849	17	0.923	11	0.939	32
153	Syria	0.551	133	0.62	132	0.637	132
46	Taiwan	0.78	72	0.807	37	0.844	60
91	Tajikistan	0.691	82	0.787	124	0.661	121
148	Tanzania	0.559	157	0.488	129	0.65	149
84	Thailand	0.704	95	0.762	42	0.827	72
100	Timor-Leste	0.676	126	0.664	94	0.725	126
141	Togo	0.575	146	0.525	68	0.779	144
75	Tonga	0.724	107	0.726	71	0.769	54
101	Trinidad and Tobago	0.674	67	0.816	119	0.68	82
81	Tunisia	0.714	104	0.739	96	0.724	70
73	Turkey	0.725	63	0.822	79	0.76	91
112	Turkmenistan	0.653	109	0.725	126	0.658	113
157	Uganda	0.534	159	0.479	167	0.544	160
107	Ukraine	0.66	81	0.788	45	0.822	60
56	United Arab Emirates	0.763	84	0.785	24	0.87	68
40	United Kingdom	0.793	15	0.925	91	0.731	2
65	United States	0.737	3	0.956	44	0.824	40
68	Uruguay	0.734	79	0.793	77	0.762	72
98	Uzbekistan	0.681	82	0.787	145	0.606	133
120	Vanuatu	0.628	134	0.617	66	0.782	89
128	Venezuela	0.612	99	0.756	152	0.589	104
63	Vietnam	0.744	57	0.833	85	0.741	66
172	Yemen	0.474	148	0.522	171	0.529	180
154	Zambia	0.548	136	0.596	165	0.551	143
159	Zimbabwe	0.528	125	0.67	178	0.47	151

Country	Equality & Inclusion score	Health & Wellbeing rank	Health & Wellbeing score	Peace & Security rank	Peace & Security score	Political & Civic Participation rank	Political & Civic Participation score
Sri Lanka	0.798	58	0.778	72	0.778	12	0.395
Sudan	0.663	65	0.756	162	0.392	164	0.173
Suriname	0.844	126	0.602	98	0.71	128	0.238
Sweden	0.959	43	0.808	11	0.931	64	0.318
Switzerland	0.951	51	0.786	5	0.943	14	0.392
Syria	0.752	157	0.505	172	0.357	136	0.227
Taiwan	0.903	19	0.848	43	0.864	164	0.173
Tajikistan	0.79	100	0.691	84	0.753	45	0.34
Tanzania	0.69	135	0.571	116	0.641	134	0.228
Thailand	0.878	123	0.614	114	0.653	68	0.315
Timor-Leste	0.769	92	0.714	78	0.763	84	0.294
Togo	0.709	155	0.508	147	0.508	110	0.262
Tonga	0.918	97	0.699	59	0.802	57	0.323
Trinidad and Tobago	0.862	131	0.586	127	0.589	29	0.365
Tunisia	0.881	13	0.865	110	0.657	175	0.13
Turkey	0.835	21	0.843	155	0.446	80	0.305
Turkmenistan	0.805	117	0.628	76	0.768	153	0.205
Uganda	0.653	150	0.522	118	0.621	7	0.41
Ukraine	0.903	158	0.502	171	0.364	58	0.322
United Arab Emirates	0.885	65	0.756	30	0.891	155	0.198
United Kingdom	0.988	67	0.752	18	0.91	45	0.34
United States	0.942	144	0.538	95	0.716	131	0.234
Uruguay	0.878	63	0.77	70	0.786	148	0.212
Uzbekistan	0.75	84	0.731	55	0.811	95	0.276
Vanuatu	0.836	168	0.445	83	0.756	85	0.293
Venezuela	0.816	141	0.548	148	0.497	58	0.322
Vietnam	0.887	72	0.743	52	0.822	92	0.28
Yemen	0.44	129	0.589	175	0.316	158	0.197
Zambia	0.714	170	0.427	96	0.711	75	0.31
Zimbabwe	0.678	177	0.399	124	0.603	43	0.345

Table A2.4 2020 Commonwealth YDI overall and domain scores[2]

Commonwealth Overall Rank	Global Overall rank	Country	YDI Overall score	Global Education rank	Global Education score	Global Employment & Opportunity rank	Global Employment & Opportunity score	Global Equality & Inclusion rank
Very High Youth Development								
1	1	Singapore	0.875	4	0.946	1	0.969	13
2	4	Malta	0.859	23	0.913	5	0.953	33
3	18	Cyprus	0.825	41	0.874	22	0.886	28
4	19	New Zealand	0.824	30	0.901	14	0.914	48
5	29	Australia	0.807	29	0.903	61	0.796	46
6	36	Canada	0.798	21	0.917	20	0.901	21
7	39	Maldives	0.794	47	0.857	80	0.755	54
8	40	United Kingdom	0.793	15	0.925	91	0.731	2
High Youth Development								
9	47	Barbados	0.779	8	0.936	59	0.799	57
10	49	Brunei	0.777	17	0.923	69	0.778	46
11	50	Malaysia	0.775	59	0.83	23	0.881	66
12	54	Mauritius	0.766	77	0.795	33	0.85	64
13	60	Fiji	0.748	63	0.822	51	0.812	109
14	61	Sri Lanka	0.747	92	0.769	56	0.806	117
15	66	Grenada	0.736	43	0.871	108	0.703	70
16	72	Samoa	0.728	71	0.808	110	0.701	59
17	73	Seychelles	0.725	38	0.886	120	0.675	80
18	75	Jamaica	0.724	86	0.776	47	0.818	86
18	75	Tonga	0.724	107	0.726	71	0.769	54
20	80	Saint Lucia	0.716	65	0.819	64	0.785	81
Medium Youth Development								
21	101	Trinidad and Tobago	0.674	67	0.816	119	0.68	82
22	104	Bahamas, The	0.67	57	0.833	75	0.767	100
23	108	Botswana	0.659	88	0.775	105	0.706	128
24	111	Solomon Islands	0.656	128	0.642	51	0.812	127
25	118	Kiribati	0.635	100	0.75	117	0.685	119
26	119	Namibia	0.632	121	0.692	76	0.764	83
27	120	Vanuatu	0.628	134	0.617	66	0.782	89
28	122	India	0.626	119	0.696	139	0.618	172
29	124	Belize	0.619	122	0.688	102	0.715	131
30	125	Guyana	0.617	103	0.74	123	0.663	123
31	126	Bangladesh	0.616	116	0.705	172	0.526	174

Country	Global Equality & Inclusion score	Global Health & Wellbeing rank	Global Health & Wellbeing score	Global Peace & Security rank	Global Peace & Security score	Global Political & Civic Participation rank	Global Political & Civic Participation score
Singapore	0.97	1	0.927	1	0.962	162	0.178
Malta	0.95	18	0.853	33	0.882	11	0.398
Cyprus	0.955	16	0.858	41	0.865	88	0.292
New Zealand	0.93	60	0.777	11	0.931	77	0.308
Australia	0.932	56	0.78	25	0.899	3	0.412
Canada	0.96	73	0.742	30	0.891	177	0.115
Maldives	0.918	2	0.913	45	0.859	124	0.243
United Kingdom	0.988	67	0.752	18	0.91	45	0.34
Barbados	0.912	61	0.776	102	0.696	85	0.293
Brunei	0.932	92	0.714	35	0.878	95	0.276
Malaysia	0.887	86	0.724	48	0.844	74	0.311
Mauritius	0.892	95	0.709	38	0.874	36	0.355
Fiji	0.81	85	0.727	67	0.792	36	0.355
Sri Lanka	0.798	58	0.778	72	0.778	12	0.395
Grenada	0.881	55	0.782	68	0.791	172	0.149
Samoa	0.905	77	0.74	59	0.802	109	0.264
Seychelles	0.866	67	0.752	66	0.794	171	0.157
Jamaica	0.842	81	0.736	134	0.564	25	0.37
Tonga	0.918	97	0.699	59	0.802	57	0.323
Saint Lucia	0.864	102	0.682	119	0.612	80	0.305
Trinidad and Tobago	0.862	131	0.586	127	0.589	29	0.365
Bahamas, The	0.82	145	0.536	131	0.578	104	0.27
Botswana	0.763	138	0.559	91	0.73	77	0.308
Solomon Islands	0.765	140	0.549	99	0.709	22	0.377
Kiribati	0.791	170	0.427	80	0.761	17	0.39
Namibia	0.847	166	0.462	136	0.559	34	0.358
Vanuatu	0.836	168	0.445	83	0.756	85	0.293
India	0.61	101	0.683	106	0.679	51	0.332
Belize	0.753	148	0.529	130	0.58	77	0.308
Guyana	0.779	159	0.498	133	0.566	53	0.328
Bangladesh	0.561	42	0.809	105	0.681	151	0.208

(Continued)

Commonwealth Overall Rank	Global Overall rank	Country	YDI Overall score	Global Education rank	Global Education score	Global Employment & Opportunity rank	Global Employment & Opportunity score	Global Equality & Inclusion rank
32	131	Ghana	0.608	123	0.675	159	0.568	118
33	131	South Africa	0.608	113	0.714	100	0.717	69
Low Youth Development								
34	138	Sierra Leone	0.58	162	0.447	107	0.705	148
35	139	Kenya	0.577	123	0.675	126	0.658	140
35	139	Gambia, The	0.577	150	0.503	143	0.61	151
37	142	Rwanda	0.574	156	0.495	167	0.544	142
38	144	Papua New Guinea	0.572	154	0.499	71	0.769	115
39	148	Tanzania	0.559	157	0.488	129	0.65	149
40	152	Eswatini	0.553	127	0.652	157	0.581	97
41	154	Zambia	0.548	136	0.596	165	0.551	143
42	157	Uganda	0.534	159	0.479	167	0.544	160
43	160	Cameroon	0.527	144	0.529	148	0.596	136
44	161	Nigeria	0.52	154	0.499	173	0.52	157
45	162	Pakistan	0.517	152	0.5	146	0.603	165
46	163	Lesotho	0.511	142	0.539	121	0.67	145
47	171	Malawi	0.484	172	0.375	175	0.514	160
48	173	Mozambique	0.46	174	0.37	155	0.586	166

Country	Global Equality & Inclusion score	Global Health & Wellbeing rank	Global Health & Wellbeing score	Global Peace & Security rank	Global Peace & Security score	Global Political & Civic Participation rank	Global Political & Civic Participation score
Ghana	0.793	141	0.548	107	0.675	40	0.35
South Africa	0.884	173	0.405	157	0.426	23	0.375
Sierra Leone	0.691	161	0.495	61	0.799	3	0.412
Kenya	0.723	161	0.495	170	0.365	25	0.37
Gambia, The	0.678	127	0.601	103	0.688	28	0.367
Rwanda	0.716	121	0.618	92	0.729	30	0.362
Papua New Guinea	0.8	173	0.405	123	0.604	71	0.314
Tanzania	0.69	135	0.571	116	0.641	134	0.228
Eswatini	0.826	180	0.384	135	0.561	114	0.257
Zambia	0.714	170	0.427	96	0.711	75	0.31
Uganda	0.653	150	0.522	118	0.621	7	0.41
Cameroon	0.736	167	0.461	158	0.422	53	0.328
Nigeria	0.655	129	0.589	168	0.373	23	0.375
Pakistan	0.64	124	0.61	156	0.438	181	0.06
Lesotho	0.704	181	0.378	164	0.389	122	0.245
Malawi	0.653	172	0.417	94	0.719	52	0.331
Mozambique	0.639	178	0.392	163	0.39	42	0.348

Endnotes

1   In this table, 181 countries are listed by their overall YDI rank based on scores achieved in relation to the data available at 2018.

2   In this table, 48 Commonwealth countries are ranked based on the overall YDI scores achieved in relation to the data at 2018. The Commonwealth overall rank, global overall rank and global domain rank are shown.

YDI Technical
Expert Group

A3

Annex 3

YDI Technical Expert Group

A diverse group of experts drawn from development organisations, academia, governments, research institutes and youth networks reviewed and provided feedback on the updated methodology of the Youth Development Index (YDI). The following members met in 2019 to develop and refine the 2020 YDI, including the choice of indicators, particularly for the two new domains on *Equality and Opportunity* and *Peace and Security*. Their advice and recommendations have ensured that as many countries could be included as possible and that the best available data was employed to estimate levels of youth development. Their recommendations will also influence future iterations of the index as new data becomes available.

Table A3.1 Members of the Expert Group

	Name	Designation and Institution
1	Mr Ademola Sylvester Adesina	Head of Partnerships, African Union
2	Ms Amanda Chukwudozie	Policy and Advocacy Officer for Youth, African Union
3	Dr Ann Hagell	Research Lead, Association for Young People's Health, UK
4	Dr Chris Locke	Founder, Caribou Digital, UK
5	Dr Christian Gapp	Technical Officer on Indicators, World Health Organization
6	Mr Christopher I. Morris	Head of NGO and Civil Society Centre, Sustainable and Climate Change Department, Asian Development Bank
7	Prof. David Gordon	Professorial Research Fellow, Centre for the Study of Poverty and Social Justice, University of Bristol
8	Dr Philomen Harrison	Director of Research, Caribbean Community
9	Ms Elvisia Karuuombe	Senior Youth Officer for Research, Ministry of Sport, Youth and National Service, Namibia
10	Mr Haiduwa Tangeni	Chief Youth Officer, Ministry of Sport, Youth and National Service, Namibia
11	Mr Emmanuel Ruhumuliza	Partnership Manager, Rwandan High Commission, London
12	Ms Eshani Ruwanpura	Programme Manager, Adolescents and Youth, United Nations Children's Fund
13	Ms Gemma Wood	Consultant, Numbers and People Synergy, Australia

(Continued)

	Name	Designation and Institution
14	Ms Talia Hagerty	Consultant, Institute for Economics & Peace
15	Mr Gerald Chirinda	Entrepreneur and Founder of Future Africa Forum, Zimbabwe
16	HE Orville London	High Commissioner, Trinidad and Tobago High Commission, London
17	Ms Katie Acheson	Chief Executive Officer, Youth Action, Australia
18	Ms Kemberley Gittens	Operations Officer, Social Sector Division, Caribbean Development Bank
19	Ms Larasati Indrawagita	Senior Officer, Education, Youth and Sports Division, Association of Southeast Asian Nations Secretariat
20	Ms Leituala Kuiniselani Toelupe Tago	Director, Social Development Programme, Secretariat of the Pacific Community
21	Dr Mema Motusaga	Team Leader, Youth and Social Inclusion Human Rights and Social Development Programme, Secretariat of the Pacific Community
22	Mr Li Zhou	Associate Social Affairs Officer, United Nations Economic and Social Commission for Asia and the Pacific: Subregional Office for East and North-East Asia
23	Dr Maria Kypriotou	Youth Focal Point - Ethics, Youth and Sport Division, United Nations Educational, Scientific and Cultural Organization
24	Ms Joyce Asamoah-Koranteng	Minister/Commonwealth & Diaspora, Ghanaian High Commission, London
25	Ms Nafula Wafula	Vice Chairperson for Policy and Advocacy, Commonwealth Youth Council
26	Mr Namir Chowdhury	UK Young Ambassador to the Commonwealth, British Youth Council
27	Mr Paul Dowling	Senior Researcher Manager, Ecorys, UK
28	Ms Qairunnisa Md Alias	Counsellor, Malaysian High Commission, London
29	Mr Rafiullah Kakar	Policy & Social Development Specialist, Pakistan
30	Ms Ritash Sarna	Department of Statistics, International Labour Organization
31	Dr Robert Tanton	Research Director, National Centre for Social and Economic Modelling, University of Canberra
32	Ms Roma Vedamuttu	Member, Commonwealth Youth Forum 2021 Task Force
33	Ms Thimuthu Dissanayake	Second Secretary, Sri Lankan High Commission, London
34	Mr Usman Dar	Special Adviser to Prime Minister on Youth Affairs, Prime Ministers Office, Pakistan